OF VICTORIANS AND VEGETARIANS

I dedicate this work to my family

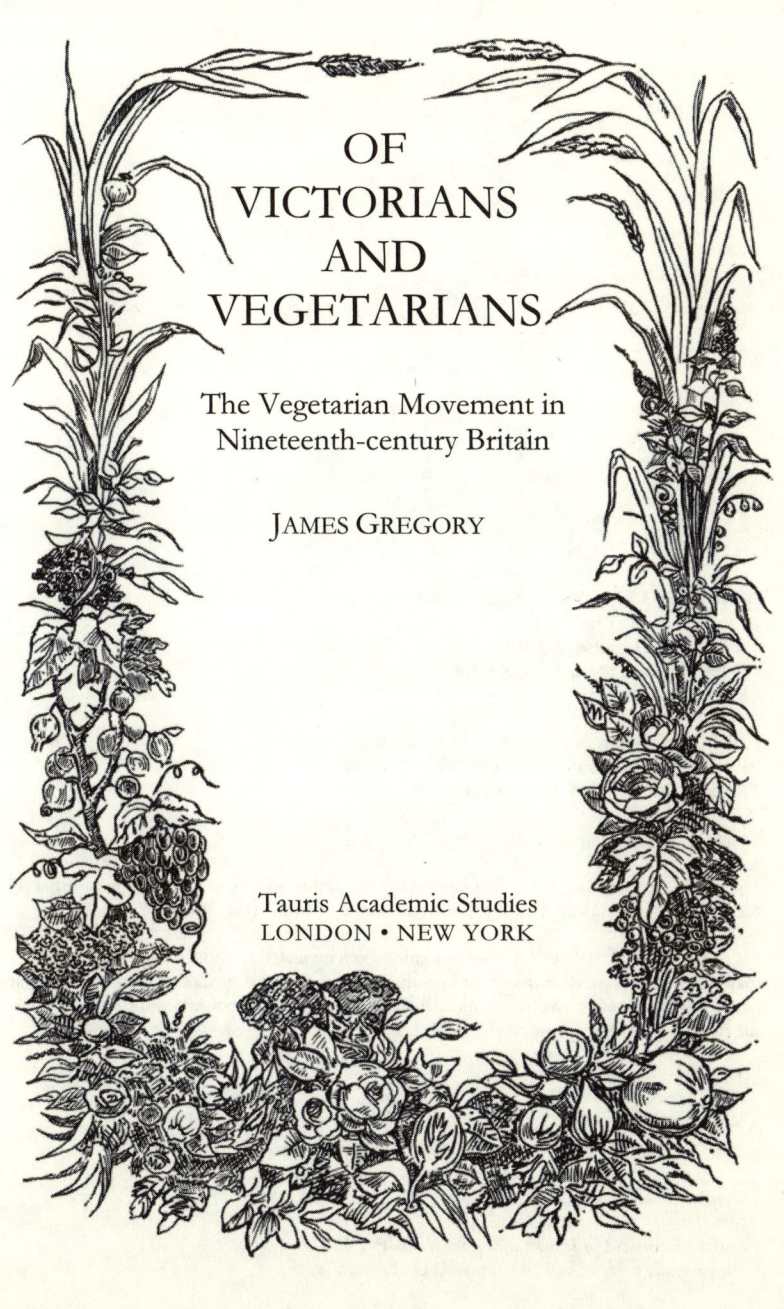

OF VICTORIANS AND VEGETARIANS

The Vegetarian Movement in Nineteenth-century Britain

JAMES GREGORY

Tauris Academic Studies
LONDON • NEW YORK

Published in 2007 by Tauris Academic Studies,
an imprint of I.B.Tauris & Co Ltd
6 Salem Road, London W2 4BU
175 Fifth Avenue, New York NY 10010
www.ibtauris.com

In the United States of America and Canada distributed by
Palgrave Macmillan a division of St. Martin's Press
175 Fifth Avenue, New York, NY 10010

Copyright © 2007 James Gregory

The right of James Gregory to be identified as the author of this work has been asserted by the author in accordance with the Copyright, Designs and Patents Act 1988.

All rights reserved. Except for brief quotations in a review, this book, or any part thereof, may not be reproduced, stored in or introduced into a retrieval system, or transmitted, in any form or by any means, electronic, mechanical, photocopying, recording or otherwise, without the prior written permission of the publisher.

ISBN: 978 1 84511 379 7

A full CIP record for this book is available from the British Library
A full CIP record for this book is available from the Library of Congress

Library of Congress catalog: available

Printed and bound in India by Replika Press Pvt. Ltd
Camera-ready copy edited and supplied by the author

CONTENTS

List of Illustrations	vii
Abbreviations	ix
Acknowledgements	xi
Introduction	1
1. The Vegetarian Movement, *c.*1838-1901	21
2. Physical Puritanism and Medical Orthodoxy	69
3. Beasts and Saints: Zoophilia and Religion in the Movement	88
4. Radicalism and Fadicalism	111
5. Feeding the Vegetarian Mind and Body	125
6. Class, Gender and the Vegetarians	151
7. Representing the Vegetarian	174
Conclusion	187
Notes	195
Bibliography	271
Index	305

LIST OF ILLUSTRATIONS

Front cover
Gordon Browne, 'All A-Growing, All A-Blowing', *Punch*, 12 February 1898, p. 72, ©Punch Ltd, www.punch.co.uk. [Miss Nicholson spoke of the facility with which vegetarians might, if they pressed their demands upon their tradesmen, obtain vegetarian boots and vegetarian gloves – *Report in Daily Paper of Meeting of the Vegetarian Federal Union*.] OUR LUNATIC CONTRIBUTOR THINKS THIS IS AN EXCELLENT IDEA. BUT WHY NOT HAVE VEGETARIAN COATS, AND HATS, TOO – IN FACT, VEGETARIAN CLOTHING FROM HEAD TO FOOT?

Title page
The ornamentation is based on a wood engraving designed by James S. Hibberd for the bound collection of William Horsell's *Vegetarian Advocate* (1851).

Integrated
All images appear courtesy of the Vegetarian Society, except for Figure 4, which appears courtesy of Kevin Beurle, Figure 5, which appears courtesy of the University of Southampton, Figure 7, which appears courtesy of Dundee City Archives; and Figure 19 *right*, in the author's collection.

FIGURE 1.   The *Vegetarian*, organ of late nineteenth century metropolitan vegetarianism, promoting a specious origin for the word 'vegetarian' (2 May 1896). [p. 10]
FIGURE 2.   James Simpson, *left*, and William Horsell, *right*, founding figures in the Victorian vegetarian movement. [p. 32]
FIGURE 3.   A typical lecture by the first President of the VS, in 1855 (*Vegetarian Messenger*, 1936, p. 43). [p. 42]
FIGURE 4.   George Dornbusch, a leading figure in early London vegetarianism, and also an activist in anti-vaccination and peace organizations (Image courtesy of Kevin Beurle). [p. 47]
FIGURE 5.   The Vegetarian Society banquet at Freemasons' Tavern, 1851, from the *Illustrated London News*, 16 August 1851, p. 223. [p. 49]

FIGURE 6.   The 'vegetarian van' spreading the gospel of vegetarianism (frontispiece, *Vegetarian Messenger*, August 1898). [p. 53]
FIGURE 7.   Poster for a dinner under the auspices of the Dundee FRS (Dundee City Archives, GD/Mus36). [p. 59]
FIGURE 8.   Arnold Frank Hills, *left*, from the frontispiece, *Vegetarian Messenger*, January 1898; and Charles Walter Forward, *right*, from *Vegetarian Messenger*, February 1894, p. 56 [p. 63]
FIGURE 9.   An illuminated address recognizing the role of Arnold Frank Hills in the revival, reproduced in the *Vegetarian*, 1897. [p. 67]
FIGURE 10. Delegates at the VFU congress in Portsmouth May 1891. At the front are Josiah Oldfield and M.K. Gandhi. *Vegetarian Messenger*, October 1936, p. 318 [p. 68]
FIGURE 11. Oriolet Hospital in Essex. *Vegetarian Messenger*, April 1896, p. 108. [p. 79]
FIGURE 12. Promoting a muscular image for vegetarianism: the champion runner John Barclay. *Vegetarian Messenger*, March 1898, p. 117. [p. 81]
FIGURE 13. Butchers Row, Aldgate. *Vegetarian*, 1 January 1898. [p. 90]
FIGURE 14. The Jewish method of animal slaughter investigated. *Vegetarian*, 8 January 1898. [p.91]
FIGURE 15. Josiah Oldfield: student of the occult, fruitarian and leader of the late-nineteenth century anti-capital punishment movement. *Vegetarian*, Christmas supplement, 21 December 1891. [p. 97]
FIGURE 16. Council Room of the Order of the Golden Age, Barcombe Hall. *Herald of the Golden Age*, 1900. [p. 109]
FIGURE 17. Caldwell Harpur, who favoured metrication, nationalization of property, Saturday for Sabbath, and Oliver Cromwell as national hero. *Vegetarian*, 7 December 1895. [p. 117]
FIGURE 18. A ticket for an anniversary banquet for the Vegetarian Society, 1891. *British Vegetarian*, January-February 1963, p. 39. [p. 127]
FIGURE 19. *Left*: Pitman Vegetarian Hotel, Birmingham, from *Vegetarian Messenger*, January 1899, p. 16. *Right*: Charing Cross Vegetarian Hotel, from an advertisement in C.L.H. Wallace, *366 Menus*. [p. 139]
FIGURE 20. Front cover, *Vegetarian Messenger*, August 1898. [p. 142]
FIGURE 21. *Left*: front cover, *Almonds and Raisins. The Vegetarian Society Annual for 1888*; and *right*: front cover of *The Herald of the Golden Age*, 1897. [p. 148]
FIGURE 22. Unemployed workers given work (and vegetarian food) by Arnold Frank Hills. *Vegetarian*, 3 December 1898 [p. 154]
FIGURE 23. A branch (Camden Town) of the Ivy Leaf Society established by Frances Boult. *Vegetarian*, 2 December 1899, p. 574. [p. 165]
FIGURE 24. Alexandrine Veigelé, *left* and her daughter Adrienne, *right*. *Vegetarian*, 7 December 1895. [p. 167]
FIGURE 25. Leading black and white artist of the late-Victorian period Phil May's comment on the appeal of vegetarianism to the fashionable. *Vegetarian*, September 1894, p. 419. [p. 179]

ABBREVIATIONS

Allinson Papers	Thomas R. Allinson Papers, Special Collections, The Library, University of Edinburgh.
Baume Papers	Pierre Henri Baume Papers, Manx National Heritage, Manx Museum, Douglas, Isle of Man.
DNB / Oxford DNB	*Dictionary of National Biography/Oxford Dictionary of National Biography*
DR	*Dietetic Reformer*
Forward, *History*	Charles W. Forward, *Fifty Years of Food Reform. A History of the Vegetarian Movement in England* (1898).
FRM	*Food Reform Magazine*
GMCRO-VS	Greater Manchester County Records Office, Vegetarian Society Records.
Gregory, 'Vegetarian Movement'	James R.T.E. Gregory, 'The Vegetarian Movement in Britain c.1840-1901. A study of its development, personnel and wider connections', 2 vols (Ph.D., University of Southampton, 2002).
HGA	*Herald of the Golden Age*
HH	*Herald of Health*
Johnson	John Johnson Collection of Printed Ephemera, Bodleian Library, University of Oxford.
LFRS / NFRS	London / National Food Reform Society
LVS	London Vegetarian Society
NMW	*New Moral World*
Twigg, 'Vegetarian Movement'	Julia M. Twigg, 'The Vegetarian Movement in England from 1847-1981: a study of the structure of its ideology' (Ph.D., London School of Economics, 1982).

UKA	United Kingdom Alliance
VA	*Vegetarian Advocate*
VFU	Vegetarian Federal Union
VM	*Vegetarian Messenger/ ~ and Health Review*
VS	The Vegetarian Society. With prefixed name: a local society e.g., Portsmouth VS.
WTE	*Weekly Times and Echo*
WVU	Women's Vegetarian Union

In the Notes, other sources, including material from less-frequently cited archives, are abbreviated to surname and short title following the first citation. If a later edition of a work has been used, the date of the first publication is also given.

ACKNOWLEDGEMENTS

This book is based on a doctoral dissertation at the Department of History, University of Southampton (May 2002), which was made possible by a full-time research award from the Arts and Humanities Research Board. I would like to thank my supervisor Professor John Rule and examiners Dr Waltraud Ernst and Professor Edward Royle for their comments and advice, and Professor Miles Taylor for his support. I would also like to thank the University of Bradford for a grant which contributed towards the cost of a dust jacket and the copyright fee for a cartoon from *Punch* (reproduced with permission of Punch Ltd, www.punch.co.uk). I am especially grateful to Chris Olivant of the Vegetarian Society for his help, particularly with the task of locating and scanning many of the images that appear here as illustrations. I am most grateful to the Vegetarian Society for their generosity in granting me the use of these images.

I have benefited from the help of many scholars and library staff and it is a pleasure to record my thanks to Dr Jackie Latham, Alexander Tyrrell, Professor Kathryn Gleadle, Dr Richard Allen, Dr Ben Marsden, Dr Hilda Kean, Dr Chien Hui-Li, Dr Lesley Hall, Dr Christine Garwood, Dr Ruth Livesey, Molly Kramer, Dr Lyssa Randolph, Dr John Parry, Leslie Price, Sam Calvert, Dr Arouna Ouedraogo, Tristram Stuart and Edgar Crook. I am also grateful for advice from Professor Peter Brang, Professor Roger Cooter, Professor John Belchem, Dr Malcolm Chase, Professor Gregory Claeys and Professor Sir Brian Harrison. Others have given me their assistance through that wonderful global community, the Victoria Listserver. I am indebted to descendants of George Dornbusch, Job Caudwell, and Charles Walker for granting me access to material in their possession. Judith Crowe made research at the the Institute of Alcohol Studies a pleasure. Roger Sims kindly granted access to the papers of the extraordinary Pierre Baume at the Manx Museum. Staff at the following institutions kindly sent copies of rare or unique material: the Livesey

Collection at the University of Central Lancashire, the Seligman Collection at the University of Columbia, Cheethams Library in Manchester, New York Public Library, Kansas University, Glasgow Library, and Regents College Library in Oxford. I would also like to thank staff at the British Library, the University of Edinburgh Special Collections, Greater Manchester Records Office, the University of Dundee Archives, Dundee Local Records Office, Trinity College Cambridge, the University of Southampton Special Collections, East Sussex Records Office, Northampton Records Office, Friends' House Library and the Co-operative College.

Some of my work on vegetarians appears in the *Dictionary of Labour Biography*, *Dictionary of Nineteenth Century Scientists* and *Oxford Dictionary of National Biography*. Essays on vegetarian-temperance connections and White Quakers have been published in the *Social History of Alcohol Review* and *Quaker Studies*. I am most grateful to the editors for the opportunity to publish this research. Other essays on the wider context of vegetarianism across Europe, America and in British India have had to be pruned from this study due to lack of space. Readers curious to find out more about vegetarian branch societies, restaurants and biographies of the rank and file are advised to read the second volume of my doctoral dissertation.

My thanks to Professor Dilys Hill for her editorial and stylistic advice on an earlier draft, to Dr Anne White for her meticulous reading of a later version, to Audrey Daly and Carolann Martin for their expertise with the final copy, and to my editor at I.B.Tauris, Elizabeth Munns. I also wish to thank the anonymous publishers' reviewers for their advice, which I have attempted, where appropriate or possible, to follow. Above all, I am grateful to my family for their encouragement and support through the years in which I have pursued dietetic heretics. This work is dedicated to them.

James Gregory, 2006

INTRODUCTION

Believing that their cause was 'favourable to health, peace, and happiness, and has a tendency to abolish everything that makes us miserable in this world', a select group of Britons established the first vegetarian society in the modern western world in 1847 and struggled thereafter to reform the diet of their contemporaries.[1] A seemingly marginal phenomenon, vegetarianism actually involved much that was of concern to the culture of Victorian Britain.[2] Whilst never a mass movement, and certainly far from attaining the level of support it now enjoys, vegetarianism became a vocal movement which attracted attention that ranged from the serious response of scientific men, the incorporation of vegetarian recipes in cookery books, to the skits on vegetarian dinners, restaurants, animal-free clothing and enthusiasts which appeared in satirical journals and theatrical sketches. The responses to the various challenges vegetarianism offered means that a study of the movement is important for our understanding of Victorian society.

Of the challenges to Victorian practices and attitudes, the most obvious were related to *food*: a subject involving a host of major questions about, for instance, supply and national sufficiency, national and social identity, charity and the working-class budget, and sociability. But vegetarianism also had implications for the relationship of man to animals, and for violence between humans (thus vegetarians were often against war, against capital punishment and violent punishments in general), and also had things to say about the role of women, through claims, for instance, to liberate women from unpleasant kitchen duties. Most Victorians assumed the vegetarians were 'radical' in their associations, it being understood that dietetic heresy went with other heresies of bodily self-culture, politics, and religion. However, through its connections to a wider temperance movement (teetotalism) and spiritualism, vegetarianism was actually part of broader movements rather than a fringe concern. In its gender roles this seemingly counter-cultural movement actually reflected Victorian *mores* rather than fulfilled any radical potential. And like temperance, many contemporary working class and socialist opponents thought vegetarianism played into employers' hands in its guise as a campaign for thrift and economy, for many advocates saw it as a way of living on small wages (though with the beneficial result of using the savings for self-improvement), or as a cheap but wholesome form of soup philanthropy. A more general, non-vegetarian 'food reform' was concerned with teaching the working classes about food values, economic recipes and substitutes at times of economic hardship. This wider food reform could potentially give the vegetarians a sympathetic audience, and they attempted to attract support through lectures, pamphlets and classes, by addressing the plight of the malnourished poor.

Thus, though vegetarianism was far from being a 'central' concern to most people, it was not neglected by the mainstream. Many cultural figures commented on the movement when it emerged in the mid-nineteenth century, and when, revitalized, it returned to prominence in the late nineteenth century. Some leading Victorians indeed, investigated the diet and dabbled in dietetic reform. From the unfamiliar perspective of Victorian vegetarianism, through a study of the movement and its reception, this book provides an entry into a broader world of reform of body and soul, habits and manners, and of society.

It is as a *movement* that this study primarily treats vegetarianism, rather than as an ideology. The latter aspect has been well studied before, in the undeservedly neglected and unpublished doctoral research by Julia Twigg. Although Twigg was concerned primarily with analyzing this ideology (and published two essays which reflected this focus on ideology), the movement's general history from *c.*1847-1980 was ably set out as part of a wider 'field of social relations' giving meaning to the ideology. Here, whilst building on Twigg's insightful research, I am keen to study the social history of the movement with the level of detail that her broader canvas made impossible.[3]

The study provides an in-depth treatment of the movement as a 'lived' experience, and as a campaign. As the latter, British vegetarianism began with the creation of the Vegetarian Society (hereafter abbreviated to VS) by a few hundred men and women who had already been promoting vegetarianism as part of their religious beliefs, hygienic reform or utopian experiments. The transition from private endeavour to public movement in order to further the adoption of their diet led to provincial branches, lecturing campaigns, printed propaganda and a range of alternative commodities. Though the movement lacked a 'Meat Bill' equivalent to the prohibitionists' 'Drink Bill' or any likelihood of prohibition it occasionally lobbied government and politicians. This agitation attracted adherents in sizeable numbers by the late-Victorian period, so that by 1899, when several other organizations were also active in Britain, the senior vegetarian society had almost six thousand members and associates. Since one member often represented a family group, and since throughout the period there was an unquantifiable number of experimenting 'considerers', the total number of deliberate vegetarians (as opposed to the many thousands practically vegetarian through poverty) was much higher.

This book is a study of the movement but inevitably also of vegetarianism itself. Though the primary concern is not to explore ideology, one needs to understand the various elements to vegetarianism to understand its appeal and challenge. Through a study of its hygienic, religious, zoophilist, radical and 'fadical' aspects, a study of the diet is a study of Victorian culture. Though some of these aspects have been touched on by historians working in various different disciplines, these themes are brought together here in order to fully understand this polyvalent and multivocal movement.

One could open this study out to consider the movement's associations with what by the late-Victorian period was an international phenomenon, with North American, continental European and imperial connections. Indeed, from its earliest days British vegetarianism was connected to an international elite of ultra-temperance and other reform movements.[4] This included Grahamism, an American health movement based on the ideas of Sylvester Graham which incorporated vegetarianism and whose heyday was in the 1830s.[5] The Dutch Marxist historian Jan Romein presented vegetarianism as a component of the 'little religions' in his study of the European *fin de siècle*, and interpreted these as expressive of 'the bad conscience of a ruling class that was no longer convinced of its divine right to rule but not yet under sufficient threat to take full stock of its shortcomings'.[6] The German 'Natural Living' movement and German vegetarianism have been the focus of numerous studies. Attitudes to animals in France, where vegetarianism failed to flourish, have also been examined. The Russian movement has recently been analysed in detail.[7] Mahatma Gandhi's association with the London vegetarians in the late-Victorian period is perhaps the most famous episode in the relationship between vegetarians in Britain and the subcontinent. Not the least of its political aspects was the challenge vegetarianism presented in an empire where 'British' food habits encountered the dietetic 'other'.[8] However, reasons of space prevent any study here of the links between the British vegetarians and others.

This study ends in 1901. Apart from the wish as a 'Victorianist' to illuminate the nineteenth century and keep the work to manageable length, the twentieth century presents a larger scale movement, though there are often echoes of the Victorian movement in later activities. General histories of western vegetarianism covering the recent past already exist, such as Colin Spencer's well-known survey history of vegetarianism.[9] In the twentieth century developments in food technology and food science, altered attitudes to non-western diet and religion (and general developments in religious belief), mean a different context to vegetarianism: making it, in many ways, an easier practice to follow (through manufactured substitutes, greater understanding of nutrition, proliferation and specialization of food retail and retail of culinary equipment, and the decline in the force of scriptural injunctions for most Britons).

The vegetarian movement was a topic of debate and interest in the nineteenth century. Though the British public never became enamoured of the movement to a great extent, or even to the degree that a few of its contemporary reforms enjoyed, its concerns were of relevance in the broader world of reform (partly because vegetarians were often not merely vegetarians), and more generally in British culture. If the movement has been one of the few under-explored British reform movements of the era, and is practically ignored by the popular historiography on the period, this study argues that the movement was a significant phenomenon.

In an age worried about overpopulation, environmental catastrophe, and the ethics and health risks of industrialized food production, vegetarianism has acquired an acknowledged relevance in western discourse. Sociologists identify it as one of the components of movements that make non-materialist concerns about 'personal identity' and 'lifestyle' the focus of politics, the so-called 'new social movements' (also including feminism, environmentalism, lesbian and gay movements) that they argue were a development of post-industrial western societies. But concern to reform lifestyle is not a recent or 'post-modern' development: for critics have shown that these movements descend from or reiterate nineteenth-century concerns.[10] This book examines the origins of these present day concerns and responses.

As a consequence of the diversity of motivations for adopting vegetarianism and the variety of forms vegetarianism took, exploration of the Victorian movement needs to draw on research by scholars working in a number of fields. The most obvious category, histories of western vegetarianism, is an expanding one, which has offered broad narrative, exploration of ideology (in the case especially of Twigg), and sociology, including its gendered dimensions (in the case of Carol J. Adams most famously[11]). The most recent large-scale study has been Tristram Stuart's fine cultural history of Western responses to Indian vegetarianism from the seventeenth century.¹² Modern scholarship has also included smaller scale work on the vegetarian-teetotal Cowherdites (or Bible Christians) active in Salford and Manchester after splitting from mainstream Swedenborgianism in 1809, and the progressive press in the Isle of Man which, in exploiting legal loopholes, produced vegetarian periodicals in the 1840s.¹³ But from the beginning of the movement there was an internal genealogical impulse which demonstrated the diet's *antiquity* through essays which constructed a 'canon' descending from classical and biblical times.¹⁴ This can be explained as a response to the novelty of organized endeavour and anxiety about vigour and reach. Precociously, the vegetarian organ in the 1850s (the *Vegetarian Messenger*) collected material for a history of the first few years.¹⁵ Charles Forward produced *Fifty Years of Food Reform* for the movement's jubilee in 1897. This, despite some sketchiness originating from its basis in short articles, was essentially accurate, and candid about the strains between the two major societies of the period, the Manchester-based VS and the new London Vegetarian Society (hereafter abbreviated to LVS).¹⁶

As Forward's history makes clear, vegetarianism frequently positioned itself as 'ultra temperance'. Like much research on Victorian reform movements, this study is indebted to the work of Brian Harrison who has emphasized the interconnecting reform interests of temperance leaders and rank-and-file, and who uncovered a rich body of material in his study of the temperance press.¹⁷ The close study by medical and social historians of hydropathy, medical botany, mesmerism, and other contemporary (and often associated) medical unorthodoxies, also provides this work with a wider context of hygienic reform. Another important area in which vegetarianism has previously been briefly considered is in histories of animal welfare and human/animal relations, vegetarianism being interpreted as an outcome of the growth of 'humane' feeling, also reflected in more mainstream zoophilist movements and in antivivisectionism. If many vegetarians were animal lovers, their sympathies were not limited to animals, and the ethical dimension to the movement also involved concern about human suffering and pain. Vegetarians supported campaigns against violent or capital punishment; their organization took off at the same time as a revived anti-capital punishment movement and experienced similar lack of public sympathy.¹⁸

Those associated with anti-capital punishment efforts were often radical reformers more generally, and one key area for previous treatment of vegetarianism has been histories of radicalism. Such radicals include the poet Shelley, who saw carnivorism as the 'root of all evil' and whose espousal of vegetarianism was shared by others in Romantic circles in the early nineteenth century. Working-class radicals also adopted vegetarians.¹⁹

This association between dietetic heresy and other radicalisms was also apparent during the next period of radical ferment, the first Victorian decade. The so-called 'moral radicalism' of the Quaker Joseph Sturge and his followers provides one middle-class location for vegetarian sympathies, along with other social, moral and 'physiological reforms'. As this research demonstrates, personal reform can be *political*, and recent work on radical middle-class women and the private sphere in the early-Victorian period has also emphasized the political nature of health reforms.[20] Vegetarians themselves, competing in the marketplace of reforms, stressed their cause's radical or fundamental implications for society.

Advocates asserted vegetarianism's indispensability for personal and social regeneration. Like temperance, vegetarianism was advocated on the basis of plebeian or lower middle-class self-improvement and self-help in institutions such as mechanics' institutes from the late 1840s. Another area where the plebeian element to vegetarianism can be seen is spiritualism, a movement with a strong plebeian following. Studies of spiritualism mention the interest in diet as part of a range of concerns for a self-styled 'advanced' movement. Historians of late-Victorian esoteric movements which attracted women as members and leaders have also noted the vegetarian dimension. Such associations prefigure vegetarianism's place in the modern 'New Age'.

Utopia, whether actual experimentation, or fictional and prospective, invariably involves dietetic radicalism. Food reform surfaced in several utopian experiments in England and America in the 1840s. Vegetarianism is an under-explored aspect of the radical world of Owenite socialists, 'new move' Chartists and others in the 1840s. It was the community at Alcott House *c.*1838-49 (which despite its links to Owenism was not Owenite) that coined the word 'vegetarian'.[21] Similarly, a 'back-to-the-land' movement in the late nineteenth century (with parallels in continental Europe, North America and South America) provided another location for vegetarian activity combined with social and moral reforms.[22] By the 1890s vegetarianism was a *cliché* of utopian fiction.[23]

This practical and literary dabbling in dietetic reform by late-Victorians reflected the revival of the British movement from the 1870s and an ensuing vigour and publicity which was unparalleled. It took its place amongst esoteric religions and anti-vivisectionist efforts in the 'late-Victorian revolt' (continuing in the Edwardian period) when there was 'an unusual amount of activity of radical-eccentric nature'.[24] In that famous diatribe, Max Nordau interpreted vegetarianism as another sign of *fin de siècle* degeneracy.[25] Vegetarianism was also acknowledged as a feature of the *fin de siècle* in the classic early studies by R.C.K. Ensor (himself vegetarian) and Holbrook Jackson, though surprisingly it is ignored in more recent work on the 'Eighteen Nineties'.[26]

This period also saw the emergence of socialism, and the reformed diet became a topic for debate in the socialist press and clubs, not least because, if some leading socialists were sympathetic, others viewed vegetarianism as a capitalist tool.[27] *Fin de siècle* efforts to create a new morality involved food reform, and so vegetarianism is occasionally glanced at in studies of, for instance, the early Fabians who included vegetarians such as Bernard Shaw and Edith Nesbit, the writer of children's literature. One 'advanced' location of vegetarian discussion in this period, the feminist and pro-labour journal *Shafts*, has been studied, and the significance of vegetarianism for some late-Victorian and Edwardian feminists has been recognized.[28]

Despite vegetarianism's association with the radical and progressive the transformation it offered was not necessarily liberating. Identified along with other physiological reforms as a form of 'physical puritanism' in the 1850s, it can be associated with a more general Victorian 'puritanism'.[29] If plebeian adherents saw it as a means to self-mastery, another interpretation might be that dietary 'regimen' was primarily a bourgeois response to urbanization and industrialization: a disciplinary effort especially directed at working-class bodies. Thus the sociologist Bryan Turner, who has proposed a theory of the 'somatic society' where personal or political problems are problematized and expressed through the body, has charted changing dietary regimens, from those advocated for the professional and urban classes in the eighteenth century to those stimulated by anxieties about the labouring classes from the second half of the nineteenth century, when working-class diet became a subject of concern through anxieties about public health, urban poverty and national efficiency.[30]

The first part of this study provides a history of the movement in a single chapter. It first examines the background to the establishment of the VS, through a survey of activity from around 1840-46. It then outlines the Victorian movement, identifying and analyzing some of the main features of the movement in terms of location, institutions and activity, and personnel. Previously this has had no detailed attention, with published work concentrating either on communitarian locations or on activity in Manchester and the 'industrial north'. The metropolitan and provincial activity across Britain shows the movement's place in a larger radical or progressive world, but also shows how vegetarianism was applied to social problems as an additional force in mainstream philanthropic dissemination of 'bread and knowledge'.

The second part of this study dissects the movement by exploring and contextualizing the varieties of (or dimensions to) vegetarianism, with a chapter on 'physical puritanism' and vegetarianism's relationship with medical orthodoxy (chapter two); a chapter which examines vegetarianism as an animal welfare movement, its religious dimensions and relationship with spiritualism (chapter three); and a chapter examining its radicalism and 'anti-everythingarian' tendency (chapter four). The latter chapter emphasizes how categories were blurred not simply as a propagandist convenience, but because followers were not monomaniacs with a dietetic obsession despite the frequent pejorative labels that also appeared in criticism of other 'anti' movements confronting customary behaviour ('faddish', 'crankish', 'crotchety', 'eccentric', and 'sentimental'). The second part then, is an attempt to define the movement, with the conclusion that like temperance and other health reforms, the movement was a personal physiological reform, a moral crusade and social movement, with 'political' associations despite a tension between more obviously political movements.

The third part is concerned with the vegetarians' dietetic practice in private and public, the role of a vegetarian press, and the movement's social base. It begins by considering vegetarians' own culinary practices and gustatory attitudes, and then explores the movement's physical manifestation through its own commodities, and restaurants and press (chapter five). The vegetarian press emerges as an important aspect to the movement. The examination of restaurants continues the exploration of vegetarianism's geographical and institutional locations. Their roles in vegetarian activism and as locations for allied radicalisms are examined. Study of the restaurants' growth and fortunes provides evidence about the growth of the movement, and also about the social base which is further examined, alongside gender, in the next chapter (chapter six). The relative appeal of the movement to the 'classes' of Victorian Britain and the specific attempts to attract plebeian support are considered, by examining the literature which explicitly addressed contemporaries in terms of the dietetic needs of classes, and the response to the movement from socialists and co-operators. The role of women is examined, through study of gender roles in general and consideration of the Women's Vegetarian Union in particular. Finally the movement's representation by others (chapter seven) is studied. The chapter is a consideration of literary responses to the diet and its practitioners: the discourse on vegetarianism in a variety of prose works, including works of fiction and in the national or local press, was extensive, and certainly more than one might assume. The ambivalent relationship of the movement to 'modernity', which is one of the themes apparent in the discourse on the movement, is considered in the conclusion.

Vegetarians, trusting to the power of the printed word, were prolific writers and their journals, books and pamphlets are core material for this study. Apart from the sparse documentation of the early years (1847-55) there are extensive minute books for the VS, the London Vegetarian Auxiliary, and LVS. In addition, there are minutes and related material belonging to the St Pancras branch, the Dundee food reform society and traces of material from the Liverpool Society. Their activities and those of many other vegetarian societies were fully reported in the vegetarian press. Material relating to the Women's Vegetarian Union is in the British Library, and the John Johnson Collection in the Bodleian Library, which also has other vegetarian ephemera. To assess the status of vegetarianism within a wider reform world, I have also examined periodicals promoting philanthropic or progressive causes in general, and specific concerns such as temperance, anti-tobacco, peace, phonetic reform and spiritualism. Because many who were not simply reforming their diet for purely personal health reasons were concerned with other causes (though being the former did not exclude the latter), the broader survey has been crucial for understanding this particular group of so-called 'anti-everythingarians'.

These 'ultras' were not however, merely agitators for a nexus of *negatives*. This is made clear by studying the lives of prominent individuals such as James Simpson and Arnold Hills, the early and late-Victorian leaders of the movement. Regrettably their papers do not exist, nor are there any papers belonging to William Horsell, the first secretary of the Vegetarian Society. However, privately-owned material does exist relating to the London vegetarian George Dornbusch and the teetotal-vegetarian publishing partner of Horsell, Job Caudwell. A unique view of early vegetarian and associated radical circles in London is provided by the recently discovered papers of the eccentric Pierre Baume. The papers of Thomas R. Allinson, the late-Victorian naturopath, in Edinburgh University, include a rare archive of vegetarian ephemera, as does the archive relating to his contemporary labour activist and vegetarian Joseph Edwards at the Liverpool Records Office. Glimpses of vegetarian activity may be found in the papers of the social and moral reformers Lord Mount Temple and his wife Georgina, at the University of Southampton.

This study uncovers the unfamiliar and exploits new material, avoiding a concentration on the activities of the Cowherdites and well-known vegetarians such as the social and sexual reformer Edward Carpenter, the Fabian and playwright Bernard Shaw and those other Victorians whose vegetarianism is identified (or in some cases ignored) in entries in the *Dictionary of National Biography*. The commitment of the updated *[Oxford]*

DNB to broadening national biography has involved the inclusion of others, such as William Horsell. Detailed research on pioneering vegetarians such as Horsell, the poet James Elmzlie Duncan and the grain merchant Dornbusch, underpin this study. A unique glimpse into provincial activity in the early movement was possible through the diary of one mid-Victorian vegetarian in Worcester.[31] Apart from this, the close study of obituaries, testimonies and interviews in the vegetarian press and those of other reform movements provides much on the humbler vegetarians, and allows a prosopographical approach to replace the assertions made by the VS through their propaganda (including statistical analyses), with concrete and rich information on the religious affiliations, occupational background, varied motivations and interconnections of adherents and sympathizers. If historians need to relate the movement to larger developments such as urbanization and secularization, we need to know and ask questions about *who* was attracted to the movement and how they saw their place in the 'age of reform'.[32] Since vegetarianism often formed a part of an *omnium gatherum* of radical positions, it offers an entry into that 'anti-everythingarianism' which has been noted by historians of Victorian reform, but has not received close treatment. In fact, study of the vegetarians is an especially fruitful means of investigating this phenomenon because, as an extreme, it attracted fewer supporters than more mainstream reforms, and so provides the researcher with a more manageable group to deal with. Also, because what was involved was a reform of *life* style, the movement's journalism contains many detailed biographies and membership lists, in contrast, for instance, to the paucity of rank-and-file information for the anti-vivisection movement.

FIGURE 1. The *Vegetarian*, organ of late nineteenth century metropolitan vegetarianism, promoting a specious origin for the word 'vegetarian' (2 May 1896).

Specialist diets played a part in separating vegetarians into various schools, so that the appropriateness of the word 'vegetarian' became questioned. The commonsense etymology (deriving 'vegetarian' from the eating of vegetables) was obfuscated in the 1870s to counter the popular view that the diet was composed of raw vegetables. But as Kenneth Romanes pointed out in the German vegetarian journal *Vegetarische Warte*, an etymology derived from the Latin for spirit, *vegetus*, was 'entirely an after-thought of the scholars and ... had no place whatever in the minds of the originators of modern vegetarianism'.[33] Those who wanted to attract wider support also spoke of 'dietetic reform'.[34] Proponents, like other reformers, used a multitude of justifications, but when one comes to examine individuals, a neat classification into 'ethical' or 'hygienic' is often unhelpful. But controversies over the name echoed differences of opinion over rationale and emphases, reflecting the sometimes competing ethical, medical and economic motivations. Internal debates about what constituted the best diet, morally or physiologically led to 'fruitarianism', a coinage of the later 1870s; and stricter definitions of a bloodless diet brought a few people to a position which, though it was to be distinguished by a separate name only in the 1940s (veganism) existed well before then.

Though this necessary *excursus* on etymology highlights the part specialist diets had in separating out the vegetarians, the study's primary concern is not the food they promoted but the movement's social history and connections with other reforms. The reader will find only morsels of vegetarian cuisine, perhaps in keeping with that strand in vegetarianism concerned to divert people from sensuality to higher things. Another reason for not privileging food is that, despite its etymology, vegetarianism was from the start concerned with other forms of consumption. But given that many people took the reform at face-value as an agitation concerned with eating, it makes sense to contextualize this study by a brief consideration of the Victorians and food.

Food and the Victorians

> Moral, religious and political considerations no less than the natural promptings of appetite, influence the individual and community in the preference for certain articles of food and the rejection of others.[35]

Though their critics often treated their efforts as time wasted on worldly and insignificant matters, to be a committed vegetarian was to engage in debates on food which took in the ethics and economics of its production, its nutrition and aesthetics. Food was a significant and pervasive subject in Victorian culture, offering a 'culinary nationalism', signifying the march of 'progress', or imperilling it through faulty supply and adulteration, featuring in the 'gospel of thrift', and prominently figuring in social life. The gustatory dimension to nineteenth-century culture, expressed in such diverse forms as the novels of Charles Dickens and the celebrations surrounding all manner of local and national events, was substantial. Examination of 'foodways' therefore provides a constituent element rather than a mere 'flavour' of the past.

Fears of a Malthusian crisis of population outstripping food supply stimulated a great deal of early nineteenth-century writing, with solutions sought in emigration, 'home colonization' and the exploitation of wastelands, even (for a few advocates) birth-control.[36] It was a matter of national policy and security. Politics was focused on the 'staff of life' during the Corn Laws agitation; conflict between free traders and protectionists concerned 'taxes on food', many of which were abolished or lowered. The Irish famine also made food a major question. The imperial dimension was reflected in colonial imports and the export of British foodways. Crises, such as Indian famines, were matters of imperial policy. Always the concern of local authorities (with food riots into the mid-Victorian period), food was increasingly regulated as health reform, chemistry and food technologies developed. Although food manufacture only became industrialized late in the century, the production and processing of food were major sources of employment throughout the period.

Scientists synthesized flavours and explored new ways of preserving and manufacturing foods, such as the 'extract of meat' promoted by the chemist Justus von Liebig in 1865.[37] Improvements in food production and quality could be identified as 'keeping pace with the progressive movement of the last fifty years'.[38] Technology was also applied to domestic food production, with the emergence of gas-fuelled fires, refrigerators, cookers and, by the end of the period, electric cookers. By contrast, for social reformers, poor diet was a sign of the failure of modern society, the pursuit of good food a theme in propaganda and part of the vision of a reformed world. Diet was one of the vexed questions to be dealt with by prison and workhouse authorities. The modern age, for reasons of economy or social hygiene, seemed to involve the proliferation of specialist dietaries. Social investigators explored the food budgets and cooking habits of the poor. Following their late-eighteenth-century forebears, Victorian philanthropists and health reformers agitated for cookery classes, cheap utensils and fuel, and alternative foods.[39]

Working-class self-help and mutuality involved food provision; the 'movement culture' of working-class radicalism included the marketing of alternative foodstuffs.[40] Dietetic aspirations fed into the programmes of working-class social reformers such as Chartists and co-operators. The early-nineteenth century radical leader William Cobbett's oft-quoted remark 'I defy you to agitate a fellow on a full stomach' expresses another link between availability of cheap food and the fortunes of radical activity.[41] The opponents of later radicals were acutely aware that food provided 'excuse for the work of political incendiaries of all kinds, and for the fatal endeavours of democrats'.[42]

Food was a marker of class, gender and age.[43] The proliferation of domestic and culinary guides reflected both a general growth in the press and revealed the social significance of dining as a way of maintaining appearances and marking membership of the upper and middle-classes, through conspicuous consumption and rules of etiquette that provided pitfalls for the *arriviste*.[44] The working class devoted the largest proportion of their earnings to food; their womenfolk sacrificed health to provide men with a more nutritious meal to fuel their hard and lengthy manual work.[45] Men were defined as breadwinners: interference in their right and duty to provide food for their dependents was seen as a violation of the sanctity of the family and a 'desecration of the freeman's dignity'.[46]

Diet was also a marker of nationality, region and locality and helped identify racial and religious differences.[47] It has been argued that 'after language, food is the most important bearer of national identity'.[48] Certainly the association between roast beef and Englishness was long established, and symbolised 'manly English virtues' and the 'natural', against the dietetic other of artifice, luxury, the *potage maigre*, or frogs' legs of the French. The nation's wealth was indicated through meat consumption: Britain was the heaviest consumer of meat in Europe.[49] This 'culinary nationalism' haunted vegetarians: the anthem created by Fielding and Leveridge in the eighteenth century, 'The Roast Beef of Old England', was the hostile chorus to their crusade. A poster condemning the dish, produced by the London Food Reform Society, was one response.[50] In practice most Englishmen ate beef rarely: for the poor, protein came from the sea (as in the Cornish diet), or from pigs, so vegetarians stressed the dangers of eating pork, and the serious problems with the meat consumed by most people.[51] In 1863, Professor Gamgee's researches for the Privy Council revealed that, though only a small proportion of meat was ever formally condemned, over one-fifth of the meat sold was unfit for consumption. The authenticity of meat products was suspect: Bobus Higgins the sausage-maker, in Thomas Carlyle's *Past and Present* (1843), and Ford Madox Brown's 'Work' (1852-63), enriched by his adulterations, was not alone in anticipating the French Hippophage Society's introduction of horse flesh as a cheap article of food.[52]

Opponents repeatedly assured vegetarians that British pluck was based on beef, and beer. The *Morning Chronicle* found in 1849-50 that most

English agricultural labourers rarely ate meat (especially in southern England), and though there were improvements by the 1860s, butcher's meat remained a rarity. Yet the 'spare diet' was stigmatised as a sign of poverty or asceticism. Henry Mayhew observed it was not something that English men liked to admit to: 'Many a poor untaught Englishman will shrink from speaking of his spare diet, and his trouble to procure that; a reserve, too, much more noticeable among the men than the women.'[53] A mixed diet in which flesh meat was a constant element was 'practically the sort of diet to which all classes aspire', the late-nineteenth-century vegetarian and former Eton master Henry Salt had to admit.[54]

The other great culinary symbol of Englishness was the plum-pudding: it was not surprising that vegetarians should publicise their substitute for the suet-based symbol of Christmas conviviality.[55] Similarly, 'porridge and Scotland went together'[56]: vegetarians gestured to the Scottish diet of oats as proof that national vigour was compatible with vegetarianism. Nutritionally the diet of the poor Scot was probably good, but it may not have been perceived thus, since it may have represented a recent deterioration in the quantity of animal foods available and hence been experienced as a decline.[57] Ireland provided proof too, for vegetarians, that a largely vegetable diet allowed physical efficiency. But many writers on diet believed the Irish dependence on potatoes was a sign of a lower civilization and the spread of potato dependency a mark of pauperization.[58] Diet provided a key to the hierarchy of races or nations. Experts on these topics maintained that the British had become civilised, had become modern, through a mixed diet. But diet, or the methods of cookery, needed to be improved to make the most efficient use of the material (whether it was the foodstuffs, fuel, or time required).

The journal *Food* told its readers in 1884 that 'even now the great struggle for food mainly occupies the thought, the care, and the industry of the nation'.[59] The questions of population and self-sufficiency were certainly integral to vegetarian polemic from the movement's earliest days.[60] Since meat was deemed to be crucial in the nation's diet, vegetarianism often surfaced in debates about population and national or European food supply in meetings of savants such as the British Association; usually to be dealt with dismissively.[61] The supply of meat could be disrupted by epidemics as in 1866, when rinderpest threatened livestock; it could also be disrupted by the instability of foreign sources. But Victorians, even when their fears about a Malthusian crisis were calmed, worried about the strategic implications for a nation which depended on foreign food to feed its population. Groups as diverse as Tory anti-free traders and liberal members of the Land Nationalization Society (established in 1881) sought to exploit these fears in linking their reform to concern about dependence on foreign supplies; so too did vegetarians.[62]

Agricultural improvements helped increase domestic production, and further solutions to potential shortages were advocated, such as the introduction of small proprietors proposed by Joseph Fisher in articles in the *Morning Chronicle* (1866) or the improvements to soil fertility suggested by the land surveyor and agricultural engineer John Ewart, who argued that increasing and improving the arable pasture would support the additional livestock required.[63] Whatever the proposals, increasing the meat supply was seen as a *major* question.

It is not surprising, given these meat-centred anxieties, that preserved meat featured at exhibitions such as the International Exhibition at South Kensington in 1862.[64] Stimulated by population growth and the problems with domestic meat supply, new preservation technologies were tested. The Society of Arts established a prize for a method to transport raw meat into Britain. Tinned and salted meat came from Chicago, but its greasiness and stringiness made it unpopular. Meat supplies from Australia and New Zealand were reported in newspapers. In February 1869, *Public Health* discussed the 'great Food Question' in relation to imports of colonial meat, and noted the Duke of Edinburgh's recommendation that this was sweet, juicy and solid.[65] The journalist and statistician Michael Mulhall thought that New Zealand offered an alternative supply of meat if the Americas were insufficient, demonstrated that the population could not be sustained on the domestic supply of cattle, and remarked that new sources of meat for Britain were a strange outcome of the industry of a small number of settlers who had transformed cannibal islands.[66] However, this meat was generally of poor quality and in 1871-72 a couple of workhouses even rioted against Australian meats.[67] If the meat had not improved by the 1880s (when preservation by ice became satisfactory), nevertheless the supply came to be depended upon by the working classes by the end of the Victorian era.

Entrepreneurs and philanthropists promoted alternative sources of protein, such as fish, or 'acclimatized' exotic mammals – whose relocation expressed domination of non-European fauna.[68] Hippophagy was perhaps the most controversial alternative, widely discussed in the mid-Victorian press, but on the whole in a bantering tone. Horse-flesh was seen as a solution to a dearth of meat during the cattle-plague of 1865-67; but attempts to emulate the Parisian *banquet hippophagique* of 1865, itself stimulated in part by official concerns about the low consumption of meat in comparison with the British, were unsuccessful. A 'Society for the Propagation of Horseflesh as an Article of Food' hosted a dinner at the Langham Hotel in 1868 to promote the meat. There were lectures on the subject and subsequent French propaganda revived the idea in 1875, but the British response remained unsympathetic.[69]

Food adulteration was pervasive in nineteenth century Britain due to urbanization, industrialization and the particular circumstances of trades (such as competition in the retail of beer and tea), with profound medical, social and economic effects.[70] It became a matter of medical or scientific concern from the early 1850s, for men such as John Postgate, Henry Letheby, John Simon and Arthur Hassall. The findings of analytical chemistry, printed in *The Lancet* from 1851-54, were widely reported.[71] The evidence of widespread adulteration led to the formation of a national society, the Anti-Adulteration Association, and local societies, to agitate for 'prompt and efficient legislation'. At Birmingham, for instance, six meetings were held and in February 1856 there were resolutions on municipal food and drug tests, and the Home Office was petitioned.[72] In parliament the question was treated by radicals and Tories as a test of free trade. Those who called for legislation against adulteration risked being accused of treating the populace as infantile rather than informed and rational consumers free to avoid the patently fraudulent goods. Tory opponents of Free Trade depicted the 'poor man' as at the mercy of the retailer.[73] Commentators pointed to the implications for national reputation from the wholesale fraud being committed.[74]

The poor, the main victims of adulteration, whose stomachs were (in the words of the co-operator G.J. Holyoake) 'the waste basket of the market', organized to secure the purity of their food through such establishments as flour mills created in the eighteenth century, and in the co-operative movement.[75] Holyoake noted that the co-operative People's Mill in Leeds 'wisely' supported the local Anti-Adulteration Society's efforts in 1855, judging this involvement to demonstrate respect and interest for the community.[76] Food supply co-operatives were recommended by philanthropists partly for their protection against adulteration and poor quality. The purity and genuineness of foods came to be stressed in advertisements in the 1850s but adulteration remained a problem even after legislation enabled local authorities to appoint public analysts from the 1870s.

Samuel Smiles's opinion that the 'spirit of self-help is the root of all genuine growth in the individual; and, exhibited in the lives of the many, it constitutes the true source of national strength and vigour' received much support.[77] Amongst the virtues retrospectively seen as characteristically 'Victorian', thrift has been given prominence, though it was not confined to British culture.[78] Part of the 'hard way' along with 'character', punctuality and duty, thrift helped fuel the Victorian engine of self-help.[79] Though thrift was a necessity for middle-class families keen to display their respectability, discourse on thrift was directed especially at the poor by their betters, in sermon, lecture, tract, newspaper article and visitation. Thrift was about self-sacrifice and abstinence quite as much as it was about recycling and avoidance of waste, to make the poor moral and useful. Poverty and destitution, it was believed by many, could be eradicated partly through thrift. But this virtue was, according to Smiles, 'the growth of experience and example'.[80] The organizations established to exemplify and promote thrift ranged from the local savings clubs to penny banks, the Penny Office Savings Bank (established 1861) and a variety of social reform societies.

Edwin Chadwick's *Report on the Sanitary Condition of the Labouring Population of Great Britain* (1842) accounted for poor health partly through domestic mismanagement which amounted to lack of thrift: the 'huckster dealing' in an improvident manner, the extravagant purchase of small quantities of food, indulgence in meat and drink.[81] Thrift concerned domestic management in general, not simply advocating foresight in savings. Food was part of the problem, and hence the outrage of food reformers who wanted to eradicate adulteration. Foods made cheap because of adulteration were deceptions, their existence prevented accurate domestic economy. Waste was to be deplored in the kitchen, hence the value placed on equipment such as the 'digester', designed to convert all the scraps into nourishing soup, and the stockpot and the eulogising by domestic economists (and early apologists for factory conditions), of the French soup: a 'potage economy' where nothing was thrown away. Newspapers and journals reported on schemes for cookery classes throughout the period. Much of the advice on food thrift was irrelevant to the poor however: too expensive in terms of equipment, fuel, and time.

The promotion of thrift as virtue and social panacea had its critics. The vegetarian movement's place in the discourse of thrift is one theme in its dialogue with the working classes, and will be explored more closely in a later chapter. It is sufficient at this stage to point out that some vegetarians found the economic argument offensively selfish and preferred more 'ideal' arguments to those of the 'breech pocket'. But there was a wider attitude towards food which saw pleasure as something to be avoided. Vegetarianism can partly be seen as a dietetic form of puritanism, with the promotion of 'simplicity of taste' as a moral rather than aesthetic virtue, though vegetarians were not necessarily ascetics. Old Testament-derived scruples about eating foods with blood or which derived from strangled animals might also figure. In Samuel Butler's dissection of his evangelical childhood, when Christina Pontifex agitates herself about insufficient spiritual-mindedness, in *The Way of All Flesh* (begun in the 1870s but published in 1903) she worries about her past enjoyment of 'forbidden' black puddings.[82]

Evangelical Protestantism with its concern to avoid soul-imperilling sensual gratification might condemn a preoccupation with food after hunger was gratified. Although corpulence was associated with health for most of the nineteenth century, over-indulgence in food represented greed, one of the sins to be combated by evangelical parents. Diet must be seen as part of a regime in which 'everything was restricted and controlled'.[83] One result of sabbatarian scruples was that Sunday meals were largely cold affairs; in Colin Spencer's acclaimed history of British food puritanism is blamed more widely for culinary decline. But puritanical response to food was not the only attitude: there are too many contrasting references to enjoying eating.[84] One writer who has referred to the 'horrid little books for the instruction and intimidation of the young... against the sin of gluttony' also asserts that the sternest Puritans of the early Victorian period 'felt no sense of guilt in enjoying the pleasures of the table'.[85] Moreover, a criticism of asceticism did not necessarily mean a belief that material comfort was enough. Richard Jefferies, for instance, stressed that 'when the highest wages of the best paid artisan are reached it is *not* the greatest privilege of the man to throw mutton chops to dogs and piles of empty champagne bottles'.[86]

The lack of vegetables in the national diet was deplored by non-vegetarian food reformers who appreciated the nutritional value of vegetables, or who wished to see a wider consumption of meat through the wealthier consumers foregoing some of their meat for vegetables. Cookery writers and gourmets also deplored the British habit of overcooking their vegetables.[87] Tom Jerrold condemned the attitude of English cooks and their employers, that except as an accompaniment to meat, vegetables were 'nasty foreign messes'.[88] English culinary antipathy was attacked by other writers on food: Joseph Brown, a Sunderland doctor, condemned John Bull's hostility towards garden stuffs; the writer of a tract promoting maize deplored the antipathy towards 'foreigners, vegetable or human'.[89] Significantly, a late-Victorian edition of Mrs Beeton's *Cookery* argued that the greatest boon of vegetarianism, its popularization of a wider range of vegetable dishes, brought 'us more on a level with our Continental neighbours'.[90]

There were popular and expert prejudices. Vegetable soups were associated with Gallic culinary ingenuity attributed to the low quality of French ingredients or poverty.[91] Scientists revealed that vegetables required more effort to digest than animal foods and argued that in order to obtain an equivalent amount of nutrition large quantities would need to be consumed. Vegetables were associated with certain classes: thus onions were the staple of the poorest, whose strong and uneducated stomachs required their stimulus; turnips were avoided except in dire circumstances.[92] Garlic was obviously foreign. Lentils and pulses, treated today as vegetarian staples, were difficult to get and associated with animal foods. Rice was not commonly used.[93] Fruits were associated with summer diarrhoea and imagined to be dangerous for children. Medical writers stressed the danger of parasites on raw vegetables.[94]

A major problem (obviously important for vegetarians) involved urban and rural availability. Production for urban markets meant that vegetables might not be cheaply available to the rural poor, so that, as the great chef Alexis Soyer noted, 'excepting in large towns' vegetables were scarce.[95] But their price for city-dwellers was high, as one newspaper noted in 1875, the monstrous price of fresh vegetables rendered bacon and cabbage, 'the humble fare of the country', almost unattainable.[96] Tinning of fruit and vegetables, which cheapened them, did not happen until the 1880s. Between 1815 and 1850, Britain was 'a population existing permanently on the verge of starvation'.[97] From the 1870s working-class diets improved, as a result of rising real incomes, cheap imported foodstuffs, and standardised and pre-packaged foods through multiple retailing, which helped reduced food adulteration. Railways made feasible the expansion of the trawling industry to supply urban consumers. Even agricultural labourers' diets may have improved. No longer was bread the 'staff of life': Britain was in the vanguard of a dietetic revolution that saw the democratization of meat and protein in Europe.[98] School textbooks of the late-Victorian era presented the pennyworth and ha'porths of meat as a sign of poverty which progress had abolished.[99] Macaulay's dream in 1848 that the twentieth-century artisan would 'be as little used to dine without meat as they now are to eat rye bread' was to be realized.[100] Made possible by steam-trawling, railway transportation and ice preservation, fish and chip shops were well-established by the late nineteenth century. They were a significant contribution of protein for the working class and an addition to the 'fast food' that had always been sold by stalls and street vendors.

The adulteration scandals had probably helped to educate people's tastes towards milder flavoured, less vibrant foods, through the revelations of dangerous substances used to 'sophisticate'. If adulteration was less widespread by the end of our period, there were new concerns about the use of chemical preservatives and flavourings. For the middle class, the movement was towards a more mixed and lighter diet, possibly influenced by vegetarianism.[101] It also represented the trend towards self-control in feeding, which had already been the response of the aristocracy as food supplies became stable and plentiful in the modern era.[102] But if diet generally became more varied and improved in quality, the domestic cookery that began to be taught in some cities ignored the *pleasure* of food. Victorian cuisine was also less sophisticated than it had been, because of the prestige of French cuisine and the disruption of culinary traditions through urbanization.[103]

Eating together, as a method of creating sociality, is a sociological truism. Food was publicly consumed in a variety of places, from hotels and public houses, to the restaurants that proliferated during the second half of the nineteenth century. Roast beef, white bait and turtle soup were dishes associated with public dinners for the humble (for beef was commonly given to the poor at feasts marking great occasions such as coronations) to the most exalted civic and government officials. The vegetarian was an intruder who sat at these events eating cold potatoes and, like the teetotaller he or she often was, imbibed water to the dismay of fellow guests. Those observing a vegetable diet had to choose between swallowing their scruples and eating meat in public, thus undermining the cause in the eyes of the more rigid, or consolidating their reputation for eccentricity. Verse in *Punch* which depicted the vegetarian's Christmas fare was one expression of the pity or contempt directed at those who, through their dietetic heresy, seemed to be foregoing festive hospitality. It was not surprising, then, that the one vegetarian recipe which London adherents inserted in *The Times*, was for Christmas pudding! Vegetarians were encouraged to entertain their friends at parties to demonstrate the attractiveness of their new diet: the desire to show its reasonableness could lead to mimicry of meat dishes. What vegetarians actually ate is studied in chapter five, how they campaigned in order to alter the food of the majority is now considered.

1

THE VEGETARIAN MOVEMENT, *c.*1838-1901

The immediate origins of the Victorian vegetarian movement lie in attempts by a few hundred pioneers to encourage the diet as part of their religious beliefs (as members of the Swedenborgian sect of Bible Christians or Cowherdites in Salford and Manchester), or as a result of their temperance beliefs, or compassion for animals, though to be sure, such motivations are not neatly divided. Here the movement's history is provided, beginning with the nurturing of vegetarianism by another group of people in the 1830s, radical communitarians. This first part concludes with the establishment of the VS. The next section studies the movement's development in the Society's first two decades and examines key aspects of vegetarianism as an organized, propagandist and 'lived' (that is to say, embodied and enacted) movement, before its apparent eclipse in the 1860s. Aspects of its social base are brought out here and through a study of London vegetarians. The third section studies the movement's revival from the 1870s through a brief examination of some key areas for activity across Britain, and again through a study of London, which became a centre for vegetarianism to rival its earlier heartlands in the north of England.

Before the Vegetarian Society

The followers of the failed merchant and theosopher James Pierrepont Greaves provided one highly significant source of vegetarian propaganda through their activity at a community founded in 1838 at Richmond in Surrey, known as the 'Concordium' or Alcott House. Greaves' self-ascribed label of 'sacred socialism' and the involvement by several Owenites in the community have led to a misinterpretation of the community as an Owenite one.[1] For Greaves and many followers ignored contemporary politics and economics, believing individual moral reformation and the development of the 'love-spirit' (or divine spirit) was necessary before the social reform proposed by Robert Owen. Greaves was transformed by a spiritual experience in 1817, and as a disciple later advised, 'you must think of him as an inspired man, or at least as a man who truly believed himself inspired'.[2] The *New Moral World*, reviewing Greaves' posthumously published letters, spoke of his 'peculiar philosophy ... It was emphatically to live in a new world to hear him talk'.[3] Despite his strange phraseology the emphasis on spiritual reformation before any meaningful 'physical socialism' is clear. His vegetarianism, from about 1817, was for mystical and moral reasons (he thought the physiological motives had been well-argued); humanitarian concerns joining fears of animalization and sexual stimulation. A celibate, his teachings included expressed anxiety about (as Jackie Latham expresses it) 'a new kind of original sin'; engendered by unregulated marriage and intercourse without the 'divine creative love-law'.[4] Dietary reform would remove a sexual stimulant and separate man 'from the animal world'.[5]

Greaves' salon at 49 Burton Street, London, from about 1837, was open to all and he attracted radicals and literary figures to weekly meetings of his 'Aesthetic Institution'. Of his disciples, the most important female follower was Sophia Chichester, a wealthy aristocrat who also gave covert financial support to several other theosophers and radical reformers, such as 'Zion' Ward and 'Shepherd' Smith.[6] In July 1838 Greaves and Chichester established 'Alcott House' school on Pestalozzian lines at Ham Common village, Surrey. A school existed throughout this period, with an average of thirty pupils (a few were day pupils) recruited from radical families and the neighbourhood.

Promoted by followers before 1838, and central to the community, was vegetarianism. The prospectus which records the community's reorganization in 1841 details the diet (oatmeal, porridge, bread, fruit and water), dress and timetable for work, meals, classes and recreation. The 'Concordium' consisted of 'united individuals ... desirous, under industrial and progressive education, with simplicity in diet, dress and lodging, etc., to retain the means for the harmonic developement [sic] of their physical, intellectual and moral natures.'[7] Graham bread with raisins was baked on the premises, a garden was planted to promote self-sufficiency, and a shoemaker/tailor was recruited. The establishment was open to visitors, especially on Sundays when there were lectures; many hundreds may therefore have become acquainted with the community and its dietetic reforms. To disseminate their philosophy and recruit, a press was established. Tracts, motto 'wafers' for sealing letters, and two journals, *The Healthian* and *The New Age*, were published. These devoted much space to vegetarianism (a neologism it helped make current). Other physicalpuritanisms discussed included hydropathy (which the community pioneered from late 1841). The Concordium experiment was recorded in the *New Age*'s 'Concordium Gazette'. The 'progressive' cause of phonetics was endorsed. Works by American transcendentalists were advertised and Graham's physiology reviewed.

America, already a place of physiological reform ideas and the location of the new moral world, was important for sacred socialists (and Owenites). The Concordists printed and promoted American texts in favour of vegetarianism such as William A. Alcott's *Vegetable Diet Defended* and Sylvester Graham's *Lecture to Young Men on Chastity*, and hoped to raise funds for a visit by Graham. The association of Greaves and his community with the infinitely more talented New England transcendentalists was serendipitous.[8] Greaves' disciples hoped the educational reformer Bronson Alcott would visit, and run the eponymous school; when he came shortly after Greaves' death, he was charmed by the community. Greaves had intended to establish a community in America; Alcott brought back three of the Concordists – Charles Lane, his son, and Henry Gardiner Wright – with him in September 1842. Wright found America uncongenial and returned, but Lane stayed with Alcott to establish a short-lived but famous community, Fruitlands, near Harvard. The disaster at Fruitlands did not, at least, shake Alcott's faith in vegetarianism (he joined the British VS in 1850).[9]

Despite talk of withdrawal from 'the external discordance and disagreement of actual society', there were attempts to connect the diet with the peace movement and attract converts through tours in 1843. Three Concordists went out as missionaries to exhibit their 'simplicity of living' in tours of the Midlands, Hampshire and Sussex, and generated discussion by their manner, and costume of white trousers and checked shirt, *sans* necktie or hat. The *New Age* thought that the sympathetic response 'augurs well for humanity'.[10] The paper itself was an important means of propaganda but circulation was limited despite advertisements (in the *New Moral World* and J.E. Smith's *Family Herald*).[11] An obvious group to cultivate was 'advanced' teetotallers. Whilst the *Healthian* mystified the *Temperance Lancet* in 1841[12], some teetotallers' sympathies were reflected in a teetotal excursion to the Concordium in July 1843.[13] A teetotal reader of the *New Age* advised linking it as an 'acceptable journal ... sowing good seed', to the 'nine million' teetotallers and anticipated 'high patronage'. The journal's title was altered to *The New Age, Concordium Gazette and Temperance Advocate* after the sixth number.[14]

The Concordists also promoted physiological reform societies, beginning with a 'Health, or Physiological Association' whose secretary, G.J. Ford, was involved in vegetarianism into the 1860s.[15] The *Healthian* approved its simple, pledge-free rules and reported its intention to hold public and private meetings, print and circulate literature, and offer personal example on health and physiological law. The committee was open to members of either sex.[16] Every Monday in October discussions on an 'interesting topic' took place at 11, Leathersellers' Buildings, London Wall. On the 19th of October, a crowded assemblage for the departing Bronson Alcott included the pioneer vegetarian William Lambe who approved 'the object and the means'.[17] The Association then disappeared from the *Healthian* which itself folded in February 1843. Another attempt to promote vegetarianism through organized propaganda and missions was launched in mid-October 1843 in the shape of a 'British and Foreign Society for the Promotion of Humanity and the Abstinence from Animal Foods,' to disseminate 'correct principles of universal peace, health of soul and body, and on the prolongation of human life'.[18] The society was to have fourteen officers and members of both sexes. Chichester was made president, perhaps to secure funds from her after Greaves' death.[19] The few members included a lady of ten years' vegetarianism who had resisted meat when eight despite her servant's pressure. One of the few reported meetings debated man's relationship to the animal world.[20]

Internal power struggles followed Greaves' death, with William Galpin, resident from summer 1843, exercising an increasingly bleak rule that repelled many. Recast as the 'Universal Concordian Society' the community eschewed animal materials, limited food, and avoided cookery. The Owenite Alexander Campbell, failing to win control, left in 1844, and undeterred, established a short-lived educational and vegetarian community at Hampton Wick. A 'Fruit Festival' in summer 1847 demonstrated the waning Greavesian ethos in discussing the 'Social and Political Condition of Women'. A conference in early July 1847 was an unsuccessful attempt by William Oldham and Charles Lane to reinvigorate the community by associating it with efforts to promote vegetarianism. By 1848 the community had dissolved, the house became an orphanage for cholera-orphaned girls and the grounds became a strawberry garden.[21]

Although Spencer has described the Concordium as 'well outside the perimeters of what society in general would have thought acceptable', there were radicals who supported it.[22] Holyoake, for instance, distinguished between the mysticism that he deplored, and the physiological reform that he admired (he dabbled in vegetarianism). His account in the *Cheltenham Free Press* was notably appreciative of the health reforms: members looked healthy and appeared happy, the plain vegetable diet was contrasted with the 'disease-engendering food of the epicure' and the dress and beards were excused as symbols of independence: 'We have a strange propensity to ridicule the slightest deviation from custom's worn and hackneyed way, however harmless in itself that deviation may be.'[23] Holyoake, who declined an invitation to teach at Alcott House, was dismayed and exasperated by the Concordist papers which he published in the journal *The Movement* (1844).[24] But though critical of the perversions of Greavesian philosophy by disciples, his later journal, *The Reasoner* presented Greaves as the 'great logician of personal reform', who had originated the 'personal reforms that are destined to extend their operations over the people'; dietary reform being the most important of those personal reforms that needed to precede public or political reform.[25]

The debate on vegetarianism involved several other leading reformers. An important contemporary, J.E. Smith, formerly a visitor to Greaves' salon, devoted *The Shepherd* to sustained critical discussion of sacred socialism and vegetarianism in 1837. Smith possibly visited the Concordium: he is probably the 'J.E.S.' writing to the editor of the *New Age* pointing out vegetarian inconsistency in 1844.[26] From May 1843 Smith edited the weekly *Family Herald*, a 'family religious journal' which in its heyday had a circulation of half a million. In its early years it published and replied to many inquiries on subjects which included Southcottianism, socialism, astrology, phrenology and vegetarianism. In 1843, responding to a letter from Oldham (hoping for publicity for the community), he maintained that a two-year experiment was insufficient and that diet remained a question of individual natures. Vegetarianism, kindred to celibacy and the common life, would be brought forward with the growing influence of 'Puseyism' upon an established church which alone made such discussions respectable.[27] In 1844-45, the *Herald* published an advertisement for *New Age* and texts associated with the community and Smith returned (not for the last time) to diet in an article on the sixteenth-century Italian vegetarian Luigi Cornaro.[28]

Greavesian experimentation attracted the attention of even more distinguished figures. Alcott and Owen were the most important visitors, though (presumably by report) it was known to Friedrich Engels and Karl Marx. The *New Moral World* published a letter from Engels referring to 'Ham Common folks': the community must be included in their attack on utopian socialism.[29] Carlyle's relationship with Greaves, whom he characterized as a 'blockhead' and a 'tail' of Emerson in England, has been examined.[30] Through Emerson, Alcott was received by Carlyle in 1843 and exasperated him with the 'Potatoe-gospel' [sic]. One of Alcott's visits was witnessed by Robert Browning who ridiculed the diet, though he had been vegetarian in the 1830s through Shelley's example.[31]

One disciple, Francis Barham, considered Greaves to be greater than Coleridge; Lane described him as a 'colossus'.[32] Yet his posthumous reputation, beyond his followers, was slight. An essay in *Westminster Review* in 1852 described him as vegetarianism's modern apostle and identified the poet Henry Septimus Sutton, author of *Evangel of Love*, as a successor.[33] These references apart, Greaves and the community were unknown beyond the small world of (transatlantic) utopian and radical reformers. Hundreds may have boarded with or visited the community, but this generated no public fame. The radical *Douglas Jerrold's Newspaper*, reviewing Lane's vegetarian tract of 1847, demonstrated its previous ignorance of the community.[34] The one satire on Alcott House which might have reached a larger audience, in a novel by Mary Kelty published in 1851, has been entirely ignored.[35] Yet the Concordium's reputation for ascetic fanaticism was preserved by the memoirs of the radicals Thomas Frost, Holyoake and William Linton.[36] Late-Victorian and Edwardian vegetarians, interested in tracing lineages, examined the Concordium and drew on the memories of the few surviving participants.[37]

The efforts of the Concordists had some resonance with other reformers. Pure diet, good health and physiology in dress were components of the 'community movement' central to Owenism.[38] High-thinking and plain-living Owenites saw temperance as a virtue and could naturally investigate vegetarianism, especially when the *New Moral World* which catered to Owenite artisans and advanced liberals discussed the diet.[39] Vegetarianism was promoted by native Owenites and by non-British communities reported by the Owenite organ, such as the community planned in Ohio which intended to 'wholly exclude the animal kingdom' for humanitarian, physiological and timesaving reasons (the time thus released for mental culture).[40] The organ of William Hodson's breakaway Owenite community at Manea Fen published an account of Alcott House school by John Firmin which supported the diet for socialist children but questioned its suitability for adults. With 'the assistance of a light trade, well directed and well governed' it would make children wholly or practically self-supporting. The savings would go to community funds, 'toil and disagreement' in food preparation would be abolished and time could be spent in more rational and useful activity.[41] The frequency of the discussion explains why, when the projected Norwood Co-operative Industrial Association advertised in late 1843, it eschewed all 'sectarianism', including the 'edible'.[42]

But the relationship of vegetarianism to Owenism was ambivalent. At the Owenite community of Harmony Hall, vegetarianism was adopted to address financial and organizational deficiencies and partly espoused on principle (indeed one youthful convert, Alfred Slatter, continued to advocate it as a means to social reform into the 1870s). Not all the members relished the diet, although Alexander Somerville said half of the community were vegetarian.⁴³ One of the governors of the community, James Rigby, was a life-long vegetarian⁴⁴; his successor John Finch was a teetotaller whose testimony before a Commons committee, that in the rational state of society 'all those who will eat beef, mutton, veal, and pork, must in turn kill the animals for themselves,' suggests his vegetarian sympathies.⁴⁵ Finch's second governorship inaugurated a spartan regime, with a committee formed to create a 'cheap and rational diet' but a lack of consensus led to separate vegetarian and non-vegetarian tables, the former containing the merriest diners according to Holyoake.⁴⁶

The Owenite relationship with the Concordium was equally ambivalent. Metropolitan Owenites treated it as a radical country resort; the 'attractive yet convenient position ... made it a good goal for visitors from London, particularly if they could avoid the food'.⁴⁷ Owen visited thrice, in the summer of 1840, with Lambeth Owenites, in spring and August 1843.⁴⁸ A rural excursion, during which socialist forms of government were debated, was reported in August 1841.⁴⁹ Another Owenite group visited in that year.⁵⁰ Charles Lane, so important in the Greavesian community, had had an early interest in Owen, attending the first public exposition of his ideas in London, in 1818.⁵¹ A more committed Owenite was Alexander Campbell, one of the Owenite 'social missionaries', who was converted by Greaves and joined the community in 1842, but remained an Owenite propagandist. After Greaves' death he edited some of his letters for publication by the community. The *New Age* reported Owenite congresses and activity at Harmony, but criticized Owenite 'sectarianism', and condemned the use of hired and animal labour at Harmony. Concordists hoped for support from the *New Moral World*, social missionaries and tracts in the preparation of 'all' for the abandonment of meat, 'injurious and superfluous luxuries'.⁵² Some Concordists, for example Wright, lectured to metropolitan Rational Society branches. Wright twice lectured on the 'advantages of a vegetable diet' at Goswell Street Road, Branch 16 of the Rational Society, and gave a well-attended lecture on 'Fruit Diet' to the Lambeth branch which 'gave great satisfaction' according to its secretary John Firmin.⁵³ In 1840 a Mr Body of A1 Branch had presented Harmony with the book *Vegetable Cookery*, and four years later Campbell gave a lecture on Concordist principles and practice to the same branch.⁵⁴

The appeal of mysticism, shared millenarianism and the desire for paternal leadership explain the migration of some of the collapsing Harmony Hall's disillusioned inhabitants to the Concordium.⁵⁵ William Galpin, vice-president of the Rational Society, obeying Owen's call for him to leave Harmony, found refuge there, with disastrous consequences. Hannah Bond, who had taught children at Harmony, joined after its collapse. Samuel Bower of Bradford (who went with Lane, Wright and

Alcott to America) also joined. For some (like the widow of the prominent radical Richard Carlile, Eliza Sharples), residency was simply an alternative to destitution.[56] As the wider Owenite movement dissolved in the mid-1840s into a variety of institutions promoting education, self-help, or secularism, for a few it became identified with a 'new eccentric world where individual self-expression signified the beginning of the supercession of irrational social prejudices'.[57] In this context vegetarianism was viewed by critical socialists as a characteristic of less sane, or 'dissident' followers. Socialism now harboured 'moral and intellectual delinquents – empty-headed young men bordering on idiocy, babblers and quibblers, long-haired, bearded and vegetarians, etc.'[58]

Similar ambivalence can be found in the Chartist movement. The Chartist utopia involved a transformation in diet. For, as the *Northern Star*, the movement's leading newspaper observed, those who reared the cattle did not taste flesh food.[59] The paper reported the projected vegetarian conference in July 1847, but printed comments against dietetic totalism.[60] Earlier it had favourably reviewed the *New Age* and described the Concordists as an 'interesting body of Social reformers, who seem to realize practically (so far as possible) what god-like Shelley only dreamed of in his Queen Mab'.[61] A fair review of the *Healthian* characterized the diet advocated by Concordists and a 'large number of isolated individuals' as 'whole-hog teetotalism and no Mistake!'[62] Yet vegetarianism attracted some Chartists: and perhaps vegetarianism may be classed as one of the sectional successors to Chartism.[63] The most well-known examples are Charles Neesom and, at least to the extent of writing a vegetarian essay, Robert Gammage.[64] Charles Kingsley's character John Crossthwaite, in *Alton Locke* (1850), was an idealistic Chartist and vegetarian, 'to which perhaps, he owed a great deal of the almost preternatural clearness, volubility, and sensitiveness of his mind'.[65] Other Chartists of course, were vegetarian because of their poverty, such as John Bezer, whose published autobiography included the apology to any vegetarian readers for his backsliding from 'vegetable marrow'.[66]

The influence of vegetarian believers reached beyond the mainstream to more fringe movements. For example, Concordists published tracts by John Etzler, leader of the 'Tropical Emigration Society'.[67] Etzler, his wife and a disciple, C.F. Stollmeyer, briefly resided at the Concordium, where Etzler delivered a course of public lectures in 1843-44.[68] A materialist, Etzler at least came to share the faith in vegetarianism, claiming that the man of 'science and reality' could see no need to butcher animals for food and use, or quarrel and rob fellow man for a living: 'there is an endless variety of vegetable foods much pleasanter in taste, sight, smell and much more wholesome, than carcasses of animals'.[69] The Etzlerite 'Co-operative

Emigration Society' endorsed vegetarianism in 1844. Members decided following 'long and earnest enquiry' to restrict themselves to a vegetable diet (excepting milk, butter, eggs and other products not requiring killing) for economic, social and moral reasons. The principle was so important that they urged it upon the attention of 'all advanced reformers' and made a 'public declaration of their views on morals, diet, practical measures &c'.[70] Etzler's pro-vegetarian statements appeared in the Etzlerite organ *Morning Star* which was founded and initially edited by a youthful enthusiast and vegetarian propagandist, James Elmzlie Duncan, connected to the Concordium.[71] Duncan's mediocre literary output included a chapter of an unfinished novel entitled 'Edward Noble, or the Utopian' which featured Greaves and a vegetarian essay which referred to Shelley and the 'Healthian diet' of 'the London Vegetarians'.[72] He advertised a *Guide to Health and Longevity* in the *New Moral World*, and in 1848 announced an expanded serialization of his 'romance of progression' whose heroes included Greaves, Owen, Etzler, the Unitarian W.J. Fox, the temperance figure Father Mathew, and Richard Cobden. Duncan's continued interest in physical puritanism is shown by his subscription to William Horsell's *The Truth-Tester* and *Vegetarian Advocate*. Horsell published Duncan's final journal in 1849.[73]

Another communitarian experiment which incorporated a school and food reform was promoted by the Barmbys (1843-44).[74] A pioneer communist, John Goodwyn Barmby was influenced by Greaves, the Concordium and White Quakerism. One of the 'societarian wants' he listed in *The Promethean* in 1842 was 'medicinally prepared diet'; the tenth was common or contemporaneous consumption of food.[75] In 1843 he and his wife Catherine (an Owenite feminist) established 'Moreville Communitorium' at Hanwell, Middlesex. His costume and hairstyle at Hanwell were modelled on the Concordists'.[76] His dietary rules (reprinted by the *New Age*) partially promoted vegetarianism.[77] A follower of Barmby and Greaves, Henry Fry of Cheltenham, endorsed vegetarianism in his *Educational Circular and Communist Apostle*.[78] An attack on the Barmbys' small Communist Church sect (*c*.1842-49) in the *News of the World* (1846), treated dietary radicalism as part of the creed.[79]

The high ideals of such communities are apparent in yet another, established by William Galpin at Little Bentley on the Tytherley estate in 1845, with Isaac Ironside of Sheffield (a visitor to the Concordium).[80] Members of the Rational Society were informed by them 'that man has a nobler destiny than that of being a mere eating and drinking animal, or one that receives his highest gratifications from sensual objects'.[81] They hoped that members of the Harmony community would find refuge from the 'old world' here. Members were to abandon worldly ties and connections, 'That God may be all in all.' Galpin's 'divine message', to gather a nucleus of the Universal Church before Christ's second coming, was dutifully, if scornfully printed in the *Reasoner*.[82] Holyoake rightly identified the ultra-puritanism promoted there as influenced by White Quakerism.[83] A newspaper reporter, although spicing his account, wrote that members equalled 'the most ascetic cynic of old' in their self-denial.[84] It proved too much for many members including Ironside, who felt that Little Bentley involved 'absurd and repulsive austerities – ridiculous and repugnant fanaticism, little short of insanity'.[85]

The contentious White Quaker community, established by the schismatic Quakers Joshua Jacob and Abigail Beale, became another location for ultra-asceticism and vegetarianism. Though they rejected Greavesian celibacy, they practised community in goods, wore undyed linen clothing, and the men grew beards and long hair. They were visited separately by reformers such as Barmby, Campbell, Ironside and Owen, and attracted other radicals.[86] Ironside collected sympathizers from Manchester's branch of the Rational Society, some of whom joined the sect.[87] After Little Bentley's collapse, Galpin joined, with marriage to Joshua's sister Mary cementing his 'Jacobism'.[88] Given the sect's aim to return to primitive values they espoused simplicity in diet: at one community house in a former hotel in Dublin, 'some twenty or more' practised vegetarianism.[89] Probably due to Galpin, the community committed itself firmly to vegetarianism. In summer 1847 a visitor saw the dining table at the sect's new home, Newlands, piled with wheaten bread, butter, cheeses and dried fruits. When the English reformer Joseph Barker visited the sect in 1850 the diet was rigidly vegetarian, with bread and potatoes made available to impoverished visitors. A bleak account in the *Family Herald* reported the sect's decline, the correspondent suggesting that Jacob ate secretly since he was thriving despite the diet of 'half boiled green cabbage, raw corn, and water'.[90]

Vegetarianism as a result of such experimentation was a familiar topic in journals associated with Owenism and 'infidelity', and came to be supported by a number of Chartists. Communitarianism continued to have associations with vegetarianism but from 1847 vegetarians had the wider community of an organized movement for support.

Establishing the Vegetarian Society

By the late 1840s, vegetarians sought a national association. The VS was founded by remnants of the Concordium, a few advanced teetotallers and the vegetarian Cowherdite sect. Its establishment owed much to the Cowherdite James Simpson, who became the first president. Also among the prime movers was the temperance reformer William Horsell who had become vegetarian in 1846 in the process of writing a populist health manual. His journal, *The Truth-Tester*, presented vegetarianism as 'the next practical moral subject which is likely to call forth the virtuous energy of society' and published dialogues, maxims, verse and letters in support of the diet. In April 1847 Horsell printed a letter from a young teetotaller called William Bramwell Withers, of Whitehurst in Hampshire, calling for such a society. Vegetarians met in Alcott House on 8 July to discuss the project. A further meeting on 30 September, at Northwood Villa in Ramsgate, the hydropathic infirmary managed by Horsell and his wife, formally established the VS.[91]

The rules had already been drawn up by James Simpson, who had corresponded with Horsell to reassure him that his advocacy was worthwhile and that many readers would support him.[92] The Cowherdites also sent their endorsement to William Oldham.[93] The Concordist contribution included advertisements for Alcott House, a letter by Hannah Bond, and essays by Charles Lane. Members of Alcott House wanted to be involved in the project, and Oldham invited interested parties to a 'physiological conference' (8 July 1847) to publicly initiate preparations.[94] The meeting attracted some fifty vegetarians including James Simpson, Joseph Gunn Palmer (a Birmingham Quaker who acted as chairman), and Horsell. Bond's dishes united 'the innocence of the hermit's repast with the refinements of art, and the labours of domestic experiences'.[95] In the afternoon the group, which had increased to one hundred and thirty vegetarians and others, congregated in the shade of a large tree in the 'beautiful and productive garden'. Lectures followed, with Horsell chairing one at Ramsgate Primitive Methodist chapel. He published an address by Simpson and, several weeks before the date arranged, printed a verse 'Invitation to the Physiological Festival' by Fanny Lacy, an aristocrat associated with Barmby and the Concordium.[96]

The establishment of the VS involved the support of a well-known figure, the Cowherdite Joseph Brotherton MP, who presided at the inaugural meeting which included fellow Cowherdites such as James Scholefield and James Gaskill.[97] Simpson was elected the VS's president, Horsell was appointed secretary (a post he held for three years) and William Oldham became treasurer (for a year). One hundred and fifty members were immediately enrolled; in 1848 the VS comprised 265 members spanning the ages 14 to 76, with Cowherdite families providing almost half of the members.[98] Although the Cowherdite element to the early movement is a well-known one which need not be examined here, an analysis of the role of one of its members, James Simpson, is crucial to an understanding of the VS from 1847 to 1859.[99] Simpson provided it with the necessary financial support for its public activities, and leadership.

Horsell later acknowledged that the establishment of the society was 'principally under his own generous and judicious guidance'.[100] Given the low profile of vegetarianism in Victorian historiography, it is unsurprising that Simpson has a minor profile as a reformer.[101] Yet he was one of those leading provincial citizens so important for reform movements and provincial politics.

FIGURE 2. James Simpson, *left*, and William Horsell, *right*, founding figures in the Victorian vegetarian movement.

Simpson was the son of a wealthy Scottish calico printer who had become a Cowherdite in 1810. Education in London and Berlin prepared Simpson for a legal career but this was abandoned because he disliked the prospect of pleading for guilty clients. Inherited wealth meant he could devote himself to philanthropy and politics; in large part his early death at forty-eight was due to overwork in the cause of reform. According to one obituary, he bore the 'sins and sorrows of others' with him, even though 'moving gracefully in the higher walks of life, and amongst those who feel but slightly the heavier cares and anxieties of others'.[102] As part of the small Cowherdite sect, he was connected with many prominent Manchester and Salford men, such as his father-in-law William Harvey and Joseph Brotherton.

Simpson's career was launched when he gave his first public address at Northwood Villa. Yet vegetarianism was merely the most prominent of his causes, which included the teetotal United Kingdom Alliance (whose prohibitionist principles he accepted despite his voluntarist ideals), the peace movement, anti-capital punishment, phonetics and the allotment movement. His temperance work alone involved much travel and platform activity. In 1856 he attended the *Congres de Bienfaisance* (Brussels) as a United Kingdom Alliance delegate. Participation in this congress, and peace congresses as a member of the Peace Society, allowed him to advocate vegetarianism in other reform circles. He was one of the leading benefactors of the Anti-Tobacco Society. Like many middle-class reformers he had been involved in the anti-corn law agitation, and vegetarianism may indeed be seen as a new claimant for reformist and philanthropic attention with the apparent victory of this agitation.[103] Simpson was prominent too in local government, as a magistrate, and as the chairman of the Blackpool Local Board of Health. Some of his wealth was devoted to the expensive task of collecting data for a campaign to have Accrington made the centre of a new electoral and poor-law union district. A Liberal, he was active in the Lancashire Liberal world, being a generous benefactor of the Liberal Registration Society for North Lancashire but declining to contest a seat for Blackburn. A range of 'political reforms', such as financial and parliamentary reform, concerned him. He often arbitrated in disputes between workmen and employers. He promoted allotments as sanative and character-building, setting up 'Temperance Garden Allotments' at his Foxhill residence 'as tending to develope [sic] in the minds of working men a taste for the beautiful, as well as a love of the useful'.[104] He subscribed liberally to the day and Sunday schools and planned a school for Foxhill Bank.

His vegetarian advocacy before the VS's establishment included the publication of several tracts, and provision of vegetable soup for the starving in Manchester in 1845. On the day of the VS's formation, his anonymous *A Few Recipes of Vegetable Diet*, dedicated to it, was published.[105] He publicly acknowledged that his vegetarianism resulted from the influence of a 'fond mother' who had been 'staunch and firm as rock': his father was not vegetarian. For Simpson, scientific education endorsed inherited views. As the *Truth-Tester* noted in reviewing one of his works, he came from the school of chemistry of Justus von Liebig.[106]

Simpson was no dour puritan, for the secretary of the Liverpool vegetarian association recalled him as 'pre-eminently a happy man,' who 'delighted in seeing others happy about him'.[107] An obituary in the *Manchester Examiner and Times* stated that 'though he might be termed an enthusiast, yet he never indulged in anything which savoured of dogmatism or bigotry, but ever treated an opponent with courtesy and respect'.[108] His death at a comparatively early age was a financial and moral blow to the movement. Into the 1890s the VS reiterated his own view that the key debilitating factor was overwork.[109] His secretary, Henry Clubb, recalled a daily workload of up to fifteen hours and (as a phrenologist) his 'nervous encephalic temperament'; another secretary claimed it was brought on by a chill caught at an Aberdeen hydro. Pollution, ironically in part from the Simpson calico works next to the family home, was also blamed. In an anecdote revealing Simpson's spiritualist interests, Clubb noted that a visitor, the vegetarian clairvoyant John Beach, had sensed the place's unhealthiness.[110]

The role of the new organization which Simpson led was to be crucial to the development of the movement as a national force. The next section considers the importance of the early years of the movement both nationally and in its metropolitan dimensions, to the development of the vegetarian cause.

The movement c.1847-1870

The VS spread vegetarianism beyond Manchester and Salford and its other isolated pioneers, using the standard techniques of movements, such as print media and meetings ranging from private discussion group to public lectures. The first annual report announced the preparation for lectureships and proposed local secretaries for large towns or counties to build on private advocacy.[111] Copies of the report and other publications were widely circulated. The campaign started to attract prominent press notices, *Punch* noting facetiously a 'great Vegetarian movement' whose missionaries were inculcating the 'doctrine of peas and potatoes'.[112]

Vegetarianism was strongest in urbanized, industrialized northern and midland England. There were societies in Manchester and Salford, Accrington, Rawtenstall, Bolton, Darwen, and Liverpool. In the West Riding, there were associations at Leeds, Sheffield and Barnsley. There was scattered organization and activity elsewhere across the north, in Barnsley, and at Great Houghton. In the north Midlands there was a society at Boston and activity elsewhere, in Derby and Bridgnorth. In the south Midlands there were supporters at Birmingham, Northampton, Worcester and Gloucester. Organized vegetarianism in eastern England comprised a secretary in Bury St Edmunds in 1852, Henry Clubb's efforts in Essex around 1848-1849, and a presence in Colchester. Southern England had few activists despite the fact that Whitchurch in Hampshire had been the home of William Withers, the temperance advocate whose letter had occasioned vegetarian organization. Efforts were made to agitate Andover in 1851, and a Brighton association briefly existed. In Cornwall, the temperance lecturer Bormond claimed there was 'A Whole County Alive to the Importance of a Bloodless Diet' in 1850.[113] His lectures there were by public request and 'numbers' investigated vegetarianism; but no association developed out of activity in Padstow despite the support of northern vegetarians and local teetotallers. In Scotland there were associations at Edinburgh, Glasgow, Paisley and Thornliebank. Though the Society's Office was briefly at Kirkcaldy (when the secretary, Henry McIntosh, lived there), there were only 41 Scottish members of the VS in 1866. Irish vegetarianism was even more minor, although not without its defenders and press coverage: *The Nation* recommended the *Dietetic Reformer* and stressed the scientific proof for vegetarianism provided by the Irish; *The Irishman* felt it contained 'much useful and curious information' and was an 'excellent magazine for 3*d*'.[114] Welsh vegetarianism was negligible.

Many other places were targeted by the vegetarians and had their efforts briefly reported. Some of these were urban areas where little impact was made despite a tradition of radicalism. The 'radical' Leicester around 1870 was a location for vegetarianism and other 'isms' in Mary Ward's *History of David Grieve*, a bestselling novel of 1892, but local vegetarianism in the 1850s lacked dynamism.[115] The failure to win support in the countryside will be discussed shortly.

The movement's urban geography

Because it was the home of the Cowherdite sect, the Manchester and Salford area was a central location for the early VS. The sect, vegetarian since 1809, provided leading activists and the VS's offices. Their King Street chapel library was used for meetings in 1849. Locally important and with an offshoot in distant Philadelphia, the sect was all but unknown nationally in the early Victorian era, though it received scornful publicity in Samuel Brown's essay on physical puritanism. Although some of their officers might be based elsewhere, annual meetings of the VS rarely strayed from the area until the 1870s.[116] A Manchester and Salford Vegetarian Advocates Society was formed in August 1849 and a vegetarian eating house briefly operated in Manchester in 1850. Local temperance halls invited lecturers; and branches developed in neighbouring places such as Accrington, Miles Platting, Liverpool, Rawtenstall, Darwen and Bolton.

As William Horsell wrote, vegetarianism seemed destined to find an important place 'among the moral reforms which so eminently characterise the people of Lancashire'.[117] He could have added Yorkshire, for the English 'North-west-and-Pennine' region in general nurtured the various medical unorthodoxies, Chartism, Owenism, secularism, spiritualism and other later 'currents of plebeian independence' (Social Democratic Federation, Labour Churches, Independent Labour Party).[118] Stimulating these movements of innovation or renovation was the region's strong religious nonconformity. In the case of vegetarianism, the Bible Christian concentration in Manchester and Salford and the area's strong temperance activity played an important part in making northern England a centre.

Features of the urbanized and industrialized north encouraged and sustained radical activity: high literacy and a strong belief in self-improvement which had institutional expression in friendly societies and mutual improvement societies where topics such as vegetarianism were earnestly debated. Mrs Gaskell, when contrasting north with south, thought that things seemed 'purpose-like' in the former: such earnestness was apparent in physical puritanism as well as work.[119] William Cooke Taylor, explorer of the new urban world, identified obsession with business as a defining feature of Mancunian modernity, with science, religion and charity as favoured leisure-time pursuits. Commentators such as Engels and de Tocqueville made similar observations.[120] If this environment brought new disciplines and restrictions it also allowed the literate and more independent to congregate and consume the fruits of the urban-based press, freed from the rural world of custom or pulpit-focused communication.[121]

It was a Victorian *cliché* that the future of humanity lay in cities, which 'naturally develop the democratic principle ... well-organized municipal institutions, in which the government is in the hands of the citizens, afford continual nourishment to the spirit of freedom throughout a country'.[122] Reason and intellect were urban requirements; mere physical strength was being replaced by technology.[123] Urbanization and industrialization were generally seen as concomitants of civilization and progress, though some feared the survival of 'serf-like' habits.[124] Cooke Taylor wrote of a new mentality developing in Lancashire factory districts: a dread of the countryside and rural work.[125] Vegetarians did not ignore rural areas but their rural campaigns were, as in Bury St Edmunds in 1853, unsuccessful.[126] The informed debate which vegetarian campaigners prided themselves on was alien to the peasantry, and radicalism in the countryside meant isolated individuals such as the Quakers who organized temperance activity; or the few independent tradesmen, cobblers and carpenters who might be their locality's 'Bradlaugh'.[127] Vegetarians feared a lack of support in the countryside, though the *Vegetarian Advocate* emphasized the importance of visiting villages as there was 'suitable mental soil for cultivation, amongst those who live in accordance with *nature* in other respects' or who (as one correspondent expressed it) enjoyed a state of 'primitive goodness'.[128] Bury St Edmunds' secretary believed that rural Suffolk would show no interest because of vegetarianism's appeal to reason and intellect, and he limited himself to tract dissemination.[129] An exception was the short-lived interest amongst 'husbandmen' in Chesterford in 1851.[130]

Urban civilization presented great and unprecedented social problems which in turn stimulated moral and social reform efforts. Environmental factors peculiar to the early Victorian towns and cities also help explain the appeal of physical puritanism. A 'general assault on the senses' involved food adulteration (peaking in the 1840s-50s), drabness, dinginess and noise. An 'enfeeblement of elementary taste-discrimination' in a degraded urban environment is the context in which reformers sought a return to 'nature'.[131] Workers sought escape from overcrowded and filthy townscapes in the countryside and hymned the purity of nature.[132] The pursuit of natural harmony took more exotic form amongst some reformers such as the Concordists and White Quakers with their drab or undyed costume displaying their desire for purity and alienation from the modern world. Urban experience sustained the utopian archetype of the rural colony and 'back to the land'/'return to nature' sentiments can be seen in vegetarianism.

Although industrialization and urbanization were attended in Britain by democratization in meat consumption, which encouraged non-vegetarians to identify civilization with rising meat consumption, modernization also provided the preconditions for vegetarianism by replacing mere subsistence with choice and selection in the market.[133] Urbanization also encouraged that zoophilia which led to vegetarianism through an altered relationship with animals, now sentimentalized through a detachment from husbandry and agriculture. But this distance can be exaggerated, since animal exploitation and maltreatment were omnipresent features of the urban environment throughout the period. Moreover, though Mancunian poets praised the countryside, there is truth to Twigg's observation that northern vegetarians in the late 1840s were 'too recent emigrants from rural poverty for the romanticism of nature or of cottage life'. This came later.[134]

The inadequate and sickness-engendering diet of the proletariat was targeted by vegetarians, for one form of vegetarianism addressed the pathology of urban and industrial living. Beyond matters of health, vegetarians appealed to the needs of the new urban and industrial society. Identification of the reformed diet with self-control and economy was frequently made in vegetarian journalism, and this vein of propaganda may be considered supportive of capitalism. Quite plausibly, Twigg sees some of the vegetarian apologetics as equivalent to E.P. Thompson's depiction of methodism as a potentially 'cooling' force promotive of temperate behaviour.[135] The commercial and disciplinary interests of textile manufacturers, it has been noted, could be served by the temperance cause which several of them supported.[136] Several vegetarians were manufacturers, such as Charles Tysoe, a partner in a spinning firm which was noted for its exertions in promoting 'the social comfort and improvement of their workpeople'. Tysoe and his partner Harney were teetotallers and 'lose no opportunity of inculcating the advantages of temperance upon their workpeople'.[137] Those entrepreneurial qualities eulogised by Samuel Smiles could be easily endorsed by vegetarians and teetotallers.[138] But it would be wrong to interpret vegetarianism as primarily (or latently) about social control.[139] Rather, it was about voluntary control of the self; and rightly, Twigg has stressed the consonance of self control with a radical outlook. Many Chartists and freethinkers after all, supported temperance.[140] Nor did the economic rationale for a fleshless diet predominate over ethical concerns about violence and abuse of power. Yet testimony from plebeian converts delighted at the new capacity to work with limited sleep was rarely prefaced in the vegetarian press by criticism of their appalling and debilitating working or living conditions.[141]

To the statement uttered at one vegetarian soirée that 'from Manchester had flowed, as it were, the lifeblood which sustained the varied philanthropic efforts throughout the land in public works of many kinds' might be added the famous slogan of the era: 'What Manchester thinks today, London thinks tomorrow.'[142] Certainly tension between an innovatory northern England and a lagging metropolis, condemned by critics as hostile or apathetic, characterized Victorian reform and is evident, to an extent, in vegetarianism. But London was not a negligible location for early vegetarianism and became far more prominent from the 1870s. From that period northern vegetarianism, for lack of novelty when contrasted with the varied and imaginative efforts of metropolitan neophytes, rather than through any substantial decline, figured less prominently in the vegetarian crusade.[143]

Personnel and propaganda

The Cowherdite role is evident in a Manchester and Salford Vegetarian Association (established 1849), which nevertheless was in decline by 1858, reputedly through infirmity, competition from other philanthropic movements and middle-class lack of interest. The Cowherdite role was also evident in James Simpson's hometown of Accrington, a centre for calico printing, the secretary of its association was the Scotsman William Sandeman (Simpson's private secretary). The Bolton association was led by another Cowherdite, Peter Gaskill.

Other nonconformists were important too. Their interest in allied reforms was the factor however, rather than denominational affiliations. Bolton's secretary was a methodist, John Cunliffe, active in the Bolton Benevolence Society and various 'movements' (anti-Corn Law, peace, freehold and franchise reform). By the time he established the liberal

Bolton Guardian (1859), he was a town councillor. At Great Houghton in the West Riding, the Primitive Methodist Joseph Wilson led a group of converts and encouraged many experimenters. Wilson had progressed from mill worker to business man by 1888 and continued to be active in philanthropy until his death in 1926. A Chartist at fifteen, active in the Chartist Sunday school movement and temperance, his compassion for animals led him to ask Horsell for literature. The nonconformist minister William Sharman was important in energizing a vegetarian association in Sheffield in 1858.[144] But Sharman, a prominent lecturer who moved to Birmingham and then Aberdeen, abandoned the diet following illness.[145] In Methven, Perthshire, the Reverend G. Bruce Watson distributed vegetarian literature and lectured on anthropology and phrenology.

A number of Quakers gave public support. In Bradford James Simpson's lecture (accompanied by a Cowherdite minister from Philadelphia) was chaired by the Quaker temperance and peace worker John Priestman. At Norton in County Durham in 1857, the anti-smoker John Longstaffe addressed Quakers. In Gloucester, where an association operated in 1858, support came from the Quaker Jesse Sessions, brother-in-law of the Quaker philanthropist Samuel Bowley, later a mayor of Gloucester, and supporter of anti-slavery, peace, education, free trade, free press and free religion. The Bury St Edmunds local secretary in 1852 was another Quaker (and a dispensing chemist). By contrast, few Anglican clergymen were visible. One was the Reverend Barnes from near Dorchester, undoubtedly the teetotaller, philologist and dialect-poet William Barnes.[146]

Not surprisingly, those who had been writing in favour of vegetarianism gave their support. Most important was John Smith of Malton, whose *Fruits and Farinacea* was a major text for the movement. Through his influence there was activity in his home town in the North Riding in 1848, with an association presided over by James Simpson. Smith gave a lecture in York in 1855. The next year he became president of the Hull association and encouraged the *Hull Advertiser*'s editor to try vegetarianism. In Derby, Luke Hansard, a member of the family of parliamentary printers, encouraged activity in 1848. Hansard was a 'thoroughgoing Vegetarian and a writer of some note', who had advocated vegetarianism for moral and health reasons in *Hints and Reflections for Railway Travellers* (1843), challenging entrepreneurs to create synthetic parchment and fur, and offering a 'premium for the best work upon Vegetable Cookery'. He lent literature to a physician and a clergyman who had previously been scornful.[147]

Activists included men who were significant local figures. Thus in the Shropshire market-town of Bridgnorth (which had eleven members in

1850) an adherent reported that some of the 'most influential' inhabitants were 'gallantly going forth pleading the great truth of Vegetarianism, believing that it should go hand in hand with the temperance reformation'.[148] Influential individuals elsewhere included two significant figures in Boston radicalism. John Noble the younger was secretary and Peter William Clayden was treasurer of the association. Noble's father, a Baptist bookseller prominent in municipal reform and 'moral radical' reform since the 1830s, was town councillor from 1836. His son, involved in local support for the Anti-Corn Law League, was vegetarian from early 1850 and lectured for the cause. He then became active in municipal and financial reform, and the London Political Union. Clayden was the town's Unitarian minister but he became a famous journalist, as assistant editor of the liberal nonconformist *Daily News*.

Temperance leadership is discernible in many cases. In the Rawtenstall and Crawshawbooth association (founded in 1854) much depended on the energies of William Hoyle, later a national temperance figure. Reading had led him to vegetarianism when a young mill-hand. He attributed his advance to mill-owner by the 1860s to an ability to resist the world's 'follies and fashions'.[149] The association was noted by Simpson in 1856 as being 'for some time, the most active of any connected with the Society'.[150] Elsewhere the temperance input is clear: the vegetarian message was brought to Bridgnorth by the temperance lecturer Joseph Bormond at the request of temperance supporters. Activity in the Cornish seaport and 'retired' market town of Padstow came through efforts by northern vegetarians to stimulate local temperance figures such as the surgeon and Wesleyan preacher Henry Mudge and John Darke Martyn, both from Bodmin. In Edinburgh assistance came from the temperance activist Robert Reid, who was acquainted with American reformers such as William Lloyd Garrison and Frederick Douglas and became a more visibly important figure in late-Victorian vegetarianism.

A generous reform outlook can be identified in a number of provincial activists such as the president of the Barnsley association (from 1859), the commercial traveller W.H. Barnesley. An attendant at the Paris Peace Congress in 1849 and supporter of the UKA, Barnesley briefly ran a vegetarian-temperance hotel in Manchester. The secretary of the Newcastle upon Tyne's association, John Mawson, was an anti-slavery activist whose wife organized contributions for the Boston Anti-Slavery Bazaar in 1856. James Larner of Framlingham, a Wesleyan preacher, was a member of the Liberation Society, Peace Society, opposed capital punishment, led temperance activities in the region and sought involvement in all *progressive* movements. He attributed the stamina necessary for business, evenings at institutions and societies, and preaching, to his diet. Alfred Gassion, the zealous secretary to Brighton's association, supported spelling and notational reform, inaugurating a column devoted to the duodecimal system in the *Phonetic Journal* (whose Swedenborgian extracts eroded his Catholic faith; he became a spiritualist). In Liverpool, John Calderwood and the clerk Aquila Kent were also involved in the phonetic movement.

In their attempts to win over support, vegetarians used standard techniques and activities associated with 'movements' of the period. These included distribution of tracts and copies of the vegetarian journals. The forge-worker Perkin distributed tracts among workers in Burley in 1853, for instance. Unusually for a local society, Birmingham produced tracts. In Northampton in 1856 vegetarian publications were sold by a homeopath who admitted being a lapsed adherent at a later meeting. This literature then became the focus of local study and debate. In Sheffield in 1861 for instance, fortnightly discussions were introduced and focused on G.H. Lewes' recently published, anti-vegetarian *Physiology of Common Life*. The Glasgow association even published a tract, *Vegetarianism Attacked and Defended* (1855).

A few societies made elaborate arrangements. Liverpool, for instance, which hosted the annual banquet in 1851, and which had an association with offices at the 'Vegetarian Depot' in Dale Street, formed a joint-stock company to provide soirées with plate and glassware. In York, where the local secretary was a music teacher, a musical festival and banquet was arranged in 1856. In Padstow in 1850, vegetarianism was such a novelty that inhabitants offered time, talent, and equipment to make the event 'worthy of the town, and the occasion worthy of the principle of mercy and kindness which it was intended to serve'. Literature was distributed to a ship of emigrants to show them that vegetarianism made their departure unnecessary. Flowers, fruit and mottos testified to the 'ideal, poetic and intellectual character' of vegetarianism. A band provided music and a subsequent banquet catered for working people. In Edinburgh one meeting featured fruit, music, addresses, and a lecture (aided by plant specimens) on the text 'Behold I give you every green herb bearing seed' (which was derived from Genesis 1: 29).

Lectures by prominent vegetarians such as James Simpson (who lectured from the early to mid-1850s across England and in Scotland) were intended to generate local press coverage, inquiries for information and demand for books, and ultimately, new members to the Society: as was reported to be the case after Simpson's visit to Newcastle-upon-Tyne.[151] The moral suasion exerted by these events depended partly on the support of ministers of religion, other local worthies and members of the medical profession, support which would be stressed in published reports.¹⁵² At Bridgnorth, a crowded meeting included several ministers. In Padstow the guests at the banquet included a surgeon. But the medical professionals present tended to be the unorthodox, such as Dr Ryan of the *Homeopathic Review* who chaired Horsell's lectures at the Sheffield Council Hall in October 1859.¹⁵³ Often meetings were ticketed affairs, organized by the society activists, though occasionally meetings may have been through local pressure, for instance in Andover in 1851, where Horsell gave a lecture with 'good [paying] attendance' at the Mechanics Institute at the request of two or three local people.¹⁵⁴ The size of audiences varied from those in Brighton attracting almost fifty people, to those in their several thousands where funds and energies and interests were less limited. In Birmingham a meeting chaired by an alderman attracted over a thousand, and another, in the Odd Fellows Hall, also proved popular.¹⁵⁵

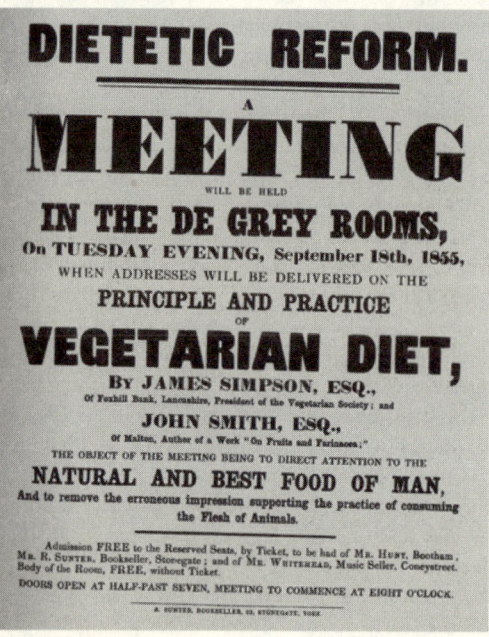

FIGURE 3. A typical lecture by the first President of the VS, in 1855. (*Vegetarian Messenger*, 1936, p. 43)

The size of the vegetarian associations tended to be small even if there were sizeable numbers of non-affiliated vegetarians, such as the forty experimenters reported by the Hull secretary in 1856 as 'backward' in enrolling (there had been supporters here since 1846); the thirteen reported in Colchester in 1856, or the 'one to two hundred' that the Birmingham society claimed were in its sphere in early 1854.[156] Brighton was smaller, with a society of eight (including wives) based in a schoolroom. Leicester's society, despite the circulation of literature, monthly socials and banquets, was a small society of some seven adults, only three of whom were VS members. Where there was insufficient support to justify associations, activists were isolated and, like the boot maker John Sully in Market Harborough, the subject of curiosity. Another example is the local secretary in Colchester, John Beach, a rate-collector, cooper, clairvoyant and father of a British Fenian spy ('Henri le Caron'). His family was considered an oddity, with passers-by pointing out his shop as the abode of vegetarians.[157]

The social base of vegetarianism in this period can be understood from the society's statistics and the reports of activities. In Leeds the plebeian background to vegetarian activity is apparent. The association established in 1853 included a bricklayer, railway-worker, and a forge-labourer. The latter was George Perkin, who abandoned tobacco and novel-reading, believing the diet preserved him in a dangerous and laborious trade and provided time for culture, and sympathy for a host of other *-isms*.[158] The Sheffield association's plebeian support can be seen from its 'customary' meeting place at the Working Men's Reading Rooms in 1860.[159] In Birmingham the edge-tool maker Nathaniel Griffin proselytised amongst his fellow workmen.

Members of mechanics' institutes discussed vegetarianism.[160] Periodicals taken by the Huddersfield mechanics' institute in 1850 included the *Vegetarian Advocate* alongside peace and teetotal titles; Sheffield institute's copy of Graham was heavily used.[161] Twigg notes that mechanics' institutes were more middle-class in tone than the mutual improvement societies, the latter offering another location for vegetarian discussion.[162] Organizations for civic and self-culture like the Chester Literary and Scientific Institution, where a 'few young men' were vegetarian in 1850, were environments where vegetarianism could be considered.[163]

Only a few women gained visibility in vegetarian reports, for instance in Liverpool, where the committee included wives of other officers in 1856. In Harrogate a 'zealous female member' was reported amongst the few supporters in 1848.[164] Wilson of Great Houghton's ten converts in 1870 were mostly women and (noted as a favourable sign of female willingness to join the movement), a female weaver was the secretary.[165] Perhaps most important was Elizabeth Horsell, the wife of the vegetarian entrepreneur, who pioneered vegetarianism in Worcester: it was she who possibly sent the *Worcester Herald* the report on the Ramsgate conference.[166] When a soirée took place in the Natural History Society's rooms in Worcester (involving guests such as James Simpson and Dr Balbirnie of Malvern) the local press reported a 'good proportion of the fair sex' amongst the seventy guests.[167]

So far, the account of the provincial movement suggests little difference from the approach of other movements. Attempts at communities provided one point of difference. A 'home colony' at Stratford St Mary in Suffolk was established to further local temperance, vegetarianism and 'mutual improvement' in 1845. Its leaders were the siblings Henry, Robert and Sarah Clubb. Henry had left Colchester Post Office to join the Concordium as a shorthand teacher. A Chartist activist, he became Simpson's secretary (the Clubbs had been Swedenborgian, Henry joined the Cowherdites) and a vegetarian lecturer. In June 1853 he emigrated to the United States and became an abolitionist journalist, senator, and Cowherdite pastor. Sarah published a children's vegetarian tract. Robert was the VS's local secretary in 1849. The colony obviously drew on Concordist experience in combining land cultivation with 'artistic, literary or mechanical pursuits' including phonetics. Henry took the message to neighbouring villages. In 1850 there were public dinners and a meeting at the village, with Bormond and a follower of Greaves, William Ward, present.[168] A more ephemeral colony involving physical puritanism was the 'Renunciation Society' established by Gustav Struve, exiled from Baden following the revolutions of 1848. Land in Yorkshire was given to him by an old Englishman, as a joke according to Marx and Engels. Struve and his wife were joined by a man called Schnauffer, a 'Swabian canary' and a 'few good men'. It was dissolved, and Struve became a 'wet [white?] Quaker'.[169]

This was not the last community experiment attracting British vegetarians. Henry Clubb, newly arrived in America, originated another project in 1856. The *Preston Guardian* reported that several English vegetarians had contacted Henry's brother Robert, then a bookseller at Kirkdale in Liverpool, who was the corresponding secretary of a New York company planning a vegetarian colony near Neosho City, Kansas. The 'American Octagon and Vegetarian Settlement' plan was not officially sanctioned by the British or American vegetarian societies. Simpson was unhappy about colonies since 'most of us are needed here, in the busy stirring scenes of life'. Benn Pitman, a brother of Isaac Pitman the phonetic reformer (and vegetarian), who was resident in Cincinnati, published a phonographic account, as did the *Manchester Examiner and Times*. By September 1857 it had been established on the ground and the Kansas *World of Freedom* reported seven Englishmen and three ladies, one Scotsman and lady as members. The colony rejected pigs, meat, alcohol, tobacco and slavery. An 'Octagon' at the centre of the planned settlement was to be the place for discussion of scientific, political, theological and moral subjects. The project failed through poor management, and it was not reported in the British vegetarian organ after November 1857.[170] It stirred some interest in home colonies, but though the vegetarian journal in 1858 published a series of agitated letters by Dornbusch of London on a scheme for a fruit-growing colony, editorial comment was unsympathetic about the colonies.[171] Dornbusch's motives for seeking the comfort of a colony will be apparent after examining the London movement.

Metropolitan vegetarianism

Most of the vegetarians recorded in Forward's jubilee history of the movement as assembling to form a metropolitan association in 1849 would be unfamiliar to historians of mid-nineteenth century Britain.[172] But many were active in various reform movements. Many were temperance activists such as William Horsell and his sometime partner in a 'Vegetarian Depot', Frederick Towgood, and James Shirley Hibberd, later a famous horticultural writer. A few were medical unorthodox practitioners such as the Polish Graf Johan von Viettinghoff, whose radical sympathies are indicated by letters and advertisements on homeopathy in the Owenite *New Moral World* and secularist *Reasoner* (several vegetarians were converted through his advice). A few had followed Greaves or associated with the Concordium.[173] Some were Chartists, such as the veteran radical Charles Neesom, who preached and taught 'in true apostolic style, with a sonorous and emphatic voice, the primitive, humanizing, elevating, and health-giving principles of Vegetarianism.'[174] Several were Owenites, such as Samuel Houghton who had been involved in Harmony Hall, or the middle-class Frederick Hurlstone, a London representative in the Owenites' Sixth Congress as a member of the Central Board and a well-known artist who became President of the Society of British Artists. Freethinkers included Edmund T. Gooch of Poplar (who also supported communism, utilitarianism, phonetics and teetotalism), Henry Lestar Harrison, and William Turley (who became a spiritualist).

Interest in phrenology characterized many London vegetarians, through the shared membership of an 'Anthropological Society' which (according to Viettinghoff) was to promote scientific inquiry about sensation, mental processes, and the role of environment on the mind, with the view to shaping future mental development.[175] Colin Mackenzie Dick, formerly a sugar planter, and one of the officers of the Association, operated as a 'practical phrenologist' at Horsell's Depôt, offering 'male and female heads, lithographed'. Others were involved in education. One meeting place for vegetarians in the 1850s, Harrison and Turley's Aurora Villa at Hampstead Heath, echoed Alcott House in being a vegetarian school. Vegetarians were also linked to Johannes Ronge and his wife, German émigrés who were pioneers of the kindergarten. One London vegetarian, the autodidact Joseph Bentley, inspected schools (styling himself the 'first school inspector') and inspected life assurance and 'other means of provident care of working-man's earnings'. George Vasey, who taught briefly in Alcott House, was secretary of the London Phonetic Association, ran a school on vegetarian lines, was on the Anthropological Society committee, and joined Sheffield Vegetarian Association in 1860.

Many London vegetarians were nonconformists. In the support for Ronge there was also a close connection with reformed religion, since he had become famous by attempting to reform German Catholicism, and vegetarians were associated with his 'Humanistic Society'. Another religious reformer was the Reverend William Forster of Kentish Town. Spiritualism was soon to interest several prominent London vegetarians. Given their anti-violence sentiments it is natural to assume Quaker sympathy, but though a widely reported banquet at Freemasons' Tavern in August 1851 was attended by many Quakers, their support was not striking. The exception was the family of William Bennett of Croydon, a retired tea-dealer, botanist, author, acquaintance of Wordsworth and Hartley Coleridge, and friend of Greaves and the writers William and Mary Howitt.

The metropolitan movement probably numbered about sixty 'fairly committed' to socializing in this period, though eighty of the *known* vegetarians responded to an invitation in 1853. Others were not affiliated to the society, since it was claimed 'almost daily we are hearing of some Vegetarian who had abstained from flesh-eating for many years, without having heard of the existence of the Society'.[176] In 1875 London members of the VS included a letter-press printer, lecturer, artificial florist, shoemaker, merchant's clerk, accountant, naval engineer, timber merchant foreman, medical student, author, linen draper, banker's clerk, gentleman, clerk in orders, japanner, i.e., a range of occupations excluding heavy manual work. Many prominent metropolitan vegetarians/or sympathizers were middle-class, but there were 'plebeian' supporters whose involvement was sought privately by the secretary George Dornbusch (who resisted calls for admission charges); and attracted through lectures, open-air addresses and distribution of tracts. Those attracted were artisans, Owenites and/or temperance supporters interested in self-improvement and thrift. In 1856 a Mr Bottle recommended the diet to his fellow working men as a cure for intemperance.

Several were artists: George Cruikshank (at least in sympathy[177]), engraver Richard Anelay (also perhaps present in sympathy) and Hurlstone and his wife Jane. In the scholar Frederick J. Furnivall there was a connection with Christian Socialism and London literary circles. Horsell and Job Caudwell were publishers. A man prominent in the future progressive press, John Passmore Edwards, was briefly involved. Hibberd became famous as a horticultural writer. If no prominent man of letters supported the cause, a minor poetess, Fanny Lacy, attended some meetings. She had been acquainted with and published by the Concordium. Her story 'The Vegetarian' appeared in the *Metropolitan Magazine* in 1846, and *The Truth-Tester* printed her verse invitation to the 'Physiological Conference' preparing the way for the Society.[178]

FIGURE 4. George Dornbusch, a leading figure in early London vegetarianism, and also an activist in anti-vaccination and peace organizations.
(Image courtesy of Kevin Beurle)

There was a cosmopolitan element. The Dornbuschs came from Germany and the Austro-Hungarian empire, Viettinghoff from Eastern Europe. London harboured exiled German revolutionaries including the vegetarian Gustav Struve, apparently known to Dornbusch.[179] One vegetarian meeting was attended by the homeopath C.F. Zimpel, who heralded the association as 'one of the signs of the coming of the Lord, and preparation for the fulfilment of the prophecies'.[180] In 1853 efforts were made to win over another émigré, Pierre Baume, a wealthy and eccentric supporter of radical reforms, and dietetic experimentalist. Horsell published an advertisement for Baume when he was keen to establish a North American community.[181] Baume visited Dornbusch at the Vegetarian Cottage and became a regular participant at Humanistic

Society meetings. Although resisting requests for money in propagating vegetarianism he had several meetings concerning bequests for the UKA. An irascible man, when he fell out with the London vegetarians he wrote: 'Is Vegetarianism a SECRET SOCIETY!?! Des Culcons?!?'[182]

The work of women in the London movement included the central provision of food, and decoration of/and presence at venues. Some went beyond passive support of their spouses, and their efforts were welcomed by the men.[183] When one meeting was presided over by a woman this was delightedly received as recognition of the dignity of women. A 'Ladies Domestic Committee' was created.[184] Elizabeth Horsell distributed bouquets to an audience at one lecture, spoke at others and hosted soirées, and published a recipe book. Other activists included Jane Hurlstone, who travelled to Manchester for the second Annual Banquet and was influential in organizing events at the Talfourd Tavern and Whittington Club. Amalie Dornbusch supported Horsell's *Truth-Tester* and corresponded about the diet's worth for young mothers. Mrs Dorcas, another member of the Association, had earlier lectured (at the Owenite John Street Institution) on the 'Rights and Position of Women'.

Clearly many of the London vegetarians were not in the mainstream in their political and social views, though most were not out-and-out 'outsiders,' by intent or in practice. Though Aurora Villa mixed dietary radicalism with secularism and gestured towards George Sand (i.e., Aurore Dupin, Baronne Dudevant) through its name; Horsell rebutted a press comment connecting vegetarianism with Owenite free-love.[185] Yet Horsell was evidently too radical, too independent of Manchester, or perhaps too eccentric for some despite this. James Simpson proposed William White and J.G. Crawford as local secretaries with Dornbusch in May 1856. This was a response to Horsell's election as secretary in the place of the Austrian, whose continued services had been rejected on the basis of alleged lameness, a disability he had disproved. Horsell's private reputation, Simpson feared, would harm the cause in London, '& bring it under the imputations & objections which ought carefully to be avoided'. The additional secretaries would advance vegetarianism by opening up fresh circles of society to the influence of the movement, 'any steps taken by the association at all unfavourable to the general interest of the movement being thus somewhat modified, as far as our control of the public influence of Vegetarianism in London will permit'.[186]

When vegetarianism was first agitated, Londoners responded with enquiries, applications for lectures, and attentive, animated and prolonged debates. Early meetings at Browning's Commercial Coffee House had extended over three evenings until a vote in favour of the diet was reached. Coverage of the movement in *Punch* also helped generate interest, and other papers published comments on the new movement; when *The Times* (which published advertisements for Horsell's publications) condemned the cruelty of Smithfield on Christmas day in 1850, it felt obliged to deny any 'vegetarian pangs' and referred to Shelley and James Elmzlie Duncan.[187] The significance of a vigorous and co-operative metropolitan presence was recognized by Simpson and others travelling 200 miles south to participate in several meetings, including the meeting during the Great Exhibition of 1851, at the Freemasons' Tavern. The banquet, attended by temperance reformers, was announced in *The Times*, had wide coverage and a graphic record in the *Illustrated London News*.[188] An Annual Meeting was again held in London in 1862.

FIGURE 5. The Vegetarian Society banquet at Freemasons' Tavern, 1851, from the *Illustrated London News*, 16 August 1851, p. 223.

Vegetarianism was a novelty. But the London movement was too small, too poor (in 1856 the annual report showed a balance of £10!) and scattered to exploit and sustain this, or make any great impact, although the national press (based in London) did report national activity (and indeed an Association meeting was reported by the *Morning Advertiser, Nonconformist* and *Patriot* in 1854). Dornbusch in 1852 pointed to the difficulties that all reformers knew, with 'penetrating and moving' this 'immensely huge metropolis', and even in expounding their principles to their circle of friends.[189] Not surprisingly, one London convert (Charles Herve) in 1854 had not heard of the VS before.

Although the *Vegetarian Messenger* publicized the London Association, and although it did continue to campaign, it remained tiny. In a cosmopolitan and fashion-conscious environment vegetarianism possibly had more of a tendency to be an ephemeral enthusiasm (to be satirized indeed, in 'Bloomerism, or Follies of the Day' at the Royal Surrey Theatre in 1851). Though the *Daily Telegraph* in 1859 thought it symptomatic of other agitations begun by 'idlers, rattle-brains, and wool gatherers, whose babblings are frequently so loud as to threaten us with the organization of a permanent nuisance', London vegetarians had insufficient vigour for prolonged and imaginative campaigns in the 1860s.[190] There were other priorities. Dornbusch said simply getting a living diverted energies.[191] He sought relief (and refuge) in a vegetarian communitarian scheme. By 1870 Dornbusch was reporting that for the last year there had only been a few lectures and 'practice in private families'.[192] Metropolitan vegetarians, as elsewhere, found more urgent reforms (disestablishing the Church, education, prohibition) and calls to re-establish an association went unheeded.[193] But in this decline, the metropolis merely mirrored the movement as a whole.

A movement in decline

Encouraged by the VS, nineteen English and five Scottish associations were established. These depended on financial and moral support from the leadership and Simpson, who was also the financial prop for the *Vegetarian Messenger*, was president of many.[194] Often they were no more than the 'local secretaries' listed in the *Vegetarian Messenger*, and were an attempt to exaggerate strength.[195] In Worcester, despite the secretary Charles Walker noting 'great curiosity' in 1853 the only other member of the society in 1851 had been (he recorded in his diary) a 'crazy boot maker'.[196] Associations depended on a few activists; when they left the area, abandoned the cause or died, the society could collapse. In Brighton this happened with Gassion's departure and the local president's death. Even a place which seemed highly promising to the Society, like remote Padstow in 1849-50, which had sixteen new members enrolled, tracts and a vegetarian 'ever-circulating magazine', could decline from a state of public zeal.

In the decade of the Crimean War and Indian Mutiny, a movement associated with peace and mercy struggled. In late 1856, *Blackwood's Edinburgh Magazine* observed that, after soirées in various towns, and public munching of their food, people had 'heard nothing of them for a long time'.[197] The *Messenger* lamented the current, inimical, spirit of belligerence, one local activist emphasizing the absence of 'a calm and patient hearing' for an anti-violence movement.[198] In Padstow activity was limited to anti-vaccination petitions by 1856, conversations by a shopkeeper with his customers and lectures by Bormond in 1858. Novocastrian vegetarianism declined in the late 1850s into private discussion and papers in debating societies or Young Men's Associations. Leeds had hosted the annual meeting in 1854 and had even been intended as the permanent location for annual meetings, but by 1858 its association's public activities were suspended. Manchester Association itself had a 'do-nothing policy' in 1858. With James Simpson's death in 1859 most remaining branches became dormant and the survival of the Society itself was uncertain. The Executive Committee acknowledged, as Simpson was dying, that 'a far greater burden of the means of carrying on its operations, fell upon the President than there ought to do' and some of the secretaries of the associations still in existence in 1859 accepted the blame 'for having done so little'.[199] The Society narrowly missed disappearing.

Nurturing the new *Dietetic Reformer* preoccupied the committee in its first year and though there were a few lectures at Manchester, London, Sheffield and more parochial locations, there was little centrally directed activity in 1861. The 1861 Report gestured to inquiries, gratuitous distribution of tracts and more than average sales of literature, but referred to the 'great bulk of the community' being inert about the question.[200] Ferocity of spirit engendered by the American Civil War was blamed.[201] The weakness of associational activity can be exemplified by Liverpool, where meetings were poorly attended, leaving one member to simply post up advertisements. By 1862, though there were twenty members, the association limited itself to private quarterly meetings involving essays and discussions rather than aggressive propaganda. At a time when, due to serious cattle disease the movement should have been making headway, a Sheffield paper noted the quiescence of local and national efforts.[202] Yet the VS's annual meeting was held in the city in 1862. The Report for the year 1865-66 noted that the spiritualist James Burns's labours had 'been more abundant than all other lectures'.[203] His journal *Human Nature* commented on the Society's inactivity.[204]

One site for activity that received public attention was the experimental co-operative farm at Blennerhasset, Cumberland – equipped with market garden, artificial manure works and ploughing machines – established by William Lawson, brother of Sir Wilfrid Lawson the temperance leader.[205] In 1863 the *Dietetic Reformer* reported an experiment in which several of his workers lived as vegetarians; the outcomes, including loss of weight and energy, were unfavourable. In 1866 a free Christmas 'vegetarian fête', reported in *The Times* (silent on further vegetarian activity until 1871), incorporated Burns's lectures on diet, physiology and phrenology. Tickets were distributed locally and guests told to bring spoons and musical instruments. Unsurprisingly (as *The Times* and other papers reported), the 'extraordinary messes' of boiled grains, oatmeal gruel and linseed boiled to a jelly repelled the 'beef-eating peasantry'. The *Dietetic Reformer* believed Lawson's servants were either ignorant about the diet or played practical jokes in presenting unintentionally raw vegetables. Whilst doubting the propagandist wisdom of a 'cheap' Christmas meal the journal praised his commitment. Subsequent festivals involved lectures on typical reformist subjects: capital punishment, shorthand, diet, dress and smoking. Henry Pitman's *Co-operator* reported its leading ethos as 'the provision of good things and the prohibition of bad things'.[206]

This was a rare public display of vegetarianism. The 1867/8 Report expressed the sentiment that lacking many new recruits 'we have yet to congratulate ourselves that the society does not decline in its enrolled strength'.[207] But determining the movement's precise size is impossible in this or any period. Membership of the VS did not often include the other family members who became (reluctant or willing) vegetarians and women were under-reported.[208] As in modern times there were principled but unaffiliated vegetarians. Horsell claimed a thousand-strong Society in 1856 with 'thousands who, though not enrolled members … are practically carrying out its principles'.[209] This generous estimate, small compared with other movements, is in keeping with the self-image as the 'elite' of the temperance and moral reform world.

The vegetarian press frequently reported experimenters and occasionally vegetarians who were reluctant to enrol. John Davie asserted that many 'would not think or take the trouble to connect themselves with the society'. Some refused to join for fear of ridicule; others were tardy due to isolation.[210] 'C.L.B' was perhaps unusual in refusing to enrol on the grounds that vegetarianism was not *moral enough*. The bookseller and former Chartist T.P. Barkas, vegetarian since 1840, had a reasoned objection, arguing that as many struggled to obtain fresh vegetables, vegetarianism could not be a choice free to all.[211] Francis Newman when joining the Society, referred to frequent discussion in his circle, of acquaintances who tried and abandoned vegetarianism. Whatever the number of adherents, at the start of the 1870s vegetarianism as a movement was quiescent. Provincial survival relied on private advocacy and the distribution of literature by men such as Davie in Dunfermline, William Couchman at Newcastle or Joseph Wilson at Great Houghton. But the movement's fortunes were about to change.

The movement c.1870-1901

In 1874 *Chamber's Encyclopedia* noted incorrectly that since 1861 there was no vegetarian organ and few disciples; and the *Dietetic Reformer* complained that the press rarely discussed vegetarianism and when they did it was 'generally with slight or for jest, often with high contempt and much misrepresentation'. Yet in 1874, Francis Newman's suggestion concerning an 'associate grade' to invigorate the movement was accepted, and the Society grew rapidly.[212] In 1876 the *Graphic* published four leading vegetarians' portraits.[213] One of these, William Gibson Ward, a trustee of the Northern Agricultural Labourers' union, and contributor to the *Labourer's Union Chronicle*, played an important role in the revival through letters to *The Times* advocating vegetable alternatives for the working classes at a time of concern about the cost of food. Ward and the VS were inundated with requests for information as a result.[214]

In the late 1870s, as the movement revived, an effort was made to reestablish local organizations; but real moves began in 1888, with preparations for local society membership and the establishment of a number of branches.[215] A sense of a *national* movement was encouraged by the introduction in 1876, at Newman's suggestion (based on long-standing evangelical practice), of May Meetings which acted as social outings, conferences and press campaigns.[216] In 1889 the Vegetarian Federal Union (VFU) was formed by London vegetarians, who carried out many high-profile provincial missions.[217]

FIGURE 6. The 'vegetarian van' spreading the gospel of vegetarianism (frontispiece, *Vegetarian Messenger*, August 1898).

Organized vegetarianism in the provinces

By 1900 a total of 58 English societies had existed. Many of these were weak, short-lived or resuscitated on several occasions, but there were a few strong centres such as Bolton, Sheffield and Exeter. The north of England remained important in the movement.[218] In the 1880s the VS offices were at Princess Street, Manchester. There were several vegetarian restaurants in the city; one at Fountain Street (opened 1884), with lecture hall, reading and smoking rooms, provided a venue for lectures targeted at groups such as teachers, doctors and temperance workers.[219] The Society established a shop about 1893 at Peter Street, close to the Deansgate tram route. The window on the main street had a large display of commodities which helped attract enquirers.[220] Such new showiness reflected the growth of the national movement and also the vigorous efforts in London in the late nineteenth century.

In Bolton a society was established in 1890, after three residents sent out a mass of leaflets and gave a cookery demonstration. The president was John Nayler, a Methodist and journalist specializing in commercial matters. William Farrington, the secretary, was a Congregationalist and post worker. The vice-president was a Unitarian minister, H.M. Livens (who preached vegetarianism). One of the members, John Fletcher, was a socialist, miner and president of the local field naturalists' society. Other members included a decorator, a machinist/engineer, a businessman (and Sunday school teacher), a steel worker (who was a Primitive Methodist), and a farmer. Others were mostly young men, nonconformist and temperance workers. Nayler reported 'much opposition and indifference' in 1892. In 1893, as a preliminary to managing a restaurant, the society became a limited company. By 1898 there were nearly seventy members and associates. Activities included lantern lectures, indoor meetings, tract dissemination, and adverts inserted in the local press. A lithographed food diagram by Farrington was to be given to English and Welsh public schools in a scheme which cost nearly £1400 (with £800 probably given by Arnold F. Hills, a vice-president in 1898, on whom more shortly). Bolton vegetarianism should be seen in the local context of late-Victorian radicalism, with an active labour church and Independent Labour Party supporting various advanced causes.[221]

A few other examples of associations in England must suffice. Sheffield society was formed (in 1889) through support by Liverpudlian and Mancunian vegetarians and advice from the engraver and inventor Henry Swan, an associate of Ruskin. A Scottish Quaker, R. Barclay Murdoch, was the honorary secretary; a postman, W. Addy Hall, 'a reformer in many ways,' was president c.1896. The society continued into the late 1890s, with the provision of a restaurant. The city's radical tradition found contemporary expression in the *Sheffield Weekly Echo* which supported Kropotkin, feminism, social purity and anti-Contagious Diseases Act agitation; and in community experiments which involved vegetarianism. The radical reformer (and vegetarian) Edward Carpenter lived in Sheffield and corresponded with the *Commonweal* on the local Ruskinian Totley farm community, later attributing its failure to fear of surveillance by blue ribbonites, vegetarians and other puritans.[222] In 1898 six young Sheffield workers 'returned to Nature' through a Kropotkinite tomato-growing colony at Norton. Strict vegetarians, the *Vegetarian* heralded them as pioneers of 'true socialism'.[223] Though the colony attracted hundreds of visitors from the city it was short-lived and members joined the Starnthwaite colony near Kendal.

Vegetarian associations required frequent re-invigoration, as exemplified by the history of Birmingham vegetarianism. A dietetic reform club formed in 1877 was revived three years later, when its president was a physician, Dr T.G. Vaudrey. Thirza Tarrant, author of a vegetarian cookery book, managed a vegetarian restaurant in Pall Mall; another, the 'Garden,' opened late 1881 and was reported in local satirical journals. A restaurant and fruit store was also opened at Paradise Street. In the late 1880s a new branch was led by the Unitarian minister James Street. The committee included James Newey, a member of the teetotal UKA, prominent in methodism and chairman of the Directors of Newey Brothers Ltd., button, eye and hook makers. Another committee member was the Swedenborgian schoolmaster Thomas Cochrane Lowe. The society was relaunched with outside assistance in April 1894, but it was a 'hard uphill fight' to sustain. In late 1898 the Society debated and passed a motion to abolish the associate grade in membership. In spite of these problems, a 'Pitman Vegetarian Hotel' (with restaurant and health-food shop) was established.

By contrast vegetarianism flourished in Exeter and Devon through efforts by J.I. Pengelly, a magistrate's clerk who wore vegetarian boots, and Augustine Honey, an engineering student. They invited the prominent American-born vegetarian advocate Dr Thomas Low Nichols to Exeter in 1882. Francis Newman also came, attracting an audience of nearly three hundred. Agitation took the form of letter writing, essays and lectures in the region's literary societies, mutual improvement societies and Good Templar societies. Practical demonstrations, refreshment stalls, and food and flower exhibits were organized. In 1882 there were sixty full and associate members, presided over by a 'practical vegetarian' alderman. Two years later the May Meeting was held in Exeter and backed by the mayor and local worthies, yet Pengelly lamented aloofness by the upper classes, professionals and 'intelligent persons of all ranks'. The president in the 1890s was the Reverend J.H.N. Neville, friend of the hygienic reformers Joseph and Chandos Wallace. By 1896 there were almost ninety associates and members, and a branch society in Salcombe. There was also the stimulus of Pengelly's work with Sidney Beard at Ilfracombe, in the vegetarian Order of the Golden Age. Here, a society previously associated with the proprietor of a vegetarian restaurant resurfaced in 1899 as a branch of the Order. The local press, favourable to vegetarians' claims to combat poverty and illness, reported their activity.

The movement's extent is not to be measured simply by societies for there were other locations for activity and support through the work of individuals or families. Two examples must suffice: in the Northamptonshire village of Tuxford the eccentric veterinary surgeon R.S. Wilson provided, from about 1889, a venue for meetings and vegetarian food provision on his estate despite 'stubborn prejudice and other obstacles'; in Stockton-on-Tees the steel pen manufacturer W.M. Wright joined forces with a Quaker George Emmett and his daughter in a 'Flower, Fruit and Love Mission Band' in 1889.[224] Other locations included vegetarian restaurants and stores (discussed later), 'colonies' and schools. Percy Harrison, who supported spiritualism and vegetarianism, established a 'Progressive College' in 1875.[225] G.W. Sibly's Wycliffe College in Gloucestershire (founded in 1882) and Abbotsholme school, founded by a follower of Edward Carpenter in 1889, also encouraged vegetarianism.[226]

Vegetarianism was strongest in England, but there existed food reform societies (fourteen in all) in Wales, Scotland and Ireland. The VS, conscious of a linguistic barrier, produced a translation of its explanatory pamphlet, appealing to notions of Welsh thrift and idealism.[227] Activity was mainly limited to lectures, house-to-house visitations, tract distribution and press campaigns conducted by the VFU's secretary for the 'South West', G. Cholwick Wade. He created a Newport society, presided over by a telegraphist and supported by members of the Salvation Army in 1899. He moved his base from unreceptive Newport to Cardiff, where he organized banquets and established a society. His account of 'Four Years Crusade in Wild Wales' makes it clear that apart from interest during a miners' strike in 1898, results were limited to individual conversion, a demand for reformed foods (hampered by the lack of stores), press coverage, and attempts to introduce the question at Eisteddfod and Gorsedd.[228] Wade, formerly a solicitor, had become vegetarian to cure rheumatism. A life of 'social ostracism' followed from his anti-vaccinationism, teetotal-vegetarianism and Swedenborgianism.[229] Another arch-individualist vegetarian was the famous Dr William Price of Llantrisant. Formerly a Chartist, Price combined being a physician with druidry. He opposed vaccination, would not treat smokers, washed all his coins and refused to wear socks. He fathered a son in old age, and when the infant died he was burned on a hilltop, creating a scandal and resulting in a trial in 1884 which helped lead to the legalization of cremation.[230]

North of the border, by the late nineteenth century there were societies in Aberdeen, Arbroath, Dumfries, Dundee, Dunfermline, Edinburgh and Glasgow.[231] This reflected native efforts and outside influence. John Davie of Dunfermline, active in the Society's early days, remained a leading figure until his death. Prominent English-based vegetarians lectured in Scotland throughout the period: Thomas Low Nichols paying particular attention to the formation of Scottish food reform societies.[232] A 'Scottish Vegetarian Society' was founded in 1892 in response to a sense of *weakness* and to ridicule as cranks, and began shakily with the press dwelling on the farcical nature of some meetings. Probably there were fewer than a thousand members or associates of the VS in the mid-1890s, for when the *Glasgow Evening News* noted a recent Glaswegian vegetarian boom had petered out, the vegetarian John Barclay replied that there were five hundred members affiliated to a Scottish Vegetarian Union, and 'many' Glaswegian members of the Manchester VS.[233] A May meeting was held in Glasgow in 1898, and the first Scottish 'Summer Conference' was held at the Bridge of Allan hydro in 1899 – the banquet was attended by 130. A journal, *Scottish Health Reformer*, covered Edwardian vegetarianism.[234]

Glasgow was connected with food reform through Hay Nisbet, Thomas Low Nichols's publisher.[235] Charles Ottley Groom Napier and Arthur Trevelyan sponsored a popular banquet here and in Edinburgh in 1876. A 'Scottish Food Reform Society' was established in 1879, with an active president, David Fortune and the support of Nichols. Most members lived in the Crosshill suburbs, where the American-born phrenologist, vegetarian and spiritualist James Coates also resided. Aspinwall suggests that the Glasgow movement was 'particularly strong', perhaps owing to temperance support. Though this overstates its vigour at the expense of London and other centres, he points to the existence of a short-lived cookery school under the direction of Miss Thirza Tarrant and an American universalist minister, Dr Caroline Soule. Nichols was not alone in his support; the local press covered a banquet attended by the Englishmen William Gibson Ward and the Bible Christian Reverend James Clark. In 1884 a new food reform society was established. Mrs Macbean, who gave cookery classes, published a recipe booklet in 1890, when, if the society still promoted a wider food reform, the tendency was towards vegetarianism. The secretary, Ernest Clark (the son of the Reverend James Clark and a 'life vegetarian') managed to attract an audience of six hundred to a meeting at the City Hall, but with his departure the society faltered.

A Glaswegian movement was sufficiently vigorous to support several vegetarian restaurants. A Scottish Vegetarian Society, independent of London and Manchester, was formed in Glasgow in late 1892 through the efforts of Joseph Knight, late secretary of the VS. Its headquarters were in the Athenaeum in Buchanan Street. H.S. Bathgate, the president, was a builder, life teetotaller and non-smoker, active in the peace movement and Church and Sunday school work. He gave generous financial support to Scottish vegetarianism. In 1895 there were about three hundred Glaswegian members of the several vegetarian societies, 'chiefly young men', although a third were women, and practically all teetotallers (the Scottish Temperance Life Assurance Co. had a vegetarian section), and seventy members of the Scottish Society in 1896. With several successful vegetarian restaurants established by Leonard McCaughey, the society was hopeful, declaring 'things will be made to "hum" in Scotland when they have consolidated themselves'. Assistance with lectures came from the London vegetarians.[236]

The Dundee 'Dietetic Reform Society' was founded in 1877; by 1882 it had eighteen members and a group of sympathizers. Newspaper accounts indicate that its activities were uncontroversial. It had mixed success as a mutual support group, since social events were often poorly attended, and frequently business could not be transacted because of an insufficient quorum, as the minute book (a rare survival for branch societies) reveals. There was little attempt to spread the cause by directly lecturing to the 'poorer classes' (i.e., the majority of the local population) though these were referred to as the beneficiaries of a 'reformed diet' on several occasions. The diet was highlighted as a therapy for illness, although non-physiological aspects were expounded in discussion. Its activists initially were men, whose wives participated infrequently. Forbes Marshall, a Quaker and retired confectioner, supported abolition of capital punishment, teetotalism and anti-tobacco and the Peace Society. Other members included a bookseller, a mechanic, an architect, and a supporter of phrenology, who gave an illustrated lecture on heads at the first banquet. But in January 1878 it was agreed that women could attend meetings and later they were permitted to join the standing committee.[237] Perhaps the most significant Dundonian vegetarian was Margaret Parker. The English wife of a merchant, she was a national figure in social reform; her home was often visited by American and European reformers. A representative of the Scottish Good Templars in America in 1875, she was instrumental in the creation of the British Women's Temperance Association and a leading advocate of women's rights. Her progressive career culminated in the Women's International Congress in Chicago which she helped organize in 1893.[238] Another important participant, from

March 1880, was James Scrymgeour, a former Chartist sympathizer associated with vegetarianism in 1857, and now agent of the Prison Aid Society. His son Edwin was to become a Prohibitionist MP.

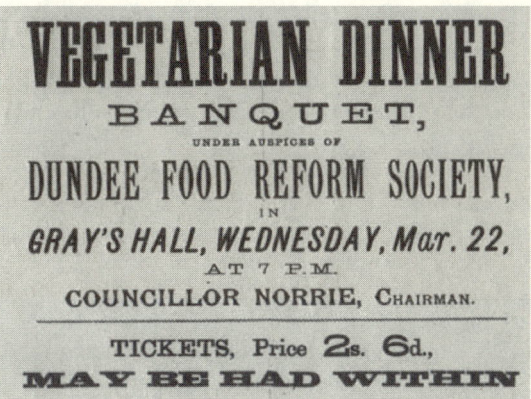

FIGURE 7. Poster for a dinner under the auspices of the Dundee FRS (Dundee City Archives, GD/Mus36).

Like other activists, the Dundonians' strategy involved lectures and cheap literature, and the secretaries were ordered 'to get one or more booksellers to push the sale of some of the cheaper publications'.[239] Notices and weekly advertisements were published in the local press. Discussions and testimony were important parts of the meetings. Papers 'on some topic of vegetarian interest' were arranged by ballot and included talks on consumption (blamed in great measure on 'the large use of highly oxidised substances such as sugar'), on the mental effects of the diet, on the earth as a place designed for man (with fossil evidence to show grains had arrived with man) and coffee as a deleterious food.[240] Picnics, walks and public 'fruit and bread' festivals were also arranged. There was also an attempt to enlist temperance support, which was manifested in an address from the Dundee Temperance Society at their small festival in early January 1879.

As with many of the vegetarian societies funds were limited, and in early 1883 the public activity was abandoned. Dundonian vegetarians had failed to inspire the town with their teachings, and if this was partly due to limited resources, they had been unable to capitalize on Dundee's dire problems of inadequate diet, poor sanitation and housing. Nor seemingly, were they part of the town's 'network of radicalism'.[241] A revival was attempted at the turn of the century. The conversion of the Reverend

Walter Walsh 'every inch a reformer' was seen as encouraging. Walsh had preached universal salvation and the extinction of hell, in Northern England, and lectured in secularist halls. Becoming influenced by Tolstoyan ideas of a spiritualized social reform, he succeeded his friend David Macrae (famously expelled from the Presbyterian ministry for heresy over future punishment) who had established the Gilfillan Memorial Church on the 'broadest Christian basis'. Walsh established a 'Free Religious Church' in Dundee, and was active in housing reform and local philanthropy. [242]

In Ireland, previously of limited significance in organized vegetarianism, there developed a centre for activity in Belfast when the British movement revived in the late 1870s.[243] Some propaganda had been undertaken by the Reverend Collyns in lectures at Victoria Hall in 1877, supported by the Reverends Charles Seaver, James Street, and A.M. Morrison, James Haslett (later knighted), and Robert L. Hamilton JP. A society was established in 1877 by a number of young men including John Herron (an advertising manager), who had become a vegetarian in the late 1860s. A Congregationalist, active in the Good Templars, and a 'lively' social reformer despite his retiring nature, he published a *Vegetarian Almanack* from 1879. His wife, a student of Swedenborgianism and theology, was vegetarian too, and wrote (contributing poetry and doing much of the editorial work for the *Almanack*) and spoke privately on the subject.

As the 'Belfast Vegetarian and Food Reform Society', vegetarians met monthly in a room at the Evangelical Union Church school in 1880, published W.H. McLester's *Vegetarianism Popularly Considered*, and ran a shop. At that period the president was the Reverend A.M. Morrison and the honorary treasurer, Thomas Strain, was an anti-vaccinationist. Belfast also had Leonard McCaughey's 'XL' vegetarian café.[244] Members of Belfast's Trades Council supported the movement to the extent that a deputation requested assistance in 1899 in provision of cookery classes for slum-dwellers who had 'lamentable' ignorance.[245] There were lantern lectures, open-air meetings involving temperance songs and concertina playing, banquets, cookery demonstrations and visits to Good Templars. Literature was 'always eagerly sought'.[246] Religion remained a key issue in Belfast vegetarian discussion, indicated by correspondence on the subject in the *Belfast Evening News* in early 1899.[247]

A later organizational development in Belfast was the Irish Vegetarian Union. Its creation in 1890 was stimulated by the London vegetarians who had previously sent the Reverend Bristow to lecture. It was established by the Reverend John Bruce Wallace, then editor of the *Belfast Evening Star*, and known for his 'advanced' social and political views. In 1892 the paper reported his efforts, after visiting West American colonies, to set up a

'Voluntary Co-operative Commonwealth'. He became an important member of the 'Brotherhood' movement. The first president was a biographer of Swedenborg, the Englishman George Trobridge, headmaster of the Government School of Art and a life vegetarian. Members of the Union's committee included John Coulter of Belfast, an anti-smoker who published moral-reform verses; the Scotsman John Straiton, pastor of the Christian Brethren community in Belfast and opponent of vaccination and vivisection; and another Scotsman, R. Semple, general secretary of the Irish Order of Good Templars and editor of *Irish Templary*.

Dublin vegetarianism was marked by the involvement of women and the literary elite. A society existed by 1890 and the *Dublin Evening Telegraph* reported the extension of a vegetarian café in early 1894.[248] Five years later Adrienne Veigelé helped establish a society for 'the Study of Food Reform' (twelve only of the initial members were vegetarian) with a long standing vegetarian, Mrs E. King-Flewitt, and the vegetarian Mrs Sophia Gough, wife of the proprietor of a temperance hotel in Exchequer Street. Vegetarianism was one of the causes espoused in *fin de siècle* Dublin in an advanced circle that included W.B. Yeats, 'A.E.' (George Russell), James Joyce (*Ulysses* depicts a 'literary etherial' vegetarian couple, the man – Russell – in homespun, beard and riding a bicycle), James H. Cousins and Margaret Cousins, and the Sheehy-Skeffingtons. The associates and members of this circle, which gathered at a vegetarian restaurant, supported the militant Irish Women's Franchise League, Gaelic revival, anti-smoking, anti-vaccination and theosophy.[249]

These societies at Belfast and Dublin, with two others, at Lisburn near Belfast in 1878, and Londonderry in 1898, represented the extent of the Irish movement. According to Herron, the Irish were 'stiff-necked' and opposed to vegetarianism. Semple attributed lack of progress to inherent Irish conservatism and stupidity. The most responsive class was the 'fairly well educated artizan class' including the women-folk. Resistance came from religious and temperance quarters (the latter feared vegetarianism would act as a 'red herring'). The best arguments to use with Northern Irish yeomen were economic.[250]

The London movement

With a national revival, London vegetarianism was organized on a broader footing than in its earlier days, but the growing pretensions of its vibrant and controversial efforts strained the relationship with the more staid Manchester-based Society.[251] Though the Society's provinciality was itself being challenged by the more cosmopolitan and higher profile leadership of Francis Newman (1873-1884) and the Cambridge classicist J.E.B.

Mayor (1884-1911), the national movement was transformed through London's awakening by Arnold Hills, his protégés, and others. The London movement, eventually organized through the LVS and local societies, was independent-minded, and more vigorous through the good fortune of having Hills, a millionaire with the zeal of a recent convert. Activity by the 1890s was well-directed, well-publicized, and recognized as a feature of modern metropolitan reformist, radical, or progressive life. The press, if still viewing it as unorthodox, treated it as worthy of attention.

A new London association emerged after several efforts in the mid-1870s. Then, vegetarianism appeared in the Reverend C.M. Davies's *Heterodox London*, because if it represented 'thinking differently', it also followed a current tendency to examine 'the basis of things, and accept nothing as final until proved by argument or experience' and because it was a social topic due to the 'famine levels' of meat prices.[252] Vegetarianism was discussed by a 'Social Progress Society' in Clerkenwell in 1874 and secularists and republicans in 'heretical' Hackney in 1875. There was a 'Diet Reform Society' led by Charles Ottley Groom Napier, who established another, also short-lived, in the later 1870s.

The 1870s saw an attempt to attract non-vegetarians in philanthropic organizations such as thrift and temperance societies, through the broader notion of 'food reform'. The London Food Reform Society was formed in 1875. It owed its existence in part to an obscure and elderly supporter of co-operation and industrial reform, Martin Nunn, who lived a life of 'almost ascetic self-denial'. Free, twice-monthly lectures and debates on food were held at the poky Franklin Hall (off Oxford Street). Strangers were encouraged to participate and introduce kindred subjects. Audiences gradually increased as a group of eager young men and well-known food reformers gave their support.[253]

The London society's high-class *Food Reform Magazine* referred opaquely to Manchester when referring to 'living-down' of opposition from a quarter which should have been supportive. The Manchester society thought its own organization sufficient but London vegetarians, often new converts who knew little about the movement's historical geography, disagreed; there was even talk about moving the national offices to the metropolis.[254] The London society's annual meetings in 1882 and 1883 debated broadening ambitions to make a 'national' claim; but critics thought this would generate hostility, and that funds could hardly support this. But the society's title was changed to '*National* Food Reform Society'. This lasted only until October 1885, when the VS paid off its debts, and, due to metropolitan pressure, established an 'auxiliary'. The results were disappointing. The VS failed to keep the good will of 'food reformers' and lost the reversionary interest of the Food Reform Society's subscription list. Manchester closed the office but agreed to an auxiliary with independent financial responsibility. Conflict grew around the issue of 'advanced' literature which the Society refused to accept without prior approval.[255] The inevitable split came in 1888, when the LVS was formed.

An indication of the newly independent society's ambitions was its impressive journal, the *Vegetarian*. Hills funded it 'and in point of fact the history of the Vegetarian movement in London from 1889 to the present time has been in a great measure the history of Mr Hills'.[256] Though Forward recalled a 'rough-and-tumble' period, the general mood was optimistic, reflected in plans to establish a 'Charing Cross Vegetarian Hotel and Restaurant'.[257] Several branches existed, and new workers were attracted, with affiliated societies at Oxford, Nottingham, Brighton, Guildford and Reading. Due to increasing business, in 1889 the LVS and *Vegetarian* offices moved to the Congregationalist Memorial Hall (Farringdon Street) thus placing their cause at the heart of London-based reform, since Memorial Hall not only hosted their meetings, food exhibitions and congresses, but also meetings of land reformers, women's temperance organizations and others. National (1885, 1899) and international congresses (1890, 1897) were held at London.[258]

FIGURE 8. Arnold Frank Hills, *left*, from the frontispiece, *Vegetarian Messenger*, January 1898; and Charles Walter Forward, *right*, from *Vegetarian Messenger*, February 1894, p. 56.

As an expression of the movement's growth, a number of specialist societies, clubs and independent organizations developed, catering for children, athletes, ramblers, musicians and sketchers. As we shall see later, vegetarian restaurants proliferated in this period and served as meeting places for various reformist groups. In 1889 the LVS created a national 'Federal Union', to the consternation of the VS which resented Hills's view that it was obsolescent. Affiliated societies included local metropolitan and suburban societies. By 1901 twenty-one societies had been established (although some were short-lived); these were co-ordinated from 1895 by a London Vegetarian Association.[259]

One important experiment in vegetarian sociability involved the 'Ideal Club' at Tottenham Court Road, funded by Hills and operative from 1893-98.[260] This was conceived as an 'agency' for practical application of temperance and purity, and identified with thrift and benefit societies, co-operative production and distribution, and food reform. It involved the co-operation of both sexes who would be educated in the duties of citizenship and local social needs. It was intended to support itself through mutual ownership, and stimulate similar institutions. It had a café and restaurant, and clubs, lectures and amateur dramatics were projected. By October 1894 there were a thousand members of whom just over a third were women. The men came from neighbouring businesses, but there were some artisans and medical students. Contemporary political and social questions were debated at the 'St Pancras Parliament' meeting there. It was recalled enthusiastically by the Labour politician Margaret Bondfield as a place 'where one could have discussions, dances, drill and fun ... in the club we gloried in being pioneers'.[261] Other attempts to promote sociability included the 'Vegetarian Rambling Society' which offered outings from the city in the summer (to Down House, St Albans and Arundel) and cultural visits in the winter. The spiritualist James Burns described it as free from 'intrusive familiarity' or favourites; a company united by diet and personal purity.[262] Its first offices near the British Museum included a tea room, drawing room, ladies' room and back room.

Apart from the 'Women's Vegetarian Union' and the anti-cruelty Humanitarian League with its headquarters and many key officers and supporters in London, there were twelve other London-based societies advocating food reform. These stopped short of, or deviated from, vegetarianism, or incorporated vegetarianism in wider rules for 'Higher Living' (and prolonged living), or were specialist manifestations of vegetarianism, or represented dissatisfaction with Hills's 'religion of vegetarianism'.[263] Other locations for vegetarianism involved unorthodox medical establishments. The American-born Thomas Low Nichols began his British activity with the publication of *How to Live on 6d a Day* (1870). His 'Hygienic Institute' in Bloomsbury hosted lectures and social meetings, displayed health reform goods for sale and published the *Herald of Health*.[264] *Forward* emphasized that the well-known Nichols attracted people of 'all sects and opinions'.[265] Three hospitals supported and managed by anti-vivisectionist, anti-vaccinationist and teetotal-vegetarians, were located around London.

Organizations associated with the 'simple life' tendency of the so-called 'late Victorian revolt', whose calls for simplification were in sympathy with vegetarianism, included the essentially metropolitan 'Fellowship of the New Life' which was formed in 1883 and which attracted the young middle-class intelligentsia and lower-middle-class clerks, teachers and journalists.[266] Another sympathetic organization was the Croydon Brotherhood Church, with its associated Brotherhood House at Kingsland that included a co-operative store from 1894 selling vegetarian and other 'advanced' periodicals and literature. During the 'International Vegetarian Congress', humanitarian sermons were given at the church. Also in this area were Theosophical, New Fellowship, anarchist and Social Democratic Federation groups; highlighted along with the local vegetarian society in a letter published in the (socialist) *Clarion* in 1896. The Croydon VS gave lectures at the Brotherhood Church.[267] Another cluster of vegetarians was the group of Russians led by William Frey (described by the *Pall Mall Gazette* as possessing the 'suave manners of a Russian gentleman'), which followed a vegetarian-Tolstoyan lifestyle in 'one of the dreariest streets of the Finsbury Park district'.[268] Also closely connected with London, through personnel and supporters (city workers) and press coverage, were a couple of 'back-to-the land' colonies in Essex involving vegetarianism: Purleigh which was founded in 1896, and Wickford, created after a meeting at the Central Vegetarian Restaurant in Bride Street in 1898.[269]

Despite all these organizations and activities, membership of societies was limited. The Food Reform Society's small membership size is indicated by its finances; it began with a 'magnificent' fund of £15. An appeal in April 1882 stated work was 'crippled' though lecturers were unpaid and there was no 'ornamental staff'. Publicity from a Free Dinner campaign seems to have increased membership and capital. At its demise it had a subscription fund of 'nearly' £250. The LVS had about seven hundred members and associates in 1899, though these figures included non-metropolitan vegetarians and under-represented the metropolitan movement because family members were not always enrolled.[270] Its income peaked in 1890 at just under £1400; by 1898 it was about £800, with £650 donated by Hills.[271]

The effort to attract working-class supporters is examined closely later (chapter six). Vegetarians sought to win workers over through free breakfasts, penny dinners, schemes involving penny banks and sewing meetings, and cookery classes. But their message of 'food thrift' was interpreted by internal and external critics as a pretext for lowering wages. The metropolitan recruits to the VS were variously occupied as writers, dairy managers, clerks, dial-writers, moulders and carpenters; to list a few joining in 1887. The high proportion of new members who were clerks is noticeable. These were often young men beginning their careers, needing to be thrifty, dabbling in self-improvement and idealistic.[272] Vegetarian restaurants here and elsewhere catered for them and they were satirized in *Punch, Funny Folks* and other journals.[273]

Many of the Food Reform Society's officers were known philanthropists, especially in temperance circles, like the Congregationalist minister Frederic Wagstaff, Manchester agent for the British Temperance League. Dr Nichols hoped for the support of luminaries such as Lord Shaftesbury or the Duke of Westminster. London vegetarianism also attracted 'ornamental' support from Lady Mount Temple, whose public support reflected the wider trend in the movement from the 1870s to accept women in public roles. In 1885, as the *Annual Register* reported, the secularist-theosophist Annie Besant addressed a meeting in Exeter Hall.[274] But although the activity of London-based female activists is explored further below, it is worth noting here that the leadership of the Food Reform Society was predominantly male and many of the members were 'active young men' who belonged to the ultra-teetotal, transatlantic Good Templar organization.[275] A London Vegetarian Club was also described as 'full of young fellows devoted to vegetarian principles'.[276]

What was the impact of this activity in the wider metropolitan world? The Food Reform Society's thrift campaigns directed at the working classes, and the food reformers' message of moderation, won approval. *The Times*, the voice of London as well as 'the nation', was perhaps representative in this, and supported the Society's dinners. Hyperbole about flesh was pardonable because of their useful work. Those who could afford it ate too much meat, including 'the whole class of domestic servants'.[277] This thrift message was picked up by George Gissing whose own experience underpinned his depiction of a London of cheap lodgings, boarding houses and shabby-genteel vegetarians. Limited means played a part in drawing people towards a fleshless diet in the city, just as it was forced on many in the countryside.

Others beyond the economically precarious were recruited, as vegetarianism became a predictable cause amongst elements of the metropolitan progressive milieu. By the end of our period there were even efforts to make it a fashionable lifestyle for the upper class; with Lady Windsor's drawing-room meeting in 1899, rightly described by the *Vegetarian* as a 'new departure'.[278] Undoubtedly there was a new vitality in metropolitan vegetarianism, and its visibility was enhanced by the greater coverage in the serious and satirical press. The movement celebrated its half century in a *fin de siècle* London favourable to it. Repeating the response at the movement's inception, vegetarianism was recognized as a 'sign of the times'. Many elements of late Victorian vegetarianism were not new: associations with temperance, religious unorthodoxy, and *soi disant* 'progressive' reform in general. Its temperance, anti-vaccination and purity connections, reflected in its journals and platform, demonstrate the continuing vigour of puritanism.

FIGURE 9. An illuminated address recognizing the role of Arnold Frank Hills in the revival, reproduced in the *Vegetarian*, 1897.

The national movement in the late-Victorian period

In 1887 the *Westminster Review* noted that vegetarianism was not dead but 'of late its voice has been almost lost in the din of political and social struggles of a more exciting nature'. In an effort to strengthen the local voice, Forward suggested to the London May conference that a new organization be formed, a suggestion which led to the Vegetarian Federal Union. Despite this, the *Vegetarian Review* complained about the lack of a well-devised provincial campaign, and a *drifting* cause failing to exploit 'its inherent basis of dynamic truth'.[279] Many of the local societies established in the late 1880s-90s had disappeared by the time Forward wrote his official history.

If the fate of some of the provincial societies suggested weakness, vegetarians could refer to increasing membership and wider interest. It is impossible to know the exact size of the late nineteenth century movement. The senior society's membership list did not take account of those who died or abandoned the diet, and thus represented a total membership rather than the society at any particular time. By 1887 the VS had attracted 3172 full members and 1335 associates. By 1899 there were 3972 members and 1823 associates. This probably does not include all *c*.700 members of the LVS who were not necessarily members of the older organization; it also concealed the family members whose vegetarian status was represented by a parent or spouse, and underplayed the tendency to abandon the diet by many converts.[280] Non-members who were subscribers to the journal may have been vegetarians or active sympathizers. It was claimed there were vegetarians in almost every town – people who were often not members of the Society – and one activist estimated Society membership was only a twentieth of the real number of vegetarians.[281] Naturally, vegetarian societies emphasized the gains (most patently when noting the addition of 'thousands' with the affiliation of Indian vegetarians, but also including some American vegetarians).[282]

The financial situation was unhealthy; a reduced income in 1894/5 of £449 was partly attributed to a depression which had lowered the sale of literature. However, the financial weakness had been an enduring problem since Simpson's death, with few significant legacies.[283] Yet the national movement could reassure itself that it was part of what was an international movement (with vegetarian societies developing in America, continental Europe, Australia, and India), expressing its sense of brotherhood through international congresses.[284]

FIGURE 10. Delegates at the VFU congress in Portsmouth May 1891. At the front are Josiah Oldfield and M.K. Gandhi. *Vegetarian Messenger*, October 1936, p. 318.

2

PHYSICAL PURITANISM AND MEDICAL ORTHODOXY

The status of vegetarianism as a health reform was an important element of debate surrounding the diet. This chapter contextualizes vegetarianism through a brief discussion of 'quackery' and examines its relationship to other alternative practices described as quackish by opponents; 'pathies' which, with vegetarianism, were classed by the *Westminster Review* in 1852 as 'physical puritanism'. The phrase nicely suggests the Victorian association of health (whether personal, or public and social) with morality and religion. It then examines the relationship of vegetarianism to the most widespread Victorian personal reform, temperance. Vegetarianism's sanative claims and hygienic institutions are then studied. Finally, the movement's reception in an influential quarter of Victorian society, medical orthodoxy, is considered. The connections which existed between health and religion through the 'physico-moral effects' of flesh-eating, and the associations between health reforms and social or political reforms, are discussed in the two succeeding chapters.

Quackery and Physical Puritanism

England was described in 1844 as a 'Paradise of Quacks' due to tolerance by government, press and public. If it was a paradise, it was because of a demand which had developed over the last century, popularizing medical knowledge and expanding the 'medical market'.[1] Victorians tried to achieve *Mens sana in corpore sano* and as one historian has aptly stated, 'worshipped the goddess Hygeia, sought out her laws, and disciplined themselves to obey them'.[2] Unprecedented population growth, rapid urbanization and a concomitant new scale of problems made public health a political issue. The body and medicine also provided powerful images for writers such as the dyspeptic and hypochondriac Thomas Carlyle who famously used the metaphor of universal quack medicine against radicals, social theorists and society in general. Vegetarianism's promotion as a panacea for social and moral ills led one observer to call it a 'Holloway-Pill' movement (equating it with Thomas Holloway's lucrative proprietary cure-all).[3] It was also treated as a quackery for its hygienic claims.

In 1851, *The Lancet*, the widely-read medical weekly established by the surgeon and radical Thomas Wakley, reported a lecture on quackery which encompassed phrenology, mesmerism, hydropathy, teetotalism, vegetarianism and homeopathy.[4] Typically this confounded commercial fraud and promotion of the medically 'unconventional'. The latter's labelling as 'quackeries', 'heresies' or 'fads', though it can be seen as part of the wider efforts to reform medicine by removing questionable practices, stemmed from the competing claims for customers in the health market, and the assertion of status and authority by a nascent profession which could not yet claim to be more successful than alternatives. We need to be sensitive about the denigratory or relative nature of terminology employed by opponents and proponents of the unconventional.[5]

The competition for authority is apparent from numerous articles on quackeries or 'medical delusions' in journals for the more orthodox medical practitioner. These attributed their appeal to popular discomfort at being left behind by advancing science. People were 'ready to turn their attention to any system which they think they can comprehend'.[6] A new 'pathy' or 'ism' was simply 'a new medical sect struggling to supplant the old one in general esteem' rather than false science.[7] The uneducated public could not discriminate, but developed (aided by popular texts by medical men) a 'self-sufficient judgement', which was the 'pabulum' for quackery and lack of respect for the 'profession'.[8] It was recognized that patronage and practitioners came not from uneducated plebeians alone, but also from clergymen, gentry and aristocrats.[9]

Vegetarianism was not quackery, but early and later opponents used the label. As a therapy, or part of a larger hygienic regimen, it was explicitly an alternative to 'allopathy'. As an organized health movement with propagandist press, it followed temperance/teetotalism, and the 'big four' of herbalism, hydropathy, homeopathy and mesmerism. Its message of temperance and natural cure had been familiarized by these. Its kinship as a health movement concerned with purity was identified in an important essay in the *Westminster Review* in 1852 (anonymous, but by the chemist Samuel Brown) investigating the hygienic, moral, social and political implications of homeopathy, hydropathy, mesmerism, teetotalism and – especially – vegetarianism.

Brown's label was 'physical puritanism'.[10] 'Physiological reform' was one of a confusing array of 'signs of the times', along with political, religious, scientific and industrial developments. Brown's treatment of the various movements was even-tempered but critical. Vegetarianism was 'a physiological heresy, and consequent project of reform, among the militant ideas and practices of the present century'. Having himself briefly tried the diet (under the influence of Shelley, Dr Lambe and J.F. Newton), his vegetarian acquaintances included a physician, electrician, painter, barrister, radical gentleman, lady-farmer and authoress. Brown was clear that the practice was not restricted to Cowherdite fanatics (as he saw them), or visionaries such as Greaves but attracted 'men of the people, phrenologists, natural-religionists, general reformers'.[11] For the moment vegetarianism was 'puny', but there were many thousands who were 'considerers'. Physiological reform was an expression of 'certain of the wants and aspirations of society' and thus had wider social and political implications. The movements represented 'a rooted and far-spreading conspiracy against orthodoxy'; perceptively, he noted their supporters among Owenites and city-dwelling artisan atheists. Despite errors of enthusiasm and extremism, physical puritanism involved the social body's salvation from long indulgence in 'poisonous and excessive pleasures'. It was an unparalleled 'vigorous, many-handed, and almost universal reaction against the final catastrophe'. At stake was the empire's health and therefore future. Predicting an Anglo-Saxon contest with European tyranny in the late nineteenth century, Brown welcomed physiological reform's recuperative role but argued that reform of the 'arts of life', education and government, rather than extreme asceticism, was the engine of progress. Temperance, as an exercise in will power, was morally better than total abstinence.

Though the article naturally antagonized medical heretics, the *Teetotal Progressionist* believed it to be fair and impartial and 'productive of beneficial results'[12] and a leading teetotaller claimed that vegetarianism received better treatment than teetotalism because the author had understood it better, stated its arguments fairly, and had in fact led several to convert to the system.[13]

The vegetarian movement and alternative 'pathies'

The overlap between vegetarianism and alternative 'pathies' is important and was both conceptual and social. As a matter of personal health, people experimented with practices to see what best suited them, combining new reforms with earlier ones, discarding those that proved redundant. Sequential movement could reflect a 'faddist' temperament, and opportunism by entrepreneurs exploiting these crazes. Thus *Punch* recounted an individual's journey through homeopathy, hydropathy, teetotalism, the 'vegetarian Dodge', electrobiology, mesmerism and clairvoyance.[14]

Medical unorthodoxy had its press, with general papers like the *Journal of Health* and specialist organs like the phrenological *The Zoist* or the hydropathic *Water Cure Journal*, and a mass of teetotal and temperance journals.[15] Often these journals showed the heretic's broad tolerance for unorthodoxy, especially given shared core beliefs and attitudes – hostility to the medical profession and its orthodoxy of 'poisons' – which overrode theoretical differences. The *Journal of Health* promoted Grahamism, hydropathy, homeopathy and temperance. The *Vegetarian Messenger* seemed similarly eclectic to the *Dublin Medical Press*, describing it as an 'organ for Homeopathy, Antivaccination, and for ought we know, Mesmerism'.[16] The VS's first secretary, William Horsell, published journals, almanacs and tracts for the various movements, retailed at his Depôt along with commodities and equipment for the range of health reforms.

One lecturer prominent in vegetarianism and spiritualism said that he combined vegetarian lectures with phrenology, physiology and health as a 'natural sequence' and because it was 'accepted much more readily than if I announced myself to lecture on Vegetarianism'.[17] Of course, unconventional medical reformers did not *necessarily* support other 'alternative' therapies. For instance, Jacob Dixon, a radical homeopathic surgeon, argued against exclusive diet.[18] The ultra-radical J.J. Garth Wilkinson also opposed it, though accepting that it might some day be important.[19] The editor of the *Homeopathic Journal* attacked it in 1855.[20]

Some critics of vegetarianism chose to highlight a superficial connection with an earlier system. Morisonianism, the panacea of the 'vegetable pill' invented by James Morison, was a precursor only in that it advocated a *vegetable* remedy; critics might have thought the connection closer when the *Vegetarian Advocate* advertised medals of Morison, as the 'Great Medical Reformer'.[21] Satirical 'transmogrification' of vegetarian consumer into vegetable occurred earlier in anti-Morisonia.[22] The connection between vegetarians and phrenology was less contrived, since although the phrenological journal *The Zoist* (1844-48) ignored vegetarianism, many early vegetarians, like Horsell with his phrenological museum and consultancy, or the Reverend G. Bruce Watson of Methven, were phrenologists. James Simpson's portrait even appeared in a Spanish phrenologist's work in 1851.[23] Despite being an exploded pseudo-science by the late nineteenth century, association continued with the *Vegetarian* advertising the *Phrenological Magazine* (1893); and offering free phrenological delineations of character (1894).[24] Another of the 'pseudo-scientific' therapies, mesmerism had been supported by Concordists and was also embodied in press and provincial societies. The coverage in the main vegetarian journals was limited but there were connections – often through spiritualism (examined in the next chapter) – though one mesmerist told a vegetarian that he could not be magnetized due to his diet.[25]

Of the few 'regularly' trained pro-vegetarian medical practitioners, a number were homeopathists. Homeopathy attracted cross-class support, but 'respectability' was furthered by its self-restriction (as a profession of homeopathic physicians) to those trained in allopathic orthodoxy.[26] This, and patronage by members of the upper-class, meant that allopaths were particularly offended by it.[27] The *Hahnemannian Fly Sheet* published one homeopathic doctor's support for vegetarianism (Viettinghoff) and the editor of the *Homeopathic Review* chaired a vegetarian meeting in 1859.[28] The VS's secretaries for Newcastle (John Mawson) and Plymouth (F.H. Foster) were homeopathic chemists. Yet one important homeopathic journal ignored vegetarianism throughout its existence[29] and homeopathic doctors quoted scriptural support for meat-eating.[30] Yet undoubtedly, as *Chamber's Encyclopaedia* stated in 1874, vegetarianism was supported by most of its disciples in combination with homeopathy and hydropathy.[31]

The 'science' of hydropathy narrowly preceded organized vegetarianism as a health craze. Its 'fringe' status was ambiguous. Many leading hydropaths were conventionally qualified physicians who maintained orthodox ideas on their role, the classification of disease, or physiological concepts. By the 1870s, as 'hydrotherapeutics', it was accepted by medical orthodoxy. The therapy's radicalism derived from rejection of traditional allopathic treatment in favour of less traumatic healing through bathing, showering and drinking water. It was supported by intellectual and cultural leaders such as the Carlyles, Tennyson and Darwin and accepted by 'official' Methodism.[32] There were practical and personal connections between the two reforms. Early hydropaths promoted a regime of simple diet and teetotalism (with fresh air and exercise). The English publicist for the water cure, Captain Claridge, wrote to the *Vegetarian Advocate* to announce he was preaching Grahamism. Unaccountably the endorsement was little exploited, a significant propagandistic error.[33] Through supporting Carl von Schlemmer, the Concordium at Ham Common had already pioneered hydropathy.[34] Schlemmer was responsible for one prominent convert to vegetarianism, Baker of Wokingham.[35] Horsell wrote a well-received popular hydropathic manual and briefly ran a hydropathic establishment at Ramsgate.[36] His *Vegetarian Advocate* reviewed hydropathic books and the *Water Cure Journal*. The latter published correspondence on vegetarianism from the Unitarian anti-slavery activist James Haughton (a future VS president). However, although 'respecting' the *Advocate*, it was wary of this new and 'hitherto unknown' reform, since scripture allowed animal food. Yet the hydropath Thomas Smethurst advocated a vegetarian diet for children. Forbes Lawrie, a vegetarian, ran a hydro at Dunstable.

Another hydro, at Melrose, supported vegetarianism because one of the founders was the prominent vegetarian John Davie.[37] Several vegetarians ran Turkish bath establishments.

The largely herbal therapy of 'medical botany' rivalled vegetarianism for popular support in the north of England in the 1850s with several large Yorkshire and Lancastrian town having societies. Like vegetarianism it had native and American antecedents. The movement was almost entirely working-class, with support particularly from plebeian Methodists, despite 'official' critique for its 'naturalism' and hostility towards orthodox medicine. The breakaway 'Eclectic' movement established by John Skelton had a national society and local branches, largely in northern England. In the 1860s the movement became less popular and more commercialized, but in the early 1850s vegetarians and medical botanists competed for local support, as an episode reported in Skelton's *Botanic Record* illustrates. A vegetarian lecturer at Bramley (Leeds) failed to convince his audience, so another lecturer was sent, and also found wanting in science: the correspondent canvassed experts in physiology and was told by one of these that 'it is not the first time *commonsense* has beaten *learning*'.[38] But the two movements were not mutually exclusive. Skelton, for instance, believed that an exclusively vegetable diet was healthier than one with animal food, and Horsell's *Vegetarian Advocate* carried advertisements for *Dr Coffin's Botanical Journal* and reviewed *A Botanic Guide to Health*.[39]

In 1854 in Salford and Manchester Alderman William Harvey chaired meetings against the Bill for Registration of Qualified Practitioners; his fellow Cowherdite Brotherton presented the petition to Parliament.[40] Vegetarians' opposition to what they saw as a monopolistic and monolithic allopathy is also evident in its support for anti-vaccination. Like the necessity for those other 'impurities,' meat and alcohol, this was held to be 'a delusion for the benefit of doctors'.[41] Many vegetarians were activists in the anti-vaccination crusade that kept the bogey of the lethal allopath alive when orthodoxy was becoming less drastic. Thus the prominent late-Victorian vegetarian, Arnold F. Hills, told the Vegetarian Congress of 1898 that vaccination touched the 'very spring and fountain head of vegetarianism itself' and anti-vaccination success would be a triumph for vegetarianism.[42] Involvement was long-standing. Though stressing that as a Society, anti-vaccination was not an official creed, the *Vegetarian Messenger* printed a petition against compulsory vaccination (the Vaccination Extension Bill) in 1853. Brotherton presented a vegetarian petition.[43] Though it was far from axiomatic that all vegetarians engaged in anti-vaccination efforts (though the *Dietetic Reformer* stated that probably 'few of our readers are aware of the amount of hardship inflicted on Vegetarians by the Compulsory Vaccination Acts') local vegetarians organized a petition in Padstow (and probably elsewhere).[44] The leading anti-vaccination polemicist, William Tebb, had earlier been a vegetarian activist, other significant vegetarian anti-vaccinationists were Thomas Baker of Wokingham, William White, Dr Walter Hadwen and the Beurles.

Teetotalism was identified by Samuel Brown as another component of physical puritanism. The movement's close temperance connections reflect strands which are less significant in modern vegetarianism: concern with self-help (including thrift), self-control, and social progress through individual reform. But if temperance became an archetypal Victorian reform associated with self-help, thrift and respectability, its teetotal offshoot was controversial in early-Victorian Britain. Early adherents, like vegetarians, were feared to be hastening their deaths.[45] Vegetarianism was a logical progression for 'extreme' teetotallers, who called it 'ultra-temperance'. Connections were close, indeed 'inevitable'. [46] Having reformed themselves in drink it was natural to adduce similar physiological, social and moral reasons for vegetarianism and if teetotalism dwarfed vegetarianism in its scale of support (perhaps a million adults in Britain in the 1860s) the temperance affiliation of rank-and-file vegetarians was standard.[47] But this did not prevent tensions. The extension of sympathy from this dietetic reform to vegetarianism was not automatic, especially as early teetotallers were advised or expected to eat meat. In an effort to emphasize the healthy, jolly and remunerative nature of teetotalism, supporters demonstrated hearty appetites, the 'rapid consumption of beef and pudding, indicative of health and vigour'.[48] Vegetarianism was attacked for harming the cause through bringing ridicule as the absurd but (so opponents who recognized a kinship might say) natural conclusion to its principles.[49] Silence on the subject of vegetarianism in one early temperance history (which included a life of James Simpson that ignored Simpson's main concern) probably indicates embarrassment and a fear of being damned by association.[50]

Alcohol-related concerns undoubtedly provided an important motivation for would-be vegetarians. Vegetarians' claims that their diet strengthened teetotalism and combated alcoholism were pressed forward most colourfully by one of the oddest characters in vegetarianism. Charles Ottley Groom Napier, self-styled 'Prince of Mantua', publicized his vegetarian treatment of alcoholism at the British Association for the Advancement of Science's meeting in 1875 and claimed to promote it a few years later at a grand fete at Greenwich.[51] Neither medical nor temperance orthodoxy accepted this assertion uncritically. But the kinship of late-Victorian temperance and vegetarianism found expression in annual temperance meetings at the Crystal Palace, when 'food reformers' wore their silver tassels and vegetarian 'Danielites' (on which more below) wore a yellow sash.[52] London vegetarians were associated with the Society for the Study and Cure of Inebriety, although its president, Dr Norman Kerr, queried its curative pretensions at the first 'Colonial and International Congress on Inebriety' (1887) despite being a supporter of vegetarianism.[53] By contrast, another teetotal activist, Samuel Morley, supported the National Food Reform Society's vegetarian meals as an advertisement for temperance.[54]

National and provincial temperance organizations were important and natural targets for vegetarian lecturers. One of the most important was the militant prohibitionist International Order of Good Templars (IOGT) which came to Britain in 1868 and typically attracted young working-class and lower middle-class nonconformists through its ritual, hierarchy and philanthropy: 'the Good Templar organization appealed to me as being a very sensible and useful one,' in the words of one Good Templar whose lodge organized a vegetarian demonstration.[55] Many lodges provided venues for vegetarian meetings and new recruits. It helped that the Grand Chief Templar, Joseph Malins, was vegetarian.[56] The Danielite Order was a 'food reform freemasonry' modelled on the IOGT, founded by a second-generation temperance worker, T.W. Richardson. Well-versed in temperance history he established it on the forty-fourth anniversary of the pioneering Preston teetotal pledge (i.e. August 1876).[57]

Vegetarian journals and pamphlets consistently emphasized the kinship of the causes; identifying vegetarianism through advert, article and notice with the wider temperance movement.[58] The link was made clear when the National Temperance Depôt was acquired by the millionaire vegetarian Arnold F. Hills's Ideal Publishing Union in 1898.[59] The *United Temperance Gazette* (1896-99), which carried vegetarian articles, also reflected his efforts to create a 'United Temperance' movement in this period.

Vegetarians criticized teetotallers for half-measures or inconsistency, often characterizing teetotalism as an incomplete reform. The prominent freethinker Francis Newman, soon a convert (and then pushed into becoming President of the VS), wrote that 'No law which levelled Barleycorn ought to stop short at the Butcher.'[60] The secularist G.J. Holyoake, sympathetic to both reforms, discussed shared tactical errors in a tract in the late 1850s.[61] In a debate with a teetotaller he spoke of the vegetarians' reasonableness in arguing that meat stimulated new passions whilst alcohol merely inflamed man's bad passions. But charges of dietetic inconsistency or half-measures could be levelled against vegetarians. The exclusion of eggs and dairy products pressed for by a few advanced vegetarians – vegans *avant la lettre* – partly replayed the temperance/teetotal development. Though calls for further consistency also reflected revulsion at all exploitation of animals (as in debates over leather and wool), the temperance connection does help emphasize the significance of physico-moral motivations apart from animal welfare.

Individuals and groups connecting teetotalism and vegetarianism existed before the Society's foundation. The Cowherdite sect, the core of the early Society, was one of the earliest groups in Britain to espouse teetotalism (*c.*1810).[62] Joseph Brotherton, who published a teetotal tract in 1821, and James Simpson, were teetotallers through their Cowherdism. Brotherton's co-denominationalist and brother-in-law William Harvey was founder member of the prohibitionist UKA, and vice-president of the Anti-Tobacco Society. The radical reformers of the Concordium had also supported teetotalism. A number of teetotal Owenites and Chartists, most notably Charles Neesom, became vegetarians.[63]

The teetotal pioneer Joseph Livesey of Preston, who was acquainted with Manchester vegetarians, was an early supporter who believed that as temperance societies had enlightened people about the proper drink, the same 'spirit of inquiry' would discover the best food.[64] He wrote of other vegetarian experimenters such as Preston Temperance Society's secretary.[65] He continued to provide support by detailing his diet and recommending vegetarian literature in his *Staunch Teetotaller* and (cautiously) approved vegetarianism in a letter to the VS for its 'encouragement' in 1876. As a British temperance celebrity his endorsement was naturally stressed in the official history of the vegetarian movement in 1897.[66] There were other prominent teetotallers who were vegetarians or supported vegetarianism. Three successive presidents of the Society – Harvey, Simpson and James Haughton – were honorary UKA officers. Frederic Lees was a supporter who won a vegetarian essay competition in 1857.[67] The Alliance's secretary, Thomas Halliday Barker, friend of William Lloyd Garrison, was a vegetarian. The editor of the UKA's journal was that Henry Sutton who had been a disciple of Greaves (and who was mentioned in Brown's essay).[68] The most striking sign of UKA-vegetarian connections was the unrealized scheme devised by the ultra-eccentric Pierre Baume, who hoped to harness the energies and reputations of Mancunian vegetarians and teetotal elite to a scheme uniting the two reforms with educational reform.[69]

William Hoyle, whose annual letter on the 'national drink bill' was published by *The Times*, was the secretary of the Crawshawbooth VS in the 1850s. Local associations were often led by and composed of teetotallers, whose own movement was also strongest in a northern, urban and industrial location. The connection was also close in London. The publisher Horsell created a temperance 'Order of Horebites' and established a business devoted to temperance literature and periodicals such as the *Temperance Star*. His *Vegetarian Advocate* promoted 'temperance in all things'.[70] His publishing partner, Job Caudwell, was also a committed teetotal-vegetarian. The London Vegetarian Association's secretary, Dornbusch, not only abstained from alcohol but also tea, coffee and tobacco (the latter another kindred movement to vegetarianism involving laymen and women from nonconformist backgrounds against the medical profession's general indifference[71]).

Teetotal connections continued to characterize men leading or supporting the VS, newer national organizations and provincial societies. The LVS, for instance, was led by a national temperance figure, Arnold F. Hills. Women were less prominent in a public capacity initially, rather like teetotalism.[72] But in the late-Victorian period, the Women's Vegetarian Union located itself in the wider temperance world and in 1895 held a reception for the World's Women's Christian Temperance Union with 'kindly thoughtfulness, and possibly an eye to future sisterhood of practical aims'.[73]

Although vegetarianism and teetotalism were established as movements within two decades of each other, in the late-Victorian period the former presented itself as a young movement requiring decades of public education before it could enjoy the toleration or inevitable acceptance accorded (it believed) teetotalism. Gone was the youthful confidence with which one pioneer had declared that 'the glory of the Vegetarian Society will quite eclipse that of the Temperance Society'.[74]

Hygienic vegetarianism and medical orthodoxy

One critic described vegetarianism as a 'siege train of physiological intimidation'.[75] Its armoury included a critique of orthodox medical opinion (and general assumption) concerning the best or 'natural diet of man'. Vegetarians marshalled physiological evidence of unimpaired physical and mental efficiency. Meat was shown to be responsible for diseases such as tuberculosis. Vegetarianism's role as a curative, prophylactic or reliever of specific (or all) diseases was rehearsed. This was with the knowledge that 'dietetics' had traditionally been an important aspect of medical treatment. Concerns about diseased and adulterated food allowed vegetarianism to be presented as a public health question.

One vegetarian was being unusually restrained when he said that the diet had not transformed them into Sampsons or 'entirely done away with every sort of ailment', but had effected 'a few things in that direction'.[76] Manifold scientific-hygienic claims were expressed in many media: books, tracts, handbills, lantern slides, posters, demonstrations and lectures. 'Diet in relation to health' and the 'curative action of the regimen' were the foci of many lectures. The first vegetarian lectures in London emphasized the diet as 'best adapted to man's constitution' through anatomy, physiology and chemistry.[77] Some provincial branches in the 1850s distributed copies of Sylvester Graham's *The Science of Human Life*, and tried to assemble their own libraries. About 1884 a VS handbill setting out the vegetarian case listed 'health' as the first (though the summary of the system in the same period privileged religion). Some of the discussion over the name of the reform reflected debate over the primacy of health, one member in 1873 suggesting 'Hygeist'.[78] A new root for 'vegetarian' was introduced which emphasized the health claims: vital, healthful and vigorous.[79]

Vegetarian journals often featured 'health' in their titles, thus *The Vegetarian* was a 'Paper for the Promotion of Happiness, Purity, Temperance, Health, Wealth and Happiness', and was advertised for 'every invalid or sufferer in health'. It was inaugurated with a 'Health' column superintended by Dr Thomas Low Nichols, whose Health Institute was an important centre for metropolitan vegetarianism. His *Herald of Health* was a recognized organ of the movement. The journals advertised 'health' foods, equipment and clothing, listed 'Sanitary Food Stores' and vegetarian boarding homes with names such as 'Hygiea' or 'Hygienic Home'. Late-Victorian vegetarians supported several 'vegetarian hospitals'. Oriolet, at Loughton in Essex, treated cancer and consumptive patients and was managed by Josiah Oldfield, a former barrister, with Arnold Hills as president. Another was the 'Humanitarian Hospital of St Francis', on the New Kent Road. Thomas Allinson ran a vegetarian Hygienic Hospital at Willesden for the working class. A Maternity Society was established to support vegetarian women.[80]

FIGURE 11. Oriolet Hospital in Essex. *Vegetarian Messenger*, April 1896, p. 108.

Vegetarianism in America formed a component of a wider Grahamite health reform in the 1830s. In Britain too, vegetarianism was generally no isolated practice, but one followed in association with other medical unorthodoxies. Further, temperance in, or abstinence from, a range of other stimulating or poisonous foods (tea, coffee, pickles, spices), was often recommended and attempted. Many were interested in exercising their bodies, reforming their clothes and cleansing their homes. If this was personal or domestic reform, it was also a crusade for public health. Early recognition of its sanitary status was shown by the *Health of Towns Journal*.[81] Later, in a journal like the *Herald of Health*, in organizations like the Wallaces' 'Physical Regeneration Society' or Allinson's 'Natural Living Society', vegetarianism was a prominent component of 'natural cure'/ hygienic reform systems.[82] Testimony shows that many became converts through consulting 'naturopaths' like Nichols, Allinson or the Wallaces, or reading their books and journals.

When vegetarians from Middleton emphasized the diet reform's subordinate role in a wider health reform by naming their association a 'Society for Promotion of Health' in 1880, they were keen to direct attention to slums.[83] Vegetarianism certainly promoted itself as an invaluable reform for the urban dweller facing pollution and overwork. Some vegetarians acted as irregular practitioners in their localities (though presumably reinforced through overlapping 'irregular' capacities as homeopaths or medical botanists), thus the Cowherdite John Monks was the 'village Aesculapius' for fifty years, Walter Hardman helped cholera victims in 1894-95 and Forbes Marshall treated people with acetic acid.

There were critics of attention being accorded to non-vegetarian health matters, or to assumptions of support for further dietary abstentions. Not everyone approved of the *Vegetarian Messenger* giving space to sanitary reforms, the reluctant president Francis Newman believing ventilation, bathing and clothing reforms formed no part of the programme.[84] Differences of opinion over what constituted the 'natural diet' provided enough controversy already to divide the movement. The most prominent late-Victorian controversy concerned a theory proposed by the American Emmet Densmore, that cereals were indigestible or non-assimilable. Heated articles and letters, reprinted as tracts, contested his 'anti-cerealism'.[85] Densmorites who had previously attempted a vegetarian diet argued that vegetarianism was dangerous. At the same time, Arnold Hills promoted the idea of 'vital foods'.[86]

It was said that the first question usually raised with a convert was: 'Don't you feel very weak?'[87] Opponents caricatured vegetarians as flaccid and lacking normal stamina.[88] Whatever the emphasis was (health, economy, animal welfare or spiritual purity), the physical health, stamina and longevity of activists were important. Vegetarian obituaries sought to stress other factors for early deaths such as those of the first president, James Simpson, or the London secretary Dornbusch.[89] From the start emphasizing the vegetarianism of vigorous workers like Constantinople's porters or Belgian miners, a collective effort to address orthodox opinion on diet and strength through displays of 'muscular athleticism' was only made later (Forward attributed this to the intellectualism of earlier vegetarians).[90]

FIGURE 12. Promoting a muscular image for vegetarianism: the champion runner John Barclay. *Vegetarian Messenger*, March 1898, p. 117.

Health scares could be 'improved' by propaganda. They were recognized as opportunities for the cause by observers like the *Exeter Daily Gazette* which thought vegetarianism was aided by bad meat and tuberculosis scares.[91] Food adulteration, as the *Sheffield Telegraph* appreciated, was a 'powerful' argument for vegetarianism.[92] One early 'vegetarian ordinary' advertised thus: 'Novelty! Cholera Prevented – Better than Cured'. Cholera was an important fear that could be addressed to win converts, the audience at a banquet in London in 1851 being told that no member of the Society had died of the disease, and a meeting in Bristol discussed it over thirty years later.[93] The novelist Mrs Humphry Ward attributed a Manchester audience for vegetarianism to cotton famine and cholera.[94]

How popular was 'hygienic vegetarianism'? Many who never joined vegetarian societies tried it for health reasons. In 1883 *The Lancet* claimed that 'physicians see in the course of their practice many who have done themselves injury by making the attempt'.[95] Testimonies published by vegetarians which included the reasons for conversion often gave dyspepsia as a causative medical complaint, other complaints included rheumatism, asthma, flatulence, even nettle-rash. One can accumulate a list of converts for medical reasons and add to these, those who chose to emphasize hygienic claims as paramount, and vegetarians who were physicians. But the adherents thus classified as supporters of a 'hygienic' claim must be incomplete as the many other vegetarians who were teetotal were often teetotal on health grounds. Nor did health motives preclude acceptance of 'principled' reasons.

Vegetarians who had tried unsuccessfully orthodox and other unorthodox therapies testified to the diet's curative power. The cost of unsuccessful orthodox treatment, pills and patent medicines, in comparison with cheap self-cure, was stressed. Pills and doctors could now be banished. It was a movement appealing for popular support and aiming at popular instruction. The *Vegetarian Advocate*'s full title proclaimed its democratic intent to instruct the people so they would be their own doctors.[96]

Like other heresies the movement often characterized allopaths, members of a licensed and registered profession after the controversial Medical Act of 1858, as a sinister priesthood. In 1872 Francis Newman identified 'opposition of medical men' as one of the most serious obstacles.[97] The leading Welsh activist testified that his worst opponent was the 'mutton chop doctor'.[98] Medical orthodoxy was convinced that a mixed diet was mankind's proper food. Climate, occupation, age (a near vegetarian diet for children was recommended in the early-Victorian period[99]), and state of health might vary it, but an omnivorous diet was best for bodily and mental development.[100] Patients were recommended meat (and alcohol) as cures for dyspepsia and as a necessity during pregnancy. The orthodox were convinced vegetarianism was fatal. Thus one early convert recalled a medical man's amazement when he was pointed out as a vegetarian.[101] The editor of the *Hull Advertiser* was advised to abandon his diet during the cholera epidemic of 1854.[102] Henry Salt in 1886 claimed a 'physician of some local repute' denied the existence of vegetarians, alleging that they were nocturnal carnivores.[103]

The movement's relationship with medical orthodoxy was complicated. Vegetarianism's antagonistic attitude stemmed from a self-help mentality on *principle*, and the hostility of medical professionals, whose own efforts at reform vegetarians ignored or treated as self-interested. Paragraphs, asides and testimonies condemned the 'faculty' and inquired whether doctors were necessary.[104] Yet vegetarians craved the 'respectable' medical profession's endorsement and claimed scientific credibility. They might contest the definition and course of scientific endeavour (as in opposition to vaccination or vivisection), but most did not reject it as a mode of analysis of the way the world functioned.[105] Science was seen as endorsing the infant VS since Justus von Liebig's chemical researches appeared to prove the nutritional value of plant foods. James Simpson had studied the chemistry of food in Berlin, and one of his tracts attending the nascent Society over which he presided, was dedicated to Liebig and Dr Lyon Playfair.[106] His claim that the new chemistry of food was unappreciated by the British medical world is supported by the failure of another vegetarian, James Haughton, to obtain any medical judgement on Liebig's work.[107]

Dietetics, 'diet administered according to principle,' for the prevention, relief or curing of disease, formed a branch of medicine 'as important as that of the Materia Medica'.[108] Yet orthodox medical journals of the 1840s recognized its neglect. The reformist *Lancet* in 1847 feared that 'diet and regimen, along with other topics of hygiene, obtain little attention from most medical practitioners' and that this created the breach through which quackery entered.[109] In 1864 *The Times*, in the wake of Edward Smith's findings on national diet, condemned the professionals' neglect of the 'chymistry of digestion' and recognized that the 'irregular' and amateur instead met this need.[110] Vegetarians certainly claimed this. The *Vegetarian Advocate*'s editor was assured by many medical men that dietetics was not part of their education or medical examination: 'What they know on this matter is learned either before going to college, or after their return. Need we wonder at their want of information.'[111] The homeopathist Viettinghoff told his homeopathic audience that 'the generality of the medical profession' failed to investigate vegetarianism and that it had been left to people unconnected with the profession.[112] Decades later, one 'regularly' qualified naturopath asserted that 'vegetarians taught me more of the science of life than all my professors'.[113]

Still, the Society wanted medical endorsement. A few physicians had already supported a vegetable diet. Historically, the most significant (for demonstrating cholera was waterborne) was John Snow, a teetotal-vegetarian when apprenticed to a surgeon-apothecary (1827-33). Abandoning the diet for health reasons, his experience was unknown to the early VS. The vegetarianism of Dr Lambe, who advocated the diet as a cure for cancer, scrofula and scurvy, *was* well-known, and publicized by the VS.[114] Dr A.P. Buchan had believed a farinaceous diet prevented pulmonary consumption. Gout, Dr Cullen had believed, was cured by a vegetable diet. The *Vegetarian Advocate* cited Charles Hogg's endorsement of the diet for children. He believed better results to be obtainable through *materia alimentaria* than through *materia medica*, and that 'temperance in all things' was the 'basis and stay of health and comfort'. The *Advocate* also published a paper by Isaac Lionel Crawcour, delivered to the Physiological Society of Guy's Hospital. Crawcour (provided with information by Lane and others) rightly pointed out Hippocrates' emphasis on regimen not drugs. When the homeopathist Dr Griffith Jones became vegetarian the London Association spoke of the advantages of a member in the 'enemy camp'.[115]

The Society highlighted some medical supporters. In January 1856 some eighteen physicians and surgeons were members; by 1866 there were ten.[116] They included hydropaths such as Forbes Lawrie at Dunstable and Bates at Malvern, the homeopath Viettinghoff, and a son of Dr Lambe. A few orthodox practitioners employed vegetarianism as a curative or prophylactic. Dr Nicolls of Longford Fever Hospital applied the diet for sixteen years.[117] Dr Norman Kerr, who had been a vegetarian as a young medical student, recommended vegetarianism in his practice. The most prominent vegetarian doctors of the late-Victorian period were also unorthodox: the American-born Dr Nichols, and his disciple the vegetarian-birth controller and anti-vaccinationist Thomas Allinson, Hadwen the anti-vaccinationist, and Oldfield the fruitarian barrister-doctor. Allinson thought doctors were unnecessary, for illness was a process of cure, and argued in print for resistance to vaccination. His medical correspondence column in *The Weekly Times and Echo* from 1885 publicized his ideas. He was removed from the General Medical Council Register in 1892, formally for malpractice – self-advertisement for professional gain – but essentially because of his medical opinions. The case received national and international coverage. Supporters depicted it as another incident where a 'trades union' had acted out of self-interest.[118]

Though Nichols and Allinson were well-known health reform figures in late-Victorian Britain, they were neither leading scientists nor medical researchers. In the analytical chemists A.W. Duncan and Wynter Blyth, they did have professionals (the movement also attracted several chemist-druggists, one of whom gave up his job out of principle). No great scientist joined the Society. The *Vegetarian* complained that though a 'great many scientists' thought flesh-eating caused most diseases, they would not give public support.[119] Reporting the annual vegetarian meeting in 1885, *The Times* was unimpressed by the scientific support, counting 'one provincial surgeon' and a 'lady doctor' (Anna Kingsford).

The Society advertised what medical support they could find through tracts, articles, and handbills. In the late 1840s the surgeon and physiologist Professor Lawrence's apparently favourable testimony had appeared on wafers.[120] A handbill quoted opponents who accepted that the diet allowed physical vigour. The attempt to present the eminent surgeon Sir Henry Thompson's advocacy of a 'lighter' diet as an endorsement of vegetarianism led to controversy in the *Nineteenth Century*. A competition sought the 'most striking' medical opinion on vegetarianism.[121]

Practical attempts to win over orthodox medical men included debates. There is little evidence for the presence of local medical men to combat heresy at vegetarian lectures in the 1850s, but certainly medical men were supplied with literature by the Birmingham Vegetarian Association and the Edinburgh society reported an 'eminent MD' had been converted in 1858.[122] Medical and sanitarian associations were targeted with little success. A paper by Dr Edmunds was discussed by members of the Medical Society of London in 1877, the president summarized the case for the diet as: advanced age, when the climate was conducive, in the treatment, especially, of illness, in the chief area of temperance.[123] Novel theories and doubtful scientific evidence exposed the cause to derision, as happened in 1888, when medical men and students were entertained at a vegetarian hotel, under the presidency of the respected sanitary reformer and sympathizer Dr Benjamin Richardson, there was ominous silence after Arnold Hills's speech on 'vital force'.[124] The vegetarians also used hygienic exhibitions and congresses. They struggled to gain a presence in the Health Exhibition of 1884, but the restaurant which was eventually allowed through the support of Richardson was a great success.[125] There was delight at the sanitary reformer Edwin Chadwick's support for vegetarianism at the Hastings Health Congress (1889).[126] But in 1891 the *Vegetarian* sent out a questionnaire to members of another Hygienic Congress, and was dismayed at their prejudices.[127] The same paper sought support through advertisements and correspondence in the *Nursing Record*.[128]

Hostile medical opinion can partly be located through the vegetarian press. Condemnation demonstrated that their message was being heard and critical paragraphs were dissected to show the ignorance of the 'faculty'. Popular lectures on diet and health by medical men made reference to vegetarianism, for instance, Dr E. Lankester's at the Bradford Mechanics Institute in 1861.[129] Popular health manuals by medical professionals and others often alluded to vegetarianism, and were similarly reviewed by vegetarians – if they advocated a 'light diet' and criticized modern excess they could lead readers to vegetarianism; if they were hostile they could stimulate a debate.[130]

The treatment in the *Lancet* and *British Medical Journal* (*BMJ*) may be taken as representative of orthodoxy (both promoted medical reform, the *BMJ* being the British Medical Association's organ). Their ignorance of the infant movement may have been a strategy of disregard. The journal which became the *BMJ*, triggered by a vegetarian banquet in Birmingham in 1855, first treated vegetarianism as the 'most ridiculous of the many absurd fallacies that even well educated men (in other respects) will sometimes fall to'. Standard problems were touched on, concerning the admission of eggs and dairy products, climate, and the fate of Eskimos. Significantly the movement was treated here as an 'eccentric sect' rather than quackery.[131] The *Lancet* was critical of the movement in reporting its General Meeting in October 1862.[132] It reported the Medical Society of London's debate in 1877. Criticism resurfaced in 1879 when considering economic dietaries, an 'important and difficult question' which, however, was left to 'certain visionary enthusiasts, each one of whom believes he has discovered a universal food'. After a vegetarian clergyman recommended a horse-bean dietary to the St. Pancras Board of Guardians the journal warned that 'fashionable' advocacy of legumes ignored the dangers of cutaneous eruptions, heating, colic, indigestion and paralysis.[133]

The defence of meat was often explicitly connected with questions of empire and authority. Arguments were unoriginal, and not peculiar to the medical profession. Considering the vegetarian 'school of social reformers' in 1881, the *Lancet* argued that herbivores, though physically strong, did not 'assert supremacy over other orders of the animal creation'.[134] An omnivorous mankind had headship of Creation. But food reform (not vegetarianism specifically) achieved a philanthropic status; recognized as attending to the physical, mental and moral needs of the people.[135] It was educational – against fashion and prejudice – and concerned with the purity and dietetic value of foods. Dietetic errors such as preference for white bread were 'at the very root of most of the evils which afflict the lower strata of society'.[136] The orthodox did, of course, criticize overindulgence in animal foods, and could accept vegetarianism's value in reducing meat consumption, an admission Henry Salt felt a 'trifle provoking'.[137] At its most favourable, the *Lancet* gave qualified praise for the Society's role in increasing consumption of vegetables, whilst fearing its essential 'utter confusion' of the natural order.[138] The *British Medical Review* praised vegetarianism's message of economy during hard times and attention to national self-sufficiency.[139] Vegetarian restaurants received friendly notice, on the basis of health and economy, in the *BMJ* and *Medical Press and Circular* in 1880.[140] Vegetarian books were reviewed, correspondence published, vegetarian meetings noted, but orthodox medical opinion was not persuaded 'to the full extent of their desires'.[141]

Ultimately, for professional and lay 'orthodoxy', the debilitating consequences of vegetarianism were clear. Conventional thought believed that a diet which excluded animal foods weakened and even fatally undermined health. It might be concluded then, since death was often 'regarded as by no means distant or improbable' that whatever motivated someone to become vegetarian, it was a health issue for relatives, friends and family doctors.[142]

3

BEASTS AND SAINTS: ZOOPHILIA AND RELIGION IN THE MOVEMENT

Many vegetarians wanted animals to be treated more humanely and humans to be less beastly. This chapter explores both aspects through studying the place of 'zoophilism' in the movement and the role of religion.

The changing relationship between humans and the animal world has been explored by a number of scholars. Keith Thomas has charted the decline of anthropocentrism and the emergence of zoophile sensibilities from the early modern period.[1] Anxieties about suffering animals in the shambles, about brutalized butchers, and the pain involved generally in meat production, had been expressed in the eighteenth century, stimulated by the growth of towns, agricultural developments, increasing dominance over wild animals and urban isolation from animal farming. But although much has now been written about the attitude of Victorians to animals, and the animal welfare movements, a focus on the vegetarian dimension has so far been missing.[2]

When vegetarians claimed that theirs was a 'moral' cause they often alluded to animal welfare. Many vegetarians prized the ethical dimension which this aspect represented, and deplored a merely hygienic or economic vegetarianism. Many converted from compassion for the suffering animal, whose image figured repeatedly in propaganda.[3] The exploration of this aspect begins with the movement's relationship to cruelty in the provision of meat and other animal-derived items, and to cruel sports. The relationship with the animal societies and anti-vivisection movement, in the light of vegetarians' claims to be the most consistent zoophiles, is next examined. Animal-centred concerns are then situated in the broader context of anti-violence and anti-pain.

The connections between a vegetarian diet and religion are extensive and ancient. Christian theologians had debated the transition from a vegetarian golden age to a post-lapsarian or post-diluvian age of meat-eating. Medieval ascetics and protestant sectarians rejected worldly pleasures of the flesh through their regimen.[4] The section examining the Victorian movement's religious dimension places it in the wider context of links between health reform and religion. Religious affiliations are then discussed. The associations with spiritualism and the occult are then explored.

Vegetarian zoophilia

Analysis of the vegetarians whose motivations are known or inferrable suggests that humane principles were less important than hygienic motives, since ethical or humane concerns and involvement in animal societies can only be identified in the case of some 120 of them. Yet humanitarian sentiments could be acknowledged by those drawn to the movement for other reasons. In Francis Newman there is the example of a vegetarian on ascetic, hygienic and economic grounds, but who was an anti-vivisectionist on welfare grounds. Private vegetarians who did not join any society must have included many on animal-centred moral grounds.

Vegetarians promoted themselves as an animal welfare movement, though not being categoric about the status of this aspect. The second cardinal principle of the *Manifesto of the Vegetarian Society* asserted none had the right to 'wantonly kill or mangle' animals as sensitive as ourselves and that there must be an urgent necessity before one sought food from an animal of a 'superior grade'. Discussion about a 'fish grade' of associates was condemned for imperilling the humanitarian aspect.[5] A legal judgment on the charitable status of the national vegetarian societies stressed their object was 'to prevent destruction of animal life for food'.[6] The *Vegetarian Messenger* noted 'with interest everything that tends to bring us into friendly relations with our quadruped fellow creatures'.[7] The journals carried sentimental stories about animal friends, discussed animal rights, and such matters as the fate of caged and wild birds and dog-muzzling. Coverage undoubtedly grew, a result of an expanded press in which to examine all aspects, and a propagandist response to questions of the day such as vivisection. But the significance of animal-centred concerns was a constant rather than increasing factor.[8]

If vegetarianism was classed by many as a personal reform, animal cruelty allowed specific public measures to be agitated for. The 'Danielites' petitioned Parliament against the employment in slaughterhouses of women and youths.[9] A fourteen-point political programme devised by the VFU in 1892 included private slaughter houses and live animal transport.[10]

The cruelty which these late-Victorian political programmes addressed was always visible to Victorian urbanites, who were far from divorced from 'real' (working, as opposed to pet) animals.[11] In cities and market towns, maltreatment by drovers and butchers was a common spectacle and could be exploited to stimulate inquiry.[12] Like animal diseases and adulteration, observers recognized the potential value to the cause from cruelty in transit.[13] The socialist Edward Aveling had to preface remarks about his sense of the cruelties of the cattle trade by affirming he was 'no vegetarian'.[14] The horrors of transportation caused a number to become vegetarian. Vegetarian societies petitioned against the cruelty of cattle transit (and in support of Samuel Plimsoll's 'Merchant Shipping Act Amendment [no.2] Bill').[15] The cattle trade's horrors were emphasized in articles and correspondence.

FIGURE 13. Butchers Row, Aldgate. *Vegetarian*, 1 January 1898.

Slaughterhouse horrors attracted attention. It was not surprising that an audience at the City of London Mechanics' Institute should support Charles Lane's argument that the Smithfield nuisance would only end through vegetarianism: the filth, stench and cacophony of the live-cattle market of Smithfield appalled many, and not simply vegetarians or zoophilites (Charles Dickens, for instance, alluded to it as a 'shameful place' in *Great Expectations*).[16] George Dodd, in *The Food of London*, noted that hypocritical shunning of the necessary stage prior to the institution of beef-eating was the basis for vegetarians' sense of moral superiority.[17] The tactic of taking readers 'behind the scenes at slaughter houses' was employed by the National Food Reform Society (and the Humanitarian League, on which more below).[18] In the *Vegetarian* in 1895, the veil concealing the slaughterhouse was lifted in a cartoon by Jack B. Yeats; in 1898 the *Vegetarian* had illustrated articles on slaughterhouses.[19] Jewish slaughter methods were investigated.[20] The public heard of a policeman becoming vegetarian after visiting shambles, and a missionary almost converted after another visit.[21] Critics like T.P. Smith MB, who accepted current standards and methods were a 'grievous blot on our much-vaunted civilization', recognized the challenge of slaughterhouse revelations.[22] An admittedly inadequate attempt to gauge the reasons for vegetarianism indicated the importance of slaughter houses in 1898.[23] Nevertheless, one humanitarian questioned the permanency of conversions on this ground.[24]

FIGURE 14. The Jewish method of animal slaughter investigated. *Vegetarian*, 8 January 1898.

Leigh Hunt had contrasted the disturbing sights of butchers' and anglers' shops with those of fruiterers in the early nineteenth century.[25] Even if killing was concealed, these shops caused offence.[26] A late-Victorian utilitarian examination of vegetarianism accepted that 'aggregate impairment' to millions through the sight was a forceful justification for the humane diet and agreed that butchers were brutalized.[27] Butchers' and slaughtermen's anaesthetized moral senses were repeatedly adverted to in *vegetariana*.[28] Loss of humane feeling had been recognized, it was claimed, by an antique law forbidding butchers becoming jurors.[29] No practising butcher was vegetarian, though a butcher from Beverley was 'a little bit in that way myself' through reading a vegetarian publication.[30] Somewhat improbably, a butcher who expressed a wish 'to get out if he could', was an occasional visitor to the Concordium.[31] A butcher's boy requested a copy of Graham's *Science of Human Life*.[32] Two vegetarians (Andreas Gottschling and Captain Darley) had been butchers, another two were butcher's sons (C.P. Newcombe, and F. Harrison of Didsbury). London vegetarians hosted a dinner for publicans and butchers in 1888.[33] Earlier, butchers attended public vegetarian meetings, including one at the Rotunda at Dublin in 1867, when butchers' boys were disruptive. Others wrote in response to slurs on their character.[34]

If the concern about butchers was heartfelt, it also enabled vegetarians to avoid the charge that their compassion was animal-centred. The culpability of customers ('butchers by proxy') was stressed. One enterprising vegetarian association made this clear at Christmas by having an advertisement with the message that flesh-eating involved bloodshed printed in the local paper.[35] Consumers were to blame, and conscientious consistency demanded a general reform of consumption. Radical movements traditionally had their alternative commodities, for loyalty, advertisement and the raising of funds. Alternative commodities offered on moral grounds (as opposed to hygienic or dietetic grounds) were *central* to vegetarianism and of direct propagandist relevance. Critics pointed to the inconsistency of adherents, and to the impossibility of vegetarian principles given the dependence of their civilization on animal-derived products in the manufacture of items as various as shoes, belts for conveying rotary power in factories, and buttons.[36] Old 'debating friends' at vegetarian lectures therefore included questions about the alternatives to leather, wool, horn and ivory. Early substitutes represented the application of newly discovered natural materials and the creation of synthetics in what was the beginning of the plastics industry. A radical vegetarian in the 1830s commissioned boots made of 'some vegetable or woolly substance'.[37] Luke Hansard discussed artificial fur, parchment and leather in 1843.[38] The *Vegetarian Advocate* advertised the recently introduced natural plastic, gutta-percha.[39] James Simpson argued that the problem of materials was simply a question of supply and demand, with clothing, fuel, and manure all having their vegetable substitutes.[40] Artificial leather continued to be investigated and exhibited throughout the period. Adherents sporting 'innocent' clothing, such as Lieutenant T.W. Richardson, created a stir.[41]

In her column in the *Illustrated London News* Florence Fenwick-Miller alluded to her late friend Anna Kingsford's extreme scruples about exploitation. She concluded that if matters were considered too closely, modern European civilization became impossible: a point Kingsford would not have disputed since she denied the status of 'civilization' to the present age. Whilst she was the proprietor of a journal, she avoided advertising goods exploiting animals.[42] She and other vegetarians were critical of female humanitarians' inconsistency in the wearing of kid gloves, furs and (with bird-protectionists) condemned 'murderous millinery'.[43]

Murderous sport was also considered. Like Aveling, an essayist in the *Fortnightly Review* had to preface his concerns with the disclaimer 'I am neither a Vegetarian nor an opponent of capital punishment'.[44] It was a surprise when the *Sporting Chronicle* published vegetarian correspondence in 1890, though at least two racing horses were named 'Vegetarian'.[45] Several vegetarians had been actively involved in blood sports, including Kingsford, Lady Florence Dixie[46] and Arnold Hills, whose novel *Sunshine and Shadow* described hunting and shooting 'as if he had once loved them'.[47] As recompense no doubt, and to public amusement, he advertised a sale of animals with the stipulation that they were not to be killed.[48] Hills's athletic heartiness no doubt explained the *Vegetarian's* publication of one inappropriate story involving game hunting, by George Henty, the writer of stirring adventure stories for boys; though the vegetarian *Merry-go-round* earlier published an interview with the hunter Frederick Selous.[49] More consonant with 'the range of our duty', the *Vegetarian Messenger* noted the formation of a Berlin elephant protection society.[50] Vegetarians were amongst the supporters of early environmental societies.[51]

The relationship with mainstream zoophile organizations

In the zoophilite crusade, wrote one vegetarian, only the vegetarian's armour was impervious to the enemy.[52] The relationship with mainstream organizations was problematic.

Forward believed that it was difficult to find a 'longstanding vegetarian' who accepted vivisection and cruel sports.[53] Anti-vivisectionism led a member to resign, but this was probably unique.[54] Vegetarianism's connections with this moral crusade have been discussed by Richard French, who notes, 'one would expect antivivisection to have a great deal in common' with it.[55] Despite vegetarians' prominence in the leadership (Francis Newman, Anna Kingsford, Edward Maitland and Ernest Bell, the chairman of the Victoria Street Society) and a shared concern about cruelty, there was no intimacy.[56] The evidence is insufficient to indicate how many moved from vivisection to vegetarianism, rather than the reverse.[57] The Victoria Street Society's branch societies did not feature many vegetarians and vegetarian sentiments were not published in the

Zoophilist.[58] French attributes this detachment to anti-vivisection's absorption with political activity such as electoral pressure rather than the expansive reformation conceived by vegetarianism.[59] His suggestion that it was also a tactical distancing from critics' arguments that their position was untenable without abandoning animal foods is highly plausible.[60] Early anti-vivisectionists were aware of the vegetarian logic, but resistance (on scriptural, physiological and tactical grounds) was maintained.[61] By contrast, vivisection was favourably discussed by the vegetarians in symposia, essays, fiction and correspondence.[62] But they asked anti-vivisectionists to be consistent by adopting their diet.[63] Acceptance of half-measures was wrong: French points out that Maitland, Newman and Kingsford were opposed to anti-vivisection societies' support for reform of slaughter houses.

The wider animal welfare movement's relationship with vegetarianism was long-standing. The *Vegetarian Advocate* received copies of the *Animals' Friend* and Lewis Gompertz's *Moral Inquiries,* and a report of the Belfast Society for the Prevention of Cruelty to Animals.[64] The receipt of material from Gompertz and his Animals' Friend Society can be explained through his vegetarianism, which led to Horsell publishing two of his works.[65] The *Animals' Friend* (1833-41) expressed vegetarian sympathies.[66] By contrast Horsell's paper queried the Belfast SPCA's humanitarian credentials. The parent SPCA had lost radical animal lovers, possibly including fellow vegetarians, when Gompertz was manoeuvred from his office as secretary in 1833.[67] Vegetarians were unwelcome in the respectable, orthodox Christian RSPCA. In 1856 Horsell and two others introduced a vegetarian discussion into its second Anniversary meeting at Hanover Square to the amusement, but probably also the dismay, of many in a large and fashionable audience including the Marquis of Westminster.[68] Institutional detachment echoed individual avoidance. Decades after the establishment of the VS even the most heartfelt pleas against cruelty could avoid reference to vegetarianism.[69]

The VS addressed the RSPCA during the latter's half-centenary in 1874, following *The Animal World*'s publication of letters from the vegetarian Howard Williams.[70] The VS's expectations were modest, simply requesting 'sympathising equity' on the basis that they had 'sentiments and interests in common, which might be aided by co-operation'. Slaughterhouses were demonstrably as cruel as anti-vivisection. Vegetarianism, rather than legislation, offered a solution.[71] Yet despite telling testimony to the logic of the RSPCA's exposure of slaughterhouse cruelty, vegetarianism was avoided by it.[72] A joint discussion between the LVS and the RSPCA in 1894 was a rarity for the latter was unlikely to associate with a movement so radical in its personal demands on supporters and its implications.[73]

Vegetarians could only criticize, along with others, the RSPCA's 'mock sentimentalism'.[74]

The vegetarian discussion in animal journals was probably not extensive: unusual enough that when it occurred vegetarians noted it.[75] When the sympathetic Sidney Trist was editor of the *Animals' Friend* he showed 'fair play' and became *persona non grata* amongst some anti-vivisectionists as a result.[76] It was left instead to individual sympathizers and activists with feet in both camps to build bridges. The Reverend Francis Orpen Morris, the famous ornithologist, was 'in theory' with the VS in its objectives, and in practice, 'almost entirely,' as he informed the *Dietetic Reformer*. The Reverend Frewen Moor included the VS in a book on the future state of animals. Matilda Cooper left £1000 to the Society to promote 'kindness to animals among children'. This funded the *Daisy Basket* children's periodical, and Memorial Lectures. The Sunderland vegetarians formed a children's society incorporating elements from a 'Dicky Bird Society' and the Band of Mercy. Alice Marie Lewis, founder of a Band of Mercy branch, always discussed vegetarianism at Band of Mercy meetings.[77]

Lewis was a founder of the Humanitarian League in 1891 which agitated for Poor Law and criminal law reforms, arbitration in international disputes, abolition of bloodsports, and reform of vaccination and vivisection laws.[78] The names had already surfaced as a possibility in debates over the title of the vegetarian society or movement in 1878.[79] It was not surprising that promotion of a 'humane diet' was one of the League's concerns, as its pivotal figures included vegetarian activists like Henry Salt, Alice Lewis, and Josiah Oldfield.[80] Its first conference had delegates from the VS and vegetarian 'Physical Regeneration Society', and there were joint meetings. A Humane Diet subcommittee (established 1896) denied covert vegetarian proselytism but contrasted itself with mainstream zoophilism's refusal fully to recognize the implications of diet. Since slaughter of animals for food was 'deplored' by many who were not strict vegetarians, the committee felt able to address the food question from a purely 'humanitarian standpoint'. The slaughter method was to be studied, and food classified according to the associated suffering. The Department would not saddle humanitarians with the final solution to the problem, which was vegetarianism.[81] Whatever individual members believed, as a body the League was uncommitted.[82] Critics thought otherwise, and its vegetarian sympathies were obvious from its journal.[83] 'Individualist' writing in *Morning* asserted it was a change of vegetarian tactic.[84] The *Meat Trades Journal* believed that if you 'scratch a humanitarian you will find a Vegetarian'.[85] The Sporting League thought it intended compulsory vegetarianism.[86]

Henry Salt deplored vegetarian impatience at zoophilites, emphasizing that there was now far more appreciation of vegetarianism among zoophilists than there had been even a few years before, and that the charge of blindness to other humanitarian causes could be laid against many vegetarians.[87] Williams regretted that 'very few, comparatively, of the rightly ardent promoters of the Dietetic Reform are found to ally themselves with an association so logically humanitarian in its aims' as the League.[88]

Those involved in the Humanitarian League were stimulated by a 'cooperative' view of evolution partly derived from Alfred Russel Wallace, co-expounder of the 'Darwinian' theory of evolution, and a vegetarian himself. Wallace's spiritualism led him to limit the role of natural selection in the case of mankind, and his rejection of competition in relation to humanity also proved influential. But the vegetarian movement had no single voice on evolution, indeed its journals printed little direct discussion about the relevance of that 'fierce and universal struggle for existence', as Oldfield, one of the few vegetarians to write on the topic, characterized natural selection.[89] Clearly vegetarians seeking a non-materialist or naturalist religion might reject Darwinian theory, and many, if troubled by the vision of unceasing conflict, perhaps shared Oldfield's view that:

> The struggle for the individual survival of the fittest, at the expense of the less fit, gives place to the sympathies of the community, where the aim of each is the common good.
>
> It may be that man has had to pass through this furnace of fierce trial, but it does not follow that he will always remain there. *Below* it is true that the big fish still eat the little fish, but *Above*, the lion and the lamb are found feeding together on the produce of the earth. Man, then, if he would move up in the direction the cosmic forces would impel him, must ever take as his type that which is *above* and not that which is *below*.

Vegetarianism would enable humanity to ascend a special evolutionary ladder.[90]

Whatever the particular views of vegetarians on evolution, by the late-Victorian period a broadened interpretation of 'humanitarianism' firmly incorporated animals. The mentality which had led to the League allowed vegetarianism to be accepted as part of the zoophilite effort. Fittingly, the *Humane Yearbook* included vegetarian societies in a directory of animal protection societies from 1899.

Vegetarianism and Humanitarianism

In 1849 the *Vegetarian Advocate* informed readers that every transgression of the law of nature was a 'purchase of pain'.[91] About the same time,

Herbert Spencer included vegetarianism in his *Social Statics* as one of the efforts to ameliorate 'the condition of inferior animals' which accompanied (as *necessarily* related characteristics) efforts to diminish human misery.[92] Animal welfare movements and vegetarianism formed parts of a broader and older campaign against pain which eventually found coordinated expression in the Humanitarian League.[93] Developments in Christian theology – rejection of the doctrine of atonement and erosion of belief in an eternal and physically painful damnation – and advances in anaesthesia, meant that 'pain lost its place as a natural part in the universe and became, instead, something to be removed or alleviated at all costs.'[94] Opponents depicted campaigns against the infliction of pain as maudlin sentimentalism and feared a world of relentlessly increasing sentimentalism where organizations would agitate to defend insects and vegetables.[95]

The slaughter of animals and the ingestion of flesh could, vegetarians believed, lead to violence against people, and ultimately to 'man-butchery'. They emphasized this causal link in asking for the support of opponents of capital punishment, and pacifists, in the late 1840s-50s. Witnessing slaughter could lead to a perverted taste for blood manifested in animal cruelty, soldiering, and murder. 'Butchers,' Lady Wahlburga Paget believed, 'often become murderers, and I have known cases where butchers have actually been hired to murder persons'.[96] Into the late-Victorian period, vegetarians were active in the anti-capital punishment agitation (Josiah Oldfield was president of the Society for the Abolition of Capital Punishment) and their journals endorsed anti-capital punishment sentiments.[97] At least one critic of the abolitionists pointed out that they had to be vegetarian to be consistent.[98]

FIGURE 15. Josiah Oldfield: student of the occult, fruitarian and leader of the late-nineteenth century anti-capital punishment movement. *Vegetarian*, Christmas supplement, 21 December 1891.

An address by the Concordium was rejected by the London Peace Society Convention in 1843, on the grounds that it was irrelevant, would lead to superfluous discussion, and because the connection between diet and war was objectionable.[99] Yet some early vegetarians became attracted to the humane diet as part of their pacific beliefs. In 1849 delegates to the Paris Peace Congress included about twenty members of the VS, including James Simpson and Horsell.[100] The *Advocate* emphasized the 'perfectly consonant' nature of peace and vegetarian principles and advertised anti-war wafers and slips. Vegetarians were present at the Brussels Peace Congress, and distributed tracts to demonstrate that 'while we are seeking to protect the lives and rights of the inferior creation we are not unmindful of those of man'.[101] The fraternalism advocated by Elihu Burritt and his radical pacific League of Universal Brotherhood was seen as a step towards one 'including feeling of sympathy with the sufferings even of the brute creation' and attracted support from vegetarians such as Dornbusch (a friend of Burritt) and John Mawson's wife in Newcastle.[102] It was therefore understandable that William Aytoun's satire on the peace movement in *Blackwood's* should feature a vegetarian who 'opined that without beef and mutton there never could be a battle'.[103] Later vegetarianism continued to have personal links with the peace movement.[104]

Vegetarians attempt to associate tyranny against fellow humans with tyranny over animals, and several vegetarians found Wells' *War of the Worlds* offered an interesting viewpoint on mankind as an inferior animal tyrannized by aliens.[105] Vivisected animal and vaccinated human faced the same 'state regulated' tyrant: the new scientific 'priesthood'. Cruelty to animals combined with old fears about experimentation on the poor and vulnerable, in Longman's radical *People's Advocate*, when he thanked God for the vegetarian Oriolet Hospital, and in a tract by the vegetarian 'United Temperance Association'.[106] The recognition of the relationship of tyranny over animals to tyranny over women or the working class was most clearly reflected in the journal *Shafts*, which is discussed in chapter six.

Vegetarianism, animals and the future state

Though some vegetarians were prepared for the extinction of ferocious animals, the movement's anti-violence was expressed in visions of the future golden age where the wolf would lie down with the sheep.[107] Fictional representations already presented enthusiasts' cats and birds dining *en famille*, coexisting in harmony.[108] Henry Pitman was probably not alone in having a vegetarian dog. As the tricolour flag at one vegetarian banquet symbolized, Nature was to be restored to its original harmony.[109] In such prospects and visions the vegetarians were heirs to earlier

Christian millenarians, whose golden age of pacific animals was also expressed in contemporary travelling shows.[110]

Concern *about* animals was not necessarily compassion for the animal. Studies of the animal welfare movements and 'animal advocacy' have explored their symbolic aspects.[111] Some early vegetarians were explicitly anthropocentric, denying humanity's animality and identifying vegetarianism and the rejection of animal labour as the necessary means to develop mankind's higher nature (the theory of evolution would soon challenge this view). This view, the philosophy of the Concordium, makes it inappropriate to describe the community as 'vegan', since the modern label obscures this unusual philosophy; though it is certain humane feeling did animate the Concordists. Their spiritual concerns were shared by many who knew nothing about Greaves the Sacred Socialist. The spiritual and religious aspects to the movement are now examined.

Vegetarianism and religion

Health reform and religion

While work has been done on the organization and social setting of health reform movements, paucity of evidence has limited the examination of grassroots beliefs. A recent attempt to do this concludes that emphasis on the primacy of material benefits as an explanation for their popularity is inaccurate and that the spiritual dimension should be acknowledged.[112] It has been argued elsewhere that 'medical heterodoxy could enhance a deep-seated repudiation of materialism'.[113] A sense of conversion found in much vegetarian testimony is merely one expression of the religious sentiment central to the movement.[114] When Edmund J. Baillie denied vegetarianism was a fad, and asserted that 'there are some of us with whom it has become a link in the chain of our faith', he was articulating what many felt.[115] For many, this faith was Christian, as asserted by James Simpson: 'Our system has well been based upon *Christian grounds*'.[116]

Vegetarianism could be taken as an expression of *Christian* mercy and/or an expression of asceticism and opposition to sensuality. Francis Newman stressed vegetarianism's opposition to fixed habit and 'luxury'.[117] For Newman and many others (including critics) vegetarianism was a *puritanical* creed. When H.G. Wells associated vegetarianism with puritanism in the autobiographical novel *Love and Mr Lewisham* (written in 1898) through the fraudulent medium Mr Chaffery's condemnation of 'The Dissenter, the Nonconformist Conscience, the Puritan, you know, the Vegetarian and Total Abstainer, and all that sort of thing' the identification of vegetarianism with Puritanism (and Nonconformity) was a truism.[118]

Vegetarians were uncomfortable about grounding their reform in a selfish appeal to health and argued that individual health had a wider significance as the necessary basis for moral, social and political reform. In sympathy with this reasoning, the *Christian Record* could describe the *Vegetarian Advocate* as 'an interesting and important publication' because of the 'intimate connexion of its principles with the health and morals of the whole community'.[119] The *Advocate* desired the 'advancement of physical truths for moral and religious ends'.[120] Philosophers and priests, it argued, were wrong in ignoring the physical man since it was there that the moral man was concealed. Bodily and mental health were as intimately connected as the body and mind, and 'flowed from the same source'. When physical habits were bad, morality could not be good.[121] This echoed the Concordists' belief that health reform was a necessary instrument for 'pure moral sentiments'.[122] Physical puritans believed that moral and physical laws harmonized.

The *Healthian*'s reviewer of William A. Alcott's *Vegetable Diet* (1843) distinguished between American and English vegetarians on the basis of the relative emphasis on religion and health. He argued that there was probably more perseverance from English reformers because religion was more important, and because they had 'unperverted constitutions'.[123] The Christian dimension to Grahamism or Alcott's physiology has been explored before. Abzug's recent study of American *antebellum* reform in temperance, abolitionism, phrenology, vegetarianism etc., stresses religious rather than materialist motivation. Abzug deploys the Weberian concept of the 'religious virtuoso' (seen as a recurring type, regardless of class or period) to characterize the era's thoroughgoing reformers. He sees them as equivalent to monastic visionaries – reforming the world because retreat was no longer possible (communitarian projects suggest otherwise). 'Virtuosity' had moved from religious reform in the late eighteenth century to reform of daily life, politics and work in programmes of 'resacralization'. Highly personal relationships and situations were now targeted, whether mind-body, gender, or master-slave relations. These fundamental targets naturally generated fundamental and large-scale opposition which made such campaigns all the more fervent. The concept of virtuosity has its uses in a British context in the emphasis on an expansive *religious* viewpoint but obscures the synchronous nature of such interests in proposing a general chronology beginning with religion and ending with the body and daily life.[124]

Religious affiliation in the vegetarian movement

Contemporaries understood the tendency of dissenting medicine to go with dissenting religion. Many vegetarians were nonconformists, and nonconformist meeting places and associated institutions provided venues for many vegetarian lectures. The first membership list (1848) listed 265 members, and Cowherdites totalled just over half with 136 members. The sect's prominence, indeed, derived from its vegetarianism and teetotalism. Established in the first decade of the nineteenth century by William Cowherd, a former curate in the Church of England who had joined the Swedenborgian church, the sect's diet attracted the favourable attention of the *Annual Register* in 1824, and its exclusion from 'the beef-steak club' and 'parish feast' was referred to by Robert Southey when opposing Catholic emancipation in 1828. As several scholars have revealed, the Cowherdites' dietetic reform was combined with an active interest in equality, education and social welfare.[125] No other sect endorsed vegetarianism in its liturgy in this period, but denominations associated with reform such as Quakers and Unitarians, not surprisingly, contributed recruits throughout the period.[126]

I have been able to identify some forty Quaker vegetarians, but this probably under-represents the Quaker contribution, despite the response by the Peace Society to Concordist overtures. Vegetarianism as an extension of non-violence and 'plaining' found a home in the schismatic White Quaker sect.[127] Largely private support came from the family of William Bennett, a friend of Greaves who published a vegetarian tract.[128] In York about 1847, 'leading members among the Society of Friends' investigated vegetarianism.[129] The VS's meeting at the Freemason's Tavern in 1851 attracted a prominent Quaker audience.[130] Meeting Houses provided venues for a few meetings.[131] In 1880 the vegetarians addressed the Society of Friends; a Quaker vegetarian society was eventually established in 1901.[132]

The fourth largest identifiable denominational group of vegetarians was the Unitarians, whose ministers were appealed to by twelve Unitarian vegetarians in 1898.[133] Other religious organizations and groupings targeted included missionaries and the Congregationalist Union.[134] In addition, leading figures in the Salvation Army had vegetarian sympathies (Salvationist support is a reminder of the practical Christian philanthropic dimension, and also reflects teetotal efforts).[135] Methodists of various sorts follow Unitarians in terms of numerical contribution. Eager to recruit Methodists, early vegetarians publicized Wesley's vegetarian experience.[136]

The movement was long frustrated at the lack of Anglican clerics who prominently endorsed the cause: so rare, one joked, that he felt he should be exhibited in a glass case (cumulatively, the number of Anglican clerics compares well with other denominations).[137] One clergyman introduced food reform into the diocesan calendar; a couple advocated it in sermons.[138] The original vegetarian Order of the Golden Age (see below) had a strong Anglican component.

Significantly, the vegetarian movement attracted few Catholics. Seven have been identified. This is in keeping with their minor representation in wider temperance and zoophilia. Modern sociology has linked temperance cultures to 'predominantly Protestant societies' and related it to the Protestant emphasis on 'individual moral responsibility for personal behaviour'.[139] Obviously Catholicism was concerned too with self-control, and also had its fasts and dietary asceticism. But the Catholic Church opposed a morality-grounded vegetarianism. Vegetarianism was therefore (with the exception of monastic diets) associated with Protestantism, and sects such as the Cowherdites, White Quakers and the 'jumpers' who followed George Meredith's 'Jump-to-Glory-Jane'.[140]

A running joke, based apparently on actual misunderstandings, was that members of the public thought vegetarians were peddling a religion.[141] Since vegetarians – like teetotallers – offered controversial readings of scripture (where many would first have encountered vegetarian figures[142]) in support of their cause, this was unsurprising.[143] Scriptural support was felt to be necessary by the pioneers, who had to reinterpret such references as the sanction (in Genesis ix.3) that 'Every moving thing that liveth shall be meat for you, even as the green herb have I given you all things'; and the warning (in 1 Timothy, iv, 1-3) that 'in the latter times some shall depart from the faith, giving heed to seducing spirits and doctrines of devils … commanding to abstain from meats, which God hath created to be received with thanksgiving'. For many otherwise convinced individuals, scripture remained the problem, with a mixed diet apparently endorsed throughout the Bible.[144] Early-Victorian opponents associated vegetarianism with the mad King Nebuchadnezzar, with heresy, and the 'latter times'.[145] The fall of man, according to Richard Govett, 'began with a question of food. The fall from Christianity is to begin from the same quarter'.[146] A member of the fleshers' trade in Glasgow associated the diet with heathen countries.[147] Yet the objections of the religious orthodox were hardly overwhelming: only one minister apparently publicly countered vegetarian propaganda at a meeting.[148]

Moralism and religion remained important components of vegetarian arguments, indeed Charles Forward in 1896 oddly thought that vegetarianism could not have been run on 'moral lines' earlier.[149] One prominent, principled critic of a purely hygienic argument was Arnold Hills. Repelled by endless discussion of dietetics his *Vegetarian* introduced other concerns and promoted a 'higher vegetarianism' (Christian in his case).[150] The spiritualist James Burns (of whom more shortly), no Christian, was also concerned about the movement 'falling into the very narrow groove of a conventional dietetic regimen and that alone'.[151]

Though in 1888 the LVS could not decide to begin committee meetings with prayers or hymns, there were plans to create a hymn and songbook for meetings; and it was still 'preferable' to have religious ministers as chairmen at local meetings.[152] Twigg has identified a decline in Biblical arguments in propaganda from the 1870s, and a non-sectarian character when it was used. Yet scripture had not been used in a 'sectarian' sense prior to this, and the formation of the Golden Age and Danielite orders and the 'Christianism' of the London and Manchester journals in this period strongly suggest this interpretation is incorrect. Her characterization of Danielites as 'essentially a social group', and their magazine as having a 'light tone' is incorrect: this was a 'vegetarian Good Templar' organization dissimilar to the 'artistic circles of Bedford Park'. It required a declared belief in the existence and power of God and based itself on the Bible, though beyond this 'personal religious views were not to be interfered with'.[153] The movement, despite new religious influences, continued to have a Christian tone. But vegetarian lecturers still had to be careful though; in Birmingham in 1898 a vegetarian activist found that all denominations 'say we must look elsewhere than the Bible'. Sensitivity was also needed in Ireland.[154]

Could the 'glorious gospel of human dietetics' be an alternative to organized religion?[155] Greaves felt that hygienic reform was 'more beneficial to man, than any national doctrinal creeds, or any churches, chapels or cathedrals'.[156] Samuel Brown believed that cleanliness and temperance were 'the very religion of the materialist' and that atheistic artisans were 'all in favour' of physical puritanism. Isaac Taylor, in a study of whims and fancies, observed the tendency for dietary 'whims' to lead their exponents 'towards infidelity, and thence on to Atheism'.[157] Yet free-thinkers and agnostics had concerns about the tone or direction of vegetarian debate. One 'insulted' freethinker threatened resignation if the *Dietetic Reformer* persisted in being 'one-sided in advocating Christianism, more than materialism or any other *ism*'.[158] Sections of the vegetarian world disliked the emphasis on a 'higher vegetarianism' to be found in the *Dietetic Reformer, Vegetarian,* or *The Herald of the Golden Age* which explicitly set out to emphasize Christianity and duty rather than 'expediency' or health. One reason for support for Allinson's Natural Living Society was distaste for Hill's 'theology and idealism' or 'Neo-Vegetarian gospel of diluted Christianity'.[159] The connection between vegetarianism, free-thought and secularism will be returned to in chapter four: spiritualism was a further link between these movements.

Vegetarianism, spiritualism, the esoteric and occult

The thematic and personal relationships between vegetarianism and various late nineteenth century religious currents (liberal Christianity, American transcendentalism, quasi-Indian religion, the religion of Nature, and socialism) have been briefly examined before.[160] Leading theosophists or 'esoterics' such as Annie Besant, Anna Kingsford and Edward Maitland, it is well known, were vegetarians. The relationship between medical unorthodoxy and the 'surrogate faith' of spiritualism has been noted before.[161] The spiritualist, and more generally esoteric, interest in food reform merits further attention as a demonstration of the interplay between self-styled 'progressive' interests.

An early link between the two 'isms' was Horsell's publications. A place was reserved for the spiritualism in his family newspaper of 1858-1859, *The Two Worlds* (a title subsequently adopted by the prominent spiritualist Emma Hardinge Britton for her journal in 1887) which enthusiastically discussed it as part of a mission to 'enquire into everything relating to human life'. He published two other early spiritualist papers and several spiritualist books.[162] Horsell saw spiritualism as an aid to religious faith: 'We are one of those who believe, – and the arguments of our secularist friends have never yet been able to shake the belief, – that man cannot be happy, no matter what improvement he may be able to make in his circumstances, until he recognises his divine origin and the inner purpose of his creation'.[163] Horsell was not alone, spiritualism was a 'widespread effort ... to believe in *something*' during a period of religious crisis and was 'squarely amidst the cultural, intellectual, and emotional moods of the era'.[164] Spiritualism and vegetarianism both shared a *soi-disant* 'progressive' stance and a critical attitude to 'gross habits'. Popular spiritualism (despite Horsell's comments) drew significantly on former Owenites and freethinkers who ensured the progressive flavour to provincial spiritualist activity.

The spiritualist involvement in vegetarianism, temperance, anti-vivisection and other movements reflects core spiritualist beliefs about the 'sanctity of life, the worth and dignity of the physical frame enclosing an immortal soul'.[165] Concern with the correct diet for spiritualistic activity was also a factor.[166] Vegetarianism certainly was advocated in spiritualist circles such as the 'Circle of Light' in Cardiff in the 1880s, though a prior vegetarianism possibly influenced such advocacy.[167] There was a strong unorthodox physiological dimension to spiritualism.[168] At one séance in Nottingham Dr Gall's spirit recommended Turkish baths. A medium attending a spiritualist conference in 1872 reported his guide's recommendation of hydropathy, vegetarianism, teetotalism and abstinence from coffee and other stimulants.[169] Vegetarianism was discussed in the working-class spiritualists' 'Progressive Lyceums', debated in the spiritualist journals and also featured in several works of spiritualist fiction.[170]

The most important spiritualist contribution to the vegetarian cause came from James Burns, a major figure in the British spiritualist world as lecturer and editor of *Human Nature* (1867-78) and *Medium and Daybreak* (1870-95). The former advocated a range of physical puritan/radical causes and had a large provincial readership; the latter was an expansive but more clearly spiritualist organ. Burns saw activity in spiritualism and vegetarianism as healthy fostering of dissent against professionals and 'cliquetarians'.[171] Personally repelled by atheism and materialism, spiritualism provided him with a religion outside the confines of a professional Church. Burns was the son of a poor Ayrshire smallholder-craftsman and 'constitutionally a heretic'.[172] His father, a hydropath and teetotal-vegetarian, was a man of 'progressive thought and philanthropy' who carried a copy of *Queen Mab,* studied mesmerism and read George Combe.[173] Not surprisingly, the Presbyterian church expelled him. His son, brought up in strict Christian worship, similarly reacted against drink, animal foods and orthodoxy.[174] Travelling south for work, James Burns became a gardener at Hampton Court and befriended James Smith, an associate of the Concordists. He then worked in Liverpool in temperance publishing. Converted to principled vegetarianism by James Simpson, he joined the VS in 1854 and became acquainted with London vegetarians.[175] From the 1860s he was a peripatetic lecturer on vegetarianism and 'allied' matters.[176] Graham crackers and vegetarian publications were sold at his Progressive Library, attached to his Spiritual Institution in Camberwell.[177] *Human Nature,* noted as 'progressive in dietary' by the *Dietetic Reformer* in 1869, began his long editorial career. In 1871 he joined a deputation to the President of the Poor Law Board to advocate better and cheaper workhouse food through vegetarianism, and the use of Turkish baths.[178]

Burns was a vice president of the London Food Reform Society and member of the Vegetarian Rambling Society and *Medium and Daybreak* prominently covered their activity. In 1878 the paper carried a prospectus for 'The Industrial and Patriotic "Good Wine" and Fruit Food Guild' which aimed to establish colonies, reform land, monetary and property arrangements, and spread temperance and vegetarianism.[179] He published free vegetarian tracts and a *Vegetarian Advocate* (quoted in the *Medium*) partly directed against Emmet Densmore's 'anti-vegetarian quackery' system. In 1888 he attempted to take spiritualism in a new direction, with vegetarianism providing the 'physical food' in a 'Threefold Food' programme along with mental and spiritual sustenance. He announced a 'Progressive Food and Cooking Society' (hereafter PCFS), inspired in part by the vegetarian Alice Lewis. Cooking Stations were to be situated in poor districts, to provide cheap and well-prepared 'Deathless Food', free meals to schoolchildren and the needy. The Stations were to provide lessons on economy, hygiene and cookery. Home visiting for aid and advice in case of illness was planned. The project was to encourage fraternity, co-operation, 'domesticity' and 'neighbourism' and combat the 'beershop and gambling pastimes of Christian communities'.[180] Cultural Colonies were to be promoted to allow urban and rural dwellers the opportunity to grow their food and spend some time each year in another environment. Food was best produced as near as possible to the consumer.[181]

Burns opposed the tendency towards bureaucracy, mutual self-regard and resource-wasting in reform organizations and criticized London vegetarianism on these grounds. To combat this, the PFCS had no membership fee. A vegetarian publishing house and restaurant was established in Clerkenwell in a neighbourhood where extreme poverty made vegetarianism unattractive and access to utensils difficult. The PCFS gave free breakfasts to poor schoolchildren, meals for a watchmakers' firm, established a club room and held Sunday services and evening meetings. Contributions were received from spiritualists, and vegetarians such as Frances Boult, the Quaker Ellen Impey, and Alice Lewis.

At the same time, Burns felt that Hills was moving London vegetarianism in the right direction – towards interest in the 'Inner Life' – and welcomed his work for human progress.[182] A letter to the VS expressed his concerns about hygienic narrowness, about seeing life in merely material terms, rather than acknowledging as pioneers such as Sylvester Graham had done, the spiritual dimension:

> Our pioneers were all men of unconventional thought in almost every way. They were not instances of respectable mediocrity, far from it. They could aspire to the reception of 'all truth' without fear of those reproaches which are the only arguments of ignorance.[183]

Vegetarianism and other 'progressive subjects' featured by Burns in his weekly meetings. He supported the VS's appeals for funds and devoted an annual meeting to fundraising for it. If the *Messenger* paid scanty tribute to his commonsense and practical contributions in debate, appreciative obituaries in the *Vegetarian* and *Vegetarian Review* emphasized his financially and physically burdensome philanthropic responsibilities.[184]

Metropolitan associates of Burns involved in spiritualism and vegetarianism from the 1850s included the VS's London secretary Dornbusch and the Swedenborgian bookseller William White, on the

London Vegetarian Association committee in 1859, (and a teetotaller, phoneticist and editor of the *Vaccination Inquirer*). The pioneering *British Spiritual Telegraph* (briefly published by Horsell) noted that the American *Practical Christian*, partly devoted to spiritualism, could be obtained through Dornbusch.[185] Dornbusch, connected with the Concordium community, supported 'true spiritualism' – without any 'dross of superstition' – as the 'best means of establishing firm faith' in God. Burns described him as one of the 'leading Spiritualists'.[186] Dalston in Hackney, where he lived, possessed an active plebeian spiritualist circle and he provided a venue and vegetarian food for the Dalston Association of Inquirers into Spiritualism in 1872. Another spiritualist colleague was the artisan William Turley, co-proprietor of a short-lived vegetarian school, steward at the second annual meeting of the VS and lecturer on vegetarianism before a Mutual Instruction Society in 1850.[187]

One of the most prominent spiritualists based in London, Chandos Wallace, was a leading figure in late nineteenth century vegetarianism.[188] She met her husband-to-be at one of Burns's phrenological meetings. Another London vegetarian prominent in the spiritualist world was the restaurant proprietor Andrew Glendinning. Their colleague in London vegetarianism, William Theobald (president of the Northern Heights VS and treasurer of the VFU), came from a prominent spiritualist family.[189] Outside London the spiritualist movement provided important locations for late nineteenth century vegetarianism. A few examples must suffice, the first from Cardiff in 1877, where a spiritualist-vegetarian-Good Templar arranged distribution of literature on these 'three noble causes'.[190] The Cardiff 'Circle of Light' had 'strict regulations' on clothing, diet and bathing.[191] The mediums A.J. Smart and George Spriggs were encouraged to become vegetarian through the 'father' of Cardiff spiritualism, Rees Lewis. They were mentors to Fanny Samuel, a medium who became a leading figure in Australian vegetarianism. In Sunderland in 1892 the new president of the local vegetarian society was the journalist John Rutherford, a spiritualist published in the *Medium and Daybreak*. The shareholders of the progressive spiritualist journal *Two Worlds* held their annual meeting at a vegetarian restaurant.[192]

The vegetarian spiritualists came from plebeian and elite backgrounds. Amongst the provincial spiritualist missionaries examined by Logie Barrow was David Richmond, a self-educated wool sorter from Darlington who became an Owenite.[193] His many communitarian experiences in England and America included residence in the Concordium. Darlington Spiritualist Society's vegetarian adherents included the journalist Mark Fooks and the wholesale and retail grocer David Weatherhead who had purchased the machinery and type for the

Spiritual Telegraph.[194] Other vegetarian-spiritualists highlighted by Barrow included Hitchcock of Nottingham, a stonemason who, with his mediumistic wife, established the first spiritualist Lyceum in 1867.[195] At the other end of the social spectrum from Barrow's plebeians were Sir Charles Isham, and Lady Mount Temple. Isham (who introduced garden gnomes to Britain), supported homeopathy, mesmerism, spiritualism (from the 1870s) and published a vegetarian tract.[196] Lady Mount Temple (who tried to interest her friend John Ruskin in spiritualism) and her husband, were seekers of religious truth, and zoophilists.[197]

Spiritualism was not the only alternative spiritual movement. Vegetarianism has long been associated with the esoteric and mystic. Greaves's 'Sacred Socialism' was a Christian mystical endeavour.[198] A 'theosophic college' planned in 1851 was to include the study of pure diets, or a 'pure fuel for the fire of life' in its curriculum.[199] A later example of a vegetarian esoteric was Josiah Oldfield, swayed when a theology student at Oxford 'by the esoteric teaching which I found in every religion worthy of being classed as a divine faith'.[200] Vegetarianism was also associated with the 'occult' reaction to materialism which was far from a fringe interest. Astrology and vegetarianism were connected in the person of the 'father of modern astrology', 'Alan Leo' (William Allan).[201]

More significantly, theosophy and physical puritanism (including diet), were closely connected, as Joy Dixon and others have noted.[202] The 'occult body politics' explored by Dixon represented an immanentist turn in which various campaigns for moral, social and political reform were combined with theosophy (or a similar spirituality) as one struggle. Vegetarians learnt of the movement's beliefs from articles and letters in the *Vegetarian*.[203] The journal published discussion about whether vegetarianism was necessary for a theosophist, with some supporting the view that it was since it promoted the required pure-living.[204] The Women's Vegetarian Union was instructed on food reform from a Theosophical point of view.[205] Theosophical journals discussed the diet, although the movement endorsed it for spiritual and psychic reasons rather than on the grounds of ethics.[206]

Well-known vegetarian-theosophists included Annie Besant, who became Blavatsky's successor as the leader of the Theosophical Society.[207] Anna Kingsford and her colleague Edward Maitland (both left the Theosophical Society) were perhaps the most important. Kingsford gave numerous vegetarian lectures and was most at ease on the vegetarian platform, for vegetarianism was central to her life: 'I must say that I think the vegetarian movement is the great movement of the age, and I think so because I see in it the beginning of real civilization'.[208] The tract, *The Perfect Way in Diet* (1882), foreshadowed her major work with Maitland, *The*

Perfect Way, several essays appeared in the *Food Reform Magazine* and her address to the vegetarians at Exeter Hall in 1885 was published. She promoted vegetarianism abroad and was instrumental in the creation of a society in Paris and efforts in Switzerland which contrasted with the limited impact of her anti-vivisectionism.[209] Her circle included the Reverend Gideon Ouseley, who 'discovered' a vegetarian gospel which is still disseminated.[210]

Just as the vegetarians emulated the Good Templars in creating the Danielites, so those vegetarians interested in hermetic orders and the esoteric also created vegetarian societies. The Order of the Golden Age founded in 1882 by the younger brother of Howard Williams, the inspiration for the Humanitarian League, does not seem to have been esoteric, but its successors were.[211] Ouseley created an Order of At-Onement to investigate Kingsford's work and purify liturgy in a humanitarian direction.[212] Sidney Beard, an honorary member of the Psychical Research Society, re-established the Order of the Golden Age. Ostensibly not occult, its organ contained articles on the 'dawn of spiritualism', the increasing cultivation of the 'psychic senses', mental healing and the fading of materialism and animalism.[213] In 1900 the ornate council room at the Order's new headquarters at Barcombe Hall in Paignton was completed: incorporating a frieze representing the unity of west and east, and past and modern Golden Ages, and rugs with symbols of the Order. Josiah Oldfield described it as a 'council chamber dedicated and sanctified'.[214]

FIGURE 16. Council Room of the Order of the Golden Age, Barcombe Hall. *Herald of the Golden Age*, 1900.

Being vegetarian did not *necessarily* lead to spiritualism or any other *ism*; nor did spiritualists always sympathize with vegetariansm. The *Dietetic Reformer*'s review of *Human Nature* (1869) would have 'nothing to say' concerning spiritualism.[215] Not all spirit advice was supportive: the reformer W.T. Stead received a message that vegetarianism, which he 'approved of', was not for him.[216] A letter in the *Medium and Daybreak*, from a doctor, criticized Burns for supporting anti-vaccination, vegetarianism, anti-tobacco and teetotalism.[217] Yet close connections were frequent and stemmed from shared attitudes and aspirations. The links between vegetarianism and new religions or esoteric Christianity in the late nineteenth century continued the connection between dietetic and religious heresy apparent in the Swedenborgian Cowherdite sect and in the White Quaker sect.

Vegetarians, spiritualists and occultists saw themselves as 'truthseekers' who created their own identities and philosophies instead of passively receiving accepted wisdom. Ideological and personal connections meant that the movements overlapped whether the location was metropolitan or provincial. The 'radical eccentric' connections exhibited in the 'late-Victorian revolt', a continuation of the long associations between heresies, were maintained into the twentieth century.[218] Vegetarianism's radical connections and 'fadical' dimension are now examined.

4

RADICALISM AND FADICALISM

The vegetarianism presented to Victorians was multifaceted: health reform and ultra-temperance, exercise in self-help, crusade against animal cruelty or pain, as the basis to a purified religious or spiritual life. Though the diet did not entail radical politics or wider enthusiasms for every convert, and one should avoid claiming an *essential* radicalism for vegetarianism, its various aspects tended to give it a radical reputation and identity for contemporaries, whether these were critics, vegetarian activists or sympathizers. Actual and reputed radicalism are examined here, beginning with the associations with those working-class or middle-class groupings whose democratic or idealistic proclivities made them susceptible to the emergent movement. Identification of particular strands of vegetarianism should not obscure such interconnections with other reforms, for vegetarianism was part of a network of causes that were mutually reaffirming and logical extensions of one another (though the relationship with vivisection and medical movements which has just been outlined indicates connections were not straightforward).[1] Through this multiplicity of causes, or because of antipathy to the individual reform, the vegetarian could be called a faddist; and the 'fadical' aspect to the movement is also discussed here.[2] By this is meant the labels that were employed by critics using a vocabulary that expressed psychological assumptions about adherents and was intended to marginalize the movement. This, ironically, proved to be influential for supporters, but also for historians who have tried to characterize the mentality of those who embraced vegetarianism.

Vegetarianism as radicalism

Roy Porter's observations that those who 'baulked at the power of princes and prelates might be no more disposed to swallow orthodox medicine'[3] and that medical heretics 'typically doubled as heretics in politics and faith as well, whilst cultivating unorthodox lifestyles'[4] in the early-Victorian period, is supported by the research of J.F.C. Harrison, whose survey of well-known figures revealed some ninety Owenites and Chartists adopting unconventional medical practices. Harrison identified a democratic theme in self-cure and in the collective self-help of those mutual-aid associations and both harmonized with the ethos of co-operatives and Friendly Societies. Harrison includes their health journals in a group of early-Victorian journals advocating a range of social and political reforms.[5] Radicals could see their medical independence as a strategy against yet another vested interest.

A powerful factor in the support for alternative medicine was its hopefulness by contrast to an orthodox medicine that was far from optimistic. It is therefore unsurprising that, as we have seen, optimistic and democratic Owenites and Chartists in the 1840s endorsed vegetarianism and other health movements as tools of empowerment (rather than tedious regulations) on the way to the new moral world. There were also links between vegetarianism and the radical movement of secularism, middle-class 'moral radicalism' and the late-nineteenth-century socialism.

Freethought was another strand contributing to early vegetarianism, which could be another act of freethought after the 'one great step'. Freethinkers' predisposition to speculate about 'wild new ideas' and investigate bold schemes for social transformation in a period of 'intellectual ferment' (the early nineteenth century in this case) has been commented on before.[6] Many freethinkers supported temperance.[7] Their involvement in reform movements including vegetarianism and other 'liberal' causes has been seen as playing a part in the liberalization of the mid-Victorian age.[8] If late-Victorian freethinkers were naturally critical of the *Vegetarian*'s 'higher vegetarian' tone, *The Freethinker* was favourable to vegetarianism, though this probably owed something to the support given to it by Thomas Allinson (who married a friend of the secularist leader Charles Bradlaugh), described in the journal as 'about the most through-going heretic in England'.[9] Allinson lectured on 'freethought in health' in Secularist Halls across London and England.

Many of the supporters and leaders of vegetarianism came from middle-class radicalism, and came from a particular subculture identified by Alex Tyrrell as 'moral radicalism', flourishing in the early 1830s. This provincial network of friends, colleagues and acquaintances shared a vital religion, which cast politics in moral terms. They came from the worlds of religious dissent and business, viewed the House of Commons and London as bastions of a corrupt aristocratic Establishment and formed pressure groups in order to influence Parliament and government.[10] Their leaders, such as the Quaker Joseph Sturge of Birmingham, esteemed the self-improving Christian and saw voluntary societies as the best mode of collective action in support of teetotalism, abolition of slavery and furtherance of denominational equality against vested interest. Reforms were promoted in the name of the 'people' against the Establishment. Politics was expressive rather than instrumental, with action prompted by the 'satisfaction of adhering to principle rather than by the prospects of success'.[11] Moral consistency whether in anti-slavery immediatism, religious voluntarism or teetotalism was paramount; pragmatism and compromise were opposed as short-termist.

Though the 'moral radicals' possessed a separate identity in the 1830s-1840s they shared attitudes with political reformers and allied with anti-Tories during elections. The similarities between voluntaryists and Chartists were admitted by the *Christian Advocate* in 1838.[12] In the 1840s they joined disillusioned Chartists in the Complete Suffrage movement and contributed to a radicalized peace movement, with campaigns for 'people diplomacy', international arbitration, world court, assembly of nations, anti-armaments and militia efforts, and universal postal and measurement systems.[13] Elihu Burritt's League of Universal Brotherhood included moral radical leaders. The height of apparent success came in the Great Exhibition Year of 1851, with the London Peace Congress. The 'party' has been interpreted as contributing to a mellowing of Liberalism, allowing a mid-century social and political consensus through sharing values with, and promoting the interests of, the working classes.

Moral radicals had a tendency to become involved in the sciences and 'pseudo sciences' of the period through their belief in millennial perfectionism. The Sturge circle espoused phrenology, homeopathy and physical exercise. If Sturge was not vegetarian himself, despite being interested in the 'Roman simplicity' of Grahamism when in America, he had connections with this world.[14] He supported Horsell's 'democratic' hydropathic establishment. His nephew, Charles Gilpin, published the vegetarian Passmore Edwards's moral radical journal *The Public Good* and co-published William Bennett's vegetarian work.

Radical subcultures of a middle-class complexion continued to explore vegetarianism in the late-nineteenth century. Vegetarianism featured as part of that larger counterculture against capitalism, traditional gender relations and positivistic science. Whilst its 'mainstream' temperance, philanthropic and social purity connections must not be underplayed, vegetarianism always formed part of what Henry James called 'humanitary Bohemia'.[15]

Some of the leading middle-class supporters of vegetarianism in the late nineteenth century were also socialists. The socialist revival of the 1880s partly had its roots in radical and communitarian traditions that kept alive earlier utopianism. But the enthusiasm with which some took up vegetarianism was despite their being condemned as cranks by 'politics-centred' socialists like Henry Hyndman.[16] A Labour politician recalled that 'uncompromising zealots' such as vegetarian advocates were given the ultimatum to subsume their enthusiasms or leave and that mostly 'we went on our way without them'.[17] This was not true, as will be demonstrated in a later chapter on the relationship between late-Victorian vegetarianism and socialism.

Vegetarianism could therefore be plausibly treated as emanating from a radical environment, promoted by liberal and reforming individuals. Joseph Barker defended the new movement as one generally originating with the liberal school in politics and theology, and 'in many cases, devout and earnest enemies of aristocratic oppression and royal tyranny'. Indeed some were republicans and some 'had given the strongest proofs of their attachment to the cause of the people, and of their wish to promote the interests of the labouring classes'.[18] Later, Oscar Wilde, writing to the poet 'Violet Fane' on the subject of her vegetarianism in 1888, noted its modern anarchist, atheist, socialist and other political associations. It was strange, he observed, that the 'most violent republicans' he knew were all vegetarians.[19]

A further question remains: how far did converting to vegetarianism trigger an individual's radical career? It was probably rarely a *source* of radicalism for most of its followers, being a position *reached* in the context of personal radicalism.[20] Yet the diet *was* a radical stance and a heresy given its interpretation of scripture and official medical belief.[21] It could act as a highly visible mark of dissent. Accepting one heresy *could* lead to rejecting other orthodoxies.[22] Observers such as *Blackwood's Edinburgh Magazine* could not help thinking 'that physical heresies involve other heresies still more portentous'.[23] The few recoverable instances include Henry Salt, radicalized through vegetarianism, Shelley and Henry George; Salt recalled that vegetarianism had been viewed as a far greater heresy than socialism at Eton, because it had required practical assent.[24]

In 1856 the *Vegetarian Messenger*, discussing 'kindred movements', made a claim for its own radical character, embracing the charge of being 'ready for anything' and reinterpreting it to mean that vegetarians were 'more radical, and go further than others choose, or would like to follow'.[25] The understanding of radicalism here was its ultra-consistency, its assertion that it was going to the root of social and moral problems. Forward (and many others) credited the dietary with exalting philanthropic faculties and widening the scope of sympathies.[26]

Vegetarianism had pretensions to be considered *the* indispensable reform. The infant VS boasted of an attention and respect that had 'seldom been enjoyed by social, intellectual, or moral movements, during the first few years of their Existence'.[27] John Belchem sees vegetarianism involved in 'competitive bidding, seeking to outdistance other forms of "expressive" reform,' and has outlined the attempt to make it 'the symbolic defining issue of "compleat" reform in the 1840s'.[28] Naturally enthusiastic vegetarians keen to stake their claim to public attention and the support of progressives presented their cause as Reform's keystone. Thus William Harvey in 1850 explained that all his vegetarian acquaintances were keen supporters of peace, temperance, education, sanitary, financial and parliamentary reform because 'their system being deeper and wider than those, comprehended them all'.[29]

Vegetarians castigated those reformers who failed to take the 'rational' step in diet. The comprehensive 'Tendency of Food Reform' was still being claimed in the 1880s-1890s.[30] Vegetarianism could also be advocated, not just as an essential reform, but the *universal* reform, as *panacea*. Though some large claims were made for it, this outlook was unusual.[31]

Anti-everythingarianism

> As a matter of fact, vegetarianism does seem somehow or other to be correlated to all sorts of strange *isms*, and it is seldom that a vegetable *solus* eater is content to be in other things like the general run of his fellow-creatures; and is pretty sure to hold new and strange views on political economy, to be a member of the Society for Psychical Research, to dress in all wool clothing, to abjure the razor, or to wear soft and unsightly hats.[32]

The historian of anti-vivisectionism points out the 'lengthy' list of interests which anti-vivisectionists supported in publications and speeches, and sees 'patterns of interest in reform movements' offering insight into shared 'latent functions'. Thus anti-vivisection, anti-vaccination and opposition to the Contagious Diseases Acts were 'vehicles for hostility toward medicine'. The phenomenon of 'simultaneous allegiance' involving no such neat patterns is itself important in revealing 'an important and under-investigated problem, the moral reform mentality in Victorian England'.[33] Vegetarians accumulated impressive lists of *antis* merely by consistent avoidance of stimulants such as alcohol, tobacco, opium and spices. Beyond this, it was 'one of the most noticeable features of the movement' that physical puritan consistency was combined with advocacy of other 'moral and social reforms'.[34]

The label of 'anti-everythingarian' was used to describe a tendency simultaneously to oppose many conventional or state-enforced activities. This label was applied to the circle of Richard Allen of Dublin, which included James Haughton, a president of the VS.[35] It was applied by Francis Newman to himself, apparently with humour.[36] It was used by *Punch* and picked up by the *Herald of Health*.[37] Its currency in provincial circles, associated with physical puritanism and claims to sanctity, is indicated by its appearance in the *Weston-super-Mare Express* (in the context of a fraudster successfully pretending to piety).[38] According to one critical observer, it was purely negative collection of beliefs, 'all for forbidding and no permitting, for undoing and no doing'.[39] Such critics represented it as an intolerant puritanism opposed to all enjoyment. Though asceticism and concern with purity were important elements, the idea that the ultra-reformer was a nihilist with no alternative was a misrepresentation. In Rider Haggard's satire on anti-vaccinationism, *Dr Therne* (1898), the faddist Stephen Strong 'indeed was anti-everything, but, which is rather uncommon in such a man, had no extraneous delusions; that is to say, he was not a Christian Scientist, or a Blavatskyist, or a Great Pyramidist.'[40] If his wife believed the English were the lost tribes of Israel, Haggard recognized that the anti-everything tendency actually involved generous enthusiasms such as Stephen's support for old age pension, graduated income tax, abolition of 'tied' housing and payment of MPs.

It is not always easy to apportion primacy to a particular interest when looking at the individual 'all-round reformer'. An individual could only commit so much energy and attention to one cause, and though it is surprising just how expansive and hardworking people were in their range of interests (particularly when their occupations are also considered), vegetarianism could be a side issue, albeit one that required to be practised (and the practice having social implications). For others it formed a central belief, or unifying concept, as seen in the previous section on the religious aspect. Where detailed biographies exist, it is possible to apportion the '*also*s' according to the subject's own understanding of their often changing priorities.

The historian's difficulty reflects contemporary difficulty. Richard French's observation that a 'significant' amount of involvement in anti-vivisection movement was motivated by the desire to *participate* quite as much as the fulfilment of aims can be applied more generally: the anti-everythingarian wanted to support all principled movements. The dilemma can be seen in Caldwell Harpur, who cheerfully admitted that he had not yet joined any vegetarian society, since there were 'so many things that the world wants reform in, and I find I sympathise with a good many of them'.[41]

Thorough-going reformers combined reforms individually, institutionally (and occasionally in communities) and in publications. One regular universal reform event (from 1841) was John Lee's 'Annual

Festival for the Promotion of Peace, Temperance, Anti-Tobacco, Universal Brotherhood and other Society Reforms (Female Rights at home and abroad, anti-slavery abroad)', held at Hartwell House in Buckingham.[42] In 1854 Horsell and a vegetarian colleague reported a favourable reception: vegetarianism had formed the 'principal topic' at Dr Lee's table. Despite the coverage of a wide range of moral radical concerns, vegetarianism never featured officially although Horsell was a frequent participant and as editor of the 1857 report probably inserted the comment that its temperance component was 'not carried to the acme of its perfection'. Another mid-Victorian festival for reformers at Blennerhasset, Cumberland was discussed in chapter one. Late-Victorian attempts to unify humanitarian impulses included the Humanitarian League, and a 'Bond of Union among Workers for the Common Good', established in August 1893 by a translator of Ibsen (and Christian Scientist) Frances Lord, to get people thinking about 'associated reform work', with Josiah Oldfield representing food reform and reports in the journal *Shafts*.[43] A humbler version of alliance in 'progressive philanthropy' of the physical puritan kind was G.B. Taylor's Progressive Tract Mission, which circulated tracts on temperance, food reform, anti-vaccination, 'morality', peace, anti-tobacco, 'health' and religion to families, to workers in factories and shops, and to a range of institutions, from hospitals and workhouses to police stations and barracks.[44]

FIGURE 17. Caldwell Harpur, who favoured metrication, nationalization of property, Saturday for Sabbath, and Oliver Cromwell as national hero. *Vegetarian*, 7 December 1895.

Taylor and less obscure reformers needed no persuading that there was a kinship of causes. The VS noted the importance of other efforts in support of the 'one great principle of truth' and emphasized that 'there is scarcely an individual on the register of the Society, who is not also actively identified, more or less, with the other great reformatory movements of the day'.[45] In his notebook one vegetarian, John Wright of Bolton, wrote that vegetarianism, teetotalism, peace and international arbitration, abolition of capital punishment and slavery, were 'of the same class of principles'.[46] They could be seen as kindred because they involved principled personal behaviour, the removal of brutality and pain, and the perfection of society. Reformers thought this natural: virtues, like vices, went together; 'all good things pull together'.[47] In one rare reflection on involvement in kindred societies, John Passmore Edwards, sometime vegetarian, recalled his activity in an array of organizations (societies opposed to capital punishment, military flogging, taxes on knowledge and the opium trade) which he saw as part of a larger 'National Reform Movement' through shared aim, spirit, motives and necessities, and which 'assisted to educate the head, heart, and conscience of the people'.[48]

Perfectionism was a central outlook and manifested itself in 'temperance' in a range of personal activities. It stemmed in part, especially in the early Victorian period, from a belief in the millennium which has been recognized as far from a 'fringe' belief in Britain and America, and was obviously a central idea in utopian communitarianism.[49] Millennialism motivated Christians and infidels, radicals and conservatives. Identifying this mentality helps unify diverse reform interests.[50] Along with perfectionism went an immediatist refusal to compromise which led Charles Dickens to condemn vegetarianism, teetotalism and peace for operating on an 'American' principle of 'whole hog'. He poured scorn on their lack of perspective: 'Stew so much as the bone of a mutton chop in the pot with your vegetables, and you will never make another Eden out of a Kitchen Garden.'[51]

Most moral reformers shared a social justification for their earnestness and apparent trouble-making, conceiving or justifying their causes as efforts for the public good. *The Times*, in its discussion of the inauguration of a revived anti-capital punishment activity in 1846, expressed the view that activism, 'invested with a halo of holy mystification', was motivated by vanity and arrogance: 'There is nothing they will not do, and better far than this there is nothing they believe they cannot do.'[52]

A unifying theme has been suggested for movements of the 1840s including phrenology, Owenism, Fourierism, Swedenborgianism, temperance and vegetarianism: a 'sociology of sin'.[53] The theme could instead be seen as a sociology of hope and striving for followers of such movements believed that progress (however defined) was possible.[54] Antipathy to authority and self-appointed experts was often a feature of these movements, with the common rhetoric of 'slavery' and 'emancipation'. The influence of religious dissent (for believers and unbelievers) continued to be important. Secularist involvement in a range of reform activities such as teetotalism, anti-vivisection or vegetarianism obviously stemmed from the freethinker's refusal to accept (medical) orthodoxy uncritically.[55]

Accepting one truth opened the way for others as the hold of prejudice loosened.[56] Vegetarians were often truthseekers who investigated the reform and, convinced of its validity, felt morally obliged to attack error. Joseph Barker expressed this sentiment in addressing his readers, when convinced about vegetarianism:

> I feel reluctant myself to urge so many reforms upon my readers and my friends; but what can I do? If I really see reason to believe that another improvement can be made by myself or my friends, and I close my lips, and leave my friends to suffer under disadvantages when a word or two might lead them or enable them to escape?[57]

For Howard Williams, they were '"Protestants" in the truest sense of the word ... witnesses of the most uncompromising kind to the truth'.[58] If, as Frederic Lees declared, 'truth was always extreme', earnest proclamation of the truth led to charges of un-English fanaticism.[59] It is time to examine more closely such charges, and the labelling of reformers as eccentrics and cranks.

Faddism

Because physiological 'reforms' seemed apolitical and because many (such as hydropathy or mesmerism) became defunct, scholars in the past treated them as embarrassing hobbies on the part of serious reformers, indicative of dilettante tendencies and a diversion from serious reforms. Historians over the last three decades have become more sympathetic towards marginal or unconventional movements, and it is no longer acceptable to refer to these as fads, crotchets or crankish notions.[60] Twigg has rightly argued that vegetarianism is a 'social phenomenon' and a 'choice made available within culture' and that discussion of personality adjustment and faddism is insufficient. Yet the language of faddism needs to be explored, since it was with this vocabulary that the movement was frequently discussed, represented and perceived.[61] The vocabulary was repeatedly used to stigmatize supporters of vegetarianism and other causes.

This language belittled both the ideas and the individual. Vegetarians were accused of being people of one idea, narrow-minded, holding an exaggerated view about the significance of their cause. This could reflect a form of insanity – monomania – in which the sufferer held an irrational view on one particular subject.[62] Their interest was a fashionable 'folly' or 'craze', an unreasonable, fleeting, enthusiasm.[63] A 'fad' was a trifle, or a foolish idea, often about social or political reform held (and promoted by the faddist) with peculiar intensity. A vegetarian was a 'crank', whose eccentric ideas went with irascibility.[64] Vegetarianism could also be described as a 'crotchet', with the same meaning of peculiarity, unconventionality and perversity.[65] Faddism could be represented as a want of judgement, the rule of a limited mind by the heart. In *Dr Therne*, Martha is described as 'amiable but weak-minded', her husband as 'goodhearted though misguided'. To be dietetically unconventional was to be suspected of some mental quirk, perhaps harmless, perhaps indicative of a more serious mental instability.[66]

That individual temperament or psychology played a part in all-round reform is undoubted. James Burns, who believed himself to be predisposed to heresy through his father, declared that 'the one who is an "odd fish" in one thing is quite likely to be so in all others, and that has been my happy lot from my earliest infancy'.[67] The historian of the 'moral radicals' has referred to 'an individual quirkiness that placed [them] amongst the most disputatious people in Britain'.[68] But what of the implications about sanity? Sir Dyce Duckworth described vegetarianism as 'one of the many "fads" so rife at the present day amongst people more or less crazy'.[69] Apart from reports of vegetarianism and physical puritanism taken to uncomfortable lengths in utopian communities – the asylum these offered often attracted the mentally unstable – critics had cases where vegetarianism was indicative of insanity. John James Daw, a convert to Judaism and vegetarianism, was believed by his friends to be insane, and in 1853 after being charged with petty larceny his eccentricity was reported in *The Times*, *Punch*, *Glasgow Examiner* and *Weekly Dispatch*.[70] Herbert Goodale, a mason from Twickenham who killed himself after murdering his family in 1899, was also reported in the press. A vein of oddity certainly existed in vegetarianism, and vegetarianism could be seen by contemporaries as a natural expression of the oddity of men such as the miser Pierre Baume, the druid William Price of Llantrisant, and the Chartist poet Duncan.

The pioneer's challenge to conventional ideas and practice invited and invites the label of 'eccentric'. People identified by historians as eccentric often played important roles in local and national efforts.[71] But it was also a contemporary identification, for dietetic experimentation featured as an 'eccentricity' in popular collective biographies of eccentrics. Nor was this just a British phenomenon, for Champfleury's collection of French eccentrics in 1852 included Duncan's French contemporary, Jupille 'le Thalysien', who tried to promote the diet of his hero Jean-Antoine Gleizes during the revolution of 1848.[72]

It was certainly appreciated by contemporaries, as well as historians, that when a movement was marginal through infancy or feebleness, it might be susceptible to cranks and faddists. G.J. Holyoake, with long experience of advanced radicalism, recalled that the co-operative movement in its nascent, 'enthusiastic period', had been beset by 'a sort of freemarket place, where everybody could deposit specimens of his notions for inspection or sale'.[73] One historian of the anti-slavery movement has seen the marginalized movement of the mid-1850s as attracting 'more than its fair share of cranks, visionaries, and habitual schismatics'.[74]

People who gloried in their eccentric status were attracted to other eccentric ideas, and movements which wanted their own unpopular beliefs tolerated might be reluctant to deny a hearing for other unpopular causes from such people. Thus the *Vegetarian* published correspondence on the flat-earth theory and articles on dress reform.[75] Obviously there was a risk. But they took to heart the message of (the briefly vegetarian) John Stuart Mill who saw so-called eccentricity as a motor for progress and a sign of liberty.[76] One response to vegetarianism was precisely to see it as a manifestation of British eccentricity. But one can find no references, in a British context, to commentators identifying it indulgently with the national self-image of eccentricity. When they used the label, they meant to marginalize it.[77]

Supporting an unpopular cause could satisfy a psychological need to be different, not in itself indicative of mental instability. It allowed the assumption of a self-flatteringly advanced and progressive persona. One former vegetarian, the horticulturist James Shirley Hibberd, indicated this motivation in a short story, where a young man, despite his awareness of the absurdities of the milieu, 'had a secret liking for all the singularities of the sect to which many plausible persuasions had attached me. Perhaps vanity aids us in putting ourselves apart from our fellow men, and thus we are enabled to set commonsense at defiance'.[78] Faddism could, as here, be associated with *youthful* radical posturing, such as Shelleyan idealism (along with flowing centre-parted hair[79]). If the critics Samuel Brown and George Lewes admitted to a youthful investigation of vegetarianism inspired by Shelley, there were others.[80] A few of the young Christian Socialists of the 1850s took up vegetarianism and progressive causes such as phonetics, and sported beards 'with most heroic indifference to public opinion'.[81] The beard did indeed join vegetarianism as a sign of the enthusiast, so that pioneers like Horsell and Duncan looked very clearly different.[82] The fact of vegetarianism alone, however, was enough to make a convert the local freak, throughout the period.[83]

An unoccupied, childless and unmarried state could motivate faddism, it was implied. Boredom and the desire for fulfilment provided recruits. The *Worcester Herald* felt that vegetarianism, the new pinnacle of extremism, was a sad manifestation of idleness on the part of men of 'education', men 'shockingly at a loss for objects on which to employ their time'.[84] *Blackwood's Edinburgh Magazine* (1859) similarly pointed to the social and psychological function of reform activity.[85] In *Dr Therne* it is certainly hinted that the Strongs' childless state is an important factor in their enthusiasms. Ennui rather than radicalism certainly explained the nature cure fads taken up by the unmarried or childless upper-middle-class characters in the humorist E.F. Benson's early twentieth century novels.[86]

Addressing Dr Lee's mid-Victorian forum for universal reforms, Edmund Fry of the Peace Society had gloried in the status of a crotchety man, for 'What would the world be now if none of the crotchety men had preceded us?'[87] Some vegetarians also embraced their faddist reputation, for instance the peace activist Richard Gill: 'Personally, I have many "fads" – most Vegetarians have.'[88] Others were ambivalent: the well-known reformers Henry Salt and Edward Carpenter, who could be accused by observers of faddism, were targeted by all sorts of 'faddists' and 'cranks', they recalled perhaps ironically, in autobiographies.[89] An Edwardian reformer glorying in the title of crank was C.W. Daniel who founded the journal *The Crank*. Its mottoes were 'Take nothing for granted' and 'A Crank is a little thing that makes revolutions'.[90]

The diversity of vegetarian motivations could be advantageous. Arnold Hills welcomed a very broad understanding of vegetarianism ('The largeness of our platform is the measure of our influence') and deplored the 'wretched bickering over beggarly elements, the narrowing littleness of alimentary absorption'.[91] Others had pragmatic concerns about the overshadowing of the primary message by ancillary interests, thus Francis Newman in 1868, on the verge of conversion, feared that by 'wandering into such topics as War and Teetotalism, and Capital Punishment, and Women's Suffrage, they exceedingly weaken the effect of their advice'.[92] Discussion of the vegetarian programme in 1886 found J.A. Thornberry denying vegetarianism necessarily meant, '(as the wits are, even now, too ready to say it does) anti-vaccination, teetotalism, radicalism, or any other "ism". One "ism" at a time is enough'.[93] Franklin Doremus, an activist in the NFRS, felt that in the 1850s there had been 'many other reforms mixed with it [Food Reform], and not until outside issues were dropped did vegetarians make progress.' The perception that vegetarianism was a religion which required acceptance of other 'antis' as articles of faith, concerned him.[94] Chandos Wallace complained that straying from the 'text' was hardly fair to other reform organizations.[95]

Personal Reform

Ultimately, vegetarianism was a personal reform because to be vegetarian was to carry out the practice as an individual: one could not be a theoretical vegetarian. But how far was vegetarianism conceived of as a 'personal reform'? Answering this question reveals the complexities of 'reform'.[96] Though reforms might be described as political, or social, or moral, the categories had a fluidity which suited polymorphous vegetarians. Activists participated in an enduring debate about the relative significance of political as opposed to personal reforms, of 'organic' as opposed to parliamentary measures. Temperance and vegetarianism were promoted as self-help, but also as necessary preconditions for national moral transformation.[97] Some reformers, though, could see their reform endeavour as combining self-reform, local activism and national politics.[98]

In 1842 Holyoake reviewed the Concordist *Healthian*, extracting from it the 'invaluable' cardinal idea of self-reform. Like charity, permanent reform needed to start at home: 'He may be an enthusiast who expects to reform mankind, but he fails in his first and most important duty who neglects to reform himself.' Reform of the individual accelerated general reform.[99] Controversial handbills produced by the LVS in 1887 declaring the reform 'more Rational, more Radical than Politics' repeated this message. It was hardly novel to speak of reform beginning at home, but reformers were interested in the domestic sphere as the object of necessary reform. As Margot Finn has argued, houses and the home 'lay at the heart of bourgeois radical culture'.[100] The alternative medical therapies espoused by many radicals, bourgeois and plebeian, were domesticated. Typical of radicalism, the new socialism of the late-Victorian era combined political and personal elements, the latter not crankishness but central to the socialist 'new way of life'.[101] The personalization of reform, the blurring of public and private, was reflected in the naming of children after radical heroes and houses after causes: signifiers of affiliation and means of advertisement. Thus Dornbusch's home was Vegetarian Cottage, Wallace Grant, a late-Victorian vegetarian from Swansea lived at Hygeia House, and one of Chandos Wallace's daughters was named Hygeia.[102]

According to critics, 'faddism' inappropriately entered the political arena, yet the personal was politicised throughout the period with anxieties over state interference with bodies, in relation to vivisection, compulsory vaccination and the Contagious Diseases Acts. Not surprisingly, *The Republican* envisaged vegetarians following other faddists in inquiring about an electoral candidate's dietetic opinions.[103] But radicals and 'fadicals', this chapter has argued, were not always distinct: personalities, ideas and movements *could* overlap, even though tensions existed between often competing organizations.

Having just examined the ways in which vegetarians who were often closely involved in other causes presented their reform credentials to fellow reformers in order to maximize appeal and sympathy (though this was a strategy of association or universality not without internal criticism, as we have seen), and having studied the way in which vegetarianism was interpreted as extremism or characterized as the expression of personal aberration by non-vegetarians, it is worth repeating the qualification that there were vegetarians whose diet betokened no radical politics or wider enthusiasm. But at the least, vegetarianism did entail a practical performance, and it is this aspect – the eating of vegetarian food – which is next examined.

5

FEEDING THE VEGETARIAN MIND AND BODY

In their provision of vegetarian publications and foods, adherents and activists were concerned about feeding body and mind. These two important aspects of vegetarian practice are studied here, beginning with the question of what vegetarians ate in private, in public display for the cause through banquets, and at vegetarian restaurants. The surprisingly diverse vegetarian press is then analysed.

Private diets and public feeding

Though interviews or correspondence in the vegetarian journals provide glimpses of the diet of vegetarians, despite all the testimony from adherents there are astonishingly few details of what they ate and even fewer self-penned glimpses of vegetarians eating *en famille*, a surprising omission given the movement's attempt to present vegetarianism as suited to family and daily life. In relation to infant and juvenile members of families, the diet was certainly viewed by proponents and critics as in some ways an explicable taste. *Punch* infantilized the early vegetarians by describing their diet as 'childish' sweet food and the movement 'a mere pretext for indulging a juvenile appetite for something nice'.[1] But the vegetarians believed that they could appeal to the 'uncorrupted tastes' of children for fruit.[2]

Some pioneer vegetarians promoted their own decidedly odd versions of vegetarian eating. For example, the socialist Samuel Bower lived on grey peas and the Christian Socialist Frederick J. Furnivall lived for some time on bread, apples, and haricot beans. Whilst a bachelor, the barrister Thomas Baker lived on uncooked fruit. John Martyn, who made experiments on diet from 1849, ate bread and raw apples when in season, having found the pea too concentrated a food for his requirements. Concerning the 'vigorous and sternly consistent' George Dornbusch,

Francis Newman commented: 'We want such men to hold us up ... Nevertheless, we must not despise the day of small things.'[3] One of Dornbusch's visitors was horrified by a meal of cold cauliflower, potatoes and rice, but was relieved by an abundance of luscious fruit.[4] Edward Hare, the retired Inspector General of Hospitals, Bengal, ate two daily meals of toasted or unleavened bread, weak tea, vegetables cooked in butter, farinaceous puddings and fruit. The late-Victorian accountant's clerk Caldwell Harpur lived on Hovis bread, nut extract, jam, apples and cold water.

Such authentic dietetic oddity would only have reinforced the public's general belief that the vegetarian diet was unpleasant. Charles Lane had noted in 1851 the 'oppressive idea of dilapidated turnips, and stale, flat, and undigestible [sic] cabbages'[5] Display of vegetarian foods was therefore a necessary, as well as a common tool of propaganda, designed to show that vegetarianism was full of variety, aesthetically pleasing, perhaps even elegant. Other displays were designed to show that it was cheap and tasty and therefore an ideal food for those with a limited budget. In order to emphasize its attractiveness dishes were accompanied by flowers and cut glass, art and music. Flowers and foliage also emphasized its 'natural' status. The food at the Banquet in 1848 included savoury dishes made of onions, parsley, beetroot and mushrooms. Desserts included nuts and dried fruits, flummery, custards, plum pudding and cheesecakes. The dishes were described as 'artistic', with garnishes of different colours and shapes. Joseph Brotherton believed that strangers would realize that the diet was not self-denial, but that 'we may enjoy the luxuries of the earth with perfect innocence'.[6] On the other hand, the meal to which London vegetarians were invited by Amalie Dornbusch and Jane Hurlstone in July 1850 was a 'plain Vegetarian Supper'.[7] Early vegetarian propaganda emphasized its moral principles, and thought that appeals to taste were only what had to be done if one could not appeal to the intellect.[8]

Public vegetarian banquets in the late nineteenth century still challenged the charge that their diet entailed monotonous eating – as if a mixed diet was more varied in practice – and press reports seemed to show an awareness of variety. The *Daily Telegraph* believed the 'boiled cabbage' reputation was now exploded.[9] By contrast, the *Daily News* believed vegetarians had yet to 'make *their fare appetizing*. Their most triumphant demonstration would be a public dinner on their own menu, at which an Alderman asked for more.' But it soon had to admit to being surprised by an elaborate and artistically served variety, including excellently flavoured soups *sans* animal stock, and confessed it was 'such as even the semi-carnivorous gourmet might well respect'.[10]

FIGURE 18. A ticket for an anniversary banquet for the Vegetarian Society, 1891. *British Vegetarian*, January-February 1963, p. 39.

A sense of what was actually offered to consumers can be gained through bills of fare. One of the smartest restaurants in the 1890s offered:

Grilled mushrooms and seakale cream	10*d*
Yorkshire pudding with sage and onion and new potatoes	7*d*
Mushroom omelette and young carrots sauté	1*s*

The *table d'hôte* menu offered:

Carrot soup or mulligatawny soup
Flageolets with cream and spinach
Fried duck's egg and green peas
Lent pie or stewed fruit
Mixed salad, cheese, dessert.[11]

Vegetable cookery

Victorian food writers and vegetarians complained about the British tendency to overcook and generally maltreat vegetables.[12] Study of diet revealed the limited vegetables consumed by elites in the past, and non-vegetarians stressed a rise in vegetable consumption, *The Times* observing 'we have insensibly become such confirmed vegetarians that ... an Englishman as a rule eats a mouthful of vegetables to every mouthful of meat'.[13] Vegetarians charted the rise of new fruits and vegetables such as lentils and bananas, and the increased use of rice, a foodstuff apparently 'little known and used' in the 1840s.[14] The Edwardian vegetarian cookery writer Jean Mill claimed that 'vegetarians as a rule use fresh vegetables practically in the same way as meat eaters do, to supplement more substantial viands. No one – to my knowledge at least – ever dines off the proverbial cabbage or turnip'. She also argued that the 'most elementary food reform' would lead to dissatisfaction with the vegetable accompaniments to meat.[15]

What was conceived as vegetarian food can also be understood from recipes in vegetarian journals, pamphlets and books. A few appeared in the *Vegetarian Advocate*: advice by 'A lover of truth' included avoiding overboiling and replacing butter with olive oil. But it was also recommended that beans be gently stewed for about ten hours, to produce a rich but cheap food! Some twenty-six British vegetarian cookery books appeared in this period (though not all were by vegetarians); of these, fourteen had female authors. Vegetarian recipes also featured in 'mainstream' cookery books and domestic encyclopaedias as the movement became more prominent; in late-Victorian editions of Mrs Beeton's there were recipes and vegetarian menus.[16] The content of the vegetarians' cookery books varied: not all engaged in debates about the diet, and some devoted more time to particular foodstuffs; thus Horsell concentrated on bread-making. They came in for their share of criticism: the publisher and vegetarian Ernest Bell believed that to 'have to live by some of them would almost make a vegetarian turn meat-eater'.[17]

The earliest cookery book for the movement was Martha Brotherton's. When it was republished with James Simpson's lengthy introduction, the moral, scientific and economic aspects were privileged, with little reference to food as a source of pleasure.[18] For its part, John Smith of Malton's cookery book argued for a combination of nutrition, digestibility and 'real sensual enjoyment', but rejected 'trifles, custards and other rich productions' for the satisfying of 'a natural appetite'.[19] But Amy Baker (writing as 'Domestica'), influenced by Grahamism, deliberately avoided the title of 'cookery' because of her aversion to cooked foods (which represented dissatisfaction with the simplicity of Nature) and her dislike of 'human manipulation'.[20] Here was no expression of Epicureanism and pleasure. The same query about the need to cook foods appeared in Ernest Bell's preface to Mrs E.W. Bowdich's late-Victorian book.[21]

The VS's *Penny Vegetarian Cookery* was a short pamphlet designed for beginners with various motives and from differing economic and social backgrounds, and had advice on portable foods for the office and workplace. Like 'Domestica', moderation was stressed, with the diet for children designed to provide lessons in 'self-denial ... kindness, humanity, temperance, and moral government ... by means of dietetic management'.[22] The *Penny Vegetarian Cookery* and other works advocated variety, to combat the idea that vegetarianism meant monotony. Chandos

Wallace's *366 Vegetarian Menus* asserted that 'a very epicure need never be afraid of exhausting the variety of dishes allowed by the reformed diet'.[23] Charles Forward's cookery book asserted that gastronomic excellence was possible and published a 'materia alimentaria' to emphasize the variety possible.[24]

Vegetarians were accused of advocating uncooked green stuffs. In a period when their consumption was seen as promoting indigestion, or flatulence, salads could be problematic. Mary Pope's *Novel Dishes for Vegetarian Households* advocated salads as wholesome and refreshing but accepted that despite the English tradition of salads and the fine vegetables grown, the English were not skilled in making them.[25] Arthur Payne, however, recorded a revolution in the art of salad-making since the 1840s.[26] Equally going against received wisdom about eating fresh fruit, vegetarians stressed the place of fruits in their dietary.[27] Although the emphasis on fresh food was common, increasing availability of tinned food was reflected in vegetarian recipes by Pope, who used tinned pears, apricots, tomatoes and okra. Payne asserted that preserved vegetables and fruits were so useful 'that they are inseparable from civilized cookery'.[28]

The message that vegetarian food should be kept simple was also pressed in the pamphlet *How to Begin*, which cautioned against costly and highly seasoned dishes, but stressed the importance of attractive presentation.[29] Others allowed a certain elaboration. Martha Brotherton's book incorporated table plans and menus for dinners, and Forward's cookery book began with a model eight-course dinner (each course featuring numerous dishes). Mrs F.J. Bruce's recipes were arranged for three course and two course menus, and also included vegetarian Christmas dinner gravies and cold savouries.[30] Such elaboration was not favoured by those who saw vegetarianism as a mechanism for simplification of life. William Horsell identified the simplification as a way of unchaining women from their domestic slavery.[31] Mary Pope thought no long-standing convert could endure 'the *olla podrida* of dishes' of the mixed diet and suggested no more than four courses to a meal.[32] But tactically it was recognized that the provision of dainty and delicious foods was necessary to combat the 'old regime'.[33]

The extreme attempt to mimic the old diet was seen in the creation of cutlets, sirloins etc., from vegetables, 'so as to imitate the detested reality' as one manager informed one amused non-vegetarian.[34] An early vegetarian had called for chefs to develop an expertise in this meat-mimicry, but it could easily seem like a lusting after abandoned flesh-pots. Vegetarian restaurants offered 'veritable frauds' of steaks, roast goose, cutlets and stews.[35] Recipes books offered alternatives to hare soups, sausages, cutlets, steaks and Melton Mowbray pies.[36] But the *Vegetarian*'s answer to critics who pointed out the oddity of this habit was telling: 'The chief mission of the modern cook is to disguise the fact that meat is on the table at all.'[37] Not only did this reflect the 'flight to gentility' of middle- and upper-class cookery of the second half of the nineteenth century, with its pursuit of the dainty and recherché, it also represented the longer process whereby the animal origin of meat was hidden.[38]

Just as high-minded vegetarianism was reflected in cookery books, so the argument about thrift, in order to secure this gentility, appeared. Arthur Payne's cookery book was designed for vegetarians and non-vegetarians, and explicitly addressed that very large class of the petty bourgeois and decent poor who had no servants but wished at all costs to keep up appearances. Though an important class, 'one on which the slow but gradual march of civilization depends', their whole life was 'one continual struggle not merely to live, but to live decently'.[39]

Did vegetarians enjoy their food? Rarely did they become eloquent in a way that would suggest gustatory delight was uppermost. William Horsell spoke of food as 'good, wholesome and nutritious'.[40] Their food was commended as wholesome, derived from 'natural productions'. The economic cookery classes and recipes sent to newspapers by Dundonian vegetarians in the 1870s aimed to promote 'delicacy of taste, cheapness, nutriment, and simplicity of cooking'.[41] Henry Salt in the *Westminster Review* in 1886 maintained that the diet entailed no monotony or blandness.[42] For Mary Pope, the diet brought a natural palate that entailed an enhanced discrimination in taste; for Payne it appealed to a taste refined and natural.[43]

Vegetarians were instructed to prepare food decently and present it in the 'best possible manner', but to aim for simplicity rather than mixtures.[44] On the other hand, an early vegetarian banquet was presented as a 'feast which could not an epicure cloy'. Other banquets were described as 'sumptuous'.[45] By contrast there were some, like the Reverend Collyns or Francis Newman, who saw the value of vegetarianism in curbing the taste for luxury and lowering wants. Newman presented this as a source of pleasure through releasing time and energies for other activities such as the pursuit of knowledge, travel and enjoyment. Vegetarianism satisfied the stomach but did not indulge it.[46] It is worth noting Stephen Mennell's verdict that 'the food of the nineteenth century English domestic cookery book was rather monotonous and above all lacking in any sense of the enjoyment of food'.[47] This puts the early vegetarian fare of puddings (boiled plum, vegetable, sago etc.) or later efforts such as the banquet of the Scottish Food Reform Society in 1879 (soups of peas, lentils, beans, marrow and macaroni, pies, rissoles, tarts, pancakes, stewed fruits, puddings, hominy and fresh fruit) in perspective.

It should also be recognized that vegetarians explored non-western foodways, although this should not be exaggerated. There was a wider awareness about the dietetic fruits of empire; as the *Daily News* noted of the colonial section to the Great Exhibition, 'the vegetarians will be delighted to find that there exists in the vegetable world substitutes for almost everything that is now drawn from the animal'.[48] And there were other food reformers who attempted to introduce new dishes to the British palate.[49] Humble continental foods, such as olive oil, lentils, haricot beans and even garlic, were advocated.[50] Lentils had been unusual as a human food in England until the 1880s; their increased popularity was perhaps due to vegetarians. Mary Pope used polenta and 'spargehtti [sic]', cooked green bananas, recommended exotic pine kernels and mangosten (although in tinned form) and told her readers that cassava meal could be obtained from West Indian food stores.[51] Mattieu Williams introduced readers of the *Gentleman's Magazine* to tofu[52]; and a stall exhibiting 'Moong dal, curry, chutney, rice, and other Eastern productions' managed by the Messrs Veerasawmy in the Memorial Hall in 1897 'was one of the features of the exhibition'. Vegetarians could rightly present themselves as combating the 'monster of custom' in championing new foods.

Vegetarian substitutes and the future of food

In 1894 the Reverend James Clark admitted that there was need for more foods to be available for those not content with simpler vegetarian foods, to 'give an amount of enjoyment'.[53] A range of vegetarian substitutes was commercially available from the late nineteenth century onwards, providing alternatives to refined flour and bread, to isinglass, to meat and fish pastes and meat in general. Cereals provided new breakfast foods. Mrs Mill, in her *Food Reform Cookery* of 1908, queried how people could complain of want of variety 'with such a seemingly endless category to choose from … for the difficulty I find is to do justice to even a small proportion of them. If one were to sample a different dish every day it would take months to get over them'.

The vegetarian Seventh Day Adventists formed the London Food Reform Company by 1897, to sell Kellogg's salt-free and dextrinised granose (designed to be easily digested), nuttose and nut butter and claimed they were motivated by 'Health and NOT merely for profit'.[54] Their International Health Company factory was established at Redhill in Surrey in October 1899. Manhu Food Co. (established in 1900) sold rolled and flaked cereal foods, some with modified starch for diabetes. Mapleton's Nut Foods included the unfortunately named vegetable fat 'Nutter', produced 'under ideal conditions' in a factory in the countryside. A vegetable fat, 'Albene,' was marketed as free of odour and flavour. The creation of nut meats significantly extended the vegetarian diet in the late nineteenth century. New brands proliferated, offering substitutes for meat in stews, curries and cold slices: Nut Cream, Meatose, Vejola, Nut-vego, Savoury Nut Meat, 'Nutton'. Other foods were concentrates. Eustace Miles created 'emprote', designed to provide 'assimilable proteid' and thus ensure that 'all sorts of men and women' made a success of food reform. Fruitarian cakes, compressed cakes of uncooked fruits and nuts, were manufactured. Concern about the stimulating effects of caffeine led vegetarians to develop cereal based substitutes such as 'Caramel Cereal' (from the International Health Association), 'Sip It' (the London Nut Food Co.) and 'Lapee' (by Mapleton). Fruit syrups and vegetarian extracts included Vejos, Marmite and Vigar Extract (by Pitman) and Nut Extract (by Mapleton).[55] There were firms which created or sold a range of health foods such as Wallace P.R. Foods, with its bakery, jams and marmalade and other Wallaceite specialities, 'free from such deleterious substances or adulterants as yeast, chemicals, artificial colouring matter, mineral salt'. They ranged from very plain foods, foods for athletes, infants and invalids, to foods designed for afternoon tea.[56] G. Savage & Sons, managed food stores, and sold goods such as 'Nu-Era' wholemeal flour, Minerva olive oil and powder-o-nuts (a rissole mixture).[57] The fruiterers Shearns developed health stores and restaurants and sold kitchen utensils.

Food stores were thus another ramification of the movement, well before the term 'health food store' became current.[58] Indeed they had their origins in 'dietetic depots' in London in the 1830s-40s. Food stores were established in the late nineteenth century, some being associated with restaurants. Canning in Liverpool, for instance, had a chain of stores and then founded a restaurant in 1882.[59] It was not just edible commodities, of course, that vegetarians required. Late-Victorian vegetarian journals carried advertisements for a range of items from Nichols's sanitary soap to W.G. Smith's vegetarian candles and soaps.[60] Several stores also produced their own tracts. A short-lived store at 30, Lamb's Conduit, London (1878) was associated with a 'Diet Reform Club'.[61] The VS managed one depot. Goods could be ordered from price lists: Wallaceite Foods posted their products from the headquarters in Battersea Park Road, London.

Introducing a new edition of her cookery book, Jean Mill observed that within four years the proliferation of foods, depots and restaurants had become so multifarious that the 'simple life' threatened to become more complex than the other.[62] These new foods were exhibited at the vegetarian exhibitions in London, where their profusion could benefit the movement.[63] The *Weekly Sun* responded to the Vegetarian Congress of 1897 by remarking that it was no longer a source of speculation as to what vegetarians found to live on, but 'rather a matter of wonder how in the name of miracles they make choice of a dinner.'[64]

An industry catering to food reformers was largely developed by vegetarians themselves since the firms were often owned by vegetarians: as with the Smiths of Kingston (makers of vegetarian soaps and candles), the Adventists, Dr Nichols, Thomas Allinson, the Wallaces, James Cook and William Allan Macdonald, an exponent of sandals who created 'Natural Ration' cakes. The cookery instructor Mary Pope sold flavourings, colourings and mills.[65] This was clearly a manifestation of the reformer as entrepreneur, and could lead to accusations of quackery and exploitation. Yet Chandos Wallace was described privately as 'terribly insistent on her own theories & researches which she's anxious to make known freely. Believe me she's not on the make, or a quack'.[66]

Vegetarians such as Chandos Wallace presented themselves as pioneers of the 'food of the future'. But this was in the context of a wider speculation about future foods, by scientists, in scientific romances, and utopian fictions such as the American Edward Bellamy's *Equality*.[67] The speculative *Martyrdom of Man* by Winwoode Reade referred to the chemical synthesis of food.[68] In these, science as well as humanity was to transform the human diet. Commercial producers of vegetarian foods stressed their hygienic credentials by noting their use of machinery. But, as in the case of the Wallaces, they were keen to stress the natural purity of food, untainted by the use of chemical preservatives and other additives that were a matter of concern in the late-Victorian and Edwardian period. Some firms were developing materials like 'prepared assimilable proteid foods' which have a modern inflection, although in fact they also echo the breakfast powders which radical leaders had marketed in the early nineteenth century.[69] They also formed part of a wider development of 'new foods', patented and 'scientific', which the journal *Food* explained was the 'result of the evils wrought in the constitutions of the multitude among us by our overwrought and artificial style of living'.[70]

Timothy Morton has argued for a linkage of vegetarianism to 'those same modern constructions of food – as nutrition – which led, through the stringencies of laissez-faire, to the current BSE crisis. This is because Romantic vegetarianism was on the whole not just opposed to cruelty, but also to flavour'.[71] He refers to a Romantic vegetarian myth of the 'unmarked food' of pure nutrition 'like nutritional supplements' but in the period 1840-1901 vegetarian food was presented as 'nature's bill of fare': pure water, fruits and farinacea rather than abstracted chemicals. Smith of Malton specifically rejected the idea of concentrating nutrition: nature had combined the nutritious with the innutritious and attempts to separate these were mistaken.[72] The VS preferred 'natural to manufactured foods' but recommended variety through a frequent use of new foods.[73] Of course, as food historians have argued, 'natural food' was something created by man through agriculture.[74]

If food retailing and family eating was the basis of the movement, what happened when vegetarians wanted to dine away from home? The answer to this question, raised in the movement's infancy, was the vegetarian restaurant.

Vegetarian Restaurants and the Movement

Vegetarians brought novelty to urban refreshment.[75] The vegetarians' rationale was not itself new. Temperance activists had long been interested in creating counter-attractions in the provision of drink and entertainment, and from the vegetarian movement's earliest days there were schemes for restaurants and 'fruit rooms', to encourage the spread of their dietetic principles and offer a resort for their converts.[76] In Manchester in the 1850s there was Barnesley's 'Vegetarian and Temperance Hotel' and Mrs Hollinworth's vegetarian dining room.[77] In London's Talfourd Coffee House a 'vegetarian ordinary' was available.[78] Temperance hotels provided vegetarian food during the 1860s – early 1870s when the movement was struggling.[79] Vegetarian restaurants were a factor (as cause and effect) in the revival and growth of the movement from the late 1870s.[80] The *Food Reform Magazine*, noting their steady advance, claimed 'they have long since passed from the transient stage, and have now become permanent institutions of the country'.[81]

The growth of restaurants in the capital city of the Empire, where in 1889 there were 34 out of the 52 vegetarian restaurants, was an important sign of the maturity and strength of the cause. From 1879 Nichols's Sanitary Depôt incorporated food reform and vegetarian dining rooms.[82] A flyer in the *Herald of Health* described it as 'The novelty of the Nineteenth century!'[83] This, the 'Alpha Restaurant', continued into the late 1890s.[84] Following the success of the 'Healtheries' exhibition in 1884, the NFRS encouraged restaurants in London, and arranged a dinner with the entrepreneur Roland McDoual who aimed to introduce continental-style cafés through a 'People's Café Company'. One visitor described his customers as having 'rather a hungry, unsatisfied, uncomfortable look about them'.[85] Soon several restaurants were established, those that flourished included Robert Reid's 'Garden', Andrew Glendinning's 'Apple Tree' at London Wall and the 'Orange Grove' (later St George's Café) at St Martin Lane. Reid had come to see the reformed diet as the root of all temperance success and when he settled with his sons in London he established the 'Garden' at 24, Jewin Street to create a 'centre for the propagation of vegetarian truths'.[86] He also wrote tracts for free circulation. Glendinning's first restaurant at 34, London Wall was opened in 1882. Another, the 'Mansion House' in the Poultry, prominently emblazoned its vegetarian status.[87] Renamed the 'Apple Tree', it offered customers seventy daily or weekly papers, including vegetarian journals, while Glendinning himself produced an *Apple Tree Annual*.[88]

The publicity afforded by the visibility of these restaurants is reflected in a Sherlock Holmes story where Holmes passes a prominently situated restaurant.[89] In 1888 London had 25, providing 4000 meals daily; in 1890 there were 33, down to 31 in 1897.[90] Their names were often floral and botanical, or superlative as in 'Ideal' and 'Acme'. Success, however, was not assured. The 'Food Reform Restaurants Company' (operating seven restaurants *c*.1880) and the 'Charing Cross Vegetarian Hotel' (*c*.1888) were failures.[91] In spite of these problems, entrepreneurs persisted. In late 1889 the 'London Vegetarian Restaurants Association Ltd' was established to develop 'Co-operative Vegetarian Restaurants', its shares being set at 10*s* to involve the poorest.[92] In 1899 a 'Vegetarian Cafe Company Ltd' was planned, to establish dining and restaurant houses, bakeries, shops, stores, stalls, schools of cookery, and retail vegetarian and other literature.

Potentially, their existence signified vigour and advance. They could provide valuable models of economy, hygiene, culinary excellence and variety. They certainly provided social centres for activists, supporters and the 'progressive' in London and elsewhere. When the 'Bouverie' was established in 1886 over Charles Bradlaugh's Free Thought Depôt, T.L. Nichols emphasized that 'tight' ceilings, floor and separate entrances rendered the freethought 'non-contagious'; but in spite of this, vegetarian restaurants could be radical meeting places. Groups such as Bernard Shaw's circle or the Humanitarian League used them, in the latter's case, for a weekly tea (the naturalist W.H. Hudson described being accosted there by a 'young devotee' who 'so terribly wished to see Edward Carpenter and other famous people'[93]). The 'Wheatsheaf' off Oxford Street, was favoured by Shaw. Briefly the home of the Rambling Club, in 1892 it had a 'Pythagorean' social club, kept reformist/progressive newspapers and offered bedrooms. In late 1885 a dinner for cabmen and their wives took place here; later it hosted health receptions and a banquet celebrating Shelley's centenary.[94] Mrs Britton's 'Pudding Bowl' had an evening institute for young women.[95] James Hayward's 'The Waverley', hosting meetings such as the conference on fruit farming and colonies in 1891, was described as more effective than many avowed vegetarian institutions.[96]

As well as serving food, establishments such as those of Reid, Glendinning, Hodge of the 'Orange Grove', and the 'Cornucopia' (32, Newgate Street) produced vegetarian literature. The menu cards of

Martin's 'Savoy Café' incorporated Oliver Goldsmith's vegetarian sentiments in 1900. There was even a short-lived *Weekly Star and Vegetarian Restaurant Gazette*, the organ of the Allinsonians (Allinson's Hygienic Hospital was supported by collection boxes outside the restaurants). There is little evidence to show what impact the literature displayed at the restaurants had.[97]

Despite these important connections, the relationship between movement and restaurants was not necessarily close. Indeed, the *Herald of Health* spoke of a 'great gulf'.[98] In 1888 only one proprietor joined the LVS committee and only one vegetarian sat on the Charing Cross Company's board of directors. Many of the restaurants were not vegetarian-owned; commercial exploitation obviously reflected the movement's popularity or at least its perceived potential.[99] Various places sold vegetarian meals as sidelines, so that Forward deplored the 'prejudicial influence' of temperance restaurants, cocoa rooms, Lyons and ABC tea-rooms. When a vegetarian restaurant itself went 'mixed' it lost its propagandist utility and became a damaging sign of weak demand.[100] Few of the speculative ventures by non-vegetarians sold vegetarian literature and the proprietors avoided association with the VS's efforts through notice-boards, contributions boxes or advertisements.[101]

Who patronized these restaurants? One observer believed that many were attracted by the novelty, some by a desire to reduce the meat in their diet for health reasons, a 'fair and growing proportion' for vegetarian sentiment but mostly by a cheap and prompt service.[102] Commentators believed many customers were low-paid young clerks or office workers who needed to have quick and cheap service.[103] The novelist George Gissing recalled 'poor clerks and shop boys, bloodless girls and women of many sorts – all endeavouring to find a relish in lentil soup and haricot something or other. It was a grotesquely heart-breaking sight.'[104]

In 1892 *Punch* depicted a group of clerks of literary turn discussing the relative merits of Swinburne, Browning, Herbert Spencer, Whitman and Milton at 'The Nebucadnezzar's Head' in the City. Their fellow guests were lady clerks who lunched 'sumptuously and economically on tea and baked ginger-pudding'.[105] The 'Alpha' restaurant was mostly patronized by Crosse and Blackwell's clerical staff in the late 1890s.[106] The 'Ceres' near St Paul's (1889-*c*.1897) was used by young men and women, but also by people working at the nearby warehouse, publishers' offices and businesses.[107] Glendinning's restaurants' *6d* three-course meals attracted office workers.[108] One American reporter noted that there was no choice of vegetables or fresh fruit because the emphasis was on illustrating cheap living for the poor.[109] But the 'poor' being catered for were members of the lower middle classes, as the vegetarian Percy Echlin, critical of the 'too high-class' metropolitan restaurants that catered for clerks, pointed out in 1896.[110] The price (when meat dinners could be almost as cheap[111]), and quantity of the food, opening times and even 'flashness' – factors rehearsed in the *Vegetarian* – prevented a significant volume of working-class customers.[112]

Yet *Figaro* noted with surprise that Glendinning's restaurant was 'crowded with customers, many of whom were evidently substantial City men'.[113] Similarly surprised was the *Boston Herald* (America) which reported that rather than cranky, 'long-haired and wild-eyed individuals eagerly devouring bran pudding, sawdust soup, or something of the kind', customers at Charing Cross Hotel were sensible looking, healthy and clearly gentlemen.[114] 'St George's House Café' in St Martin's Lane, opened *c.*1887, advertised as the 'famous house for coffee' (though also specializing in 'macaroni and egg cookery, together with special American dishes, curries etc.') attracted a wealthy clientele. Customers included Bernard Shaw, the actors Fanny Brough and Frank Wheeler, the mathematician Professor William Garnett, an 'Austrian Count', and 'some olive or darker complexioned native of the far east ... a law or medical student'.[115] One such student, Gandhi, who deliberately visited all the London restaurants, divided them into the cheap (which he frequented) and well-to-do class visited by the intellectuals.

In 1885 a food reformer had expressed concern that, whilst gentlemen could 'prowl about London and pick up a good deal of the vegetarian's diet in a perfectly satisfactory manner' it was not clear that 'ladies' could.[116] But when the food writer Lieutenant-Colonel Nathaniel Newnham-Davis, commissioned to write about eating out in London by the *Pall Mall Gazette*, visited St George's Café, there was a ladies' chess club and a ladies' room. The 'Elephant' had a ladies' tearoom in 1889.[117] With or without specific rooms, vegetarian restaurants were catering for women, reflecting the emergence of restaurants offering provision for 'respectable' women.[118] The 'Wheatsheaf' advertised the fact that 'Ladies shopping in the neighbourhood will receive every attention', other female customers included the shop assistants, who had the expense (like clerks) of maintaining a smart appearance on low wages.[119]

It was the metropolitan vegetarian restaurants that gained the most press exposure. But in the later nineteenth century restaurants and cafés were established across Britain.[120] Their geography naturally reflected the geography of the branch societies, with restaurants often providing regular venues for activities. In Bradford an extensive restaurant, established above a coach-builder's firm in the Town Hall Square in 1895, was superintended by a teacher to the VS.[121] The Liverpool Society of the late 1880s met at William H. Chapman's restaurant, whilst in Chester the society's monthly meetings were held at the 'Apricot', and at Nottingham the vegetarian association met at the St James Street restaurant.[122] The herbalist William H. Webb's restaurant and health store at Southport hosted local meetings. Vegetarians at Bristol, Salcombe and Portsmouth established other restaurants.[123]

Not surprisingly, it was the big cities where vegetarian activity or potential clientele could justify the ventures, which saw significant provision. Manchester was well-provided, with six restaurants.[124] Four were established by Frederick Smallman, who advertised his 'machine bread bakery' and restaurant lit by 'Edison Electric Light'.[125] The establishment at 6, Fountain Street had a meeting hall on the ground floor with a large restaurant above. The 'Fruit and Flowers Parlour' in Market Street, a fictional representation of a Mancunian restaurant (set, slightly too early for authenticity, in 1870) by the bestselling novelist Mrs Humphry Ward probably captures well the precious/whimsical nature of businesses operated by committed vegetarians. Ward describes the kitchen, with its many simmering pans, tables laden with vegetable pies just out of the oven, stewed fruits and heaps of tomatoes, with Lancashire lasses peeling apples. Its printed bill of fare is concluded in bold red by: 'No meat, no disease. *Ergo*, no meat, no sin. Fellow citizens, leave your carnal foods, and try a most excellent way. I.E. push the door and walk in. The Fruit and Flower Parlour invites everybody and overcharges nobody.'[126] Its clientele included many foreign (mostly French) clerks.

In Birmingham there were three establishments. The 'Garden,' owned by Alfred Hughes, became the 'talk of the local catering business' according to *The Caterer*, and was seen as the major impetus to local vegetarian activity.[127] Another, the 'Orchard', was not immediately successful and ran at a loss for its first two years.[128] More ambitiously, Isaac Pitman's contribution to the movement was commemorated in the Pitman Vegetarian Hotel, a luxurious building (at 153-161 Corporation Street) in the 'later Renaissance style,' equipped with steam-powered kitchens, electric lighting, modern radiators and 'the finest collection of William E. Harris's Oil paintings in the kingdom'.[129] Terracotta reliefs depicted carpenters (part of the building was a furniture shop), and vegetarians dining. Arnold Hills (the motive force behind the scheme) and Joseph Malins attended the inauguration in October 1898. The company comprised a restaurant, shop and hotel (including coffee, commercial and smoking rooms).[130] Its director was a vegetarian, James Cook, converted by an address by Hills in 1895.[131] Customers were 'a different class of people to those ... previously reached,' including 'many Birmingham worthies'.[132]

FIGURE 19. *Left*: Pitman Vegetarian Hotel, Birmingham, from *Vegetarian Messenger*, January 1899, p. 16. *Right*: Charing Cross Vegetarian Hotel, from an advertisement in C.L.H. Wallace, *366 Menus*.

The McCaugheys played an important part in vegetarian activity in Ireland and Scotland through their restaurants. Leonard McCaughey opened the well-situated 'Eden' restaurant in Jamaica Street in Glasgow. On two floors, there were tea and coffee rooms, lavatories, and a dining room for 200 on the first floor.[133] Steam heaters kept the restaurant's food piping hot. The McCaugheys' first restaurant, in Belfast, was managed by Leonard's wife. McCaughey and Smallman of Manchester were successful businessmen committed to the movement and not simply commercial speculators. Their success encouraged others, but few were successful. When the 'Farringdon and Food Reform Restaurant Company' failed in 1882, it was offset by the knowledge that 'new ventures' were springing up all the time. George Newnes (no vegetarian) established one in Manchester *c.*1881, to save money to establish *Tit-Bits*, the journal that initiated his successful publishing career.[134] By contrast, the Sheffield Vegetarian Restaurant Company's restaurant had to move to cheaper premises at Campo Lane, where the working classes could be catered for, according to the directors in 1895.[135] There was a dining room, smoking room, second-class room and ladies' room. Thought reading and the display of Edison's phonograph inaugurated the establishment.[136]

Mapping the spread of vegetarian restaurants adds to our understanding of the movement as a lived experience and provincial phenomenon. But how far did they contribute to the movement's attractiveness? How successful was the movement in attracting a wide range of social groups? The broader context of temperance refreshment (courted by vegetarians) was unpromising.[137] According to G.J. Holyoake in 1859, the forty best teetotal and vegetarian coffee houses had to be rolled into one to make a room as half as brilliant as ordinary refreshment rooms.[138] The teetotal restaurant and café movement relied on middle-class subsidy, and was only vigorous in the north, elsewhere the companies flourished 'like mayflies in the summer' and few lasted into the last decade of the century. The overtly religious interior decoration of many coffee houses made them uninviting as places for refreshment and recreation.[139] Rather than epicurean relish, observers saw a similar 'zeal' operating in vegetarian restaurant.[140]

The fortunes of the restaurants were widely discussed in articles, meetings and conferences. Forward found it 'difficult to form a satisfactory opinion' about their effects. He feared 'prejudicial influence' from temperance restaurants, cocoa rooms, Lyons and ABC tea rooms where non-flesh foods could be bought. The value of businesslike, hygienic and attractive enterprises was offset by 'so-called' vegetarian restaurants mismanaged by inexperienced and commercial speculators. These hindered the cause through their badly cooked, adulterated or insect-infested food, whose public recollection by people attending his lectures largely undermined his efforts.[141] This was echoed by the journal of 'scientific socialism' *To-day*, which asserted: 'Half cold soup, sodden and sloppy cabbage, ill-boiled potatoes, a horribly starchy, watery mixture called "melted butter," these – served upon a dirty tablecloth, are not the delicacies to attract the descendants of generations of meat-eating Englishmen.'[142] Little wonder that when a gastronomer sought guidance from 'one of the high priests' of vegetarianism he was advised against trying any of the restaurants.[143] Complaints about food quality in the *Vegetarian* led one metropolitan restaurant to ban it.[144] Yet criticisms about pricing and quality were also levelled against provincial restaurants.[145]

Despite the complaints of vegetarians and opponents alike there was demand: one London vegetarian complained of the 'greatest difficulty' in getting a seat for lunch because of crowded rooms.[146] Undoubtedly the restaurants had novelty value for the metropolitan and local press, and though there was much to criticize, they also received favourable coverage. In 1880 there was a 'first rate notice' of dinners, in the *Graphic*.[147] *Punch* poked fun at the clientele but was appreciative about Spiers and Pond's restaurant in 1886.[148] Even the medically orthodox *Medical Press and Circular* and the *British Medical Journal* gave appreciative notices about a restaurant at Farringdon Street.[149]

Restaurants were important signs of the movement's earnestness and the reformed diet's perceived commercial viability. A restaurant prominently situated in a town could not be ignored and proved the possibility of the diet beyond the home circle. The propagandist and practical value of restaurants and ordinaries had long been appreciated but for much of the period the movement had to rely on the power of the platform and print. The latter – the 'vegetarian press' – is now examined.

The vegetarian press

Vegetarianism, like other reform movements, stimulated a 'movement culture' incorporating educational, leisure and social functions.[150] A movement entailing inherently different consumption and production, it developed specialist clubs, stores and places for eating, even agencies for marriages and servants were attempted. Another of its 'counter-cultural' resources was its press. For although vegetarianism was spread through public lectures, demonstrations, debates and privately amongst personal acquaintance, the dissemination of serial literature and other publications by national and local societies was also important. The press was designed to attract new members, to create a national (and international) movement, to inspire its adherents through this sense of community and through the information it published on favourable conditions or evidence of the spread of its ideals.[151] Just as with the provision of foodstuffs, however, the literary needs of the movement were also supplied by entrepreneurs hoping to make a living in the 'trade of agitation' and reform.[152]

Vegetarianism was first prominently advocated in the Concordist journals and James Duncan's journals. Horsell's *The Truth-Tester*, which intended 'to grapple with most questions affecting the social, physical, intellectual and moral Health of Man', continued this effort, his association of temperance and vegetarianism requiring 'some degree of courage'.[153] Sales suffered as a result of this advocacy despite Simpson's funds and sympathizers' efforts to increase circulation.[154] With some trepidation Horsell published the *Vegetarian Advocate*, the VS's first organ and the first avowedly and specifically vegetarian paper. The 2d *Advocate* (published in the Isle of Man until Manx postal privileges were abolished), was earnest and ably-produced.[155] Despite appreciative reviews in some progressive temperance/health reform journals and nation-wide subscription, circulation was small. The arrival in 1849 of another official vegetarian magazine (intended to be complementary rather than a competitor), led to its demise with some financial loss, but throughout the 1850s Horsell's other reform journals supported vegetarianism.[156]

The newcomer, the *Vegetarian Messenger*, was funded by James Simpson.[157] It began as a plain production. Artistic sensibility was not to emerge until the 1880s. It was similar to the *Advocate* in its essays on aspects of vegetarianism and broader reform concerns. There was a correspondence page, reports of local and annual meetings, and a supplement.

In addition, in 1851-52 the VS published two ha'penny periodicals *The Vegetarian Controversialist* and *Vegetarian Treasury*.[158] Circulation in 1854 was *c*.21,000 copies independent of copies for friends and booksellers. Following Simpson's death, in December 1859 it ceased and the VS hired four pages in Horsell's *Journal of Health* and planned to disseminate stock of old volumes and Prize Essays.[159] The preferred situation, the possession of a distinct journal, was reached in 1860 with a new quarterly, the *Dietetic Reformer*, which subtitled its concerns as 'temperance, long-life, happiness, humanity, thrift, health, plenty, peace, love'. Its first number had a print run of 'more than 800' and 100 of the second number were sent to prominent papers and magazines. The leading temperance publisher William Tweedie offered to publish it in 1863.[160] Some 6000 copies in stock in 1871 show that sales were below expectation.[161] Yet the journal survived, if not thrived. 12,000 copies were despatched from October 1883 – January 1884, indicating a monthly circulation of 3000.[162] Despite revamping the cover, in 1884 any suggestion of coloured paper or ink was rejected as too expensive and probably the stimulus of the London vegetarians was required to make the journal more attractive.[163] It was renamed *Vegetarian Messenger* in 1887 and briefly added '*and Review*' in 1898 during a short-lived amalgamation with the London movement's *Vegetarian Review*.[164]

FIGURE 20. Front cover, *Vegetarian Messenger*, August 1898.

Press comment about the journal was rare though the appreciative remarks by two Irish papers in 1862 have been mentioned earlier. A few letters indicate readers' attitudes. In 1862, a teetotal schoolmaster who had read an advertisement for it in Pitman's *Co-operator* – and who had previously viewed vegetarianism as 'a sort of safety-valve, by means of which a number of peculiar individuals allowed their eccentricity to find vent' – was persuaded by the paper's *wit, talent* and *logic*.[165] Another vegetarian (the architect William Larner Sugden), produced a handbill advertising the journal along with other 'progressive literature', including the *Secular Chronicle, Republican Herald, Labour Union Chronicle* and *Women's Suffrage Journal*.[166]

The range and diversity of vegetarian serial literature expanded in the late 1870s as the movement revived, with specialist publications such as annuals and children's papers. The London movement had its own serials and there were several other pro-vegetarian health reform journals. This development began in July 1875 when Thomas Low Nichols's penny monthly *The Herald of Health* was launched. In its first year it covered London's emerging food reform efforts and continued to cover vegetarianism in detail throughout its relatively long life.[167] It began as a four-page *Journal of Sanitary and Social Science* (a copy sent to the *Dietetic Reformer* elicited the understandable comment that there was 'hardly anything we dread more than the appearance of another journal').[168] Its initial circulation was mostly free, with over 50, 000 copies distributed in a month as Nichols appreciated the returns in terms of advertisements for his books, commodities and Institute.[169] Since there were already sanitary reform periodicals he stressed a more personal approach. The *Herald* was more concerned with individual health and less with the health of towns. Nichols hoped to alert people in the United Kingdom and, if possible, the English-speaking world, to health as the 'solid basis of all genuine reform and true progress in man and society'.[170]

He was candid about the puffery involved: 'The more a man believes he can benefit his fellows, the more personal he becomes.'[171] Nichols's earnestness took the form of articles on such subjects as esoteric anthropology (the title of his famous sexual health manual), hydropathy, Count Rumford's reforms, cataracts and consumption, national food supply, vaccination, and political subjects such as female suffrage. His column answering medical inquiries probably provided the example for Allinson's correspondence column in the *Weekly Times and Echo*. In the first year circulation reached 20,000 – 60,000 and he estimated the true readership at five times that figure.[172] With the formation of a public company the *Herald* was put on a paying basis, but his hope to make it a weekly was unrealized.[173] The *Norwich Argus* described the *Herald* as full of nostrums of all sorts: 'Everything that is, is bad, and can only be made better by entrusting the body and soul, to Dr Nichols and Mrs Nichols. Those who like extremes will find this journal to their taste, for a more extreme production we never met with.' By contrast the Scottish *Christian Leader* described it as a 'lively health paper, full of bright, crisp sayings'.[174]

On Nichols's retirement the journal was continued by his publisher, James Salsbury and edited by Forward.[175] From May 1890 after Salsbury's 'repeated and earnest request' it was edited and published by Chandos Wallace, who made it the organ for the 'Wallace System of Therapeutics' and her husband's 'Physical Regeneration Society'. Alex Owen has wrongly described her *Herald* as devoted exclusively to dietary matters with the dropping of 'Sanitary and Social Science' from the title, because it remained eclectic (though concerned largely with health). In taking it over, as Wallace wrote to Salsbury, she intended it to be profitable and not merely philanthropic; if it was worth reading, it was worth its cost: 'I will see that it shall be indispensable to every household that has once given it an entrance.'[176] Like Nichols, Wallace harboured ambitions for a weekly paper. The *Herald*'s coverage of the various *antis*, anti-vaccination, anti-vivisection and anti-tobacco, continued. It became the *Women's Vegetarian Union*'s official paper in 1897. Its tone, even in the serialized fiction by Wallace and others, was earnest.[177] One story, *Mary Jane's Experience among the Vegetarians*, was illustrated by Jack Yeats.[178]

Several other metropolitan journals competed in this crowded market. One motive was individual eccentricity, as in the case of Groom Napier's short-lived quarterly *Burlington House*, which represented his food reform society around 1878.[179] There were numerous self-penned articles on vegetarianism, as a solution to trade depression, strikes, as a way of accumulating wealth, as a cure for consumption, and the answer to the 'Threatened Supremacy' of vegetarian Chinese workmen.[180] Another, more rational journal, was the LFRS/NFRS's high-class quarterly *Food Reform Magazine* (1881-85), which expressed its ambitions by a series of lithographs of food reformers, beginning with Sylvester Graham. The periodical contained essays and verse, and reported the society's administration and activity. Contributors included the brothers-in-law Henry Salt and James Joynes, and Anna Kingsford. The domestic readership was 'several thousands', with subscriptions from the USA, Africa, India, Russia, Germany, France and Switzerland.[181]

Edward Curtice, a temperance publisher and Good Templar, planned another journal but it was the leader of the London movement, Arnold F. Hills, who introduced the next journal after securing copyright and goodwill from Curtice. The penny weekly *Vegetarian* was produced from 1888 (continuing, less frequently, to 1921). Like others, he wished to make the movement more appealing, and conceived it as an 'Independent journal' to be published 'under a more comprehensive title' than that of 'Vegetarian', but when it was launched it adopted the name.[182] Despite the title, it certainly reflected Hills's concern that vegetarianism should be recognized as a necessity to the 'ideal'. The prospectus announced its aim to be a 'radical, yet rational reformer, cutting at the roots of our national vices and sorrows, by breaking down the prejudices which protect them' and argued that food reform was directly related to problems of urban life such as overcrowding, lack of housing and food for the poor. These topics, and fashionable solutions such as resettlement of the unemployed in the 'natural home' of the countryside, figured in future issues. It was funded at a heavy loss by Hills, who responded to criticism of his mystical and idealist articles by emphasizing that the journal was not the LVS's official organ.[183] However, since he was the driving force behind London activity the distinction was slight; and the journal carried detailed reports of metropolitan and provincial campaigns. By 1895 it was accepted as the Vegetarian Federal Union's organ.[184]

The first year saw a serialization of Hills's story 'Sunshine or Shadow', a health column conducted by Dr Nichols, vegetarian and temperance biography, a series by Professor J.E.B. Mayor on 'cognate reforms', vegetarian tales from the East End (by Harry Phillips, illustrated by Jack Yeats) and an essay on 'Individual Liberty and State Compulsion' by the political philosopher and vegetarian, Auberon Herbert. There was a four-part study of Dr Barnardo's work (Barnardo was a contributor in 1892-93). Later, an interesting feature was Raymond Blathwayt's short series of interviews with celebrities.[185] There were sections devoted to women and children. Columns dealt with cookery, gardening, sports and even the theatre, art and legal inquiries. Political and social topics included land reform (and a controversy over the 'feudalism' of the countryside), old age pensions, trade unions and the McKinley Tariff. Some of these questions were represented in page-length cartoons by Sidney H. Sime and Jack Yeats.[186] There were even commissioned or reprinted short stories by Quiller-Couch, the Queen of Rumania and oddly, George Henty.[187] Not surprisingly, by 1891 it described itself as a 'general newspaper covering all topics which tend to benefit humanity' rather than a vegetarian paper.[188]

The journal was artistic, reflecting a transformation in publishing and London's more sophisticated aesthetic sensibility, also represented by highly decorative handbills and posters. The latter had their critics amongst LVS officers who condemned excessive ornamentation.[189] Preciousness also characterized an advertisement in the late 1890s, when the *Vegetarian* was advertised as gathering up the seeds that had been scattered by sages ever since the world began, and the jewels that were to be found embedded in every religion, and 'pointing to that Ideal Future when LIFE and PEACE shall be twin sisters through out all the world'.[190] The *Vegetarian* aimed at being eclectic and universal, promoting itself as 'a radical and rational reformer' with expert articles on agriculture, horticulture and fruit-culture.[191] It was 'a weapon both of attack and of defence ... every effort will be made to secure the best, the wisest, and the wittiest writers on behalf of the Reform advocated'.[192] It certainly gained recognition from the American *Universal Republic* as one of the world's leading reform papers and from the progressive *New Age* as 'spirited' and 'earnest'.[193] Even the critical *Fife Herald* acknowledged the paper was 'smartly' edited.[194] W.H. Smith's reported increasing orders in 1898.[195]

Since the *Vegetarian* aimed to demonstrate a 'many-sided Liberalism' on all current issues it necessitated a certain tolerance and/or selectivity by readers. Some clearly misunderstood its founder's intentions. One critic wrote that it was 'hardly the proper medium in which to discuss advanced social and political questions', though this was because it had readers of 'so many different shades of politics' who might be driven to throw the journal on the fire.[196] By contrast a shop assistant, at a time of labour unrest and debate on working hours, asked the *Vegetarian* to take a position on political matters.[197] A clerk in a large store wrote to show his appreciation of an article by Tolstoy and report the favour the journal found at home; *despite* articles which questioned the 'necessity of death' he was now circulating copies.[198] Another reader found it worthwhile to divide the *Vegetarian* according to the temperament of his correspondents (sending out sections on health and beauty to his daughter).[199] The Anglican clergyman Alfred Bodington had to remove 'eccentric' articles discussing nudism 'before venturing to circulate your otherwise admirable as well as bright and sparkling "weekly" '. Another reader referred to the paper's 'peculiar class of literary matter in its pages, ranging from agnosticism to the doings of ladies who have figured prominently in the divorce courts'. Whilst some ultra-puritans were concerned about theatre reviews, others praised its moral tone, 'markedly its own, and differing greatly from the common order of "New Journalism" '.[200]

There were attempts to bring some financial viability to reform publications including vegetarian journals, through the profit-sharing limited company called the 'Ideal Publishing Union'.[201] It attempted what may be described as a 'humanitarian *Strand Magazine*', but the budget and talent were too limited to make the venture successful.[202] In 1898 the Union acquired the 'National Temperance Depôt', in order to extend its value as an educational agency for the temperance movement in general.[203] But outside the Union, proliferation continued. In the 1880s Allinsonians produced the *Weekly Star and Romeike's Register of Houses, Apartments etc.*, which became the *Weekly Star and Vegetarian Restaurant Gazette*.[204] It featured articles by Allinson, coverage of his 'Natural Living Society', letters of inquiry on health, recipes, articles on Edward Bellamy's utopian novel *Looking Backwards*, and notes on the various 'anti' concerns. The *Hygienic Advertiser* (1891-92), a monthly owned by Ernest May, printed by the New Fellowship Press and devoted to 'Natural Living, Physical Culture, Health Reform etc., etc.,' stepped in to take its place when it failed and promoted the activity of Allinson's society, without being its official organ. Renamed the *Hygienic Adviser* to correct the impression it was a commercial venture, columns offered health advice on aspects of natural living such as reformed dress, fresh air, swimming and anti-vaccination, and news on the NLS. It endorsed phrenology and Ida Ellis's 'Universal Phrenology Society'. A biography of the vegetarian Positivist, William Frey, was serialized. It advertised the Humanitarian League, Free Russia cause (starting an appeal for Russian famine victims) and *Malthusian Advertiser*.[205] The *Hastings News* fairly assessed it as having 'a great deal of the American style of gross exaggeration in some of the "fad" portions of the little pamphlet', but was appreciative and other favourable notices came from the *Charity Record*, *Belfast Morning News* and other provincial papers. *The Vegetarian* thought it had the appearance of a quack medicine almanac and simply promoted its proprietor.[206] The journal briefly continued after May's split with Allinson.

Journals advocating food reform were relatively common by the 1890s, for example, Daniel Kress's *Life and Health*. Kress had worked at Kellogg's vegetarian sanatorium at Battle Creek in Michigan and Kellogg penned the journal's first article.[207] Another was Burns's *Vegetarian Advocate* from 1890, a ½d monthly that carried a great deal of material and was given out free at open-air meetings.[208] Yet more specialist journals existed, stimulated by the existence of groups with their own slant on vegetarianism. Richardson's *Danielite Herald* was published in shorthand from September 1878; in 1900 he claimed it was the 'oldest shorthand ever-circulator'.[209] The *Danielite Star* (1887-1931), its masthead the Hebrew 'Danielim' surrounded by rays, and modelled on the Anti-Tobacco Society's *Monthly Letter*, was for scattered Danielites. *The Herald of the Golden Age* (1896-1918), was the Order's smartly-produced and illustrated penny monthly and from 1897 the Scottish Vegetarian Society's official monthly. It advertised itself as advocating hygienic common-sense, practical Christianity and social reform; and claimed to circulate in twenty countries and colonies, including New Zealand, West Australia and India.[210] Articles were penned by members such as Pengelly, Forward and Oldfield, and other vegetarians such as the novelist Mona Caird and J. Howard Moore of Chicago. Many illustrations were by Charles Dawson, a designer of 'rational' (i.e., reformed) costumes and covers for several other reform journals.[211] Advertisements appeared for similar 'moral reform' journals like the American *Esoteric*, *World's Advanced Thought*, *Theosophical Review*, and probably for its Tolstoyan connections, the *Anglo-Russian*.

In addition, there were specialist serials such as annuals, almanacs, yearbooks and juvenile literature. *Almonds and Raisins* (1882-88) was the VS's Christmas annual, its second editor, Beatrice Lindsay, emphasized its function was encouragement and exhortation, not amusement. The Irishman John S. Herron produced an illustrated *Vegetarian Almanack* for over two decades from 1879, containing poetry, essays, vegetarian news, recipes, publication notices and obituaries.

FIGURE 21. *Left*: front cover, *Almonds and Raisins. The Vegetarian Society Annual for 1888*; and *right*: front cover of *The Herald of the Golden Age*, 1897.

Also offering recipes and articles was the *Apple Tree Annual* (1886-*c*.1891) produced by the restaurateur Glendinning. The 1891 edition sold 30,000 copies, and contained recipes and articles which were 'broad and enlightened'. Issued first in 1889 the VFU's *Vegetarian Yearbook* provided biographies, polemics, portraits, dietary advice, interesting facts, directories of restaurants and hotels, calendar and publications for the vegetarian.[212] Children became an important target audience. In 1893-94, the attractively produced but pious *Daisy Basket* was published for the children's 'Daisy Society'.[213] Conducted by 'Uncle' Joseph Knight, this incorporated book reviews, correspondence, short stories and verse; but the limited pool of correspondents emphasizes the Daisy Society's small size. This was followed by Frances Boult's *Rainbow*, and, in the Edwardian period, her *Children's Garden*. This reported the activity of her juvenile Ivy Leaf society and featured vegetarian children and their families, to be succeeded in 1906 by *The Children's Realm*, conducted by George Bedborough, who had gained notoriety as editor of *The Adult*, a pioneer sexological journal.[214]

Who consumed these journals and where could they be found? They were partly a standard propagandist tool to win converts to a cause; other movements had their 'organ', subsidized by a few wealthy members who also enabled the sending of gratuitous copies to mechanics' institutes, mutual improvement clubs and other institutions. Vegetarian articles were reprinted as tracts and the message also spread through letter 'wafers', charts, and posters.[215] These were sold at the societies' depôts and alongside other 'forward' publications by provincial agents. Henry Cook in Bristol sold them with titles such as the *Progressionist, Working Man's Friend, Cooper's Journal,* and *Medical Journal*.[216] The leading liberal Glaswegian bookseller and Thomas Cook of Leicester were agents for the *Vegetarian Advocate*; William Bremner the *Vegetarian Messenger*'s Manchester publisher (a vegetarian) retailed literature on 'religious, temperance, peace and kindred subjects'.[217] At the end of the century a Christian Scientist at Devonport sold American esoteric journals and literature on 'metaphysics, divine science, mental science, vegetarianism, and reform in religion, business, medicine and food'. He advertised in the vegetarian Joseph Edward's *Labour Annual*, which detailed the vegetarian press as part of the social reform world.[218] We have also seen that some vegetarian restaurants disseminated literature.

Since James Simpson financed distribution of journals to mechanics' institutes, literary institutions and libraries across Britain, it was not always necessary to purchase a copy to follow the early movement's activities.[219] The *Messenger's* first editors hoped members would circulate it amongst religious and philanthropic societies, and called for lists of volunteers for such work. Earnest vegetarians – like the schoolmaster in Wrexham in 1873 (not a Society member), who had his bookseller display copies – circulated old issues and subscribed for several numbers.[220] Later, 'XYZ' in 1889 framed assorted vegetarian literature outside his shop under the title 'health and wealth'.[221] Sometimes response to this literature was hostile. One Church Guild and Young Men's Institute's copy of the *Herald of the Golden Age* was removed and torn up by several butchers in the choir.[222] Although the chief of the Young Women's Christian Association approved of copies of the *Herald* in reading rooms, the Beckenham secretary banned copies.²²³

Forward, an editor of several vegetarian journals, deplored reform papers' *outlandish* names. The English feared the 'faddist' label and who would buy a journal entitled 'The Hyperborean' or 'Transcendentalist' for a train journey?²²⁴ If vegetarians sometimes gloried in their faddist reputation, letters reveal readers' recognition of the reputation of their cause in the *unreformed* world and their occasional pique when additional pet fads were criticized. Others, posing as purely *rational* food reformers, were dismayed when things got too 'faddist' or too 'progressive'. This was particularly the case with the late-nineteenth-century weekly, *The Vegetarian*, produced in London.

For some enthusiasts, buying a journal was insufficient. They produced their own. From the 1840s phonographic (shorthand) and phonetic 'ever-circulators' allowed small groups to discuss pet reforms through their own little magazines. The VS operated a circulator for local secretaries in 1854; and vegetarianism was the subject of another circulator.²²⁵ A shorthand *Vegetarian Herald* with a minute circulation was produced by the shorthand expert Richard Sheldrick, whilst two vegetarian youths, Harvey of Andover in the mid-1880s and Walter Godfrey in the late 1890s, produced their own quarterlies.²²⁶ There were also journals which were planned but never produced, such as *Grub*, to be edited by Bernard Shaw and the monthly magazine, *The Servant of the Age*, to be produced by a Crimean veteran and butler, E.N. Radford of Somerset, for workers in temperance, vegetarianism and social purity.²²⁷

Success was always unlikely. Horsell had suffered the pioneer's fate but his later progressive journals of the 1850s also failed. The movement's small scale and the fragmenting nature of food reform, with its rival centres and schools in the late nineteenth century, meant that the few enduring vegetarian journals made no profit (especially with their free copies for public institutions). Their protagonists' commitment meant that, in the context of generally unprofitable and frequently short-lived reform periodicals, the *Vegetarian Messenger*, *Vegetarian*, and *Herald of Health* survived for a relatively long period.²²⁸ The vegetarian butler's projected journal for servants, bizarre though it was, reflects the reformers' fervour. Since the more 'broad' food reform periodicals struggled, this scheme was unlikely to succeed, but it raises again the question of the movement's class dimension. The next chapter begins by examining this question more closely.

6

CLASS, GENDER AND THE VEGETARIANS

Consideration of 'class' offers an important dimension to the vegetarian debate. Thinking about 'class' partly means identifying the movement's social location but it is also involves attending to how vegetarian propaganda for vegetarians spoke to the public and themselves as 'classes' as well as in terms of individuals or society. Whatever qualms some historians now have about the concept of 'classes' in this period vegetarians and their public thought it meaningful to relate support to social background. Although they asserted that all classes of men and women would benefit, from manual labourer and office worker to aristocrat, the level of working-class support for the reform is considered more closely here. In this chapter, explanations are offered for the failure of the movement's efforts to attract working people in general. Its food-thrift propaganda positioned vegetarianism as a form of self-help pertinent to their needs or aspirations but it also implicated vegetarianism in middle-class philanthropy, with potentially damaging consequences, especially when it was recommended as a dietary for institutions such as workhouses. [1] Abstinence from animal foods for economic reasons brought such propagandists into disagreement with labour and socialist organizations in the late-Victorian period; but the relationship with socialism that forms another theme in this chapter was more complex than straightforward rivalry and conflict.

The vegetarian societies claimed to represent all classes and appealed to both genders, and the second section of this chapter explores gender. One direct way in which the cause could be presented in female guise was iconographic. When late-Victorian vegetarians in London chose to depict their cause on the covers of journals, the alternatives seemed to be either a feminine-looking angel, or a healthy English woman (not *déshabillé* like her Dutch sister in the journal *Vegetarische Bode*). Beyond imagery, we have already glimpsed female involvement in the cause, before the VS, and in the early London movement, and in vegetarianism's relationship with spiritualism and the esoteric. This section studies in detail female participation throughout the period and its implications for the movement. In particular, the hitherto obscure Women's Vegetarian Union is investigated. Its leading members, activity, and place in the movement are examined and its links to a wider and rich feminist culture in the 1890s are identified.[2] This appraisal of women's roles is preceded by a brief consideration of the 'natural' link between the feminine and vegetarianism.

Mapping the social base of the movement

Samuel Brown's essay on physical puritanism in 1852 alluded to support amongst his middle-class and upper middle-class acquaintances. Nearly half a century later, vegetarian journals were clearly struck by the novelty of 'vegetarianism in Mayfair'. In the *fin de siècle*, the social elite's acquaintance with vegetarianism was also manifested by debates at the Oxford Union and Eton College (where a majority of two were in favour of it).[3] Yet Francis Newman had privately observed in 1885 that 'the Aristocracy will be humiliated politically more quickly than they will consent to forego Fleshmeat and killing beautiful birds': at least for radicals the aristocracy's treatment of animals was comprised of exploitation and cruelty.[4]

Typically the social location of affiliated vegetarians was humbler: the movement was essentially middle-class and upper working-class. If the *Daily News* of late 1855 therefore erred in its belief that the movement was comprised of a few hundred 'working men', they were certainly avidly courted from the start.[5] In London, for instance, George Dornbusch's private meetings were intended for working men, and the Liverpool association held a soirée to demonstrate the cheapness and plenty to the working-class. Audiences were described as 'respectable', suggesting that early vegetarians were preaching to the already converted self-improvers. The Society's statistics (publicizing the diet's relevance for all classes and occupations) indicated the importance of working-class support in the pre-1859 period but made no distinction between labourer, mechanic and tradesman, in order to emphasize the movement's popular appeal.[6]

Plebeians who combined self-reform and social reform, such as Perkin the forge-labourer, were undoubtedly attracted to the new movement. Vegetarian from 1849, he asserted that the diet allowed him to survive in a dangerous and laborious (12-14 hours daily work) trade and still have time for mental culture. Another working-class supporter was Nathaniel Griffin, whose presence on the platform as a representative 'independent working man' indicates the limited pool of suitable labourers for early propagandists.[7] The 'independent working man' and the self-made man continued to figure in propaganda. The anonymous subject of Charles Groom Napier's well-publicized 'Autobiography' rightly thought he should be an 'appendix to Smiles's *Self Help*'.[8]

In the later-Victorian period the occupations of new members of the senior society were published, allowing a detailed occupational profile of the movement. This information suggests (as it was intended to) a movement with wide-ranging appeal. There was no doubt a desire to record plebeian voices but these were uncommon. The rare statements on the class appeal of vegetarianism, such as those published in the *Vegetarian* from provincial secretaries in 1898, indicate that the most responsive were the 'upper working class and middle classes', and not, as the *Herald of Health* claimed in March 1890, the 'sons of toil'. Twigg presents the vegetarianism of the late nineteenth century as somewhat more middle-class than in its earlier days, attracting the support of a new metropolitan white-collar population (the key users of the vegetarian restaurants) rather than 'labour', but the plebeian support in the earlier period should not be overstated.[9]

How should this prominence by the middle and lower middle classes, which was not limited to the British movement, be explained? There are mono-causal explanations for their involvement such as the need to assert self-control in order to maintain a precarious social position, or re-directed social guilt (as in explanations of zoophilia). Although there may have been an element of keeping up appearances through a vegetarian gloss on poverty, and although self-help for the upwardly mobile or precariously 'respectable', and charitable provision for the poor were important aspects to propaganda (as we shall see shortly), the movement cannot be reduced to an alleviation of bourgeois anxieties or (as discussed already) a servicing of capitalist needs. It may be, as argued in the context of German life reforms, that vegetarianism addressed middle-class fears of failure in relationships and careers, by restoring a sense of agency to the individual whose body might be reformed though other aspects of life such as employment could not be; a creed of self-restraint marked off the vegetarian from aristocratic or plebeian members of the irresponsible classes.[10] But non-material aspects to physical puritanism must not be neglected. Furthermore, there were good practical reasons for the relative prominence of the middle class in the official membership. Their income and leisure time allowed access to vegetarian materials and permitted sustained participation and activism.

The appeal to working people

In the 1860s the VS's annual reports expressed the opinion that 'exceptional prosperity' was inimical to the cause.[11] Vegetarians throughout the period appreciated the enhanced opportunities offered by economic hardship and seasonal unemployment for demonstrating the practical benefits to vegetarianism.[12] Such philanthropic work won vegetarians a measure of public support. In the late nineteenth century this dimension to vegetarian propaganda was expressed in a National Food Supply Association (1893) which, stimulated by the example of Henry L.J. Jones's efforts in Liverpool, combined London vegetarians with the Bread Reform League in the provision of hot food from metropolitan depôts.[13]

The ambitious and enthusiastic world of metropolitan vegetarianism in this period attempted to attract working-class interest. If the Ideal Club catered for the 'common soldiers' in the ranks of labour, their unemployed members were also targeted. Arnold Hills was a paternalist greatly interested in industrial and social problems and spent several years studying his employees by living above his office in Canning Town, in order to improve working conditions and workers. The Ironworks had a hall for entertainment and lectures on temperance, vegetarianism and purity, and a Dramatic Company used in vegetarian missions. But one such mission in Canning Town in 1888, involving displays, electric lighting and flags, only half-filled a marquee.

FIGURE 22. Unemployed workers given work (and vegetarian food) by Arnold Frank Hills. *Vegetarian*, 3 December 1898.

Hills also linked vegetarianism with agricultural work through an 'Unemployed Farm' at Billericay. In the decades of dockers' and match girls' strikes, Salvation Army crusades, settlements and sociological investigation, Hills and others sought to link food reform to fears about poverty and unemployment, fears that found their symbolic expression in the East End. The *Vegetarian* discussed General Booth's *In Darkest England and the Way Out* and reported activity (cookery classes, dinners and efforts to form a society) in the East End.[14]

There were certainly serious attempts to reach out to 'workers'. Partly this was done through lectures, demonstrations and latterly the 'van'. If the 'vegetarian press' in the late nineteenth century *was* predominantly middle-class/lower middle-class in tone and readership (judging from correspondents), the working-class papers owned by the philanthropist and sometime vegetarian John Passmore Edwards purveyed vegetarian wisdom. The *Weekly Times and Echo* featured Dr Allinson's medical column, correspondence, and paragraphs on the vegetarian movement.[15] Allinson noted 'a lot of signal men, tailors, etc ...' inquired about his hygienic system.[16] The *English Mechanic* also featured inquiries.[17]

Efforts to convert working people had to confront some powerful prejudices. Plebeian vegetarians like Perkin knew that most Britons (and not simply the oft-stressed Irish and Scots) were largely vegetarian of *necessity*. At the same time, vegetarians had to combat a general desire for a mixed diet in which butcher's meat was more than a mere flavouring. Association of material advancement with a more frequent consumption of animal foods was something that had to be faced. Eleanor Orlebar, a middle-class writer interested in the food question as a result of William Gibson Ward's vegetarian letters in *The Times*, asked her maid what her family ate and was told 'Why beef and mutton, ma'am, every day! Working people *want* their meat.' If servants were an important occupational group for middle-class vegetarians to convert, the importance of winning over manual workers to the practicality of vegetarianism was also appreciated.[18] Unfortunately, not only did most Britons believe a mixed diet was best-suited to the climate, but conventional wisdom assumed that hard physical work required a mixed diet, and workers appreciated the value of animal foods as a source of energy.[19]

Frustration at working men and women's lack of interest in the movement was explained as 'stupidity' by Anna Kingsford: 'you cannot hammer anything into their minds. They have an idea that there is a certain fund of strength in meat which they cannot get out of anything else'. For her, it was chiefly the middle classes that would comprehend and sympathize with the movement since the poor were too ignorant and the rich were too self-indulgent.[20] The inability to remove such dietetic errors from working-class minds was emphasized too by the temperance physician Dr Norman Kerr, who said that they were convinced porridge was 'cheap and nasty', by Dr Alfred Crespi who condemned plebeian provisioning and cookery as 'laziness', and by one discouraged vegetarian who described the working man as a natural conservative in diet, addicted to beef, beer and bacca. Even the plebeian James Burns deplored the 'perverted' and 'fastidious' tastes of the near-destitute.[21]

But apart from dietetic prejudice and sheer ignorance about the movement,[22] there were economic barriers to the diet which were too often ignored. Low demand for vegetarian specialities meant high prices or lack of supply, whether for wholemeal flour (flour-mills were an additional expense) or for exotic items such as lentils.[23] Henry Mayhew noted that fruit was bought by 'clerks, shopmen, small tradesmen, and the children of mechanics of the lower grade of middle class people', fruit and vegetables remained too expensive for poor Londoners to afford at the end of the century.[24] Recipes could be too elaborate, and thus, ironically, suggest an expensive dietary.[25] Even if they were not elaborate, soups or broths which vegetarians (and others) advertised as aids to the poor, took too long to cook.[26] Experimentalists found the diet was not necessarily as economical in money or time as propagandists repeatedly claimed.

Lack of supply was not just an urban problem; as farmers saved their crops for the market these might be more expensive in the countryside.[27] It has been seen how limited organized vegetarianism was in rural districts. If London vegetarians were careful to relate their cause to the problems of modern urban living, much late-Victorian propaganda also suggested that problems of agricultural depression, poverty and depopulation were to be solved by vegetarianism, fruit growing and colonies. Vegetarianism was cast as 'patriotic' and the labourer's friend. The fact that the active vegetarian William Gibson Ward was a trustee of the National Agricultural Labourers' Union helped make this slightly more plausible. Land reform was another agitation to make connections with, as the London vegetarians' land reform conferences demonstrated.[28]

Vegetarian concerns were part of a wider interference by the middle classes with the diet of the 'poorer classes', represented by hundreds of tracts for them, and essays or conference papers discussing their inadequate domestic cookery (though middle-class cookery was, as in the wider world of domestic science, also condemned).[29] Food-thrift as a means of survival on low wages or during unemployment, as well as a means of social advancement, was another aspect to the vegetarian movement. But this was not simply directed to the working class: a thrift message obviously attracted the 'shabby genteel' and the new male and female office workers too.[30] This aspect, now absent from much western vegetarian propaganda, is reflected in the NFRS's association with the National Thrift Society whose secretary believed that when food reform was 'connected with economy, and the connection is by no means a slight one, so far does it legitimately come within the range of the Thrift Society to advocate'.[31] And vegetarians believed that it was the economic aspect ('breeches pocket Vegetarianism'[32]) rather than the 'sentimental' which would appeal to the working classes: there was little talk of zoophilia and non-dietary aspects, in the literature directed to men and women conceived as 'working people'.[33]

Vegetarians were keen to ground their cause, in part at least, in economy, whether individual or national (since it could be related to concerns about food supply and defence).[34] Chester's society was unusual in being a Food Thrift Association but a number of tracts clearly identified the diet with individual economy; others advocated the diet for prison (therefore, ironically, answering the outrage of those who pointed to prison fare being more generous than that obtained by the decent and honest poor), school and workhouse.[35] One orphanage was indeed run by J.W.C. Fegan on vegetarian lines in the 1880s.[36] A critic from within the movement equated such propaganda with 'a patent fire-stove that saves one-half the fuel, and calculations made as to what will produce the greatest amount of energy with the least expenditure of Food'.[37]

Vegetarianism and late-Victorian socialism and co-operation

Concerns about 'class' and the condition of labour were also expressed in the exchanges between vegetarianism and late-Victorian socialism and co-operation. In the 1890s vegetarian efforts to attract working-class support added Labour Churches, Social Democratic Federation meetings, Independent Labour Party halls and Women's Co-operative Guilds to traditional lower middle-class venues such as IOGT and YMCA groups.[38] In Blackpool Women's Co-operative Guild vegetarian principles 'found a place with many' and Padiham socialists reputedly showed 'much desire for knowledge'.[39]

The early vegetarians' associations with radical working-class politics have already been put in context, as earlier chapters in this study revealed links to Chartism, metropolitan secularism and millenarian and communitarian experiments. These links came to the fore in the late nineteenth century, when the *Labour Annual* counted vegetarian and temperance societies as part of a more general pro-labour reform movement. Certainly the areas of vegetarian growth in England (in the industrial north, especially Yorkshire, and around London) were strong areas for ILP. Other linkages are more individualistic. For some middle-class socialists (such as the Fabians) and working-class socialists vegetarianism was an important personal cause.[40] It has been seen as part of the 'bohemian influx' into socialism in the 1890s; one of the key 'personal panaceas' (along with reform of marriage, anti-vaccination, birth control and faith-healing) that the 'orthodox' members of the socialist movement had constantly to combat or keep in their proper place.[41] This sense of working-class political parties beleaguered by vegetarians and kindred reformers echoes Friedrich Engels' own observations about such 'honest fools', in the same period.[42]

One important leader of English socialism, Robert Blatchford, who became a vegetarian in 1905, was a member of the Humanitarian League's 'Humane Diet' department and reported the movement in his popular *Clarion* paper.[43] The Clarion movement had coffee-houses in the West Riding and a propaganda van which similarly inspired the VS to 'go out to the people'.[44] Margaret Sibthorp – associated with Joseph Edwards of the *Labour Annual* and Blatchford in the Humane Diet department – edited the feminist *Shafts* which was the clearest direct association of the 'working classes' with vegetarianism. Vegetarianism was part of the temperance and 'clean living' observed by many socialists. Tom Mann's vegetarianism has been noted before, but Keir Hardie's support is less well known.[45] Whilst the leader of the Marxist Social Democratic Federation (Henry Hyndman) famously lumped vegetarianism with 'humanitarians ... anti-vivisectionists and anti-vaccinationists, arty-craftys and all the rest of them', and felt it kept 'a lot of useless people alive'[46] it certainly appealed to ascetic socialists.[47] Indeed, it has been well argued that Hyndman's attack is unrepresentative of grassroots socialism in the SDF in this period, and that a distinction should be made between organizational hostility towards such reforms and the attitudes of individuals (as for instance, the Bolton journalist Allen Clarke[48]). The larger point is that there were various socialisms in this period, and those with ethical emphases or concerns about 'embodiment', were as much a part of the socialist movement as their ultimately more successful 'scientific forms'.[49]

The hostility in some socialist and 'progressive' quarters towards vegetarianism did force socialists such as Henry Salt into print to defend their cause from accusations of faddism, asceticism, and penny-pinching.[50] For, quite apart from the occasions when vegetarians promoted themselves as a prophylactic against socialism, vegetarians' proposition that their diet was cheaper generated controversy in the socialist and progressive press.[51] The NFRS was described as a combination to reduce wages and a tract addressed to working men suggested vegetarians were derided by the 'common man'.[52] Expressions of anxiety about wage levels as a result of dietetic economy became a common response to vegetarian lectures. In autumn 1885 vegetarianism was attacked on these grounds in the secularists' *National Reformer*. Correspondence in the organ of William Morris's Socialist League debated the 'Capitalistic Advantages of

Vegetarianism' in 1887,[53] and the *Clarion* in 1896 also condemned vegetarian economics.[54] Such suspicions were in keeping with Marx's own critique of capitalist schemes for worker abstinence.[55] Vegetarianism was debated in other organs of the labour movement, though not necessarily rejected. Michael Davitt's *Labour World*, for instance, aired pro-vegetarian comments through its serialization of John M. Davidson's *The Book of Labour*, its health notes and recipes for 'Women Workers'.[56]

How the vegetarian journals responded to the struggles of organized labour in this period is important. The VS's journal avoided any party political tone (whilst clearly falling within the Liberal pale). Avowedly 'not Socialist, Individualist etc ... But Vegetarian' it was with some discomfort that it published the socialist clerk Walkden's anti-capitalist letters which promoted land cultivation as the future of vegetarianism.[57] On the other hand, the hostility from some British socialist quarters led the *Vegetarian Messenger* to stress the sympathy of a *Greek* socialist paper.[58] The *Vegetarian* was more outspoken in its politics, even emulating satirical magazines in its full-page cartoons on current affairs. It posed as a balanced paper critical of 'capitalist or unionist when either transgresses the rules of justice', and whilst it printed letters from exhausted shop assistants it debated individualism *vs.* socialism.[59] More radical vegetarian associations were expressed in the *Weekly Times and Echo*, *Shafts*, the Tolstoyan *Seed-time* and Andreas Gottschling's similar 'little journal', *Home Links*.[60]

Whilst the journals reported, supported or condemned the struggles of labour, some vegetarian groups were actively pro-labour. Financial support for the striking London dockers in 1889 was organized by the Allinsonian Natural Living Society.[61] Allinson also encouraged working-class co-operative vegetarian provision. It is well known that several early co-operators were vegetarian. Henry Pitman's *Co-operator* supported vegetarianism. In the 1880s a leading co-operator, Mary Lawrenson, trod the vegetarian platform and the *Co-operative News* printed vegetarian letters and recipes. A few co-operative societies supported vegetarian work.[62] The Hygienic Co-operative Society, established at the vegetarian 'Central Restaurant' in 1888, was another manifestation of working-class support. Its formation followed suggestions by Gottschling in the *Weekly Times*. He declared that as much as he valued vegetarianism, temperance, and other great movements, 'yet all these put together are but calculated to culminate in that great object of co-operation'. Vegetarianism would benefit because co-operative retail made vegetarian foods cheaper.[63] Unfortunately, as critics warned, vegetarian co-operators were too sparse and scattered to develop the society beyond a narrow metropolitan location, though Alderman Phillips was reported to be interest in establishing an East End branch. Allinson chaired an early meeting and a campaign was planned to spread the message of 'hygienic co-operation'.⁶⁴ Support also came from Mrs Allinson and other women, including the president of Chelsea Women's Co-operative Guild, Mrs Benjamin Jones. The society grew to 115 members, with £116 raised by the sale of shares. By March 1889 a land reformer John Barry O'Callaghan was president.⁶⁵ The secretary was Isidore Phillips, who had been scandalized at 'penny a day' arguments peddled by one vegetarian lecturer (William Manning, something of a liability for vegetarian propaganda).⁶⁶ Other officers included Peter Newbould, a prominent temperance worker and member of the South East London VS, and W.H. Sullivan, president of the vegetarian Rambling Society. It transformed itself into a 'Co-operative Food Reform Store' selling 'pure, unadulterated vegetarian and other foods and articles'. The premise of the store was sensible, but the demand was too limited and in late 1889 it merged with the Socialist Co-operative Federation Ltd.⁶⁷

If a desultory end to vegetarian experiment was not limited to such working-class efforts as the vegetarian co-operative, clearly working-class lack of time and money presented a greater barrier to success. These practical problems would limit the appeal of the movement in the absence of cheap, attractive and easily prepared foods. Added to this was the failure to persuade the general public that their dietetic prejudices (like those of the medical profession) in favour of a mixed diet were wrong. It was noted in the Introduction, how interference in working-class diet could be treated as an attack on the rights of the freeborn Englishman, or an erosion of the duties of parents. It could also smack of charity, thus the association of vegetarian messes with soup-philanthropy and institutional dietaries harmed the appeal to working people. Yet it was strategically and morally important to win the support of the labouring man, so the struggle to win this was never abandoned. Equally important, the movement needed to appeal to that wider category of toiler, women. Their role in the movement, always significant but increasingly documented and elaborated as the movement developed, is next examined.

Gender and the Movement

Whilst the movement had diverse politico-economic, religious, animal-welfare and health implications, and a public status through propaganda and restaurants, as a matter of diet and dining and as health reform, it was, by contrast with the issue of class, essentially *domestic*. Indeed the *Vegetarian* asserted it was 'essentially based upon the home and home life'. This sphere, if not simply a feminine one, largely concerned women and so their responses were an important concern for vegetarians. Domestic reform was one area where women were indeed encouraged by men to lead, emphasizing differentiated gender roles. That eminently 'Victorian' figure Samuel Smiles, no less, emphasized the importance for 'all true female reformers' of the 'unaccountably neglected' question of improved food preparation and economizing in his best-selling *Character*.[68] The wider non-vegetarian food reform movements that tackled questions of 'domestic science' such as standards of cooking, the provision of fuel and utensils, involved women as targets and agents of reforms presented as central to the health of the nation. Household management belonged 'naturally' to women, though the most famous manual of domestic economy, Isabella Beeton's *Household Management*, initially rejected vegetarianism as offering inadequate nourishment.[69]

In modern times, when a significant proportion of vegetarians are women, a connection between feminism and vegetarianism is recognized. The association has been touched on by Twigg, has surfaced in discussion of late-Victorian British and Irish feminism and in the context of Edwardian suffragettes, and is the thesis of Carol Adams' polemical *Sexual Politics of Meat*.[70] The identification of women with animals as victims of male cruelty,[71] the idea that housewives could create a new moral world through dietetic reform, and vegetarianism's association with other purity campaigns, have been discussed before as explanations for female involvement in vegetarianism.

It was therefore 'natural' given cultural norms, for vegetarians to argue that true femininity and women's aptitudes were consonant with their cause. But if a connection between it and femininity are claimed by modern apologists, the activities of female British vegetarians have received little attention. Adams' study is sketchy on British vegetarianism, and her enthusiastic identification of a feminist-vegetarian literary and historical tradition is demonstrated largely through American examples. Her claim that vegetarianism was 'an integral part of autonomous female identity' needs to be grounded in more detailed study of the British movement.

Women and the early movement

Female support for vegetarianism was not, despite the impression conveyed by some historians, a new phenomenon of the *fin de siècle*.[72] Women had been important in the Cowherdite sect and their significant contribution to the Concordium has been examined.[73] The strong-minded and 'coming woman' who seemed to be heralded by American imports such as Bloomerism and female lecturers in the 1850s, was recognized as including vegetarianism, and cartoons of early vegetarians did include women.[74] The role that women played in the early movement was important, but unfortunately their documentary presence is fugitive. We can glimpse some of this activity through the London Association, which had a ladies' committee that included Elizabeth Horsell, author of a cookery book and an occasional lecturer on vegetarianism outside London.[75] Another important member was the artist Jane Hurlstone, who supported Owenism, animal welfare and Italian nationalism.[76]

So significant was the female role that although it was generally overshadowed by male activity, one contributor to the *Vegetarian Advocate* felt:

> that if the men were only *half as much* in earnest about the business as are the ladies of the Vegetarian Society, and went about the work, as if they meant *doing* it, instead of talking about and telling others to do it, we should long ago have escaped from the wilderness which lies between Egypt and Canaan ... [77]

This is an important statement given the impression conveyed by the frequent complaints in vegetarian journals of female resistance.[78] The VS's secretary complained that wives failed to join their husbands as members and interpreted this as the result of sensuality or a serious neglect of husbandly 'duty'.[79] The reform required 'favours of others' rather than mere abstinence and was therefore vulnerable to 'household opponents'.[80] Fictional representations of vegetarians touched on the power of women to 'drag' idealistic spouses down.[81] But as one woman observed, male willingness to adopt vegetarianism was possible because of ignorance of cookery and blindness to all but the 'economy of the system': men did not appreciate the problems that could ensue.[82] On the other hand, it must have been the case that many were converted through female advocacy in the family circle, although published references are rare.[83] Statistics from 1866 suggest that in this period when there were a total of 701 members, 22.5 per cent were female; but figures and names (published in the journals) are problematic since a husband's or parent's name *might* represent a household. Although this circumstance reflects the general condition of *coverture*, the ideal that vegetarians promoted was partnership.[84] Not surprisingly, the divisions that might be engendered by dietetic conversion were not dwelt on. The author and vegetarian Mrs C.W. Earle's statement that 'a united Vegetarian family I have never been fortunate enough to come across' was unusually candid.[85]

Vegetarians were urged to be 'unceasing' in their efforts to convert women to the new cause.[86] Then, and throughout our period, notions of femininity and domestic ideologies were exploited. In 1848 the *Vegetarian Advocate* printed a letter from a woman, then a rare circumstance; this asserted that feminine love and kindness found the 'most comprehensive interpreter in Vegetarianism' and that women were pivotal in 'making the domestic hearth a shrine of peace and happiness'.[87] More usually, such claims were made by men, such James Hibberd in 1851, who stressed the power of 'fireside reform', deployed conventional ideas about innate female kindness, and appealed to womanly 'refined feelings'. Almost forty years later, the spiritualist James Burns appealed to women 'possessed of domestic insight, refinement and womanly sympathy'.[88] A natural repugnance to meat on the part of young women was assumed by Francis Newman and identified by others.[89] Women's maternal role — their 'extensive influence on the present and future generations' — was stressed (with examples that included the mothers of James Simpson and the French poet and statesman Alphonse de Lamartine).[90] As the formation of the Maternity Society shows, the diet continued to be promoted as an aid to expectant and new mothers.[91] Liberation from the kitchen or gross culinary preparation was stressed, and the occasional feminist statement appeared.[92]

Women's cooking of dishes for public dinners, superintending of banquet tables, arranging of entertainment and presence as audience or dining partner were important contributions to the cause.[93] Their evident good health at the banquet at Freemasons' Tavern in 1851 was reported in the national press.[94] But it was rare outside London for women to address meetings and the penning of an essay by one was treated as a novelty in 1854.[95] A few were on local committees but never as leading officers. Absence from the public sphere in anything but a supporting role reflected contemporary social mores and the practice in other reform movements such as temperance; despite the fact that it could be seen as naturally a women's question.[96]

Given the concern to attract female support, it was obviously important to target propaganda. However, no tracts addressed women specifically and no lectures to female organizations are reported in this period. Of course, this did not mean that women were necessarily ignorant of the new reform. Vegetarianism would be known to female readers of *Punch*, *The Times* or other leading newspapers. Coverage in the local press and temperance organs brought the subject before them. The *Lady's Newspaper and Pictorial* even serialized an essay on vegetarianism, after publishing a profile of Simpson (with portrait) and the VS.[97]

Women and the later movement

Complaints about female intransigence continued through to the end of the century.[98] But at the same time, and reflecting developments in philanthropy and general social trends, women were far more prominent on the national and local platform. From the late 1860s, as the provincial movement was revived, local association officers included women, and they fulfilled important practical and honorific offices in the national societies. Though as late as 1895 the VS seems to have felt it a novelty to have a female chair a meeting, this was indicative of continued conservatism in some quarters, rather than a reflection of the true state of female participation.[99]

The VS membership included a sizeable proportion of women. As a percentage of the total of new recruits, female participation (excluding associates) in the period 1874-85 stood at 12.78 per cent (140 out of 1095). In the period 1894 – to early 1899 women formed 20.65 per cent of the new members (57 out of 276). But whilst at least 35 per cent (49 of the 140) in 1874-85 were married to/daughters of vegetarians, in the later period some 22.8 per cent (13 of the 57) clearly fall into these categories, suggesting that by the late nineteenth century, the nature of female recruitment reflected women's growing emancipation.

Certainly, in this period, vegetarianism presented itself as a cause for 'progressive' women.[100] The newly artistic vegetarianism personified itself in female garb.[101] *Shafts*, the journal produced by Margaret Sibthorp from 1892-99 ('for women and the working-classes,' latterly 'a magazine of Progressive Thought')[102] and Andreas Gottschling's *Home Links*, associated vegetarianism with female emancipation and other 'progressive' causes.[103] This was a different 'New Woman'.[104] The vegetarian 'New Woman' condemned the 'fungrous growth' of the fashionable lounger and was horrified by any aping of masculine errors such as smoking.[105]

The revival and expansion of the movement from around 1870 involved a few prominent women who were already in the public eye for their activities or achievements.[106] In Paris, the mystic and zoophilite Anna Kingsford studied the subject for her medical degree, published her research, and then lectured on the subject for provincial societies across Britain and abroad.[107] The VS singled out her 'loving devotion' in 1882.[108] The previously secularist Annie Besant was another prominent woman who addressed the VS, though her main interests were elsewhere.[109] The spiritualist and magnetic healer Chandos Wallace who moved away from spiritualism towards food reform also played a prominent role as a leading vegetarian entrepreneur by the turn of the century, with her husband the Irishman Joseph Wallace.

The LFRS, though reportedly composed largely of 'active young men,' had female participation in soirées, 'at homes' and cookery demonstrations. The philanthropist Lady Mount Temple, Anna Kingsford and Chandos Wallace were associated.[110] Female involvement was recognized as a crucial factor at the annual meeting in 1885 when one male speaker expressed his happiness that a large number of the audience were ladies, 'while the ladies stand outside they are an immense force against us'.[111] The endeavours of the sisters Ellen Hawkins and Emily Harding were cited by James Burns as examples of 'what might be done by ladies of leisure and means in elevating mankind and improving the tone of society'.[112] Emily, moving to the East End in 1884 to engage in philanthropic work amongst the poor, spread the vegetarian message through church, temperance and other organizations. Ellen hired a hall for cookery lessons. Years before her activity in the Humanitarian League, Alice Lewis inspired Burns's East End food depôt and then brought the cause to the attention of the Women's Congress in Paris in 1889.[113] Another prominent worker in the 1880s-90s was Frances Boult, founder of the Northern Heights VS, a popular cookery instructor, and skilled speaker, who created the children's vegetarian Ivy Leaf Society and *Children's Garden* magazine.

FIGURE 23. A branch (Camden Town) of the Ivy Leaf Society established by Frances Boult. *Vegetarian*, 2 December 1899, p. 574.

The Victorian feminist movement had, in addition to involvement in the anti-Contagious Diseases Act agitation, many connections with health-related movements.[114] Anti-vivisection and anti-vaccination were naturally related as movements of dissent. In Wallace, vegetarians had a female prophet of health for the nation's physical regeneration but there were also a couple of female medical practitioners with orthodox qualifications who were associated with the movement: Kingsford and Frances Hoggan.[115] Female temperance workers like their male counterparts could be drawn to vegetarianism, though one doubts Adams' suggestion that the 'homosocial world' of British temperance and feminist workers *accentuated* vegetarianism,[116] female temperance certainly provided a key location for vegetarian activity and support; and feminist activity was linked to temperance and purity.[117] We have seen how vegetarianism appeared in women's co-operative circles. It was also the case that vegetarianism was promoted or debated in other women's journals, including some trade journals.[118]

Women's participation was by no means purely domestic; it formed part of a wider movement from the period of revival after 1870. VS journals were edited by a woman (Beatrice Lindsay), Chandos Wallace edited a journal into the 1920s, and Sibthorp's *Shafts* was specifically for women.[119] Women contributed articles to vegetarian journals, a few had these or lectures published as tracts, and published letters in newspapers. Women penned some fourteen out of the twenty-six vegetarian cookery books produced in this period, as mentioned previously.

Though Victorian women were no more prolific as vegetarian authors than men, despite Carol Adams' demonstration of a 'feminist-vegetarian canon', the record of their other activities in the movement show their increasingly public roles. Women were listed as the 'managers' of private households to be contacted by vegetarians seeking accommodation. Though women solely managed few restaurants their joint management was an important contribution; certainly male commentators appreciated their decorative value as waitresses![120] It was assumed that they prepared the dishes for public meetings; hence the interest at the 'unwonted scene' of men publicly cooking dishes, which was described (by the male reporter) as the world 'turned upside down'.[121] The VS announced a ladies' committee and encouraged these for local societies.[122] There were women in the Humanitarian League diet department.[123] Members of the Vegetarian Rambling Society (which had a ladies' clubroom) rambled together 'with benefit' and, with due regard to social proprieties, 'no ill-effect'.[124] A ladies' section to the Vegetarian Cycling Club existed from 1896. There was also a *women's* society, established in London in March 1895 and existing for about five years.[125] Its story has never been told: in the single-minded devotion of its two central figures the moral fervour and enthusiasm of the vegetarian cause is very evident.

The Women's Vegetarian Union (hereafter WVU) was established by Alexandrine Veigelé, 'an enthusiastic little French lady' and 'very earnest worker for women' who was already a vegetarian activist when she joined the LVS.[126] She became vegetarian initially for economic and health reasons in 1888. A member of the Women's Progressive Society, she was to be honorary secretary of a Women's International Progressive Union founded by her daughter Adrienne, a teacher who was closely involved with the WVU. A letter to Joseph Edwards, editor of the *Labour Annual*, indicates their dedication: Alexandrine largely abandoned her teaching to concentrate on vegetarianism, whilst Adrienne supported herself and her mother's philanthropy through teaching French and music.[127] Her primary motive was to remove the barrier to the movement's success from wifely opposition.[128] But early overtures were snubbed and many early recruits apparently joined the Union simply to humour Veigelé since she did 'look so terribly in earnest over it'.[129]

The Union's declared aim was the amelioration of the moral and physical condition of mankind by promoting a 'purer and simpler dietary'. The arguments they used differed from those used when vegetarians addressed 'the working classes'. The Union based its existence on the 'natural' maternal responsibility to promote the 'future well-being and prosperity of the human race'. A mother's duty was to raise children who were strong, intelligent and humane. The diet's relationship to animal welfare, to temperance, to peace and the elevation of women by 'relieving them from that which is degrading and repugnant in the preparation of meals' was also stressed.[130] The Union was to interest women of 'all classes,' through precept and example. Subscription was set at a minimum of 2s 6d.[131]

FIGURE 24. Alexandrine Veigelé, *left* and her daughter Adrienne, *right*. *Vegetarian*, 7 December 1895.

The Union was sufficiently independent-minded and earnest to issue printed reports. These make clear the small scale of the organization. By 1896 the society had attracted about 200 members and associates. Initially the members were wholly British, but though London remained the headquarters, the metropolis was not the limit of its ambitions. Within a year the Union had expanded to over 300 members and associates. Many foreigners enrolled after the Union's reception for the World's Women's Christian Temperance Union (hereafter, WWCTU) in 1895 and there were French, Belgian, German and American vice-presidents. But finances remained limited, and in 1898 income was still under £40.[132] By the time of the sixth annual report there were over 350 members and associates, but the Union remained small and poor.[133]

Despite the novelty of a female society, the Union's activities did not deviate from the general modes of activity which women had already performed: soirées, lectures, monthly cookery demonstrations. Lecturers visited female organizations such as Mothers' Meetings groups and Women's Co-operative Guilds (thus providing a link with the wider labour movement). Linkages with other organizations were attempted: Good Templar branches, the Co-operative Brotherhood Trust, a Clapham branch of the Independent Labour Party, Brixton Progressive Club, the Camberwell Socialist Society and the Tolstoyan Society. The Union was represented at conferences and gatherings (vegetarian and women's congresses, meetings of the Medical Society for the Study of Inebriety, the Church Penitentiary Association and the annual Crystal Palace temperance festival). There was a public reception during the national Vegetarian Congress in 1898, and a general meeting at the Athenaeum Hall, with physical education demonstrations.[134] Monthly and advertised lectures or discussions (occasionally with musical entertainment) were held, often at Charlotte Eamonson's home at Limehouse.[135] Reports were sent to the vegetarian and non-vegetarian press. The Union distributed and sold literature; Veigelé hoped for a small monthly magazine.[136]

Veigelé opened a depôt – a 'Vegetarian Universal Provider' according to the *Daily Telegraph* – and soon established a General [employment] Agency which allegedly co-ordinated 'many' employers and employees. Growing demand led Veigelé to move the depôt in 1898 (to 87, Praed Street, Paddington). She wanted rooms for headquarters, a cookery school and a club offering bedrooms and meals. A provident fund for employees was established. In 1899 a refreshment room was to be opened but this does not seem to have happened.[137] The thwarting of these ambitions was echoed in the Union's failure to sustain a local branch organization. A short-lived Lambeth branch was established in 1897, Adrienne Veigelé gave lectures and demonstrations in Aylesbury in 1898 and led open-air meetings in the East End and Hyde Park in late 1899, but no further English branch was formed.[138] A Dublin society was created.[139] French and American branches were planned but the 'international' network was limited to a Belgian branch which formed its own library and produced the first Belgian vegetarian journal. This reflected the connections already made by food reformers such as May Yates.[140]

The rules of the Union required members to be 'earnest women who have at heart the health, prosperity and happiness of the human race'.[141] This was an accurate description of the recruits: many were prominent vegetarian workers in their own right or active in other moral and social reform movements; such as Wallace, Sibthorp, Yates, Sarah Sheldon Amos, Laura Ormiston Chant, Emma Wardlaw Best, Anna Allinson, and Adelaide McDouall. Wallace, indeed, covered the organization's activities in her paper (the Union's official organ in 1897). She also gave lectures and made her home available for social gatherings.[142] The Union was established at Sibthorp's offices which provided a frequent meeting place for it and other reformers. Veigelé had (from February 1894) advertised her pedagogic services in *Shafts* which announced the new society, reported its activity and published Alexandrine's vegetarian recipes.[143] Sibthorp's time was largely devoted to producing *Shafts* but her support for vegetarianism was recognized by a photograph in Foward's *History*, a rare glimpse of a woman who, having 'a great aversion to have myself written about either by myself or any one', is frustratingly fugitive.[144]

Concern with purity characterized Sibthorp and other members. Sarah Sheldon Amos, an associate of Josephine Butler and member of the National Vigilance Association was recalled by Bertrand Russell as devoted to 'Good Works, especially Purity' and of 'fanatical religiosity'.[145] Chant was a celebrated (or notorious) purity activist also involved in temperance and women's suffrage, who became associated with the WVU, although previously merely 'sympathetic' to the movement.[146] Wardlaw Best, whose aphorisms were published by *Shafts*, was honorary treasurer. Strangely, she was a member of both the social purity National Vigilance Association *and* the sexual reform Legitimation League.[147] The only extended study of *Shafts*, by Brady, treats the journal's 'liberal feminist' core as participants in a 'new counterculture of vegetarianism, "rational" dress and liberated female behaviour ... combined with a social purity ideology, highly derivative of an earlier reformist tradition'. Yet vegetarianism's presence in *Shafts* presents less of a 'strange duality' than Brady supposed. Although a *fin de siècle* fad with avant-garde associations (Brady identifies *Shaft*'s 'Bohemian outlandishness'), it was also part of the puritanism which fuelled the purity campaigns.[148]

If vegetarianism was a natural concern for women interested in moral and social regeneration, the Union was also supported by the Allinsons, whose neo-Malthusianism appalled Arnold Hills. Anna Allinson had exhibited at the Royal Academy before her marriage, when she embraced her husband's activity in food and allied reforms and raised their children in 'humane principles'.[149] Their home served as a meeting place and Allinson lectured on 'rambles in North Africa' for the Union, 'dressed as a native Arab', at the *Review of Reviews* office.[150] Another supporter of the Union, whose pseudonym reflected the prejudice against women's public participation in reform activity, was May Yates – the artist Mary Corkling – who deferred to her father in concealing her real name. She led the Bread Reform League, but also supported the vegetarian cause from the 1880s, becoming secretary of the LVS in the early 1890s. Her food reform attracted the support of the Women's Christian Temperance movement, and Frances Willard supported the creation of a World's Food Reform Department.[151] Yates was appointed Superintendent, in which capacity she lectured around the world for over thirty years.[152]

McDouall chaired the 'women's session' of the vegetarian congress in 1894 and arranged the final meeting of the jubilee congress at the Central Vegetarian Restaurant in 1897.[153] Like many other vegetarians, she was interested in clothing reform.[154] Other activists comprising the committee included the sisters Caroline and Emily Coles (anti-vivisectionists), and Edith Tegetmeier (daughter of a colleague of Charles Darwin), who had joined the vegetarian Maternity Society. The auditor was Mrs Harold Cox (née Helen Clegg), wife of a Cambridge University Extension Society lecturer who had spent a year as an agricultural labourer and established the co-operative Home Colonization Society in 1884.[155] Subscribers to the Union's funds included the Quaker socialist and feminist Isabella Ford, a close friend of the simple-lifer and sexual reformer Edward Carpenter; Katharine Reid, who co-authored essays on 'modern chivalry' and the 'woman question' in the *Vegetarian*; Matthilde Wolff van Sandau, vegetarian through theosophy and humanitarianism and, another occultist, Fanny Samuel, protégé of Chandos Wallace. Margaret Bondfield, the future Labour minister, became an associate. The Union claimed success for one of its most 'important and useful' functions, the debut of new workers in the vegetarian cause.

In 1899 the conductor of the *Vegetarian Messenger*'s 'Ladies Page', cautioned against *exclusive* absorption in vegetarianism, 'lest I become a vegetarian and a woman, not a woman who is more truly and wholly woman, because I am a vegetarian'. As this brief discussion of the Union's most notable supporters indicate, they were active in several causes; their connections and affiliations suggesting that they would not have defined themselves solely or primarily as vegetarian activists. One society devoted to wider concerns, and associated with the Union through the overlapping membership and shared address, was the Women's International Progressive Union established in 1897 by Adrienne Veigelé.[156] Aiming to 'extend and develop' the freedom of women, to educate their powers of influence for good, and to place them 'securely in a position of perfect equality on all points with men', no restrictions were placed on credal, political or professional status. Honorary membership was even extended to men. Members in 1898 included doctors, Board School teachers, journalists, musicians, nurses and novelists. Its activity took the form of drawing room meetings, lectures and debates.[157] Speakers included the feminist Elizabeth Wolstenholme Elmy (a contributor to *Shafts*), Annie Besant and Wardlaw Best. Its internationalist aim (reflected in a letter of 'sympathy' to Emile Zola after his defence of Dreyfus), manifested itself in Belgian and French branches by 1898.[158] The spiritualist sympathies of one component group is clear from the account of one meeting where discourse ranged over women's suffrage, phrenology, art and holidays.[159]

If the Progressive Union is obscure, the WVU was a guest of a more familiar and similarly ambitious institution, the middle-class feminist women's Pioneer Club. Its leader, Mrs Emily Massingberd, friend of Sibthorp and Lady Henry Somerset (the British Women's Temperance Association's president) was a vegetarian and the Progressive Union's president was a member.[160] Many Pioneers were 'in full sympathy' with vegetarianism, teetotalism and anti-vivisectionism.[161] The Union's reception for the WWCTU points indeed, as a report in the *Daily News* suggested, to a shared 'sisterhood of practical aims'.[162] The connections between *Shafts* and its leader, Frances Willard (links which included Sibthorp's friendship with Willard's friend Lady Henry Somerset) have been noted before.[163] The 'shared sisterhood' was reflected in coverage in the feminist temperance journal, *Woman's Signal*.[164] It was also apparent during the temperance discussion at the International Council of Women in London, 1899 when Yates advocated vegetarianism. At the same event, Yates, Adrienne Veigelé and others made the vegetarian association of femininity with animal welfare. Yates described vegetarianism as the logical conclusion to 'a very proper and womanly conception' of our duties to the lower animals.[165]

Many of the International Council delegates accepted an invitation to Hills's home.[166] This invitation, from the London movement's financial and moral heavyweight, raises questions about the Union's relationships with male vegetarians, and with the established societies. The Union (whose first office was provided by Hills) did not jealously protect its independence from men: men could be honorary members, after a resolution passed at the first annual meeting.[167] But subscription lists and details of meetings and officers demonstrate a largely female composition. Alexandrine Veigelé was clear that the Union fulfilled the need for a society principally of ('good and sensible') women'.[168] She asserted the right and ability of women to act as independent agents just like men, but stressed that philanthropy was the better for co-operation. Women's place was not, as some believed, the drawing room or kitchen, but wherever good work was required.[169] The need to co-operate rather than segregate was also asserted by Eleanor Beeby, a contributor to *Shafts* and the *Vegetarian*, in an astute response to appeals to peculiarly *female* 'empathy' in vegetarianism or zoophilia:

> I do not think it wise to call upon women specially to interest themselves in these things, because although – whether by nature or by training – they are now less able than men to witness, unmoved, suffering in others, while, from probably the same cause, they appear better able than men to endure it in their own persons, yet this is not, to my mind, a wholly desirable state of things ... [170]

There were many male supporters. Gottschling's quarterly socialist, feminist and vegetarian *Home Links* publicized the Union. Bernard Shaw gave an address for the Union at the Ideal Club (his earlier 'vivacious and humorous' address at the Pioneer Club was succeeded by Adelaide McDouall recalling all to seriousness). That great crusader for moral purity W.T. Stead gave the two Unions a venue at the *Review of Reviews* office. His support of *Shafts*, his involvement in the National Vigilance Association, conversion to spiritualism and acceptance of the 'logic of vegetarianism' were points of contact. Alan Leo, the astrologer, hosted a meeting with his wife. The vegetarian publicist John Nugent distributed its literature. Men joined in the performance of music at soirées.[171] Yet the fact that printing of the reports was done by the Women's Printing Society, latterly also the printers of *Shafts*, reinforces the impression of a desire to support women's independent activity.

The Union was included with the other societies in the *Vegetarian Yearbook* and its activities were regularly reported in the journals. This coverage was in the context of their general efforts to make women more visible as contributors. The *Food Reform Magazine* had published papers by Wallace and Kingsford and an essay on 'Women as Food Reformers'.[172] The creation of 'Women's pages' in the *Vegetarian Messenger* and *Vegetarian*, however, did not imply a desire to segregate but to appeal to their 'special needs'.[173] Moreover, the *Vegetarian*'s policy of promoting a broad platform under the label of the 'ideal', ensured space for some explicitly feminist sentiments in the journal.[174] The London movement's 'political programme' of 1892 included consideration of female suffrage.[175] One correspondent in 1896 argued, in what by now was a cliché, that the movement's limited past success stemmed from female non-involvement; but hoped that their prominence in the Union, Ideal Club meetings, platform and in practical work relating to diet and cookery heralded a new era.[176]

Yet the Union faced critics who believed it would hinder rather than forward the movement. Veigelé evidently felt the need to stress the male support given to her, as she established the Union, by Josiah Oldfield.[177] Though the basis for criticism was not stated it can be imagined that some feared competition with the LVS and VS for funds and allegiances; or that the movement would be compromised by 'unladylike' activities. Conservative non-metropolitan elements may have seen the Union as over-ambition on the part of the London movement. Perhaps it was feared that the identification of 'Women' with 'Vegetarian' played into the hands of critics who identified vegetarianism with effeminate sentimentalism.[178] Indicative of tensions, Anna Allinson wanted the Union's affiliation with other societies to cease.[179]

The women's society proved to be short-lived. The Lambeth branch languished without a secretary, and attendance was disappointing. A late issue of *Shafts* published heartfelt words on Veigelé as an 'untiring ... worker' for the 'uplifting of humanity'.[180] Ill at the time, she declared 'I will not die before I see at least some of my projects accomplished for my heart breaks when I see all the misery some have to suffer, through wrong living, in every way'.[181] A year later she informed Joseph Edwards that work was hard in the absence of funds and that the depôt had moved to cheaper premises. Resigning the presidency due to work pressures in 1901, she was succeeded by Yates, who was opposed to the 'hard self assertive spirit' of advanced women.[182] Veigelé's life ended in poverty, with the failures of the depôt and her attempt to make a living as a magnetic healer.[183]

For women such as the Veigelés, it was fitting to personify vegetarianism as a woman. But the iconography of the vegetarian press is only one aspect to the gendered representation of the reform. Beyond the world of the movement, vegetarians were the subject of fictional presentation, often associating diet with questions of gender and occasionally with women's rights. The next chapter examines the external representation and treatment of vegetarianism in literary (and to a lesser extent visual) form, in order to gauge how far, and in what ways, the movement (and practice) permeated public consciousness. One might expect that given the period's understanding of women's nature and poetic sensibility, women would engage with the vegetarian cause in verse, at least. But in fact, as we shall see, the feminist-vegetarian literary tradition identified by Adams has few representatives in British literature of this period.

7
REPRESENTING THE VEGETARIAN

Although Samuel Brown believed that it 'must have come and gone among those small recurring topics in the experience of many' in his essay on physical puritanism, vegetarianism was not a burning issue for most contemporaries and vegetarians struggled to convert the nation.[1] Yet novelty value and its association with similar 'progressive' movements generated frequent printed discussion about vegetarianism in the 1850s. Its status as a 'question of the day' was repeated in the latter decades of the century.[2] Its claims were debated in learned and popular periodicals in a 'dietetic discourse' which ranged beyond foodstuffs because of the associations between dietary reform and a variety of subjects such as race and empire or concerns about atheism, faddism and 'sentimentalism'. As might be expected of a movement challenging contemporary practice and common sense, it was treated as a comic subject. Vegetarianism's place in Victorian culture may be studied by exploring its representation in literature and the movement's connection to the literary world. This chapter does this, through examining the treatment of the movement and diet in newspapers and journals, through outlining its presence in works by ethnologists, anthropologists and philosophers, and exploring the presentation of vegetarian characters in prose fiction and poetry.

Critics believed that excluding animal foods was harmful for physical workers and possible – but not necessarily beneficial – only for brainworkers and intellectuals. Vegetarians stressed the diet's general utility but also argued the diet aided intellectual and cultural pursuits, claims which were supported by the various 'brainworkers' (clerks, teachers, publishers and printers) listed as new members. But they also noted that raw meat had been eaten by artists wishing to fire their imagination.[3] The *Vegetarian Advocate* forcefully emphasized vegetarianism's relevance in literary circles and later vegetarians targeted the opinion-formers of the press.[4] Unlike hydropathy, which was an attractive recuperative regime for intellectuals and *littérateurs*; or mesmerism which permeated Victorian culture; vegetarianism attracted sustained commitment from few 'eminent Victorians'. Nevertheless the cultural figures who responded to vegetarianism (such as John Ruskin in *Fors Clavigera* in 1883) were not negligible.[5] The literary men and women who practised or experimented with vegetarianism included George Meredith, George Gissing, Bernard Shaw, Edward Carpenter, Edith Nesbit, Mona Caird, Henry Salt and James Joynes.

Poetic vegetarianism

Critics of vegetarianism were prepared to concede that the diet induced sentimental, idealistic or melancholic moods and was therefore a 'poetic system'.[6] They could make this connection with some justice, given the association between vegetarianism and Shelley's circle in the early nineteenth century. Thus *Blackwood's* referred to the 'feeble puny gentleman who is cultivating poetry or an incipient moustache' who dutifully became a Shelleyan vegetarian.[7] *Punch's* skits concerning the long-haired reflect this legacy. Modern scholarship has recognized the place of vegetarianism in Shelley's work and in the Romantic era more generally, with the proper diet of humanity, associated with other radicalisms and unorthodoxies, being debated in poetry, fiction, essays and journals.[8] Yet it was no mass 'movement', and attempts to present it as a tendency involving a 'significant' number of people in this period are not entirely convincing.[9]

The 'delicate and sensitive Vegetarian', Shelley, *was* a major inspiration for idealistic Victorians, but his influence on the vegetarian movement is little documented.[10] *Queen Mab*, wherein the diet was advocated, was available to working-class radicals in pirated editions such as Richard Carlile's; Carlile claimed many of his readers supported the diet.[11] Yet Shelley's influence was rarely invoked in early vegetarian meetings and a reviewer in the *Vegetarian Advocate* believed his 'vegetarianism was ignored by most of his many admirers'.[12] The long-haired enthusiasts Barmby and James Duncan were devotees. *The Times* asserted, in reference to Shelley and Duncan, that the 'poetic or the political frenzy is the exception which proves the rule' in English diet.[13] The *Vegetarian Messenger* in 1853 recorded one member's hope for the 'realization of the anticipated period looked forward to with so much enthusiasm' by Shelley.[14] Horsell partly credited his conversion to Shelley; who was also avidly read by James Burns's father.[15] A (tiny) late-Victorian survey of motivation concluded that Shelley's example was a major factor in taking up the reformed diet.[16]

Not surprisingly, given Shelley's example, a number of poets tried vegetarianism, and poetry is a minor location for allusions to it.[17] Since Shelley was a hero for young idealistic men, it is also unsurprising those later critics of the system, such as Samuel Brown and George Lewes, experienced brief vegetarian phases. But there seem to have been few poems by women expressing vegetarian sentiment. We have seen that it was a cause in tune with feminine sensibilities, according to apologists and according to critics who associated it with effeminacy or emasculation. The identification of women with poetry of sentiment, the natural world and animals has been emphasized by scholars.[18] Women were constructed as instinctive, it was to be expected that they should write heart-felt pleas for animals. Women poets such as Mary Howitt did publish poetry expressing their zoophilite sentiments.[19] But few expressions of vegetarian sympathies, and few female vegetarian poets, are known. Dora Greenwell, a supporter of women's suffrage and the right to work, as well as anti-vivisection (as expressed in her poem 'Fidelity Rewarded') was reputedly a vegetarian.[20] Anna Kingsford the mystic, anti-vivisectionist, and anti-vaccinationist, expressed her sentiments in poetry and prose. At the end of the century, Dollie Radford was another.[21] But just as New Woman novels avoided vegetarianism, women's poetry of the period apparently ignored it.[22] The *Dietetic Reformer* hoped that some day there would be an anthology of vegetarian poetry. But only the obscure Maude Egerton King seems to have published on this subject.[23]

Debates and polemics about vegetarianism

Discourse on diet appeared in a variety of locations, from works obviously about food in the context of domestic science, the developing science of nutrition and medical works, to works of anthropology and ethnology. The vegetable diet was, unsurprisingly, discussed in physiological works, and long before the Society was formed.[24] Vegetarians stressed the importance of dietetic facts obtained from parliamentary Blue Books, works of biography and travel, for their task of moral and intellectual suasion.[25] Naturally disquisition on the primitive food of man in works of zoology, anthropology, archaeology, history, and sociology, often referred to vegetarian diet.[26]

Culinary and epicurean perspectives obviously had the potential to involve vegetarian discussion, though coverage in these quarters has not been explored in this study. The celebrated chef Alexis Soyer condemned it as a dreamy attempt by a minority to return to a Golden Age of innocence, milk, honey and nectar.[27] Whilst accepting the long-standing analysis of historical dietary stages (the antediluvian frugivorous diet) Soyer asserted, conventionally, the duty and right of mankind to consume animals. Yet a posthumous collection of previously unpublished recipes was promoted in 1858 as including 'a complete system of Vegetarian dietary', although this amounted to five brief pages.[28] Debates about food supply and quality also triggered commentary on vegetarian substitutes. George Dodd's classic study of the feeding of the metropolis records the current impact of vegetarian propaganda in relation to the 'institution of English beef' and slaughterhouses, and makes reference to works such as John Smith of Malton's.[29]

Given concern over food adulteration and working-class dietary, and vegetarians' claims concerning these problems, it is unsurprising that vegetarianism should be alluded to when these subjects were discussed. The *Illustrated London News*'s essay on foods at the Great Exhibition condemned the minority who were 'phytopophagi' since to 'preserve the integrity and enterprise of the Anglo-Saxon race, the first medical authorities declare that a full meat diet must be used'.[30] Sargant's *The Economy of the Labouring Classes* (1857), it has been seen, discussed the subject at some length.[31] As a movement claiming a philanthropic, humanitarian or generally socially ameliorative role, vegetarianism naturally appeared in works discussing these subjects, including a late-Victorian utilitarian work, socialist literature such as John M. Davidson's *The Old Order and the New: From Individualism to Collectivism* (which treated it as a quack remedy along with thrift, voluntary co-operation and trade unions) and in debate about curtailment of individual liberty and the efficacy and justification of prohibition in an essay by the positivist Frederic Harrison.[32]

Another measure of a cause's contemporary significance, beyond such fleeting treatment, is the extent to which critical tract literature was generated. Vegetarianism resulted in no flood of tracts comparable to the response to some other *-isms* but there were some (eight) pamphlets. *A Future Apostacy*, produced soon after the VS's formation presented teetotalism and vegetarianism as proofs of infidelity. The *Vegetarian Advocate*, priding itself on the system's truth, advertised *A Glance at Vegetarianism* (authored by a member of that 'generally shrewd' working class), directed at the Society. One tract published just before the VS was formed, attacked vegetarianism for harming the temperance cause. A published lecture condemned *The Vegetarian Fallacy* in 1856. This is hardly an impressive body of pamphlet literature, but there may have been locally printed tracts in response to local vegetarian efforts.[33]

Another measure of public interest was coverage in periodical press. Thankfully, for the researcher, vegetarians reported both contemptuous and appreciative notices in 'influential' and purely local journals. *The Times*, although covering annual banquets and meetings, was invariably scornful of the cause as sentimental and idealistic, in keeping with its general pose as the voice of reason and 'common-sense'. But London vegetarians used the paper to announce soirées, lectures, monthly meetings, and even to disseminate a recipe for a vegetarian Christmas pudding.[34] Advertisements appeared for vegetarian books and lodgings.[35] Regular reporting of annual meetings and coverage in particular of the congresses in the late nineteenth century shows that the movement was recognized as a topic of public interest. This was the case with other papers, like the *Daily News*, *Nonconformist*, *Morning Advertiser* (which described followers as 'amiable fanatics' and the diet as 'one of the most harmless delusions of the day') or the *Illustrated London News* which thought fit to provide an engraving of one banquet.[36]

The movement could hope for some attention by temperance journals, other reformist and philanthropic journals discussed the movement's work or claims.[37] The *Mechanics' Organ* was quoted in an advertisement by the *Vegetarian Advocate* as recommending it as 'in the wake of progress, and we welcome it as worthy fellow labourer in "clearing the way".' Obscurer journals such as the *Osbornian Journal* (which called the *Advocate* a 'friend of inquiry and progress') might be supportive. But the novel movement attracted attention beyond quarters where one would expect sympathy. More importantly for spreading awareness of the cause generally, responses to vegetarian propaganda appeared in periodicals such as Charles Dickens's widely-circulated *Household Words*. Dickens attacked vegetarians, teetotallers and peace activists as extremists who lacked perspective: 'Stew so much as the bone of a mutton chop in the pot with your vegetables, and you will never make another Eden out of a Kitchen Garden'. He ridiculed the 'distinguished vegetarians' and their platform.[38] Another interesting location was *The British Controversialist*, devoted to publishing contributors' debates on issues of the day. Henry S. Clubb and others answered several anti-vegetarians' criticisms of the movement in 1851.[39] Vegetarians praised the mass-circulating *Family Herald* for good sense, benevolence, 'acuteness and philosophical acumen' when it examined the diet 'as one of the speaking signs of the times – heralds of a coming era'.[40] This association with other signs of progress or change was, of course, discussed in Samuel Brown's article in the *Westminster Review*. Another significant journal of the period, *The Athenaeum*, by contrast, saw the movement as 'fanatical' in discussions in May 1850.[41]

Responses to the movement also appeared in satirical journals. *Punch* intermittently commented on the movement from 1848, referring to it as a Manchester-based society meeting occasionally 'for the purpose of masticating mashed potatoes, and munching cabbage leaves.' The 'vegetarian humbug' was merely a juvenile appetite for sweet and nice foods. A response from vegetarians resulted in the magazine's patronizing notice of a 'movement' – with press, society, boarding houses, schools, hotels, life insurance office, stationary and missionaries.[42] The sect's diet was described as cholera-inducing and related to other reform fads. Amongst the fifteen or so references in the 1850s were notes of vegetarian leather substitutes; the 'Grand Show of Prize Vegetarians', Leech's amusing cartoon in the 1852 almanac; reference to vegetarian eating houses and annual banquets.[43] Advertisements highlighted its vegetarian skits.[44] Where Mr Punch went, others, such as *Diogenes*, followed.[45]

VIEWS OF VEGETARIANISM

ADVANCED JOHNNIE.— If using the cabbage leaf is the sign of a Vegetarian, then I'll Nebuchadnezzar it with the best of them.
CHORUS.— (in the background) Wot, call *'im* a vegetarian, w'y'e smowks!

FIGURE 25. Leading black and white artist of the late-Victorian period Phil May's comment on the appeal of vegetarianism to the fashionable. *Vegetarian*, September 1894, p. 419.

The revival in progressive movements from the 1870s brought renewed discussion of vegetarianism in newspapers and the burgeoning 'tit-bits' periodical market of the last decade of the century. Some of the journals whose comments were noted by vegetarians were quite far-flung, such as the *Levant Herald*, which reported the International Vegetarian Congress in 1898. A continued sense of the movement's oddity meant the provincial press was diligent in reporting even quite humble local activity. Often these reports and letters sent by vegetarians stimulated further correspondence and editorial comment. Though it was clearly a matter of the editors' own sympathies, the local press were often sceptics and sneerers.[46] The *North British Daily Mail* in March 1898, to cite one of many instances, said that of all the apostles of lost causes, vegetarians deserved the deepest sympathy; the *Glasgow Evening Times* in February of the same year was similarly disparaging of local efforts.[47] Other newspapers showed respect for vegetarians' philanthropic activities and motives.

Well-known periodicals featured articles or notes about vegetarianism. These included *Fraser's Magazine*, *Nineteenth Century*, *Westminster Review*, and *Pall Mall Gazette*.[48] Whereas *Notes and Queries* had avoided vegetarianism in the 1850s, there were now some inquiries, though one suspects these were planted to generate coverage.[49] Hostile commentary came from Barry Pain, a celebrated journalist and editor of *Today*, and from *The Globe*, *Wheeling* and *St James's Budget*. Not that the vegetarians missed opportunities to press their case. The *Illustrated London News*'s scientific section was conducted by an anti-vegetarian who complained that one had 'only to mention the word "foods," when there will be a hundred or more wise and learned persons to point out to you the only "perfect way in diet" '.[50] *Punch* had settled into gentle satire about banquets, restaurants, and vegetarian clothing, rival satirical journals and comics also exploited the movement's humorous potential.[51]

Utopianism

Vegetarianism's unworldly reputation drew on the connection between diet and poetic dreamer. A more substantial cumulative treatment of vegetarianism appears in utopian and scientific romance, some, like Bulwer Lytton's *Coming Age*, Samuel Butler's *Erewhon*, H.G. Wells's *Time Machine*, being bestsellers. Signifying either a racial degeneration or higher human existence, vegetarianism was a diet of the future. By contrast the demotic utopia of Douglas Jerrold's *Chronicles of Clovernook* had presented a future of plenty where meat was available to all, a message propagated at the time by the working-class Chartists.[52] Since utopia involved re-examination of quotidian habits, and a change of regimen to include diet, it is unsurprising that Victorian utopian works touched upon the food.[53]

Lytton's best-selling *The Coming Race* presented a subterranean super-race of temperate vegetarians, who initially, on examination of the human hero's teeth, plan to exterminate him as a carnivore. Lytton's sympathies for the reformed diet were made clear; ironically the beef extract 'Bovril' took its name from *vril-ya*, the electricity which powered the civilization.[54] W.H. Hudson's *A Crystal Age* (1887) depicted a future England of Anglo-Saxon vegetarians.[55] British vegetarians were naturally delighted when *Equality* (1897), Edward Bellamy's preachy sequel to *Looking Backwards*, depicted a world where humanitarianism had swept away the old dietetic habits.[56] The poet Robert Buchanan, whose father had been associated with the utopian socialist and vegetarian 'Concordium' at Ham Common in the 1840s, created a vegetarian utopia in *The Reverend Annabel Lee. A Tale of Tomorrow*, where science rendered the need for animal slaughter or a mass of vegetable foods unnecessary and people lived on rice and fruits.[57] Perhaps the most famous 'utopian-satirical' treatment of dietetic ethics is Samuel Butler's revised version of *Erewhon* which takes vegetarianism to its absurd logical conclusions in 'The Views of an Erewhonian Prophet concerning the rights of animals' and, 'The Views of an Erewhonian philosopher concerning the rights of vegetables', which Bernard Shaw (who featured a failed vegetarian in his first novel, and who presented vegetarians in his plays[58]) affected to view as an attack on himself.[59] More obscure fictions envisioned vegetarian futures.[60]

The scientist Sir David Brewster had posited pacific and vegetarian extra-terrestrials.[61] Scientific romance might also involve vegetarianism: *Punch* predicted that Saturnians would conquer Earth and enforce vegetarianism, John Munro created a vegetarian race of Venusians.[62] Thoughts of the inevitable death of the planet occasioned by a lecture given by Sir William Thomson at the Royal Institute led a group of intellectuals to discuss future society in Octave Uzanne's short story for the American *Scribner's Magazine*. A 'gentle vegetarian and learned naturalist' envisioned a future where scientific food would make obsolescent butchers, bakers, wine merchants and restaurants and transform the world into a 'fair garden, sacred to hygiene and the pleasure of the eye'.[63] Further allusions appeared in H.G. Wells's *The Time Machine* (where the master-class evolved into vegetarian cattle for subterranean plebeians), and *The First Men in the Moon*, (in which Cavor was a water-drinker, a vegetarian, and 'all those logical disciplinary things').[64] The vegetarian movement advertised the fact that Ayesha in Rider Haggard's bestselling fantasy *She* was a vegetarian.[65] It was seen as proof of the compatibility of the *aesthetic* with the reformed diet.[66] Yet Rider Haggard was concerned with indicating her *abnormality* and diet was a useful device;

the 'humane diet' resulted in no humanitarianism on the part of 'She who must be obeyed'.⁶⁷

Vegetarianism in fiction

In 1897 the *Newcastle Leader* asked why 'none of our realistic novelists have ever painted the dread monotony of the vegetarian life'.⁶⁸ Yet vegetarianism was represented in British novels and short stories, in fictions that were occasionally bestsellers, attracted a mass audience and therefore provided an opportunity, along with representations in journals such as *Punch*, for the reform to be one of those 'small recurring topics' for many. But if popular authors made the occasional reference or, rarely, more substantial comments on or representations of vegetarianism, there is no evidence that vegetarianism featured as a topic in 'plebeian' fictions.

Carol Adams' canon of feminist-vegetarian texts from *Frankenstein* to present-day literature fails to include many instances from before the Great War, a problem inadequately addressed by deploying Isabel Colegate's modern (albeit Edwardian era-located) *The Shooting Party* which features a fictionalized Henry Salt (Liz Jensen's recent novel *Ark Baby* also features Salt).⁶⁹ Further research uncovers fictional representation by British vegetarian authors in the 1840s-70s, but these were obscure (James Duncan, Fanny Lacy, Sarah Clubb) and sparse. From the 1870s, propaganda appeared in fiction and poetry produced by proponents of vegetarianism.⁷⁰ The fiction produced for and consumed by the movement was a counterpart of biographical testimony which was a staple of propaganda for life-reform movements.⁷¹

Few works of fiction by non-vegetarians in the movement's early decades featured vegetarian protagonists but a few mentioned the movement or practice *en passant*, often when condemning teetotal extremism.⁷² Dickens had the young David Copperfield experiment with the diet–an accurate reflection of the youthful dalliance with dietetic unorthodoxy especially in literary circles–and identified it with teetotalism and pacifism in an essay.⁷³ This broader ultra-progressive world provided the setting for fictional treatment of the dietetic heretic in novels with moral or social reform themes or sub-plots. Charles Kingsley's idealistic Chartist tailor John Crossthwaite in *Alton Locke* is an example. His vegetarianism helps explain a 'great deal of the almost preternatural clearness, volubility, and sensitiveness of his mind'.⁷⁴ An episode based on the 'sacred socialists' outside London at Ham Common, plays an important part in Mary Kelty's *Visiting My Relations*.⁷⁵ The connection between perfectionist communitarianism and diet also surfaces in Margaret Oliphant's *Zaidee: A Romance*, Bulwer Lytton's popular *My Novel; or, varieties in English Life*, and Aytoun's 'The Congress and the

Agapedome'.[76] The proverbial philosopher Martin Tupper's *The Rides and Reveries of Mr Aesop Smith* featured a brief critical discussion of vegetarianism as 'flatulent Cowardice', in a conversation about the inconsistency of Mr Peascod's diet in including honey.[77]

Showing her historical accuracy, George Eliot's recreation of provincial life in the 'Middlemarch' of the Great Reform Act period made reference to forming 'a Pythagorean [i.e. vegetarian] community in the [American] backwoods'.[78] Depicting transcendentalist-inspired vegetarianism and community experience in the same period were a number of American novels or short stories, including Bayard Taylor's story set in a vegetarian community in 1845, and Orestes Brownson's *The Spirit-Rapper*.[79] The inclusion of British characters as participants accurately reflects these communities' transatlanticism.[80] Vegetarian characters and references were common in American literature for various reasons: America's status as the destination for communitarian experiments, its Grahamite movement which preceded the British movement, the vigour of temperance, women's suffrage and spiritualism; and these reforms' association with the Whigs.[81]

Vegetarianism was presented as a cause for the advanced reformer in later Victorian fictions. Nevil Beauchamp and his mentor Dr Shrapnel in George Meredith's *Beauchamp's Career* (1875) draw on Meredith's friendship with the radical Frederick Maxse, whose influence led the author to experiment in diet.[82] Shrapnel is an extreme radical who opposes the age's hedonistic tendency with Beauchamp, and leads another character, Cecilia, to investigate vegetarianism.[83] Meredith's work is unusual in having leading characters as vegetarians, yet the work was hardly a piece of popular fiction.[84] Another commercial failure, Eliza Lynn Linton's autobiographic *Christopher Kirkland* (1885) similarly presented vegetarianism or dietary asceticism, in the context of social regeneration, in the Lambert family.[85] Linton describes the mother, an ultra-radical reformer, as 'one of those ascetic Bohemians who frankly prefer poverty and disorder to sufficiency and regularity... she would rather have a dish of herbs on a bare table than a stalled ox with glass and silver and damask as the adjuncts.'[86] And in Mr Dalrymple, is depicted an eccentric, effeminate and sinister character who though teetotal-vegetarian and an occultist, also partakes of opium and tobacco.[87] A more successful novel depicting an advanced reformer, who was dietetically unorthodox, was the Catholic Dr William Barry's *The New Antigone* (1887).[88]

Mary Ward's best-selling *The History of David Grieve* (1892) depicted vegetarianism about 1870, basing her treatment on research which picked up propagandist themes of increasing life-span and material advancement, and accurately located the movement in the North and Midlands of England. Adrian Lomax becomes vegetarian in a radical Leicestershire milieu of secularism, socialism and anti-vaccination; but is dismissed from his post on the *Penny Banner* for his attack on carnivorism. The novel briefly portrays a Mancunian restaurant whose appeal is attributed to an environment offering opportunities to any with novel solutions to 'those daily needs which both goad and fetter the struggling multitude at every step.' Ward was a successful novelist. Yet if the depiction of the 'Parlour' had many readers, reviewers ignored the vegetarian episode, unless to include it among the irrelevant passages in an overlong work.[89] But vegetarians advertised her work.[90]

Sherlock Holmes's journey past a vegetarian restaurant in 'The Redheaded League' symbolizes vegetarianism's presence in *fin de siècle* London,[91] a presence more prominently featuring in two Edwardian works satirising reform movements. Wells depicted the other-worldliness, absurdity, or bathos of food, dress and feminist reformers in his controversial *Ann Veronica*, published in 1909. They are identified as unattached young men and women, young artists and writers, self-supporting women or female students: people who are washed-out (the 'spectacle of failure protecting itself from abjection by the glamour of its own assertions'). Despite his exaggerations, he accurately identified important constituents and tendencies of the *fin de siècle* 'progressive world'. Wells's dislike of vegetarianism, associated in his mind with celibacy, was expressed in a number of characters and references in later works.[92] A perilously open-minded baronet also enters the world of Edwardian metropolitan radicalism in the 'apostate' Harold Begbie's satire on 'isms' such as theosophy, Christian Socialism, vegetarianism, fruitarianism and communitarianism.[93] Begbie's position as a renegade vegetarian satirising the ultra-reformer repeated what the horticulturalist James Shirley Hibberd, active in early London vegetarianism, had done in a short story of 1886.[94] Professions of ultra-humaneness are contrasted with character flaws and shown to be impractical.

The only author who dealt with vegetarianism's unglamorous thrift aspect was George Gissing, whose own experience inspired several vegetarian characters. The vegetarianism of shabby-genteel Virginia Madden in *The Odd Woman* (1893) and Tymperly in 'A Poor Gentleman', conceal their poverty. Henry Ryecroft, the eponymous hero of his most popular work, senses 'an odd pathos in the literature of vegetarianism,' recalling his own study of the periodicals and pamphlets 'with all the zest of hunger and poverty, vigorously seeking to persuade myself that flesh was an altogether superfluous, and even repulsive, food'. But even Gissing had characters who were vegetarian on moral grounds or who were involved in communitarian schemes.[95]

Some of the vegetarian characters were picked up by vegetarian journals, eager for sympathetic discussion or controversy. Others, appearing in serialised literature, such as the hero in 'A Defeated Transcendentalist' in *Blackwood's Magazine*, were ignored.[96] However, apart from the limited body of fiction which directly referred to vegetarianism, the movement was aware of a wider humanitarian literature which it took to be a sign of the purer times coming. Thomas Hardy was seen as the leading example, but there were others such as, not surprisingly, the romantic novelist and anti-vivisectionist 'Ouida', Hall Caine, Maxwell Gray, and George du Maurier, and the explicitly pro-vegetarian Leo Tolstoy, whose support for the cause was publicized by late-Victorian British vegetarians.[97]

Having documented the presence of vegetarianism through characters in popular and less popular works of fiction, it is clear that such characters were infrequent. This reflected the fact that vegetarians were uncommon. Where they featured, authors associated them with radicalism in politics and personal lifestyle in a milieu of 'Bohemian humanitary', in Henry James's phrase.[98] Dietetic nonconformity could then contribute to a satirical treatment of *soi disant* progressives or moral reformers. These representations of movement culture or restaurant clientele might be exaggerated but they often expressed truths about sociology and ideology. The actuality of youthful experimentation throughout the period was also expressed in dietetic reform as a phase for characters such as David Copperfield, Meredith's Richard Feverel or Christina in Ella Hepworth Dixon's *My Flirtations*.[99]

Dietetic and gastronomic differences were recognized forms of *otherness* in a literature of true or fictional eccentricity that reflected Victorian fascination with eccentrics. Shaped by and helping to consolidate this interest, was authorial strategy. When a writer wanted a quirky, eccentric and therefore memorable character, vegetarianism was a useful trait. Thus Crowl, the feisty character in Israel Zangwill's locked-room mystery was a republican vegetarian and the Edwardian 'railway detective' Thorpe Hazell was a health food enthusiast.[100]

If vegetarians were figures of amusement as eccentrics this situation was encouraged by their comical representation as oddities in text and cartoon in popular satirical journals such as *Punch*. When Meredith featured a vegetarian drinker and a teetotal omnivore as a couple in *One of Our Conquerors* (1892) he was exploiting the comic potential of opposites attracting, but also of 'extremes' meeting.[101] Stage farce, such as the popular *Follies of the Day* of 1851, and musical representation similarly treated vegetarianism as comic.[102] Treated as a fad along with interest in

Eastern religions or spiritualism, vegetarianism remained a target for humorists such as E.F. Benson in the early twentieth century.[103]

Victorian vegetarians, and some of their contemporaries' utopian novels and scientific romances, envisaged a more compassionate alternative. Yet the contested nature of this reform meant that popular text fictions could employ the practice to indicate degeneracy or amorality, as with Rider Haggard's terrible Ayesha, or to create a horrible irony and indicate fanatical puritanism as in the serial killer in Belloc Lowndes's *The Lodger*.[104] Striking reversals of the claims advanced by vegetarian advocates, these transgressors provide further instances of the way diet helped signify difference in fiction, drawing on the connection felt between the materiality of food and the psychic, spiritual or moral.

It has been observed that 'books with a single focus tend to exaggerate the importance of their subject'.[105] Vegetarianism never became a central question for Victorian writers; but the subject was discussed at least to a greater extent than might have been thought. Even if this was merely as a dismissive aside it raised the possibility that the reader would be led to investigate it. For a movement of the literate, for a cause whose proponents identified it with progress and modernity, with culture and civilization, the written response to vegetarianism was always going to be important.

CONCLUSION

The penultimate part of this study shifted the gaze from the movement to its representation by Victorians in a range of texts. This concluding chapter assesses the movement's achievements, and the verdict of contemporaries. The latter is approached partly through considering the movement's complicated relationship to 'modernity'. How external commentators explained the movement's emergence, how it was related to contemporary social or cultural developments and what it implied about the present age, are questions which are examined.

The achievements of British vegetarianism

There was no likelihood that the Victorian public would be won over to dietary reform. Meat-eating was too entrenched and, though the development of manufactured alternatives was advanced by the early-twentieth century, it seemed impossible for most of the period that basic animal-derived materials could be substituted. Lack of provision for vegetarians, geographical isolation or family opposition resulted in frequent returns to the 'flesh pots'. Yet it may be, as vegetarians and some of their opponents claimed, that the movement helped educate people about dietary matters such as the significance of non-animal foods and wholemeal bread for health, or the value of new foodstuffs, and caused some to ponder the economics and ethics if food production.[1] Certainly the agitation contributed to that ongoing dietetic debate about the 'proper food' – for working people, women, children, or the sedentary – and about responses to problems of price, supply and quality. One late-Victorian observer claimed that the movement, if not making abstinence from meat 'quite respectable', had largely been responsible for making personal choice in dietary matters acceptable.[2] By empowering the individual with the (dietetic) means to health and longevity it sustained that sense of personal control which resulted from traditional recourse to family medicine rather than the medical professional, but it also continued many supporters' anti-scientific attitudes (along with anti-vivisection and anti-vaccination) after medical science had started to make significant breakthroughs.

For some poor Victorians, a reasoned defence of a diet necessitated on economic grounds, may have been psychologically comforting. The worth of the diet's rational gloss, as a compensation 'for the loss of many kinds of self-esteem,' was very rarely stated, and when it was, it was often suggested by people who were not vegetarian activists, such as Herbert Spencer or George Gissing. A more common sentiment was expressed by the clerk Thorne, in Bullock's *Story of a London Clerk*: 'It would never do to let Mrs Brown think that we dined on lentils and porridge'.[3] Throughout the period, it was from the Mrs Brown-fearing classes – the middle classes and the 'aristocracy of labour' – that the movement attracted most of its support. The growth of the white-collar sector from the mid-Victorian period was reflected by the importance of clerks as new members and as customers in restaurants, but this was hardly a new bourgeois-ification of the movement. Its geography was similar to other contemporary moral and social reform movements, since northern England proved an important recruiting ground; yet societies were scattered across England and existed to a lesser extent in Scotland, Wales and Ireland. The total number of vegetarian societies in this period is surprising; their difficulties are not, since they reflected the weakness of the national movement (and the weaknesses of movements' provincial networks in general). If its fortunes partly depended on contingent personal factors such as the death of James Simpson or the accession of Arnold Hills, its emergence and revival were stimulated by the broader environment for reforms.

The movement attracted a variety of people: those who saw a reformed diet as a cure for personal ill health and no more; those who identified it as a means to moral or material self improvement; those who saw it as an additional measure to combat social problems such as poverty, in line with standard soup and thrift philanthropy; those few who identified it as part of a refashioning of society along communitarian lines; and those who saw it as a logical conclusion to other humanitarian causes, or as an integral part of their faith or philosophy. Though it was a far more radical form of abstinence than teetotalism, it was therefore both counter-cultural and conventional. Though lacking mainstream appeal, it was an expression of Victorian puritanism and liberalism. Indeed, vegetarianism was so associated with the Liberal wing of politics that it could plausibly be associated with the faddism of late-nineteenth-century Liberalism by opponents, including Conservatives wishing to appeal to the working class.[4] How far a self-described 'radical' movement could be conventional is reflected by the movement's gender roles and 'domestic ideology'.

Despite being presented as a natural 'women's question', and despite the effort by activists to harness women's energies and expertise, in its slow development of a public role for women it echoed the temperance movement and other causes which accorded women only an ornamental or supporting role in public. But though not always easily recoverable, the female role, whether in the early movement or in the late-Victorian period, was crucial. Women such as Elizabeth Horsell, Jane Hurlstone, Chandos Wallace and May Yates contributed to the development of a public female agency in reform movements. Constraints of space have precluded more extended treatment of the Horsells and Wallaces: they are good examples of the companionate marriage of reformers. On the other hand, the resistance of women to the vegetarian movement within the home – so lamented by vegetarians – indicates the power of many women in the private sphere.

Vegetarianism and modernity

The popular perception of western vegetarianism is that it is a recent phenomenon, emerging in the 1960s-70s, to be expressed in health food stores, restaurants and texts such as *Diet for a Small Planet* or *Animal Liberation*.[5] There has of course been a growth in adherents and organization over the last three decades, stimulated by concerns over the environment, animal welfare in factory-farming, the quality of mass-produced foods, and advice from medical professionals about diet. But, since the modern vegetarian movement originates in the nineteenth century, the relationship between 'modernity' and vegetarianism is older. The Victorian movement was emblematic of both modernity and 'anti-modernity'; a status revealing the complexity of the concept of 'modernity', which, though it tends to convey the sense of transformative change, ought to be understood as having 'shifting and frequently contradictory meanings'.[6] Craig Calhoun has rightly asserted that we 'need to constitute our theoretical notion of modernity not as a master narrative but in a way that reflects both its heterogeneity and contestation'.[7] As a descriptive concept it has been taken by historians to refer to industrialized and urbanized society, where radical social and cultural change was brought about by processes of technological advance, industrialization and urbanization. Contradictorily, it has been associated with both a belief in reason and progress (especially scientific and technical) *and* a break with Enlightenment rationalism and the emergence of the avant-garde modernism.

Vegetarianism clearly was a response to 'modernity' in the form of industrialization, urbanization and a separation from the natural world, as scholars such as Keith Thomas and Julia Twigg suggest.[8] Social changes brought social movements. Modernity made vegetarianism possible in a positive sense because stable and secure food supplies allowed dietetic choice.[9] In the medieval period dietary asceticism had been enjoined on an aristocracy which over-indulged: it made little sense to expect this of peasants.[10] But by the late nineteenth century the upper middle-classes could afford, if they wished to, to pursue the 'simple life'.[11] Another association of the diet with 'modernity', Morton's contention that it was the vanguard of 'a structural, modernist conception of food, now imagined as "pure" nutrition' is not, however, borne out by a study of the Victorian movement's discourse.[12]

The movement's original and primary social location was 'modern' – centres of the industrial revolution such as Manchester or the metropolis – where problematic aspects to modernity acted as stimuli. Such problems were explicitly addressed in vegetarian literature: the diet being promoted as means to cope with a degraded environment, a safeguard against food adulteration, an economy that could eke out the small wages of artisans.[13] Obviously vegetarians were keen to associate themselves with the everyday practical needs of workers but they also showed the utility of their diet for employers. The propaganda directed at factory workers reflected the movement's early geography and also identified it with a symbol of modern labour and technology. Propaganda also suggested vegetarianism was a solution to crises of unemployment. But vegetarianism was a rich and varied phenomenon and it would be wrong to stress one aspect as the central motivation for its promotion (whether explicit or implicit): it was more than a discipline for capitalist society. And when it was conceived as a response to modern social ills this was no novelty. Bryan Turner's observations concerning diet as a solution to earlier perceptions of social or moral problems, whether Luigi Cornaro's dietary solution to Reformation Italy or George Cheyne and John Wesley's diets for the upper classes and working classes in eighteenth-century Britain, are a reminder that diet was one of the remedies for earlier 'modernities'.[14] It has also been argued that the altered relationship with the natural world, whilst undoubtedly important in explaining the movement's growth, must not obscure the fact that even town-dwellers lived amongst the rearing, slaughter and butchering of animals. But it came to be true that, as James Turner notes, zoophilia was largely a 'phenomenon of cities and factory districts'.[15]

If early vegetarian apologists presented their movement as a response to modern times, it seemed 'new' (a defining sensibility of modernity) again in that second age of newness, the *fin de siècle*. Its most vigorous location, the metropolis, was at the heart of modernity. Sociologically, it was 'modern' in recruiting from that new class of white-collar workers. These included women, who as clerks, typists and shop assistants have also been described as symbolic of *fin de siècle* modernity.[16] The movement stimulated a new urban place of refreshment, new commodities and equipment, and its metropolitan organ was even described as part of the 'New Journalism'.[17] The movement was identified with another characteristically modern development: the occult and mystic revival, with spiritualism and theosophy.[18]

The vegetarian sympathizer Amelia Lewis noted in 1876 that the 'rapid strides which Vegetarianism is making show that our social arrangements are altering dietetic rules, and that new ideas are coming up'.[19] Vegetarians, because of the nature of their reform and their involvement with allied causes, were acutely aware of the novel emergence of humanitarian tendencies, and presented a narrative of European progress involving a growth in humane feelings.[20] They also observed dietetic transformation, noting the increased consumption of meat in the second half of the century.[21] But vegetarians did not engage in sociological study: there was no extensive exploration of vegetarianism in relation to material conditions, although plenty was asserted (about the diet in relation to poverty for instance). It was presented by practitioners as an obvious and natural development, a natural reaction by thoughtful, humane, progressive or Christian men and women to circumstances. Adherents did not feel it necessary to provide a detailed explanation of the relationship of their cause to changing 'social arrangements' or to dissect their cause as an expression of modern social ills.

Vegetarians were aware of their novelty. Novelty could be profitable; as we have seen, the Alpha Food Reform Restaurant's advertisement traded on its newness.[22] But vegetarians were also aware of the risks to their reputation from the accession of those attracted merely by fashion, who lost their faith, and who helped give the movement its faddist label. Vegetarians used the language of progress, thus identifying their cause with what was understood to be a defining feature of their era.[23] The age was typified as one of scrutiny and vegetarians associated their efforts with other reformers' questioning of customs and traditions.[24] They presented themselves as truth-seekers, people who dared to think, and consequently could offer 'dietetic enlightenment'.[25] They identified themselves with other 'movements of a progressive civilization' in an age of movements, saw themselves in the 'foremost stages of human progress' or in 'the van of liberty and progress'.[26] If it was presented as a response to immediate problems, some vegetarians also stressed its role in creating a different future. It was described as a 'keystone to a higher civilization'.[27] Anna Kingsford saw her task as 'building up a new system for a new day'.[28]

Throughout the Victorian period, vegetarians situated themselves in the vanguard of social, moral and hygienic reform. The earliest vegetarian journal, significantly entitled *The New Age*, aimed to develop 'new, noble-natured beings'. Its promoters were described as questioning life, custom, diet and everything, their community 'suggestive of new principles of life'.[29] The *Healthian* in 1842 asserted that a 'New society, originated by new beings, from new sympathies, and on new principles, will have its new practices, and we are pretty confident one of its first reforms will be a revision of its BILL OF FARE.'[30] Later papers which we have examined included the *Herald of the Golden Age*, and vegetarianism almost inevitably appeared in other progressive journals across Europe, North America and Australia. The late-Victorian movement in London advertised its paper with slogans including 'Vegetarianism is the coming subject'. The *Vegetarian* described itself as a paper of 'progressive thought', which 'points to that Ideal Future', which was 'always pushing ahead' and 'up-to-date'. But merely being 'modern' was not the justification (and the adjective was less popular for late-Victorians than the word 'new'), it was principle and practicality that counted.[31]

Modernity has been characterized by rationality and the elevation of science. But in the nineteenth century it was also typified by a critique of the claims of science. The movement certainly had an ambivalent relationship to science. In the 1850s they defended their reform on the grounds of Justus von Liebig's new chemistry and continued to draw on nutritional science to support their cause. They also cited comparative anatomy and the theory of evolution, Josiah Oldfield considering vegetarianism to be in harmony 'with the scientific foreshadowing of evolutionary development' (though William E.A. Axon and others sought clarification from Darwin on his views).[32] As Henry Salt asserted, 'it has been reserved to modern times to demonstrate the philosophic and scientific truth'.[33] They endorsed substitutes (edible and otherwise) and advertised the mechanical origins (and thus, hygienic production) of their foods.[34] Technology and science seemed to offer the possibility of doing away with animal exploitation, as one pioneer vegetarian and inventor, Lewis Gompertz, had hoped.[35] Vegetarians used modern technology in their propaganda. But the movement included many, such as Anna Kingsford, who opposed vivisection and vaccination and attacked 'bastard science'.[36] They did this because in their view, the new science represented moral regression. It was also true that the experimentalists' case had to wait till the closing decade of the century to be proven.[37]

Their association with communitarianism, in the 1840s and in the 'back to the land' movement of the *fin de siècle*, also reveals their critical attitude to aspects of modernity and their attempts at alternatives. As one early critic said, they were 'one of the choicer specimens of the Utopian family'.[38] Vegetarians identified their system with the 'primitive diet of man' and saw it as one response to the 'cruelties of civilization' and a solution to the decay which typified 'highly civilized nations'.[39] Often they appeared at odds with contemporaries on aesthetic, social and political grounds; condemning poor physiology, animal cruelty, exploitative relations with the natural world, and luxury. Humanitarian vegetarians of the late nineteenth century attacked the horrors of modern civilization. Communities were a flight from a prevalent form of modernity, and an attempt to create a new existence, 'free from the present competitive modes of life' as one proponent wrote in 1890.[40] Vegetarianism could, in this utopian manifestation, represent 'denouncing modern life in the name of values that modernity itself has created'.[41] As Calhoun has said, 'modernity remains visible, in part, precisely in the shape of the movements challenging it, and asking for more from it'.[42]

British vegetarians were open to the suggestion that there were other, non-western sources of wisdom and morality.[43] In fact, nineteenth-century vegetarian propagandists continued that dialogue with the real and imagined east (primarily India) which had been an important feature of vegetarian polemics for centuries, and which Tristram Stuart has recently, and in detail, examined.[44] The west was not always best, thus Charles Lane had contrasted Turkish hygiene with British steam factories[45] and imperialism was recognized by correspondents and writers in the late-Victorian vegetarian journals as destructive of valuable truths and practices.[46] Like other beleaguered innovators, vegetarians sought to stress the commonness of vegetarianism beyond Britain, in tradition, and even in 'remote history'. Acutely aware, in their propagandistic struggle and daily difficulties, of their novelty and modernity, vegetarians had the solace of antiquity. But opponents could belittle these practitioners of the 'original diet of man' as latter-day Nebuchadnezzars or, as one paper referred to them during the Indian Mutiny, proponents of 'a very ancient and low superstition'.[47]

The present-day struggle was justified by future success: the linear direction of humanity would involve vegetarianism at the end. Vegetarians seized upon any verdict from contemporaries which acknowledged their future inevitability: thus the American transcendentalist Henry Thoreau's view 'that it [was] part of the destiny of the human race, in its gradual improvement, to leave off eating animals', the Russian scholar Beketon's description of it as the 'food of the future' and the Prussian physiologist Rudolf Virchow's assertion that the 'future is with the vegetarians' were publicized by British vegetarians.[48] If in their general belief in the advance of humanity they were characteristic of their era, more specifically, vegetarians were part of the mainstream in their temperance and social purity orientation. Though vegetarians were described as unconventional, heretical, and eccentric, even the 'faddist' label that indicated the marginal status wished upon them, linked vegetarians to a modernity characterized as an age of fads, *'isms'*, and crazes.

Vegetarianism *was* perceived as new. Early critics described it as a 'new-fangled system', a 'precious class of New Reformers' and one of the 'new lights'. Contemporaries treated it as a modern movement, even if they were aware of classical antecedents, and its prevalence in the non-European world. But its significance as a 'sign of the times' when it emerged was debated. Its claims to be progressive were disputed. Early commentators, such as Brown in his essay on physical Puritanism, and Smith in *The Family Herald*, rightly identified vegetarianism as a reaction to modern-day sensualism.[49] Medical opponents could present it as retrograde: as a cause which would restrict the evolution of man, limiting food resources.[50] The pace of modernity meant that pre-digested foods were at a premium, according to Sir Henry Thompson, who thought the development of meat extracts in the 'middle third of the century' almost providential.[51] Vegetarian diet would lead to that degeneration which was also part of evolution, to defeat in the struggle for existence.[52] It was ill-suited to the 'pressure of our ordinary competitive life'.[53] To be a rigorous vegetarian was to make living 'at a European pace or after modern ideas' impossible.[54] Others could describe it as something for the millennium: for the far distant future.[55] It was described as one of the latest delusions, fads or quackeries, which would fade away as science exploded its claims. The orthodox in religion might identify it as one of the false teachings to emerge at the end of days. It could be seen as a sign of the pathology of modern civilization: for Max Nordau at the turn of the century, it was a sign of decadence, one of the many derangements which had proved popular for the German hysterical degenerate.[56]

We have seen vegetarianism develop as an organization from the 1830s, until the British movement became one part, a leading part, of a wider organized movement by the early twentieth century. The twentieth century, as in the first fifty years of its history, was to see periods of decline and periods of revival. Late-Victorian vegetarians had themselves occasionally voiced pessimism, as they struggled to attract public support: 'It would be a matter for regret if, a hundred years hence, some lexicographer should define the word "vegetarian" as "one of a small religious sect which flourished at the latter part of the nineteenth Century".'[57] If vegetarians posed as 'advanced' this was because they knew their system to be unpopular, and looked to the future for vindication, looked to the 'good times coming'.[58] In our times, when millions of Britons are reported as vegetarian, Charles Forward's belief that his cause was destined to be one of the most 'far reaching of reform movements of the Victorian age' appears vindicated.[59]

NOTES

Full publication details appear in the Bibliography.

Introduction

1 *The Truth-Tester*, 22 October 1847, p. 15.
2 Although I use the term 'Victorian' in this book, I agree with the concern expressed by many historians, from George M. Young (*Victorian England. Portrait of an Age*, 1936) and William L. Burn (*The Age of Equipoise*, 1964) onwards, that in the face of a variety of 'Victorianisms' the term has no stable meaning beyond its use as a label for a period (1837-1901) which was certainly not monolithic. For useful discussion of the problematizing of the concept, see Miles Taylor and Michael Wolff, eds, *The Victorians since 1901. Histories, Representations and Revisions* (Manchester, 2004). As Taylor notes in the 'Introduction', p. 2, 'the Victorians have been made and remade throughout the twentieth century, as successive generations have used the Victorian past in order to locate themselves in the present'. Victorian attitudes on a range of important topics (such as race, gender and sexuality) were complex; nevertheless, as I hope to demonstrate, vegetarians and others did represent a challenge to certain contemporary norms and values of their wider society.
3 Julia M. Twigg, 'The Vegetarian movement in England from 1847-1981: a study of the structure of its ideology', Ph.D., London School of Economics, 1982; 'Vegetarianism and the Meanings of Meat', in Anne Murcott, ed., *The Sociology of Food and Eating* (Aldershot, 1983), pp. 18-30; 'Food for Thought: Purity and Vegetarianism', *Religion* 9 (Spring 1979), pp. 13-35.
4 Frank Thistlethwaite, *America and the Atlantic Community. Anglo-American Aspects, 1790-1850* (New York, 1963); Peter S. Brown, 'Nineteenth-century American health reformers and the early nature cure movement in Britain', *Medical History* 32 (1988) pp. 174-194.
5 Stephen Nissenbaum, *Sex, Diet and Debility in Jacksonian America. Sylvester Graham and Health Reform* (Westport, Connecticut, 1980); Gerald Carson, *Cornflake Crusade* (London, 1959); Claudia Nelson, 'Care in feeding: vegetarianism and social reform in Alcott's America', in Claudia Nelson and Lynne Vallone, eds, *The Girls Own. Cultural Histories of the Anglo-American Girl, 1830-1915* (Athens, Georgia, 1994), pp. 11-33; James C. Whorton, *Crusaders for Fitness. The History of American Health*

Reformers (Princeton: 1982); and Susan E. Cayleff, *Wash and Be Healed. The Water Cure Movement and Women's Health* (Philadelphia: 1987).

6   Jan M. Romein, *Op het breukvlak van twee eeuwen*, translated as *The Watershed of Two Eras. Europe in 1900* (Middleton, Connecticut: 1978), p. 507.

7   Elisabeth Meyer-Renschhausen and Albert Wirz, 'Dietetics, health reform and social order: vegetarianism as a moral physiology. The example of Maximilian Bircher-Benner (1867-1939)', *Medical History* 43 (1999), pp. 323-341; Ceri Crossley, *Consumable Metaphors. Attitudes towards Animals and Vegetarianism in Nineteenth-Century France* (Oxford, Bern: Peter Lang, 2005), which partly draws on several earlier essays, including 'Attitudes towards Animals and Vegetarianism in Nineteenth Century France', in Martyn Cornick and Ceri Crossley, eds, *Problems in French History* (Basingstoke: 2000), pp. 81-103; and Peter Brang, *Ein unbekanntes Russland. Kulturgeschichte vegetarischer Lebensweisen von den Anfängen bis zur Gegenwart* (Cologne, 2002), which I have not been able to examine.

8   Stephen Hay, 'The Making of a late Victorian Hindu: M.K. Gandhi in London, 1888-1891', *Victorian Studies*, 33:1 (1989), pp. 74-98. See Edgar Crook, *Vegetarianism in Australia, 1788 to 1948. A Cultural and Social History* (2006), on the Australian vegetarian movement. I am grateful to the author for a preview of this research.

9   Colin Spencer, *The Heretic's Feast. A History of Vegetarianism* (London: 1993), republished (2001) as *Vegetarianism: A History*. Spencer draws on Twigg's research, as does Arouna P. Ouedraogo, 'The social genesis of western vegetarianism to 1859', in Robert Dare, ed., *Food, Power and Community. Essays in the History of Food and Drink* (Adelaide, 1999), pp. 154-166.

10   Paul D'Anieri, Claire Ernst and Elisabeth Kier, 'New Social Movements in Historical Perspective', *Comparative Politics* July 1990, pp. 445-458; Nelson A. Pichardo, 'New Social Movements: A Critical Review', *Annual Review of Sociology* 23 (1997), pp. 411-430; and Craig Calhoun, 'New Social Movements of the Early 19th Century', *Social Science History* 17 (1993), pp. 385-427.

11   Carol J. Adams, *The Sexual Politics of Meat. A Feminist-vegetarian Critical Theory* (1990; New York: 1994).

12   Tristram Stuart, *The Bloodless Revolution. Radical Vegetarians and the Discovery of India* (London: 2006). This work offers a richly detailed and nuanced account of cultural exchange between India and range of western philosophers, travel writers, puritans and political radicals. Though the primary focus is on the period *c.*1600-1800, Stuart discusses both the classical origins and more recent connections. I have researched the organizational and literary connections between the British vegetarians and Indian vegetarianism in the Victorian period, in an unpublished monograph.

13   Derek Antrobus, *A Guiltless Feast. The Salford Bible-Christian Church and the Rise of the Modern Vegetarian Movement* (Salford, 1997); Paul A. Pickering and Alex Tyrrell, '"In the Thickest of the Fight": the Reverend James Scholefield (1790-1855) and the Bible Christians of Salford', *Albion* 26:3 (Fall 1994), pp. 461-482; John Belchem, '"Temperance in all things": Vegetarianism, the Manx press and the alternative agenda of reform in the 1840s', ch. 11 in Malcolm Chase and Ian Dyck, eds, *Living and Learning: Essays in Honour of J.F.C. Harrison* (Aldershot, 1996), pp. 149-162.

14   See Howard William's internationally-influential *The Ethics of Diet. A Catena of Authorities deprecatory of the Habit of Flesh-eating* (London: 1883). A revised and enlarged edition appeared in 1896.

15 *VM*, January-June 1851.
16 Charles W. Forward, *Fifty Years of Food Reform. A History of the Vegetarian Movement in England* (London: 1898). The VS, objecting to Forward's account, requested its name be removed when it was published as a book. Forward's 'Forty Years among the Faddists', serialized in *Vegetarian News* (the LVS journal from 1921) from February 1922-1923 provides further information.
17 Brian Harrison, *Drink and the Victorians: The Temperance Question in England, 1815-1872* (London: 1971); Brian Harrison, *Dictionary of British Temperance Biography* (Coventry: 1973); and Brian Harrison, '"A world of which we had no conception": Liberalism and the Temperance Press, 1830-1872', *Victorian Studies* 13: 2 (1969-1970), pp. 125-158.
18 James Gregory, 'The Movement against Capital Punishment in Britain, *c.*1846-1868', unpublished M.Phil. thesis, University of Cambridge, 1997.
19 Timothy Morton, *Shelley and the Revolution in Taste. The Body and the Natural World* (Cambridge: 1994); other works exploring Shelley are cited in chapter seven A contemporary radical and vegetarian, from a working-class and Cowherdite background, was Rowland Detrosier (who died 1834): see Matthew Lee's entry in the *ODNB* (Oxford, 2004).
20 See Kathryn Gleadle, '"The age of physiological reformers": rethinking gender and domesticity in the age of reform', ch. 8 in Arthur Burns and Joanna Innes, eds, *Rethinking the Age of Reform* (Cambridge, 2003), pp. 200-219.
21 Jackie E.M. Latham, *Search for a New Eden. James Pierrepont Greaves (1777-1842): The Sacred Socialist and His Followers* (London, 1999).
22 See Arthur E. Bestor, *Backwoods Utopias. The Sectarian and Owenite Phases of Communitarian Socialism in America, 1663-1829* (London, 1950).
23 Walter H.G. Armytage, *Yesterdays Tomorrows. A Historical Survey of Future Societies* (London, 1968); Vernon L. Parrington, *American Dreams. A Study of American Utopias* (2nd, enlarged edn, New York, 1964).
24 Samuel Hynes, *The Edwardian Turn of Mind* (Princeton, 1968), p. 135. John F.C. Harrison, *Late Victorian Britain. 1875-1901* (London, 1990), p. 156, identifies vegetarianism as one of the era's characteristic reform movements.
25 Max Nordau, *Degeneration* (Lincoln, Nebraska and London, 1993), p. 209. Nordau (Simon Maximilian Suedfeld, 1849-1923) published his highly controversial work in 1892, an English translation, *Degeneration*, appeared 1895. See George B. Shaw, *The Sanity of Art. An Exposure of the Current Nonsense about Artists Being Degenerate*, first published in 1895, reprinted in Shaw, *Major Critical Essays* (London: 1932), pp. 281-332. See William Greenslade, 'Fitness and the Fin de Siècle', in John Stokes, *Fin de Siècle/Fin du Globe. Fears and Fantasies of the late Nineteenth Century* (London, 1992), pp.37-51.
26 George A. Cevasco, ed., *The 1890s. An Encyclopedia of British Literature, Art and Culture* (New York, 1993). It does not feature in Karl Beckson, *London in the 1890s. A Cultural History* (New York, 1992).
27 Norman and Jeanne Mackenzie, *The First Fabians* (London, 1977); Stanley Pierson, *British Socialists. The Journey from Fantasy to Politics* (Cambridge, Massachusetts, 1979); Stephen Yeo, 'A New Life: The Religion of Socialism in Britain. 1883-1896', *History Workshop Journal* 4 (Autumn 1977), pp. 5-56; Sheila Rowbotham and Jeffrey Weeks, *Socialism and the New Life. The Personal and Sexual Politics of Edward Carpenter*

and *Havelock Ellis* (London, 1977). See also Mark Bevir, 'The Rise of Ethical Anarchism. 1885-1900', *Historical Research* 69 (1996), pp. 143-165.

28 Norman Brady, ' "Shafts" and the quest for a new morality: an examination of the Woman Question in the 1890s as seen through the pages of a contemporary journal', unpublished MA thesis, University of Warwick, 1978. Leah Lenemen, 'The Awakened Instinct: vegetarianism and the women's suffrage movement in Britain', *Women's History Review* 6:2 (1997), pp. 271-287.

29 See Raphael Samuel, 'The Discovery of Puritanism, 1820-1914: A Preliminary Sketch', pp. 276-322, in Alison Light, Sally Alexander and Gareth Stedman Jones, eds, *Island Stories: Unravelling Britain* vol. 2 *Theatres of Memory* (London, 1998).

30 Bryan S. Turner, *The Body and Society. Explorations in Social Theory* (1984; London, 1996); 'The government of the body, medical regimen and the rationalisation of diet', *British Journal of Sociology* 33 (1982), pp. 254-269, reprinted as ch. 6 in Bryan S. Turner, *Regulating Bodies. Essays in Medical Sociology* (London, 1992), and the journal *Body and Society*.

31 Charles Walker of Worcester, Diary for 1851. Transcribed by Jean Day.

32 This biographical data forms a supplementary volume to my Ph.D.

33 *VM*, October 1895, p. 409.

34 The attempt to replace 'vegetarian' by 'dietetic reform' was inaugurated in the *VM*, September 1854, pp. 76-78, to indicate its concern with the 'whole question of dietetic habits'.

35 George H. Lewes, 'Theories of Food', *Blackwood's Edinburgh Magazine* 8:542 (December 1860), p. 680.

36 For instance, John Gray, *The Social System. A Treatise on the Principle of Exchange* (Edinburgh, 1831); Henry Fawcett, *Pauperism. Its Causes and Remedies* (London, 1871) and Charles R. Drysdale, *The Population Question According to T.R. Malthus and J.S. Mill* (London, 1892) recommended birth control. On the socialist theory of under-consumption through monopoly of the means of production, see Henry Seymour, *An Examination of the Malthusian Theory* (London, 1889). On emigration, see Caroline Chisholm, *Comfort for the Poor! Meat Three Times a Day!!* (London, 1847) and John I. Burn, *Familiar Letters on Population, Emigration, and Home Colonization* (London, 1832).

37 See Mark R. Finlay, 'Quackery and Cookery: Justus von Liebig's Extract of Meat and the Theory of Nutrition in the Victorian Age', *Bulletin of the History of Medicine* 66 (1992), pp. 404-418.

38 *Royal Album of Arts and Industry of Great Britain* (London, 1887), p. 49.

39 Stephen Mennell, *All Manners of Food. Eating and Taste in England and France from the Middle Ages to the Present* (Oxford, 1985), ch. 8 and ch. 9. Diet concerned public health organizations such as the Parkes Museum which hosted lectures from various food reformers, see Beverley P. Bergman and S.A. Miller, 'Historical Perspectives on Health. The Parkes Museum of Hygiene and the Sanitary Institute', *Journal of the Royal Society of Health* 123: 1 (March 2003), pp. 55-61.

40 Peter Gurney, *Co-operative Culture and the Politics of Consumption in England, 1870-1930* (Manchester, 1996), argues that consumption was an 'intensely political sphere' (pp. 11-12).

41 The role of 'social tension' – caused by food prices and the trade cycle – was first studied by Walt W. Rostow, *British Economy of the Nineteenth Century* (Oxford:

Clarendon Press, 1948). See George S.R. Kitson-Clark, 'Hunger and Politics in 1842', *Journal of Modern History* 25 (1953), pp. 355-374.

42 *Food*, July 1884, p. 2.
43 For a useful discussion of modern work on the patterning of food consumption by age, gender and class, see Stephen Mennell, Anne Murcott, and Anneke H. Van Otterloo, *The Sociology of Food. Eating, Diet and Culture* (London, 1992), ch. 7.
44 Lynette Hunter, 'Proliferating Publications', in Constance Anne Wilson, ed., *Luncheon, Nuncheon and Other Meals. Eating with the Victorians* (Stroud, 1994), pp. 51-70; Valerie Mars, 'À la Russe: The New Way of Dining', also in *Luncheon, Nuncheon and Other Meals*.
45 Edward Smith's government-sponsored study of working-class diet identified age and gender differences in diet. See Ellen Ross, *Love and Toil.Motherhood in Outcast London, 1870-1918* (New York, 1993) on the starvation by mothers, before the Great War.
46 *Food Journal*, 1873, p. 245. See the comment by the German reformer M.P. Wolff, *Food for the Million. A Plan for Starting Public Kitchens* (London, 1884) about 'stretching the alien hand into the very heart of the family'. See also John Burnett, in John Burnett and Derek J. Oddy, eds, *The Origins and Development of Food Policies in Europe* (London, 1994), p. 56.
47 See Keith Robbins, *Nineteenth Century Britain. Integration and Diversity* (Oxford, 1988), pp. 16-20; John G. Rule, 'Regional variations of food consumption amongst agricultural labourers, 1790-1860', in Walter Minchinton, ed., *Exeter Papers in Economic History: Agricultural Improvement: Medieval and Modern* (Exeter, 1981).
48 Ben Rogers, *Beef and Liberty* (London, 2003), pp. 2-3.
49 John Burnett, *Plenty and Want. A Social History of Diet in England from 1815 to the Present Day* (London, 1966), pp. 157-158.
50 Vegetarians, attending their public banquet in Freemason's Tavern in 1851 were told 'The vaunted roast beef of Old England was very innutritious and very long in digesting,' see *The Times*, 2 August 1851, p. 8. *The Times* condemned vegetarians, 23 January 1879, p. 9, for selling the English birthright of beef (and mutton) for pottage.
51 Richard Perren, *The Meat Trade in Britain. 1840-1914* (London, 1978), ch. 4; Francis B. Smith, *The People's Health. 1830-1910* (London: 1979), pp. 205-207.
52 Ford Madox Brown, *On Work*, 1865; the text accompanying the painting, quoted in Julia Treuherz, *Pre-Raphaelite Paintings for the Manchester City Art Gallery* (London, 1980).
53 Henry Mayhew, 'Of the diet, drink and expense of living of the Street Irish', *London Labour and the London Poor* (London, 1861), vol. 1, p. 113.
54 Henry S. Salt, 'Food Reform', *Westminster Review*, October 1886, p. 484.
55 See George R. Sims, 'The Fatal Sneeze. A Christmas Story', *Penny Illustrated News*, 17 December 1881, p. 6, for a eulogy on the pudding.
56 Robbins, *Nineteenth Century Britain*, pp. 16-17.
57 Alex Gibson and Thomas C. Smout, 'From Meat to Meal: Changes in Diet in Scotland', ch. 2 in Catherine Geissler and Derek J. Oddy, eds, *Food, Diet and Economic Change. Past and Present* (Leicester, 1993), pp. 10-34.
58 Redcliffe N. Salaman, *The History and Social Influence of the Potato* (Cambridge, 1949), pp. 522-523, p. 530 (Cobbett and Caird); *Food Journal*, October 1872, p. 357

(Carlyle). On Irish diet more generally, see E.M. Crawford, 'The Irish Workhouse Diet, 1840-90' in Burnett and Oddy, *Origins and Development of Food Policies*.
59 *Food*, July 1884, 'To Our Readers'.
60 See *Vegetarian Advocate*, October 1848, p. 30, citing Richard Phillips, *Millions of Facts*, p. 708-9.
61 *Times*, 23 September 1882, p. 6 (Nottingham British Association); 9 September 1890, p. 4: British Association.
62 See Richard Oastler's paper *The Home*, reported in the Chartist *Northern Star*, 26 April 1848, p. 5, on the danger of relying on foreign supplies; 'The Fall of Rome', *Blackwood's Edinburgh Magazine*, 59, no. 368 (June 1846), p. 697.
63 Republished in Joseph Fisher, *Where shall we get Meat? The Food Supplies of Western Europe* (London, 1866); John Ewart, *Meat Production. A Manual for Producers, Distributors, and Consumers of Butchers' Meat* (London, 1878).
64 *The International Exhibition of 1862. The Illustrated Catalogue of the Industrial Department. British Division* vol. 1 (London, 1862), p. 76.
65 *Public Health*, 1 February 1869, p. 36. See also Hassall's *Food, Water and Air*, vol. 2 (1873), p. 29 for a meeting at Cannon Street Hotel discussing Australian meats.
66 Michael G. Mulhall, *England's New Sheep-Farm* (London, 1882).
67 Smith, *People's Health*, p. 207. The working-classes' disapproval of Australian mutton was noted in James T. Law, *Law's Grocer's Manual. A Practical Guide for Tea and Provision Dealers* ... (Liverpool, 1896), pp. 56-57.
68 See Crossley, *Consumable Metaphors*, p. 79, on the 'discourse of domestication' and acclimatization.
69 See 'Working the Dead Horse', *Penny Illustrated Paper*, 10 April 1875, p. 2. Hippophagic efforts are noted by Jack C. Drummond and Anne Wilbraham, *The Englishman's Food. A History of Five Centuries of English Diet* (1939; revised edn, 1964), ch. 17.
70 John Burnett, 'The History of Food Adulteration in the Nineteenth Century, with Special Reference to Bread, Tea and Beer', Ph.D. (University of London, 1958); John Burnett, *Plenty and Want. A Social History of Diet in England from 1815 to the Present Day* (London, 1966), ch. 10.
71 See Arthur H. Hassall, *Food and its Adulterations; comprising the reports of the analytical Sanitary Committee of 'The Lancet'* (London, 1855).
72 *The Public Good*, vol. 1, 1868: articles by John Postgate in the context of the 1869 Adulteration Bill.
73 On food adulteration as a test case for the moral market, see Geoffrey R. Searle, *Morality and the Market in Victorian Britain* (Oxford, 1998).
74 Hassall, *Food and its Adulterations*, p. xxxvi.
75 Burnett, 'The History of Food Adulteration', p. 52. See George J. Holyoake, *A History of Co-operation* (London, 1879), from his speech on co-operation in Rochdale in 1843; on impure food, p. 104; and p. 287, on the Ralahine community's co-operative food store. Hassall, *Food and its Adulterations*, p. xxx, acknowledged that the poor were the principal victims.
76 George J. Holyoake, *The Jubilee History of the Leeds Industrial Co-operative Society* (Leeds, 1897).
77 Samuel Smiles, *Self-Help* (1859). The vegetarian Joseph Brotherton featured.
78 Anneke H. Van Otterloo, *Eten en Eetlust in Nederland (1840-1990)* (Amsterdam, 1990), notes the significance of bourgeois food reformers in the Netherlands,

attempting to disseminate the message of thrift and simplicity to their class and the working class.
79 Asa Briggs, *The Age of Improvement. 1783-1867* (1959; London: 1993), p. 397.
80 Briggs, *Age of Improvement*, p. 450, from *Self-Help*, ch. 1.
81 Edwin Chadwick, *Report on the Sanitary Condition of the Labouring Population of Great Britain* (1842), edited and with introduction by M.W. Flinn (Edinburgh University Press, 1965) pp. 204.
82 Samuel Butler, *The Way of All Flesh* (1903), ch. 83.
83 Ian Bradley, *The Call to Seriousness. The Evangelical Impact on the Victorians* (London, 1976), p. 182.
84 Colin Spencer, *British Food. An Extraordinary Thousand Years of History* (London, 2002), ch. 10.
85 Robert J. Cruikshank, *Charles Dickens and Early Victorian England* (London, 1949), p. 151, p. 157.
86 Richard Jefferies, *Hodge and his Masters* (London, 1880), ch. 24.
87 Drummond and Wilbraham, *The Englishman's Food*, p. 334.
88 Tom Jerrold, *Our Kitchen Garden. The Plants We Grow and How to Cook Them* (London, 1881), p. 4.
89 Joseph Brown, *The Food of the People* (London, 1865), p. 55; 'Amicus Curiae', *Food for the Million. Maize against Potato* (London, 1847), p. 79.
90 Isabella Beeton, *Mrs Beeton's Everyday Cookery and Housekeeping Book. New Edition, Revised and Greatly Enlarged* (London, n.d.), p. lxviii.
91 Wolff, *Food for the Million*, p. 135; Edward H. Hall, *Coffee Taverns, Cocoa Houses and Coffee Palaces. Their Rise, Progress, and Prospects; with a Directory* (London, 1878), p. 46, p. 75.
92 Rule, 'Regional Variations of food consumption'.
93 H.B. Proctor, *Rice: Its History, Culture, Manufacture, and Food Value* (London, 1882), p. 36.
94 *The Lancet*, 14 June 1879, p. 858.
95 François Volant and James R. Watson, eds, *Memoirs of Alexis Soyer with Unpublished Receipts and Odds and Ends of Gastronomy* (London, 1859), p. 289.
96 'Working the Dead Horse', *Penny Illustrated Paper*, 10 April 1875, p. 2.
97 Burnett, *Plenty and Want*, p. 47.
98 Vincent J. Knapp, 'The Democratisation of Meat and Protein in Europe,' *The Historian* 59: 3 (Spring 1997), pp. 541-551. Georg F. Kolb, *The Condition of Nations Social and Political With Comparative Tables of Universal Statistics* (London, 1880): p. 76 offered comparative statistics of average meat consumption.
99 Henry de B. Gibbins, *The English People in the Nineteenth Century. A Short History* (London, 1898), p. 36, p. 154.
100 Thomas B. Macaulay, *History of England from the Accession of James II*, vol. 1 (1848), a comment which appears in the section, on the 'delusion which leads men to overrate the happiness of the preceding generations,' at the end of ch. 3.
101 Burnett *Plenty and Want*, p. 180; a suggestion which some critics of vegetarianism conceded.
102 Mennell, *All Manner of Foods*, Turner, 'The government of the body', 1982.
103 Mennell, p. 231; see Burnett, *Plenty and Want*, p. 186, on 'solid and unexciting' middle-class diet.

Chapter One

1. Jutta Schwartzkopf, *Women in the Chartist Movement* (Basingstoke, 1991) p. 61; Helen Rogers, '"The Prayer, the passion and the reason" of Eliza Sharples: freethought, women's rights and republicanism, 1832-52', ch. 2 in Eileen Yeo, ed., *Radical Femininity. Women's Self-Representation in the Public Sphere* (Manchester, 1998), pp. 52-78.
2. Francis F. Barham, 'A Memoir of the late James Pierrepont Greaves Esq.' in *An Odd Medley of Literary Curiosities*, part 2 (London, 1845), p. 4.
3. *NMW*, 27 January 1844.
4. Jackie E.M. Latham, *Search for a New Eden. James Pierrepont Greaves (1777-1842): The Sacred Socialist and His Followers* (London, 1999), p. 159.
5. Latham, *Search for a New Eden*, pp. 60-61, pp. 170-171; *New Age*, 20 May 1843, p. 23.
6. Latham, *Search for a New Eden*, chs. 5-8; Kathryn Gleadle, '"Our Several Spheres": Middle-class Women and the Feminisms of Early Victorian Radical Politics,' in Kathryn Gleadle and Sarah Richardson, eds, *Women in British Politics, 1760-1860. The Power of the Petticoat* (Basingstoke, 2001), pp. 134-152.
7. *A Prospectus for the Establishment of a Concordium; or an Industry Harmony College* (London, 1841). A new prospectus appeared in 1843.
8. Latham, *Search for a New Eden*, p. 87, pp. 231-232.
9. Latham, *Search for a New Eden*, chs. 12-13; F.B. Sanborn, *Bronson Alcott at Alcott House, England and Fruitlands, New England 1842-1844* (Cedar Rapids, Iowa, 1908). On Fruitlands: Ednah D. Cheney, ed., *Louisa May Alcott. Her Life, Letters and Journals* (1889; London, 1890), pp. 33-38.
10. *New Age*, 10 June 1843, pp. 46-47.
11. *New Age*, 1 October 1843, p. 108. Copies were sent to the reformist *Precursor of Unity* in 1844. Concordist publications were advertised in Alexander Campbell's *Spirit of the Age*, 1848, p. 16, p. 48.
12. *Temperance Lancet*, 18 December 1841, p. 111. But see favourable comment on Jewish abstinence, p. 114; the editor recommended – 14 May 1842 – p. 280, the cookery book 'of the 'Coward-ites' at Salford.
13. *New Age*, 3 June 1843, p. 40. The organizer, Harrold of Greenwich, informed the *Teetotal Journal* (1844, pp. 163-165) about a Greavesian teetotal lecture.
14. 'Practical Teetotaller', *New Age*, 3 June 1843, p. 40. The title change (1 July 1843) followed the suggestion by 'Practical Teetotaller'.
15. *Healthian*, August 1842, p. 71.
16. *Healthian*, September 1842, p. 80.
17. *Healthian*, October 1842, p. 87.
18. *New Age*, 1 October 1843, p. 111. The society's advertisement is appended to the Concordium's printing of Graham's *A Lecture to Young Men* (London, 1843), pp. 145-146.
19. Latham, *Search for a New Eden*, pp. 171-172.
20. *New Age*, 1 January 1844, pp. 172-173.
21. *The Truth-Tester*, 1847, p. 121. See *The People's Press* (Douglas, Isle of Man), September 1847, pp. 235-237 and *The Times* (25 January 1848, p. 10), for efforts to recruit new pupils.
22. Spencer, *The Heretic's Feast*, p. 261.
23. *Cheltenham Free Press*, 8 July 1843, p. 213.

24   Edward Royle, *Victorian Infidels. The Origins of the British Secularist Movement. 1791-1866* (Manchester, 1974), p. 144; Joseph McCabe, *Life and Letters of G.J. Holyoake* (London, 1908), vol. 1, pp. 90-91. See p. 128 for review of the Concordist edition of William A. Alcott, *Vegetable Diet Defended* (London, 1844).
25   *Reasoner*, vol. 6, 1849, pp. 113-115; pp. 133-135.
26   *New Age*, 8 January 1844, pp. 139-140. See William A. Smith, *'Shepherd' Smith the Universalist. The Story of a Mind* (London, 1892); John Saville, 'J.E. Smith and the Owenite Movement 1833-34', ch.5 in Sidney Pollard and John Salt, eds, *Robert Owen: Prophet of the Poor. Essays in Honour of the Two Hundredth Anniversary of His Birth* (London, 1971), pp. 115-144; and John F.C. Harrison, *Robert Owen and the Owenites in Britain and America. The Quest for the New Moral World* (London, 1969), pp. 109-122; Barbara Taylor, *Eve and the New Jerusalem. Socialism and Feminism in the Nineteenth Century* (London, 1983), pp. 167-171.
27   *Family Herald*, 29 July 1843, p. 184.
28   Advertisements for Alcott House, *Family Herald*, 11 May 1844, p. 10; for Concordist publications, 18 May, p. 25; and Etzler, p. 105. Smith received vegetarian tracts, see 30 March 1844, and 8 November 1844. Though he favourably reviewed *Letters and Extracts from the MS Writings of James Pierrepont Greaves*, he thought it 'vague, incoherent, scattered, fatherless, individualism', 1844, p. 654. Vegetarianism was discussed 15 February 1845, p. 654; 10 October 1846, p. 362.
29   *NMW*, 5 October 1844, p. 120. Graves (and Barmby) are cited with others to refute an argument by Hermann Semming on 'True Socialism'; see Karl Marx and Friedrich Engels, *The German Ideology* (1846; reprinted in vol. 5 of *The Collected Works of Karl Marx and Frederick Engels*, London, 1976), vol. 2, p. 461.
30   Jackie E.M. Latham, 'Carlyle and the "Blockhead" James Pierrepont Greaves', *Carlyle Studies Annual* 2000, pp. 33-47. Through Emerson, Carlyle was informed about Fruitlands, Lane and Wright.
31   *VM*, July 1888, p. 262: 'There stands Piccadilly; there it has been for a hundred years; there it will be when you and your potato-gospel are dead and forgotten.' For Browning's encounter, see Joseph Slater, ed., *The Correspondence of Emerson and Carlyle* (New York, 1964), p. 329.
32   Francis F. Barham, 'A Memoir of the late James Pierrepont Greaves Esq.'; Walter H.G. Armytage, *Heavens Below. Utopian Experiments in England 1560-1960* (London, 1961), p. 198.
33   Henry S. Sutton, *The Evangel of Love* (London, 1847), p. 81: 'When I first tried to read James Greaves's Letters, I thought the man mad, the book seemed such a mass of raving absurdities'. See *The Truth-Tester*, 15 August 1847, pp. 3-4. Sutton's vegetarianism was based on asceticism and concern to liberate women from domestic chores.
34   *Douglas Jerrold's Weekly Newspaper*, 29 January 1848, p. 142.
35   Mary A. Kelty, *Visiting My Relations, and its Results; a series of small episodes in the life of a recluse* (London, 1851), chs. 5-7.
36   Thomas Frost, *Forty Years' Recollections: Literary and Political* (London, 1880); George J. Holyoake, *A History of Co-operation* (London, 1879); William J. Linton, *Memories* (London, 1895). A brief reference appears in 'The Culture of Emerson,' *Fraser's Magazine*; reprinted in *Littell's Living Age*, 8 August 1868, p. 372.

37 *DR*, December 1883, pp. 453-455; *Home Links*, February 1898, p. 15, and letter from former Concordist and American VS leader Henry S. Clubb, no. 2, p. 71. Clubb's recollections appeared in *HH*, May, June and August 1906. James Burns recalled Oldham and Greaves in the spiritualist *MD*.
38 E.g., 'M.L.', 'The Community Movement', reprinted in *NMW*, 16 November 1844, p. 163, on the necessity for pure diet, physiology in dress and good health. See Harrison, *Robert Owen and the Owenites*, p. 179; and Robert Owen, *A New View of Society and Other Writings* (ed., with Introduction by Gregory Claeys) (London, 1991) for the new food, clothes, medicine, and other arrangements in a rational society.
39 Frank Podmore, *Robert Owen. A Biography*, 2 vols (London, 1906), vol. 2, p. 473 reprints an Owenite 'hymn to temperance' and notes the Owenite ideal as a temperate man. See p. 474, the implicitly vegetarian verse: 'No altar smokes, no off'rings bleed'. M.D. Conway's verdict on Owenite-Chartists as 'men of plain-living and high thinking, almost ascetic in their self-denial' is quoted in Warren S. Smith, *The London Heretics 1870-1914* (London, 1967), p. 23. See Iorwerth J. Prothero, *Artisans and Politics in Early Nineteenth Century London. John Gast and his Times* (Folkestone, 1979), p. 264, for the emphasis on Owenism's *moral* reformism.
40 *NMW*, 1844, p. 371. Another, Skaneatles, advocated 'No God, No Government, No Money, No Meat, No Salt and Pepper.' David E. Shi, *The Simple Life. Plain Living and High Thinking in American Culture* (Oxford, 1985), p. 134, quotes Emerson: 'We are a little wild here with numberless projects of social reform ... One man renounces the use of animal food, and another of coin; another of domestic hired service, and another of the State.'
41 *Working Bee*, 11 July 1840, p. 43; following Firmin's letter, 4 July 1840, p. 39. Henry G. Wright intended to visit. See J.C. Langdon, 'Pocket Editions of the New Jerusalem: Owenite Communitarianism in Britain. 1825-1855', unpublished D.Phil., University of York, February 2000, p. 223.
42 *NMW*, 21 October 1843, p. 136. Thomas Frost was secretary.
43 Edward Royle, *Robert Owen and the Commencement of the Millennium: A Study of the Harmony Community* (Manchester, 1998), p. 168. Oldham spoke to colonists about diet and association; his ideas were deemed too impractical for the masses: *NMW*, 6 December 1844, p. 189. See 'A.H', *NMW*, 13 December 1844, p. 198, on the tailor's departure due to the diet; the reporter asserted 'We are in no ways ascetics, or solely vegetarians'. On Slatter, see *DR*, April 1888, p. 123.
44 Dr Dixon, *Journal of Health*, April 1861, p. 51, formerly Harmony's physician, explains his friend Rigby's vegetarianism as the result of upbringing not conscience.
45 *DR*, December 1893, p. 436, in discussion about E.T. Craig's Ralahine experiment (1831-1833).
46 Royle, *Owen and the Commencement*, p. 142; Holyoake, *History of Co-operation*, vol. 2, p. 313. The reporter, a 'Twelve Years' Socialist' in *NMW*, December 1842, p. 229, considered the vegetarian dinner 'settles at once the question of a meat diet'.
47 Latham, *Search for a New Eden*, p. 161.
48 *NMW*, May 1843, p. 22; *NMW*, August 1843, p. 56; 'A Visitor', *Cheltenham Free Press*, August 1843, p. 231.
49 *NMW*, 21 August 1841, p. 63.
50 *NMW*, August 1843, p. 104.
51 *The Weekly Tribune*, 12 January 1850, pp. 235-236.

52 *New Age*, 20 May 1843, in an address to the Congress, p. 23.
53 *NMW*, 29 January 1842, p. 48. *NMW,* 14 March 1842, p. 399.
54 *NMW*, 2 May 1840, p. 1281; *NMW,* 21 September 1844, p. 104.
55 Dennis Hardy, *Alternative Communities in Nineteenth Century England* (London, 1979), pp. 60-61; Harrison, *Robert Owen and the Owenites*, pp. 127-129.
56 Carlile had favoured vegetarianism, see Royle, *Victorian Infidels*, p. 144; Eliza Sharples's poverty restricted her to vegetarianism in later life, see Hypatia B. Bonner, *Charles Bradlaugh. A Record of his Life and Work* (1894; London, 1902), vol. 1, p. 19.
57 Gregory Claeys, *Citizens and Saints. Politics and Anti-politics in Early British Socialism* (Cambridge, 1989), p. 261. See also Logie Barrow, 'Determinism and environmentalism in socialist thought', in Raphael Samuel and Gareth S. Jones, eds, *Culture, Ideology and Politics. Essays for Eric Hobsbawm* (London, 1983), pp. 194-214, especially p. 210.
58 Claeys, *Citizens and Saints*, p. 261, quoting Lloyd Jones, writing to G.J. Holyoake, from McCabe, *Life and Letters of G.J. Holyoake*, vol. 1, p. 113.
59 14 February 1846, quoted in Theodore Rothstein, *From Chartism to Labourism* (London, 1929), p. 135. Owenism and Chartism were not mutually exclusive in the 1830s-40s, see Edward Royle, 'Chartists and Owenites – many parts but one body', *Labour History Review* 65:1 (spring 2000), pp. 2-21.
60 *Northern Star*, 10 July 1847; *Northern Star*, 21 August 1847, p. 3 (J. Dixon, from *The Reasoner*).
61 *Northern Star*, 11 November 1843, p. 3. On the same page there was a review of Barmby's *Promethean* and a reprinting of Engels's report in *NMW* comparing Saint Simonism to 'Ham Common Socialists'.
62 *Northern Star*, 2 December 1843, p. 3, preceding a review of Graham's *Lectures on Chastity*. *Northern Star* printed 17 letters from Galpin at the Concordium and Moreville Communitorium in this period.
63 As Logie Barrow suggests of medical botany, *Independent Spirits. Spiritualism and English Plebeians. 1850-1910* (London, 1986), pp. 170-171.
64 Presumably because Gammage was a medical man. His entry in a vegetarian essay competition came second to Dr Lees (*VM*, July 1857).
65 Charles Kingsley, *Alton Locke* (1850; London: Macmillan, 1878), p. 28.
66 John J. Bezer, 'Autobiography of the Chartist Rebels of 1848' reprinted in David Vincent, ed., *Testaments of Radicalism. Memoirs of Working Class Politicians. 1790-1885* (London, 1977), p. 165.
67 Gregory Claeys, 'John Adolphus Etzler, Technological Utopianism, and British Socialism: The Tropical Emigration Society's Venezuelan Mission, and its social context, 1833-48', *English Historical Review* 101 (1986), pp. 31-55.
68 *NMW* (1843-4), p. 360.
69 John A. Etzler, 'The Poetry of Reality' in *The Morning Star* 1:1, December 1844, pp. 3-4.
70 *NMW*, 16 November 1844, p. 166. According to Latham, *Search for a New Eden*, p. 163, several Concordists joined.
71 Holyoake, *History of Co-operation*, vol. 2, p. 12; and Frost, *Forty Years*, p. 50, described it as a vegetarian journal. Robert Buchanan, briefly the Concordist printer, joined Duncan as co-editor.

72 James E. Duncan, *Flowers and Fruits, or Poetry, Philosophy and Science* (London, 1843). See review in *NMW*, 27 January, 1844, pp. 242-243. The *Mirror* thought the essay a 'manful' defence; the *Illustrated London News* noted its 'vigorous defence of the use of vegetable diet' (advertisements in *NMW*, 3 February 1843, p. 256). Duncan separately a *Defence of a Vegetable Diet* (c.1843); and *Vegetable Diet for the Million!*
73 *The Divinearian, or, Apostle of the Messiahdom*, no. 3, December 1849.
74 Armytage, *Heavens Below*, pp. 196-208; Taylor, *Eve and the New Jerusalem*, pp. 172-182. The vegetarian William E.A. Axon wrote the entry on Barmby in the *DNB*.
75 Hardy, *Alternative Communities*, p. 34.
76 See Pierre H.J. Baume's description, Baume Papers, 'Journal for 1843', p. 875: 'on arriving at Barmby's I found the cold diet of Alcott House & the same contemptible self-conceit & PITY for my BLIND-PRIDE! ... I soon took leave of Barmby who is an exalted enthusiast in dress.'
77 *New Age*, 20 May 1843, p. 24. He promoted a mixture of raw, cooked, hot and cold vegetarian meals according to season, see Armytage, *Heavens Below*, p. 198.
78 Fry's short-lived *Circular* discussed the Concordium; Barmby's *Promethean* (London, 1842), no. 1, described it as 'a kind of vegetable eating Communitorium or Community lodge', but stated the diet was left 'to individual choice'. The *Healthian* was reviewed in *Promethean*, no. 3, p. 51, Oldham sent Barmby Graham's lectures (no. 2, p. 40).
79 *Reasoner*, vol. 1, 29 July 1846, p. 140, from *Communist Chronicle*, no. 40.
80 *The Moral World*, 13 September 1845, pp. 21-22. See Frost, *Forty Years*, p. 47 and Royle, *Robert Owen and the Commencement*, pp. 133-134; p. 207.
81 *NMW*, 23 August 1845, p. 497. See *Moral World*, 13 September 1845.
82 *Reasoner*, vol. 1, 13 August, 21 October and 23 October, 1846.
83 *Reasoner*, vol. 1, 1846, pp. 265-6.
84 *Reasoner*, vol. 1, 16 September 1846, from *Daily News*.
85 *Reasoner*, vol. 1, 21 October 1846, p. 272. For Ironside's letter, 28 October 1846, p. 279. See also 'Utilitarian Record', *Reasoner*, vol. 2, 1847, p. 2, for relaxation of the diet.
86 James Gregory, '"Some Account of the Progress of the Truth as it is in Jesus": The White Quakers of Ireland', *Quaker Studies*, 9/1 (September 2004), pp. 68-94.
87 *NMW*, 31 May 1845, p. 400; *NMW*, 19 July 1844, p. 459.
88 *Reasoner*, vol. 2, 'Utilitarian Record', 15 September 1847, p. 84. See letter from Galpin to Owen, 4 December 1845, in Co-operative Union Library, Robert Owen Papers, 1715. Galpin praised the sect at Harmony, see *NMW*, 7 June 1845, p. 404. *NMW*, 1845, p. 264, p. 267 excerpted correspondence between Jacob, Beale and Oldham.
89 *Progress of the Truth*, no. 40, pp. 66-67, a report by a Barmby-ite reprinted in *NMW*, 28 September 1844, p. 112.
90 *Howitt's Journal* 38, 18 September 1847, p. 181; Barker's account in *The People* was reprinted in the American *National Anti-slavery Standard*, 24 October 1850, p. 88; *Family Herald*, 1850, p. 154.
91 Ramsgate was chosen due to Horsell's invitation, Manchester and London having been considered. See Henry Pitman, 'Reminiscences of an old reporter,' *VM*, July 1898, pp. 296-299 (p. 296).
92 *VM*, July 1898, p. 296.

93 Truth-Tester, 15 March 1848, pp. 87-88, from Cowherdites of Manchester; 15 September 1847, p. 20 publishes a letter from Simpson.
94 Truth-Tester, 15 June 1847, p. 121.
95 Truth-Tester, 15 August 1847, p. 8. On the conference, see 15 July 1847, pp. 140-141.
96 Truth-Tester, 15 September 1847, p. 20.
97 The account appeared as a supplement to Truth-Tester, 22 October 1847; reissued as a tract. It was reported in *People's Journal* and *People's Temperance Journal*. Gaskill, at the 21st annual meeting of the VS, said that he 'had been warned by the ladies not to say some funny things he could tell them about that meeting' (*DR*, January 1869, p. 7).
98 *VM*, July 1898, p. 299.
99 See Antrobus, *A Guiltless Feast*.
100 *VM*, December 1859, p. 30.
101 See Antrobus, *Guiltless Feast*, pp. 72-74; Harrison, *Dictionary of British Temperance Biography*, p. 110; *VM*, 1859, pp. 120-121; *VM*, 1894, pp. 216-227.
102 *The Alliance*, 10 September 1859, p. 853.
103 *Phonetic Journal* 17 September 1859; *The Friend*, December 1856, p. 322; *The British Anti-Tobacco Journal*, October 1859.
104 *VM*, February 1851, enclosed serialized tract, pp. 6-8.
105 *A Few Recipes of Vegetable Diet* (London, 1847), p. 31. Advertised in *Douglas Jerrold's Weekly Newspaper*, February 1848. *The Productions of the Vegetable Kingdom* was reviewed by Edwin Lankester, *Athenaeum*, 28 August 1847. The *British League; or Total Abstainers' Magazine*, whose contributors included vegetarians/figures sympathetic to vegetarianism, such as Frederic Lees and P.P. Carpenter, described *Productions* as a 'Simple exposition of a question of great importance' (May 1847, p. 119).
106 *Truth-Tester*, June 1847, p. 120. His *A Few Recipes* made much (p. 31) of 'the recent application of the most established conclusions of Chemical Science' and 'the study of Dietetics'.
107 *VM*, December 1859, p. 31.
108 *Phonetic Journal*, 17 September 1859.
109 See *VM*, February 1893, pp. 48-52.
110 *VM*, March 1893, pp. 84-85.
111 *VA, late Truth-Tester*, 18 August 1848, p. 6.
112 *Punch*, July-December 1848, 'The Vegetarians', p. 140; 'The Vegetarian Movement', p. 182.
113 *VA*, 1 February 1850, p. 65; March 1850, p. 79.
114 *DR*, October 1862, p. 101. Haughton's comments on Irish diet were reported in *Transactions of the National Association for the Promotion of Social Science, 1860* (London, 1861). For press comments, see *DR*, July 1862, p. 82; October 1862, pp. 121-123.
115 Mary Ward, *The History of David Grieve* (London, 1892), pp. 329-330.
116 Antrobus, *Guiltless Feast*, p. 96. The first annual meeting was at Hayward's Hotel, Manchester, the second at Manchester Town Hall, the third at Salford Town Hall. See *VM*, June 1852, p. 41 for the decision to stay in areas ensuring a large concentration of vegetarians at annual meetings, to 'preserve the Vegetarian spirit'.
117 *VA*, September 1849, p. 1.

118 Harrison, *Drink and the Victorians*, p. 32, p. 91, p. 143; p. 219; M.H. Marland, *Medicine in Wakefield and Huddersfield, 1780-1870* (Cambridge, 1987), pp. 206-207; Jules Ginswick, ed., *Labour and the Poor in England and Wales, 1849-1851* vol. 1. *Lancashire, Cheshire and Yorkshire* (London, 1983), p. 63; Barrow, *Independent Spirits*, pp. 10-12, p. 104, p. 115 (the source of the quotation), see pp. 125-126, p. 195; Paul A. Pickering, *Chartism and the Chartists in Manchester and Salford* (Basingstoke, 1995), p. 2; R.C.K. Ensor, *England. 1870-1914* (1936; Oxford, 1963), p. 335; John F.C. Harrison, *A Study in the English Adult Educational Movement* (London, 1961).
119 Elizabeth Gaskell, *North and South* (1854; London, 1970), p. 95.
120 William Cooke Taylor, *Notes of a Tour in the Manufacturing Districts of Lancashire; in a Series of Letters to his Grace the Archbishop of Dublin* (London, 1842), pp. 7-8; Harold Perkin, *The Origins of Modern English Society, 1780-1880* (London, 1969), p. 160.
121 Royle, *Victorian Infidels*, pp. 240-242; Royle, *Radical Politics. 1790-1900. Religion and Unbelief* (London, 1971), pp. 10-11.
122 Entry on 'City' in *The Popular Encyclopedia; or, Conversations Lexicon* (new edn, London, 1873-76), p. 367.
123 See *VA*, October 1849, p. 14 (on Manchester artisans). See Keith Thomas, *Religion and the Decline of Magic. Studies in Popular Beliefs in Sixteenth and Seventeenth Century England* (1971; London, 1991) ch. 22, on urbanization's role in the decline of magic through the impersonality, literacy, population turn-over and communication of new ideas. His caveat, that the equation of industrialization-rationality is too facile, is important.
124 Fears that improved living conditions and industrial discipline had not developed self-control, so that 'the animal nature of the ancient serf appears', surface in *Transactions of the National Association for the Promotion of Social Science* (London, 1860), in Sir James Kay Shuttleworth's address, pp. 79-109.
125 Taylor, *Notes of a Tour*, p. 6.
126 Twigg, 'Vegetarian Movement', p. 92; see *VM*, May 1853, p. 4.
127 Gerald E. Mingay, *Rural Life in Victorian England* (1971; Stroud, 1990), pp. 194-195.
128 *VA*, 15 October 1848, p. 37.
129 *VM*, May 1853, local operations: p. 4. See Royle, *Victorian Infidels*, p. 212 on the 'radical deserts' of East Anglia.
130 *VM*, May 1851, p. 48.
131 Lewis Mumford, *The City in History*, (1961; London, 1979), ch. 15 'Palaeotechnic Paradise: Coketown', pp. 537-539.
132 Pickering, *Chartism and the Chartists*, p. 18.
133 Twigg, 'Vegetarian Movement', p. 64.
134 Twigg, 'Vegetarian Movement', p. 91.
135 Twigg, 'Vegetarian Movement', p. 98. See M.W. Flinn, ed., *Edwin Chadwick's Report on the Sanitary Condition of the Labouring Population of Great Britain* [1842] (Edinburgh, 1965) on stimulating food, p. 276, and p. 314, Fairbairn of Manchester's prohibition of tobacco and liquor and reduction of animal food consumption. 'Voluntary testimony' on the diet's advantages in iron manufactories, overheated mills and counting houses is referred to in *VA*, 15 August 1850.
136 Harrison, *Drink and the Victorians*, pp. 94-98.
137 Ginswick, ed., *Labour and the Poor in England and Wales, 1849-1851*. vol. 1, p. 8.

138 Examples of vegetarianism as part of a programme of self-improvement include *VA*, October 1849, pp. 13-14; the account of a teetotal-vegetarian in *Weekly Record*, reprinted in *Phonetic Journal*, 13 June 1857, p. 219.
139 Although bourgeois exploitation of the norm of 'health' and medicine in social disciplining of the German proletariat has been stressed by some historians, such as Alfons Labisch, see Michael Hau, *The Cult of Health and Beauty in Germany. A Social History, 1890-1930* (Chicago, 2003), p. 12.
140 Pickering, *Chartism and the Chartists*, pp. 126-127. Control of temperament applied to employers too, see *VA*, 1 February 1850, p. 64 on D. Morris.
141 *VA*, 1 July 1849, p. 135 and p. 138 (a London compositor and a railway worker); 15 August 1850, p. 4 (iron workers, workers in overheated mills and counting houses). A rare call for 'more liberal remuneration' – of agriculture labour – is in *VA*, supplement, January 1851, p. 6, reply to 'XYF'.
142 *DR*, January 1872, p. 21.
143 See Twigg, 'Vegetarian Movement', p. 88 for an alternative view on decline in northern and plebeian support.
144 Joseph Wilson, *Joseph Wilson. His Life and Work* (London, n.d.); William Sharman, *Plain Words to the Working Men of Sheffield, now abstaining from dear meat: with an appendix on what to eat and how to cook it* (Sheffield, 1860); *Journal of Health ... and VM*, September 1860, p. 138, feared the response to recipes on rice pudding and cabbage. *VM*, September 1858, pp. 113-114.
145 *DR*, April 1862, p. 51, p. 61. Greater Manchester Records Office, Vegetarian Society (hereafter abbreviated to GMCRO) GMCRO, G2/1/1/2, minute 11 August 1862. Sharman targeted 'thoughtful working men' and their families. See *DR*, July 1863, p. 93 for its subsequent low state.
146 *VM*, February 1850, supplement, p. 7.
147 *VA*, 15 October 1848, p. 36; *VA*, October 1849, p. 24. 'Minor Hugo' [Luke J. Hansard], *Hints and Reflections to Railway Travellers*, 3 vols, (London, 1843), vol. 3, pp. 7-20. Hansard presumably wrote 'Vegetarian', *A Letter to William Horsell, in reply to his pamphlet entitled "Emigration unnecessary, impolitic and injurious"* (Derby, 1850).
148 *VM*, December 1850, p. 155.
149 *DR*, January 1869, p. 7. He owned 1000 looms yet noted that his family of four lived on £100 p.a.
150 GMCRO-VS, VS Minutes, G24/1/1/1, letter dated 24 December 1856. For its demise, see *VM*, August 1859, supplement: p. 15.
151 In 1851 large meetings (by vegetarian standards) were held at Glasgow, Liverpool, London, Manchester, Chester, Leeds, Halifax, Bradford, Bury St Edmunds, Ipswich, Yarmouth and Boston.
152 E.g., at Malton, *VM*, January 1854, supplement: pp. 4-12; pp. 12-13.
153 *VM*, December 1859, supplement: p. 28.
154 *VA*, 1 February 1851, p. 92.
155 *VM*, July 1853, 'local operations': p. 13 (and August, supplement: pp. 41-42); December 1854, pp. 65-66. *VM*, January 1852, p. 3, indicates meetings were 'large' if from 400-1000.
156 *VM*, February 1854, supplement, pp. 15-16.
157 *VM*, July 1856, p. 62.

158 *VA*, 15 October 1848, p. 36; *VM*, report of soirée, July 1853, pp. 25-30; *VM*, November 1853, p. 60; *Dr Skelton's Botanic Record and Family Herald*, 5 February 1853, pp. 150-152; *Phonetic Journal*, 21 April 1855, p. 189, p. 271.
159 *Journal of Health ... and VM*, June 1860, p. 96.
160 Twigg, 'Vegetarian Movement', p. 103, citing Mabel Tylecote, *The Mechanics' Institutes of Lancashire and Yorkshire Before 1851* (Manchester, 1957). These institutions allowed female members, but banned their access to newspapers and reading rooms until the 1860s, see June Purvis, *Hard Lessons. The Lives and Education of Working Class Women in Nineteenth Century England* (London, 1989), ch. 5.
161 Tylecote, *The Mechanics' Institutes*, p. 218 and appendix X, subjects for discussion. The secretary in 1846-54 was the transcendentalist and radical, G.S. Phillips; the institution was genuinely working class, see John F.C. Harrison, *A Study in the English Adult Educational Movement* (London, 1961), p. 137. On Sheffield, see *VM*, May 1859, supplement: p. 10.
162 E.g., *VM*, January 1850, supplement, p. 4, Chorlton upon Medlock mutual improvement classes.
163 *VA*, March 1850, p. 75.
164 *VA*, 15 October 1848, p. 36.
165 *DR*, October 1868, p. 127.
166 'IV: Times and Seasons', *Worcester Herald*, 5 August 1848, (p. 4 of unpaginated newspaper). *VA*, 15 August 1850, p. 4 on Elizabeth Horsell's lecture.
167 *VM*, September 1850, pp. 117-128. *VA*, May 1850, p. 111.
168 *VA*, 15 October 1848, p. 36; *VA*, 1 June 1849, pp. 140-141; *VA*, 1 January 1850, p. 75 (*VM*, June 1851, pp. 45-47); *The British Controversialist*, 1850, p. 233 for H.S. Clubb's lectures on Pythagoras.
169 Karl Marx and Friedrich Engels, *Heroes of the Exile* (written but not published 1852; K. Marx and F. Engels. Collected Works, London, 1979, vol. 11, pp. 227-326 (pp. 280-281 concern the colony).
170 *VM*, June 1856, p. 45 (Vegetarian Treasury) citing *Preston Guardian*, 8 March. See Miriam D. Colt, *Went to Kansas, Being a Thrilling Account of an Ill-fated Expedition to that Fairy Land, and its Sad Results* (Watertown, 1862); Joseph G. Gambone, ed., 'Kansas – A Vegetarian Utopia: The Letters of John Milton Hadley, 1855-6', *Kansas Historical Quarterly* 38: 1 (1972) p. 65-87. On Simpson's comments on it, and its fortunes in 1856, see *VM*, July 1856, p. 52, September 1856, p. 68.
171 *VM*, January 1858, p. 32, May, pp. 59-62, August p. 180.
172 Forward, *History*, ch. 4.
173 Lane, Fanny Lacy, George Vasey, the Bennetts, George Dornbusch, G.J. Ford, J. Gowland, Pierre Baume. Horsell, no Greavesian, refers to the community, in *The Science of Cooking Vegetarian food: also the rise and progress of the Vegetarian Society, twelve reasons for not eating flesh, and answers to twenty objections to the vegetarian practice* (London, 1856) p. 87.
174 *VA*, 15 October 1848, p. 37, report by Dornbusch.
175 On the Society, see *Teetotal Progressionist*, 1852-1853, p. 205, p. 252, p. 267; *VM*, July 1853, local operations: p. 14; *Journal of Health*, October 1856, p. 46.
176 *VM*, July 1853, local operations: p. 14.
177 *VA*, 1 September 1850, pp. 15-16.
178 Fanny E. Lacy, 'The Vegetarian; or, a Visit to Aunt Primitive', *Metropolitan Magazine*, April 1847, pp. 403-413; *The Truth-Tester*, 15 September 1847, p. 20.

179 'G.W.' of Silesia, who received the *VM* and became vegetarian through Dr Zimmerman, a visitor to Ham Common, told the *VM* (February 1855, p. 18): 'Perhaps it may interest you to know that Professor Daumer of Nurnberg, foster-father of Caspar Hauser, Gustav Struve a *man* in the noblest meaning of the word, and Professor Gottfried Kinkel, who is now living in England, and other political fugitives, are practical Vegetarians.'
180 *Journal of Health*, February 1856, p. 129.
181 *Teetotal Progressionist*, 1852, p. 331.
182 Baume Papers, Journal for 15 April 1855 to March 1856, reverse of p.X. He then associated with vegetarians in Manchester after leaving London due to paranoia.
183 See Hibberd, *VA*, 1 February 1851, pp. 93-95.
184 *VM*, October 1854, local operations, p. 84.
185 *The Truth-Tester*, 15 June 1848, p. 65. See P. Thomson, *George Sand and the Victorians. Her Influence and Reputation in Nineteenth Century England* (London, 1977) on her appeal; and Crossley, *Consumable Metaphors*, p. 206, on her treatment of Rousseauan zoophilia and animal cruelty.
186 GMCRO- VS, G24/1/1/1, letter dated 5 May 1856.
187 *The Times*, 25 December 1850, p. 4. For advertisements for Horsell's publications, see 21 February 1849, p. 10.
188 Advertisements in *The Times*, 19 and 26 July 1851. Articles in newspapers included *Illustrated London News*, 16 August 1851, p. 223, *The Times*, 2 August 1851, p. 8; *Morning Chronicle, Journal des Debats* (Paris), *International Magazine of Literature, Art and Science* (New York), vol. 4, 3 October 1851, pp. 402-403. Simpson contributed £200, see *DR*, May 1882, p. 103. Another (Whittington Club) meeting attended by Simpson is reported in *VM*, July 1854, supplement: pp. 59-63.
189 *VM*, February 1853, p. 5.
190 *Journal of Health ... and Vegetarian Messenger*, February 1860, p. 30.
191 *VM*, August 1858, p. 26; *DR*, April 1871, p. 55.
192 *DR*, April 1870, pp. 4-5.
193 E.g., 'W.W', *DR*, July 1868, p. 122.
194 *VM*, December 1859, p. 29, Simpson spent *c.* £5000 in the last five years on the Society. See William E.A. Axon, *Fifty Years of the Vegetarian Society* (Manchester, 1897), for Simpson's unrecorded private financial support.
195 Model rules were provided in *VM*, May 1853, 'local vegetarian operations and intelligence': p. 2, so branches and general society would not be confounded.
196 *VM*, June 1853, local operations: p. 12; Charles Walker's diary for 1851.
197 *Blackwood's Edinburgh Magazine* 80: 494 (December 1856), p. 733.
198 *VM*, January 1856, p. 1; *VM*, August 1859, p. 17. For similar indifference to other reforms, see Royle, *Victorian Infidels*, pp. 208-210; David Martin, 'Land Reform', ch. 6 in Patricia Hollis, ed., *Pressure from Without in Early Victorian England* (London, 1974), p. 152.
199 GMCRO-VS, G24/1/1/1, 29 July 1859.
200 *DR*, January 1862, p. 2.
201 *The Times*, 6 September 1862, p. 4 (report for 1862).
202 *DR*, July 1865, p. 84, citing *Sheffield Daily Telegraph*.
203 *DR*, January 1867, p. 13.
204 *Human Nature*, 1867, p. 633. A 'Hygienic Society' – a progressive society expressing all his concerns – was announced in *Human Nature*, 1869, pp. 620-622.

205 See William Lawson, Charles D. Hunter and others, *Ten Years of Gentleman Farming at Blennerhasset with Co-operative Objectives* (London, 1874), ch. 10.
206 *DR*, July 1863, pp. 106-108. *The Times*, 31 December 1866, p. 4; *The Co-operator*, 1 February 1867, pp. 269-270; *DR*, April 1867, pp. 60-61; *The Co-operator*, 9 January 1869, p. 19. The 1866 festival was reported in many dailies and *Punch*. The festivals were intended to be plebeian equivalents to Social Science Congresses.
207 *DR*, January 1869, p. 2.
208 This was the case elsewhere; see Hau, *Cult of Health and Beauty*, p. 12.
209 Horsell, *Science of Cooking Vegetarian Food*, pp. 86-87.
210 Charles Hunter, Blennerhasset's agricultural chemist, vegetarian since 1857, was 'reminded' to join the VS in 1869, see *DR,* April 1869, p. 61.
211 *DR*, July 1865, pp. 22-23, 'C.L.B'; *VM*, May 1850, reverse of cover, 'T.P.B.'
212 The associate grade was controversial, see *DR*, 1873, August, p. 303, September, p. 318, October, pp. 334-335, November, pp. 339-341, and note C.D.H.'s comment, p. 334, that it was well known there were more *sympathizers* then *members*. See also Forward, *History*, pp. 74-75; p. 75 reproduces statistics for 1875-1896 inclusive: 2,159 members and 1,785 associates.
213 *DR*, December 1876, p. 203, reproduced as cover of *HH*, February 1876.
214 *The Times,* 24 December 1878. See W.G. Ward's letter to Eleanor Orlebar, dated 14 January 1879, reprinted in Eleanor E. Orlebar, *Food for the People. Or Lentils, and other Vegetable Cookery* (London, 1879), p. 9.
215 *VM*, April 1888, pp. 93-94.
216 May Meetings were held at Manchester, Leicester, Cambridge, Salford, London, Birmingham, Norwich, Exeter, Leeds, Liverpool, Sheffield, Portsmouth, Bradford, Accrington, Chester and Southport.
217 Forward, *History*, p. 142.
218 The sources for regional vegetarianism are vegetarian journals, *The Vegetarian Yearbook*, and local newspapers. Local societies were encouraged by the VFU to send reports, some (with financial information) were summarized in the journals. Forward, *History*, ch. 13, sketches the VFU and local societies. The branches are listed in my thesis, appendix D.
219 William E.A. Axon, ed., *Manchester Vegetarian Lectures. First Series* (Manchester, 1888).
220 *VM*, May 1895, p. 148.
221 C.E. Shaw, 'Identified with the One: Edward Carpenter, Henry Salt and the Ethical Socialist Philosophy of Science', *Prose Studies. History Theory* 13:1 (May 1990), pp. 33-57.
222 On broader Sheffield radicalism, see Sheila Rowbotham, '"Our Party is the People": Edward Carpenter and Radicalism in Sheffield', ch. 8 in John G. Rule and Robert Malcolmson, eds, *Protest and Survival. The Historical Experience. Essays for E.P. Thompson* (London, 1993); Rowbotham and Weeks, *Socialism and the New Life*, Part I.
223 *Vegetarian*, 5 November 1898, p. 704.
224 On Wilson, see *VM*, June 1892, p. 177; on Wright, see *Weekly Star*, 1889. There had been a food reform restaurant in 1879, see *DR*, April 1879, p. 61.
225 *MD*, 19 November 1875, p. 737 (also *DR*, September 1876).
226 See S.G.H. Loosley, *Wycliffe College, the First Five Hundred Years* (Stonehouse, 1982); W.A. Sibly, *Vegetarianism and the Growing Boy* (4th edn, 1942). On other schools, see *MD*, 19 September 1890, p. 605; *Vegetarian*, 12 October 1895, p. 495.

227 *VM*, January 1894, p. 6. Nichols's *How to Live on 6d A Day* had been translated, see *DR*, August 1880, p. 179, and recipes were also issued in Welsh, October 1890, p. 285 (and reproduced in *Banner and Times*).
228 *VM*, January 1895, p. 50; *VM*, September 1898, pp. 424-425; *VM*, March 1899, p. 107; *Vegetarian*, 12 November 1898, p. 729; *Vegetarian*, 12 January 1901, p. 5; *Herald of the Golden Age*, July 1899, p. 78.
229 *Vegetarian*, 7 December 1895, p. 601.
230 *DR*, March 1884, p. 89 reported that the prosecutor had discussed Price's vegetarianism until Justice Stephens stopped him.
231 On Scottish vegetarianism *c*.1892-1980s, see Leah Lenemen, *Vegetarian*, winter 1999, p. 11. For the dietary background, see Gibson and Smout, 'From meat to meal: changes in diet in Scotland'.
232 Though it exaggerates Dr Nichols's role at the expense of an already established vegetarian movement, see Bernard Aspinwall, 'Social Catholicism and Health: Dr and Mrs Thomas Low Nichols in Britain', in William J. Sheils, ed., *The Church and Healing* (Oxford, 1982), pp. 249-270. See also *HH*, March 1879; and John Davie's letters to Nichols, *HH*, May 1883, p. 58.
233 *Vegetarian*, 29 June 1895, p. 310; Barclay said vegetarians totalled 300 affiliates in Glasgow.
234 *Scottish Health Reformer* (Progressive Press, 12 High Street, Paisley) 1903-1904; renamed *Health Reform* in 1906. See *Vegetarian*, 1906, p. 2.
235 Nisbet, 219, recommended to Nichols by a London gentleman as 'good, honest, reliable', was a spiritualist, see Barrow, *Independent Spirits*, p. 168.
236 *VM*, January 1893, p. 26; *VM*, June 1895, p. 187; *VM*, February 1898; *VM*, April 1898, p. 147; *Vegetarian*, 29 June 1895, p. 310; *Vegetarian*, 1918, p. 87; *Vegetarian Review*, April 1896, pp. 147-153.
237 Dundee City Archives, GD/Mus36, Minutes and Accounts Book, pp. 2-3, p. 20.
238 Ian Tyrrell, *Woman's World. Woman's Empire. The Woman's Christian Temperance Union in International Perspective, 1880-1930* (Chapel Hill, 1991), p. 18, p. 243; GD/Mus36, p. 17; *Dundee Year Book*, 1896, pp. 78-79.
239 GD/Mus36, p. 9.
240 GD/Mus36, p. 13.
241 See Christopher A. Whatley, David B. Swinfen, and Annette M. Smith, *The Life and Times of Dundee* (Edinburgh, 1993), ch. 10. Forbes Marshall was concerned with local health and Scrymgeour's addresses brought in wider health issues. On local radicalism, see W.H. Fraser's review of M. St John, *The Demands of the People. Dundee Radicalism, 1850-1870* (Dundee), in *Scottish Historical Review*, 78:1, no. 205 (April 1999), pp. 132-133.
242 *VM*, May 1899, p. 177. McCaughey established a restaurant at Dundee High Street, see *Vegetarian*, 1 August 1896, p. 370; 5 September 1896, p. 424.
243 *Vegetarian Review*, June 1896, pp. 256-264 on Irish activists.
244 *DR*, June 1880, p. 118; p. 128, September 1880, p. 221, *DR*, November 1881, p. 244; W. Johnston, MP for South Belfast, was wrongly reported to be vegetarian, his letter in *Vegetarian*, 13 July, p. 443 condemned the journal's socialism and theosophy. See fn. 9, Leslie A. Clarkson and E. Margaret Crawford, *Feast and Famine*, ch. 1, for an advertisement for the restaurant.
245 *VM*, April 1899, p. 145.
246 *Vegetarian*, 22 August 1896, p. 401.

247 *VM*, February 1899, p. 73.
248 *Vegetarian*, 3 January 1891, p. 7; *Vegetarian Review*, July 1894, p. 51.
249 See James Joyce, *Ulysses* (1922; London, 1994), pp. 239-240; p. 248; George M. Harper, *Yeats's Golden Dawn* (London, 1974) and *Yeats and the Occult* (1975; London, 1976); Catherine Candy, 'Relating Feminism, Nationalism and Imperialism: Ireland, India and Margaret Cousins's Sexual Politics', *Women's History Review* 3 (March 1994), pp. 581-594; and Cliona Murphy, *The Women's Suffrage Movement and Irish Society in the Early Twentieth Century* (London, 1989).
250 *Vegetarian*, 5 November 1898, p. 713.
251 See Forward, *History*, ch. 12; *Vegetarian*, a major source; and Forward's 'Forty Years among the Faddists', *The Vegetarian News*, February 1922, pp. 188-193; March 1922, pp. 204-206; June 1922, pp. 263-266; August 1922, pp. 295-299; October 1922, pp. 339-342; November 1922, pp. 352-355; December 1922, pp. 371-375; 1923, p. 98. Forward's satire as A.K. Greet, *The Confessions of a Vegetarian* (London, 1893) has not survived.
252 Charles M. Davies, *Heterodox London, or Phases of Free Thought in the Metropolis* 2 vols (London, 1874), vol. 2, p. 282.
253 *DR*, February 1878, p. 34; *MD*, 9 May 1879, p. 289; *HH*, December 1879, p. 283; *FRM* January 1881, p. ii, advertisement section. See also Forward, 'Seven years of Hygienic reform in the Metropolis' in *HH*, October 1886, pp. 112-113 and November, p. 122, pp. 124-125, and Forward, *History*, p. 78. See entry in Charles Dickens Jnr., *Dickens's Dictionary of London. An Unconventional Handbook* (London, 1879), p. 147.
254 'To the readers of the Food Reform Magazine', in unpaginated advertisement section, *FRM*, April-July 1882, 'from the editors'; Forward, *History*, p. 81; Forward, *Vegetarian Review*, July 1894, p. 113.
255 Forward, *History*, pp. 108-111; GMCRO-VS, G24/1/2/1 21 July, 7 August 1887; *Vegetarian*, 14 April 1888; editorial in *HH*, June 1887, December 1887, p. 152.
256 Forward, *History* (which was dedicated to Hills), p. 111. See his later account, 'Forty Years among Faddists' in *Vegetarian News*, 1922-1923.
257 Forward, *History*, p. 112, see *VM*, April 1888 for the hotel prospectus.
258 *Vegetarian*, 2 March 1889, p. 133. Begbie, *The Curious and Diverting Adventures of Sir John Sparrow Bt* (p. 113), depicts a 'gloomy building in the middle of London, where the Vegetarian Universal League had their offices, held their meetings, and quarrelled among themselves from morning till night'.
259 *Vegetarian*, 25 May 1889, pp. 329-330. Forward, *History*, p. 148 refers to the VS's jealousy of VFU.
260 *The Merry-go-Round*, 1894, pp. 132, *Vegetarian*, March 1894, p. 144; *Vegetarian*, 23 April 1898, p. 269; *The Woman's Signal*, 11 October 1894, p. 236. On its *Ideal Club Journal*, see *Vegetarian*, 22 August 1896, p. 408; 16 January 1897 p. 36.
261 Margaret Bondfield, *A Life's Work* (London, *c.*1948), p. 27 (also p. 36, p. 46, p. 49). *HH*, November 1899, p. 163 noted her efforts for seating for shop assistants.
262 *VM*, February 1889, p. 50; *MD*, 20 June 1890, pp. 402-403; and *MD*, 28 November 1890. Activities also included lectures and dramatic evenings.
263 They are outlined in my thesis, appendix E.
264 Thomas L. Nichols, *How to Live on 6d a Day* (London, 1878) Postscript, p. 60; *HH*, July 1875 (Prospectus), p. 1. The institute moved to 429, Oxford Street (Salsbury Hall, after his friend James Salsbury).

265 Forward, 'Seven Years of Hygienic Reform in the Metropolis', *HH*, October 1886, pp. 112-113.
266 Mackenzie and Mackenzie, *First Fabians*, pp. 21-27; 179-183.
267 Advertisements for goods appear in the Brotherhood's *New Order*, January 1897, p. 8. See Nellie Shaw, *Whiteway. A Colony in the Cotswolds* (London, 1935), for recollections; and Armytage, *Heavens Below*, pp. 342-358 on J.B. Wallace, who inspired the activity.
268 'A Visit to the Russian Positivists', quoted in *Vegetarian*, 5 May 1888, p. 76. Frey's life was serialized in the *Hygienic Advertiser*. See Avrahm Yarmolinsky, *A Russian's American Dream*, (Lawrence, Kansas, 1965).
269 P. Tovey, *Vegetarian Review*, 1897, p. 358, on Purleigh. For an insider's account see Shaw, *Whiteway*, ch. 2. See also Armtyage, *Heavens Below*, pp. 342-358. Goodrich's Methwold colony (Norfolk) was closely reported (e.g. *Vegetarian*, 3 August 1891, p. 404) and briefly published a London edition of *The Methwold Express and Village Industries Gazette*.
270 *Vegetarian Review*, July 1894, p. 113 estimated 600-700 members and associates. Johnson, Box 3, *Fifth Annual Report of the London Vegetarian Society* (1893), records a membership (including associates and subscribers) of 562.
271 *VM*, April 1899, LVS and London Vegetarian Association report for 1898, pp. 139-140. The LVA income in 1897 was £959 19s (*VM*, May 1898, p. 216).
272 Geoffrey Crossick, ed., *The Lower Middle Class in Britain, 1870-1914* (London, 1977), especially Introduction; and G.L. Anderson, 'The Social Economy of Late-Victorian Clerks', pp. 113-133. Thrift related to the petty bourgeois ideology of 'personal mobility'. Youthful idealism and radicalism (opposed to parental/petty bourgeois conservatism) were other factors (see Hugh McLeod, 'White Collar Values and the Role of Religion', also in *The Lower Middle Class in Britain*, p. 78; and in the same collection, Richard N. Price, 'Society, Status and Jingoism', p. 107).
273 *VM*, February 1894, p. 45, quotes *Funny Folks*, 'City clerk's catechism', concerning a suburban vegetarian who arrives by Covent Garden van.
274 *Annual Register*, 1885, p. 4 (a meeting at Exeter Hall to publicize the results of the Exhibition).
275 *HH*, August 1875, p. 25. The first public meeting of the London Dietetic Reform Society was aimed to coincide with the Grand Lodge session of the International Order of Good Templars, see *MD*, 16 July 1875, p. 428. The membership was still youthful in 1885, see Forward, *History*, p. 81.
276 *VM*, January 1899, p. 31.
277 *The Times*, 15 December 1883, p. 9. Allinson established '*The Times* Free Dinner' (*Times*, 14 December, p. 2). See clippings in the Allinson Papers such as *Christian World*, 20 December 1883, discussing the effort in favourable terms in context of a 'food question' and winter privations.
278 *Vegetarian*, 17 June 1899, pp. 344-346.
279 *Vegetarian Review*, February 1895, p. 50.
280 The non-inclusion of a whole household is stressed in *DR*, June 1888, p. 209; on the representation of families, 'A. Stz', *The National Food and Fuel Reformer*, 5 June 1875, p. 53. A.F. Hills, in *The Times*, 17 September 1898, p. 10, claimed 20-30 per cent of new converts soon left.
281 *VM*, July 1893, p. 244; *VM*, April 1887, p. 98.

282 *VM*, February 1894, pp. 44-45, emphasized that members of the independent American, Scottish, Irish and London vegetarian societies did not necessarily join the 'parent society'.
283 See William E.A. Axon, *Fifty Years of the Vegetarian Society* (Manchester, 1897).
284 *DR*, November 1881, pp. 233-234 on the French VS's president's idea for an International Vegetarian Committee, held in Cologne, 16 September 1889.

Chapter Two

1 Roy Porter, 'The People's Health in Georgian England', ch. 6 in T. Harris, ed., *Popular Culture in England, c.1500-1850* (Basingstoke, 1995), pp. 124-142.
2 Bruce Haley, *The Healthy Body and Victorian Culture* (Cambridge, Massachusetts, 1978), p. 3.
3 'Harold', *British Controversialist*, 1850, p. 432.
4 R.M. Glover, *Lancet*, 11 January 1851, cited in Roger Cooter, *Phrenology in the British Isles. An Annotated Historical Biobibliography and Index* (Metuchen, New Jersey, 1989).
5 Robert Jütte, 'The Historiography of Nonconventional Medicine in Germany', *Medical History* 43 (1999), pp. 342-358.
6 B.W. Richardson, 'On Medical Delusions and Charlatanic Practices', *Provincial Medical and Surgical Journal*, 29 October 1851, pp. 594-596.
7 *Provincial Medical and Surgical Journal*, 17 September 1851, p. 527.
8 *Lancet*, 10 April 1847, p. 391.
9 *Lancet*, 20 November 1847, p. 555; *Provincial Medical and Surgical Journal*, 25 December 1850, pp. 708-709.
10 'Physical Puritanism', *Westminster Review*, 1852, pp. 405-442; reprinted in *Littell's Living Age* (New York), 34: 426, 17 July 1852, pp. 129-143.
11 'Physical Puritanism', p. 408
12 *Teetotal Progressionist*, p. 91.
13 Frederic R. Lees, *National Temperance Chronicle*, June 1852, pp. 275-278. For vegetarian response, *VM*, November 1852, Controversialist and Correspondence, pp. 29-30.
14 'The Quack's Diary', *Punch*, January-June 1854, p. 11.
15 'Four Strangleholds of Quackery in the Fourth Estate', *Provincial Medical and Surgical Journal*, 17 June 1853, pp. 518-520 ('bastard medical journals', p. 520).
16 *Dublin Medical Press*, 1863, p. 668.
17 *DR*, October 1866, pp. 121-122.
18 *Reasoner*, vol. 3 (1847), p. 398.
19 *VA*, 15 December 1848, p. 57; *VM*, February 1852, 'Controversialist and Correspondent', pp. 5-6.
20 *Journal of Health*, December 1855, p. 97.
21 *VA*, September 1849, p. 13.
22 'Grand Show of Vegetarians', *Punch's Almanack* for 1852 (unpaginated, p. 6). The anti-Morisonian cartoon: 'Wonderful effect of Morisons *vegetable* pills' is in the Wellcome Institute collection. It was referred to in a French report of the London vegetarian banquet in 1851, *The Times*, 2 August 1851, p. 8.
23 Roger Cooter, *The Cultural Meaning of Popular Science: Phrenology and the Organization of Consent in Nineteenth Century Britain* (Cambridge, 1984). The *Zoist* received William A. Alcott's *Vegetable Diet Defended*, see *Zoist*, April 1844, p. 141. Watson's *Phrenology and Physiology* was published by Horsell. The wood engraving of Simpson, based on

a 'truthful portrait', appears in Mariano Cubí i Soler's *Leccciones de Frenologia* (2 vols, 1851).
24 *HH*, 1893, advertised L.N. Fowler's *Phrenological Annual*; T.R. Allinson contributed articles on 'How to be Well' in *Popular Phrenologist*, March-August 1897, see clippings in Allinson Papers, MS 3193.
25 *VM*, 1 August 1857, p. 15 (the vegetarian was Dornbusch). See *DR*, October 1881, p. x for advertisement for C.L.H. Wallace's instruction. See Alison Winter, *Mesmerized. Powers of Mind in Victorian Britain* (Chicago, 1998).
26 Phillip A. Nicholls, *Homeopathy and the Medical Profession* (London, 1988).
27 See for instance J.A. Symonds, in *The Provincial Medical and Surgical Journal*, 23 July 1851, pp. 393-397.
28 *Hahnemannian Fly Sheet*, 31 October 1850, p. 78. *VM*, 1 December 1859.
29 The radical John Epps's monthly *Notes of a New Truth*.
30 *People's Magazine and Progressionist*, August 1854.
31 *VM*, April 1926, p. 67.
32 Roger Price, 'Hydropathy in England. 1840-1870', *Medical History* 25 (1981), pp. 269-280; Roy Porter, ed., *The Medical History of Waters and Spas* (London, 1990); M. Clements, 'Sifting Science: Methodism and Natural Knowledge in Britain. 1815-1870', D.Phil., University of Oxford, 1996, ch. 3.
33 *VA*, 15 August 1850, pp. 11-12. See also *Truth-Tester*, 17 February 1848, p. 74 on 'one of the most popular' physician-writers on hydropathy, trying vegetarianism.
34 Richard Metcalfe, *The Rise and Progress of Hydropathy in England and Scotland* (London, 1906), p. 43; Latham, *Search for a New Eden*, pp. 173-174.
35 *DR*, September 1877, p. 156.
36 William Horsell, *The Board of Health and Longevity, or Hydropathy for the People* (London, 1845).
37 Smethurst's *Hydrotherapia*, *VA*, 15 February 1849, p. 87; Metcalfe, *Rise and Progress of Hydropathy*, p. 84 (Lawrie); *DR*, 1872-1873, p. 19 (Davie).
38 *Dr Skelton's Botanic Record and Family Herald*, 5 February 1853, pp. 150-2.
39 John Skelton, *Family Medical Adviser* (Leeds, 1852), p. 16; Review of *Guide to Health* and *Botanical Journal* in *VA*, October 1849, p. 21; advertisement in *VA*, 1 February 1850.
40 *VM*, May 1854, pp. 54-56.
41 Dornbusch, *The Antivaccinator and Public Health Journal*, 1 November 1872, p. 223.
42 *The Times*, 13 September 1898.
43 *VM*, August 1853, 'controversialist and correspondence': pp. 17-18.
44 *DR*, February 1876, p. 29; October 1880.
45 Harrison, *Drink and the Victorians*, p. 44.
46 Harrison, *Drink and the Victorians*, p. 143. See p. 161 on teetotal health reform and vegetarianism.
47 The estimate for teetotal support is Harrison's, *Drink and the Victorians*, p. 317. Peter T. Winskill, *The Temperance Movement and Its Workers. A Record of Social, Moral, Religious and Political Progress* (London, 1892) for information on some leading teetotal-vegetarians. See also Harrison, *Dictionary of British Temperance Biography*.
48 *The London and Lincolnshire Mirror of Tee-totalism*, 1 October 1840, p. 104. N. Longmate, *The Waterdrinkers. A History of Temperance* (London, 1968), p. 69, p. 103, p. 180 on meat as part of the teetotal alternative diet and rhetoric of self-help.

49 J. Metters, *Strictures on Animal and Vegetable Diet* (Uxbridge, 1847), reviewed in *The Truth-Tester, Temperance Advocate and Healthian Journal* n.s., vol. 1 (1847), pp. 119-20.
50 Samuel Couling, *History of the Temperance Movement in Great Britain and Ireland; from the Earliest Date to the Present Time* (London, 1862).
51 The chairman of the British Association feared that intemperance would be promoted as a cure for vegetarianism, 'which very much amused the section'. See Thomas Hudson's *Recollections and Random Reflections* (London, 1875), p. 4. See Groom-Napier's *Vegetarian and Temperance Fête to his Most Serene Highness Prince of Mantua and Monferrat* ...(Dunfermline, *c.*1879), *The Cure for Intemperance* (Manchester, about 1875), *Vegetarian and Temperance Fête to 335 Welsh Miners* (Dunfermline, *c.*1879).
52 Notice of meeting, *FRM*, July-September issue, 1884.
53 Winskill, *Temperance Movement*, vol. 4, pp. 154-155.
54 *Lancet*, 4 April 1885, p. 631.
55 William J. Francis, *Reminiscences* (Southend on Sea, privately printed), p. 47, p. 68.
56 David M. Fahey, *Temperance and Racism. John Bull, Johnny Reb, and the Good Templars* (Lexington, 1996), especially ch. 2.
57 See Winskill, *Temperance Movement*, vol. 4, p. 140 on these 'vegetarian teetotallers in regalia'.
58 E.g., J. Passmore Edwards, *VA*, 18 August 1848, p. 15; Arnold F. Hills, *Natural Food of Man* (London, 1893), p. 34; and Forward, *History*, pp. 65-66.
59 *Vegetarian*, January 1898, p. 1. He aimed to extend the depôt's 'educational' value to the whole temperance movement.
60 George J. Holyoake, *The Social Means of Promoting Temperance with Remarks on Errors in its Advocacy* (London, 1860), pp. 18-19.
61 Holyoake, *Social Means of Promoting Temperance*, p. 26, p. 28.
62 As noted by Winskill, *Temperance Movement*, vol. 1, pp. 30-31.
63 See Brian Harrison, 'Teetotal Chartism', *History* 58 (1973) pp. 193-217.
64 See his *Moral Reformer*, 10 March 1838.
65 Henry Bradley; see Harrison, *Dictionary*, p. 49.
66 *Staunch Teetotaller*, 1867, pp. 374-375.
67 He became an Associate in 1874. See F. Lees, *Dr Frederic Richard Lees* (London, 1904), p. 205.
68 The *Alliance News* reprinted, 17 June 1898, p. 385 an article on Cowherdites from *Vegetarian*.
69 See material in Baume Papers, Box 5; and material (not consulted) relating to the National Public School Association in Manchester Archives and Local Studies.
70 See Belchem, '"Temperance in all things": Vegetarianism, the Manx press and the alternative agenda of reform in the 1840s,' for an examination of Horsell to about 1851.
71 *DR*, January 1886 listed the 'Anti-Tobacco Society and Anti-Narcotic League' as kindred societies. See Matthew Hilton and Simon Nightingale, 'A Microbe of the Devil's Own Make': Religion and Science in the British Anti-Tobacco Movement, 1853-1908', in Stephen Lock, Lois A. Reynolds, E.M. Tansey, eds, *Ashes to Ashes. The History of Smoking and Health* (Amsterdam, 1998); R.B. Walker, 'Medical Aspects of Tobacco Smoking and the Anti-Tobacco Movement in Britain in the Nineteenth Century', *Medical History* 24 (1980), pp. 391-402.

72 See Lilian L. Shiman, '"Changes are Dangerous": Women and Temperance in Victorian England', ch. 8 in Gail Malmgreen, ed., *Religion in the Lives of English Women, 1760-1930* (London, 1986), pp. 193-215; Harrison, *Drink and the Victorians*, p. 174.
73 *Daily News*, reported in *Vegetarian* 1895, p. 332. This reflected links between the American leader Frances Willard and British women.
74 *Truth-Tester* n.s., vol. 2 (1848), p. 53.
75 *The Times*, 15 December 1883, p. 9.
76 *VM*, February 1889, p. 41.
77 *People's Journal*, vol. 1 (1849), Appendix: 'Annals of Progress', p. 3.
78 'T.B.,' *DR*, July 1873, p. 296.
79 'Vegetus', which appeared on the *DR*'s cover and front page as well as on the cover of the *Vegetarian*.
80 *The Times*, 19 September 1898, *Vegetarian*, 7 December 1895, pp. 585-586 (Oriolet); *VM*, May 1899, p. 179 (St Francis); *VM*, May 1899, pp. 182-183, *Vegetarian*, 20 May 1899, p. 238 (Willesden). The Maternity Society excluded alcohol and flesh foods from infant-care, see *VM*, August 1897, p. 270, and *VM*, August 1899, pp. 258-259.
81 Cited in *VM*, January 1850, supplement, p. 6.
82 The title of Allinson's society copied the contemporaneous German *Lebensreform* movement. See *DR*, January 1869, p. 3, for the annual report's allusion to the German 'Natural System'.
83 *DR*, October 1880.
84 *DR*, March 1873, pp. 246-247. See the reply by the American-born medical reformer, and wife of Thomas Nichols, Mary Gove Nichols, June, pp. 273-274.
85 See for instance, *WTE*, 22 June 1890, p. 6.
86 See Mrs Stuart, reported in Hills, *Natural Food of Man*; Emmet Densmore, *Dr Allinson and Dogmatism* and A.F. Hills, *Essays on Vegetarianism, being a collection of articles contributed to 'The Vegetarian'* (London: Ideal Publishing Union, 1895). A conference in early 1893 was devoted to vitalizing food.
87 Henry S. Salt, *Plea for Vegetarianism and Other Essays* (Manchester, 1886), p. 3.
88 *The Times*, 13 January 1885; 'Vegetarianism', *Household Words*, 28 May 1881, pp. 96-97 [p. 97].
89 Forward felt it still 'worth noting' that George Dornbusch's death was partly due to a multiple stabbing, *History*, p. 71.
90 On Belgian miners, see *VA*, 15 August 1850, p. 35. Forward, *History*, ch. 14. See Whorton, *Crusaders for Fitness*, ch. 7: 'Muscular Vegetarianism'.
91 *Vegetarian*, 25 May 1889, p. 325.
92 *DR*, July 1865, p. 84.
93 *VA*, September 1849, p. 13; *People's Magazine and Progressionist*, October 1854, p. 153, *VM*, September 1849, p. 12; *The Times*, 2 August 1851, p. 8; *DR*, October 1884, p. 312.
94 Mary Ward, *The History of David Grieve*, (3 vols, London, 1892), p. 166.
95 *The Lancet*, 27 October 1883, p. 757.
96 *The Vegetarian Advocate: A Journal devoted to free discussion on chemistry, physiology, dietetics, hydropathy and other questions affecting the Physical, Intellectual and Moral Health of Man*.
97 *DR*, January 1872, p. 12.
98 *Vegetarian*, 12 November 1898, p. 729.

99 Herbert Spencer, who tried vegetarianism, abandoning it as intellectually and physically debilitating, condemned the low diet commonly recommended for children, in the *British Quarterly Review*, reprinted in *Education: Intellectual, Moral, and Physical* (London, 1861), pp. 148-162.
100 Kenneth J. Carpenter, *Protein and Energy. A Study of Changing Ideas in Nutrition* (Cambridge, 1994), ch. 5; Finlay, 'Quackery and Cookery: Justus von Liebig's Extract of Meat and the Theory of Nutrition in the Victorian Age'.
101 *VM*, May 1850, p. 81.
102 *VM*, June 1854, p. 56.
103 Salt, *Plea for Vegetarianism*, p. 19.
104 T.R. Allinson, *Food Reform Magazine*, January 1882, pp. 90-95.
105 Chandos L.H. Wallace's rejoicing that 'Pasteur is dead; I thank God' typified the attitude of vegetarians opposed to vivisection, see *VM*, May 1927, p. 93. See *Vegetarian*, 13 July 1889 onwards, for series of leading articles on 'Mr Pasteur and his Institute'.
106 See Simpson's anonymous *The Products of the Vegetable Kingdom* (London, 1847) and *A Few Recipes of Vegetable Diet* (London, 1847); and H.S. Clubb, *VM*, March 1898, p. 191.
107 *VA*, 15 December 1848, p. 63; *Water Cure Journal and Hygienic Magazine*, April 1848, p. 343.
108 Robley Dunglison, *Medical Lexicon. A Dictionary of Medical Science* (9th edn, London, 1853).
109 *Lancet*, 13 January 1847, p. 42. On the neglect of the 'cooling regimen' and hygienic physiology's backwardness, see Virginia Smith, 'Physical Puritanism and Sanitary Science: Medical and Immaterial Beliefs in Popular Physiology, 1650-1840' in Roger Cooter, ed., *Studies in the History of Alternative Medicine* (Basingstoke, 1988), pp. 174-197.
110 *The Times*, 19 September 1864, p. 7.
111 *VA*, 15 December 1848, p. 61.
112 *Provincial Homeopathic Gazette*, 1 January 1854, p. 104.
113 T.R. Allinson, *English Mechanic*, 19 January 1883 (clipping in Allinson Papers, MS 3187).
114 Richard H. Ellis, *The Casebooks of Dr John Snow* (London, 1994). Lambe was recalled by the *Medical Times and Gazette* as a 'thorough Puritan in diet, and a vegetarian' (*DR*, April 1876, p. 54), cited in Duncan's 'Vegetable Diet', in *Flowers and Fruits*; and was the subject of John Smith's dedication, *Fruits and Farinacea* (1845 edn.). The editor of the VS's reprinting of Lambe's *Diet* was Edward Hare, formerly Inspector General of Hospitals, Bengal.
115 Charles Hogg, *On the Management of Infancy. With Remarks on the Influence of Diet and Regimen* (London, 1849), printed by the vegetarians H.S. Clubb and R.T. Clubb. See *VA*, October 1849, p. 22. On Crawcour, see *VA*, 15 March 1849, p. 98; 15 April 1849, p. 111; for Jones, *People's Magazine and Progressionist*, 1 December 1854.
116 Forward, *History*, p. 58. *Vegetarian*, 22 May 1897, p. 223 discussed Smith of Malton's *Fruits and Farinacea*'s lenient treatment by medical men (Preface to 2nd edn.); its publication by John Churchill, a medical publisher, brought it into the ken of medical men.

117 Forward, *History*, ch. 7, refers to a Poor Law Commission investigation, where medical officers accepted Nicolls' claims to have the lowest death rate of any Irish Union; Kerr, *Food Reform Magazine*, July 1881, p. 18.
118 On Nichols see Aspinwall, 'Social Catholicism and Health'; on Nichols, Allinson and later naturopaths, see Peter S. Brown, 'Medically Qualified Naturopaths and the General Medical Council', *Medical History* 35 (1991), pp. 50-77, and clippings in Allinson Papers, MS 3192 and MS 3193, e.g., *Recorder* (New York) 1 June 1892; *Society*, 8 August 1892; *Figaro*, 6 August 1896.
119 *Vegetarian*, January 1898, p. 1. Pro-vegetarian scientists included Walter Wheldon, Alfred Russel Wallace and William H. Perkin, the discoverer of aniline dyes.
120 See Thomas Forster's recollections of William Lawrence: *VM*, October 1855, pp. 91-92. Lawrence had in fact repudiated Shelleyan vegetarianism, see Stuart, *Bloodless Revolution*, pp. 414-415.
121 *Vegetarian Review*, 1897.
122 *VM*, January 1854, supplement: p. 12 (presence of medical professionals); *VM*, February 1854, supplement: p. 15 (supply of literature); *VM*, November 1858, p. 28 (Edinburgh).
123 N.S. Kerr's paper on vegetarianism before the University Medical Society was opposed, *Journal of Health and Vegetarian Messenger*, p. 16; Allinson's paper before the Medical Union Society was critically received in 1883, see *Students Journal* clippings, Allinson Papers, MS 3187. James Haughton argued for the diet at the Social Science Congress in Dublin in 1861, and addressed the Royal Dublin Society's scientific meeting in 1863: *DR*, October 1861, p. 109. On Edmunds' paper, see *Lancet*, 17 March 1877, p. 391; *Proceedings of the Medical Society of London* 3 (1875-1877), pp. 169-179.
124 Hills promoted the idea that cookery destroyed a 'vital' element. An editorial in the spiritualist *MD*, 11 May 1888, p. 301, pointed out that this was not original.
125 See *HH*, 1 December 1879, p. 284. Richardson's article on 'Food Thrift', *Modern Thought*, 1880, was reprinted by the VS. He supported the Humanitarian League's diet reform, see *VM*, May 1895, p. 116. In January 1896, at the VS's invitation he lectured on food, this was published by the VS.
126 *Vegetarian*, 11 May 1889, p. 295.
127 *Hygienic Advertiser*, September 1891, p. 21.
128 *Nursing Record and Hospital World*, 16 December 1893, p. iii (advertisement), correspondence, 14 October 1893, p. 183.
129 *DR*, January 1861, pp. 38-39. Presumably the microscopist Edwin Lankester, who reviewed John Smith of Malton's *Principles and Practice of Vegetarian Cookery* (London, 1860) in the *Athenaeum*, 15 December 1860, p. 1729.
130 William Pearce, *The Treatment and Cure of Diseases Incidental to Sedentary Life* (London, 1854), p. 83. For vegetarians, a notorious lay 'expert' was George H. Lewes, *The Physiology of Common Life* (Edinburgh, 1859), see vol. 1, p. 173.
131 *Provincial Medical and Surgical Journal* (becoming, in 1857, the *BMJ*), 30 November 1855, pp. 1074-1075.
132 *DR*, 1862.
133 *Lancet*, 8 March 1879, p. 349, 'Economic dietaries'.
134 *Lancet*, 12 November 1881, p. 847.
135 *Lancet*, 18 August 1888, p. 331. It was 'One, and that not the least important, of the movements at present operating'.

136 *Lancet*, 18 August 1888, p. 331.
137 Henry S. Salt, 'Food Reform', *Westminster Review*, October 1886, pp. 483-499 [p. 498].
138 *Lancet*, 18 October 1884, p. 701.
139 Cited in *HH*, December 1879, p. 288.
140 *DR*, May 1880.
141 *Lancet*, 18 October 1884, p. 701.
142 Henry S. Salt, *A Plea for Vegetarianism*, p. 7.

Chapter Three

1 Keith Thomas, *Man and the Natural World. Changing Attitudes in England, 1500-1800* (London, 1983).
2 Harriet Ritvo, *The Animal Estate. The English and Other Creatures in the Victorian Age* (Cambridge, Massachusetts, 1987); James Turner, *Reckoning with the Beast: Animals, Pain and Humanity in the Victorian Mind* (London, 1980); Hilda Kean, *Animal Rights. Political and Social Change in Britain since 1800* (London, 1998).
3 The image was early recognized as more powerful than facts, see 'The Voice of the Tench' and correspondent's letter, *VA*, 15 March 1849, p. 98.
4 For a recent account of vegetarianism in relation to puritan sectarianism, and the polemical treatment of scripture by apologists and opponents, see Stuart, *Bloodless Revolution*, Part One, which surveys the vegetarianism of shakers, Roger Crab, Kabbalists, Issac Newton and deists; see also Thomas, *Man and the Natural World*, pp. 289-297; Alan Rudrum, 'Ethical Vegetarianism in Seventeenth Century Britain: its Roots in Sixteenth Century European Theological Debate', *Seventeenth Century* 18:1 (2003), pp. 76-92.
5 *DR*, November 1880, p. 233.
6 *VM*, March 1898, p. 100.
7 *VM*, January 1890, p. 5.
8 Kean's contention, *Animal Rights*, p. 124, that vegetarianism was increasingly seen as 'an ethical and even moral choice' is based on the growth of restaurants and shops which supported vegetarianism: this does not prove a *growing* ethical dimension, or *increased* emphasis on this aspect.
9 *DR*, July 1877, p. 126.
10 *Vegetarian*, 4 June 1892, p. 267.
11 See Kean, *Animal Rights*, pp. 29-31, in response to Thomas's thesis that sentimentalization was built on urban isolation from rural realities, see *Man and the Natural World*, p. 182, though Thomas argues this on the basis of decline in direct involvement in 'working with animals'.
12 'E.J.' of Shrewsbury, *VA*, 15 March 1849, p. 97.
13 *Vegetarian*, 23 November 1889, pp. 745-746.
14 *National Reformer*, cited in *DR*, August 1881.
15 *VM*, November 1890, pp. 315-316; *Vegetarian* 17 January 1891, p. 44. Forward's *History*, pp. 119-122 implied Plimsoll had been sympathetic.
16 'Record', *Howitt's Journal*, 26 June 1847, p. 52: Thomas ---'s revulsion to animal food since witnessing Newgate Market and a slaughterhouse. See Kean, *Animal Rights*, pp. 61-63 on the debate about Smithfield and reform of slaughterhouses.

17 George Dodd, *The Food of London. A Sketch of the Chief Varieties, Sources of Supply. Probable Quantities, Modes of Arrival, Processes of Manufacture etc.* (London, 1856), p. 254.
18 Horace F. Lester, 'Behind the Scenes', *Food Reform Journal*, October 1882; reprinted by the League (London, 1892).
19 *Vegetarian*, 7 December 1895, p. 595 [Yeats]; 1 and 8 January 1898 (p. 9; p. 25).
20 *Vegetarian*, 1 May 1897, p. 184. Forward lectured on this for the Humanitarian League and was part of a humanitarian delegation to the Shechita Board. See *VM*, December 1893, p. 471 for concern that this partly reflected anti-Semitism.
21 On the constable, see 'A. Freelance' [F.H. Perrycoste], *Towards Utopia* (London, 1894), referring to *Star*, August 1893; on the missionary, see *Vegetarian*, 22 January 1898, p. 61.
22 T.P. Smith MB, 'Vegetarianism', *Fortnightly Review*, July-December 1895, pp. 752-764 [p. 760].
23 *VM*, September 1898, pp. 429-431. 16 responded to A.W. Malcolmson's inquiry.
24 Joseph Collinson, *Shafts*, January 1897, pp. 24-25.
25 *VM*, April 1895, pp. 99-100, reprinting 'Of the sight of shops'.
26 See A.W. Malcolmson, *The Aesthetic in Food* (Manchester, 1899).
27 Michael Macmillan, *The Promotion of General Happiness. A Utilitarian Essay* (London, 1890), p. 143. See Thomas, *Man and the Natural World*, pp. 294-295.
28 'Biblius', *The Shepherd*, vol. 3, p. 94, calls butchers and slaughtermen upholders of 'the dignity of the human race'. Sutton, *The Evangel of Love* (London, 1847) wanted vegetarianism for butchers' sake; the moral contamination was stressed in the *Manifesto of the Vegetarian Society*.
29 *VA*, 15 October 1848, p. 34.
30 *VA*, 15 October 1849, p. 24.
31 *VA*, 15 February 1849, p. 91.
32 *VA*, 15 April 1849, p. 111.
33 *Vegetarian*, 3 March 1888, p. 3.
34 *WTE*, Walter Stenning, 13 January 1889, p. 16; and third generation butcher, *WTE*, 20 January, p. 6. *HGA*, January 1898, p. 7, reports hostile Devontown butchers.
35 *VM*, February 1895, p. 36, the Bolton society.
36 'J.E.S.', *New Age*, January 1844; and 'anti-cabbage', *Public Good*, July 1850, p. 209; and *Boot and Shoe Trades Journal*, quoted in *VM*, September 1894, p. 319.
37 J.E. Smith, in *The Shepherd*, vol. 3, p. 79; see *Family Herald*, 9 November 1850, pp. 444-445, on wool, 'as robbery'.
38 'Minor Hugo', *Hints and Reflections*, 3 vols. (London, 1843) vol. 3, Part I.
39 *VA*, August 1849, reverse of cover. Hence low 'selfish insinuations' the vegetarians were promoters of rubber manufacturers, *The Public Good*, Correspondence no. 3, p. 1. See also *Punch*, 1851, p. 230 on Pannus Corum Boots, directed to vegetarians.
40 *The Times*, 20 July 1854, Leeds Annual Meeting.
41 *Punch*, 18 October, 1884, p. 192. See also *Punch*, 12 February 1898, p. 72. Hygienic vegetarians also wore unconventional clothing since dress reform formed part of bodily reform.
42 *Vegetarian*, 12 September 1896, p. 433. Kingsford destroyed her sealskin, and advocated vegetarian clothing, see *DR*, June 1886. Her *Lady's Own Paper* (1872)

43   avoided advertisements for meat preparations, unhygienic apparel and harmful cosmetics.
43   *Vegetarian*, 10 October 1896, p. 483. The vegetarian Mrs Whiston wrote against murderous millinery; see *HGA*, May 1899, p. 56. See *Vegetarian*, 1899, p. 175; pp. 219-220 on cruel female attire, and Alan Haynes, '"Murderous Millinery": the Struggle for the Plumage Act, 1921', *History Today* 33 (July 1983), pp. 26-30.
44   *DR*, April 1870, referring to the historian E.A. Freeman's attack on fox-hunting, *Fortnightly Review*, October 1869.
45   *VM*, 8 May 1890, p. 185. A horse at York was called 'Vegetarian' (*Times*, 15 April 1858, p. 12); one at Ascot in 1880 was also named 'Vegetarian'.
46   Forward, *History*, pp. 125-126.
47   *VM*, July 1893, p. 265. An incident during duck-shooting made him abandon bloodsports.
48   *VM*, April 1894, pp. 130-131, the advertisement discussed in *Truth* and *Morning*. At Hills's country estate the manager was forbidden to kill foxes, see *Vegetarian*, 24 December 1898, p. 827.
49   *The Merry-go-round*, 10 April 1897.
50   *VM*, May 1895, p. 130.
51   On Lord Mount Temple, see John Ranlett, 'Checking Nature's Desecration: late Victorian environmental organization', *Victorian Studies*, 26 (Winter 1983), pp. 197-222. Auberon Herbert campaigned to protect the New Forest. The Reverend E.E. Kelly had modern-sounding concerns about land starvation, water pollution and biodegradable coffins, see *Vegetarian*, May 1889, p. 298; and, for further letter on burial reform, 2 January 1892. Allinson's Natural Living Society supported earth to earth coffins too.
52   Edith Ward, *Shafts*, 19 November 1892, pp. 40-41.
53   Forward, *History*, p. 62.
54   Dr J.J. Reynolds, see *DR*, January 1886, p. 8.
55   Richard D. French, *Antivivisection and Medical Science in Victorian Society* (London, 1975), p. 230; Nicolaas Rupke, ed., *Vivisection in Historical Perspective* (1987; London, 1990); and Hilda Kean, 'The "Smooth Cool Men of Science": The Feminists and Socialist Response to Vivisection', *Historical Journal* 40 (1995), pp. 16-38.
56   Frances P. Cobbe resisted the association, yet admitted the 'vegetarianism of Brahmins and Pythagoreans and of many modern English men and women deserving of respect, has been a protest' (*Vegetarian*, 21 April 1888, p. 44). Mrs Fairchild Allen, editor of the American *Anti-vivisector*, joined the VS, see *DR*, September 1895, pp. 303-304.
57   Jennie Brace, forced to confront her inconsistency when canvassing for an anti-vivisection petition, joined. Another, the novelist Mona Caird, became vegetarian, see her *Beyond the Pale. An Appeal on Behalf of the Victims of Vivisection* (London, 1897), p. 40, on 'the ingrained practice of flesh-eating'.
58   The vegetarians Reverend J.F. Kennard of Dover and W.G. Flynt of Southport were involved, see *Zoophilist*, 1 April 1890, p. 268; *Zoophilist*, 1 November 1890. *Zoophilist* apparently never reviewed its copies of *VM* and neglected Henry S. Salt's *An Essay on Food Reform*, received 1 June 1888, p. 25. The *VM* (January 1893, p. 6) noted its praise for Mrs Bowdich's cookery book.
59   French, *Antivivisection*, p. 230.

60 Recognition by non-vegetarians of anti-vivisectionists' inconsistency includes comments in *Pick-me-up*, cited in *Vegetarian*, 29 March 1890, p. 215; Thomas Fowler, *Progressive Morality. An Essay in Ethics* (London, 1884), and Dr Foster, *Macmillan's Magazine* 1874, cited in Ninon [sic] Kingsford, 'The Best Food for Man', *Westminster Review*, October 1874, p. 511.

61 David Mushet, *The Wrongs of the Animal World. To which is subjoined the speech of Lord Erskine on the Same Subject* (London, 1839), an SPCA competition essay, pp. 155-161, opposed vivisection but saw vegetarianism as 'impious and absurd', though practised by 'benevolent hearts' (pp. 160-161).

62 *Vegetarian*, September 1896 contained a symposium on anti-vivisectionists' duty to be vegetarian; 2 April 1898, pp. 207-209 for calls for anti-vivisectionist consistency. *HGA* supported Florence Marryat's novel, *An Angel of Pity* (1898), see *HGA*, 15 August 1898, p. 91; and published an anti-vivisection essay by Mona Caird.

63 *The People's Advocate*, 1 January 1900, p. 12; Ernest Bell, *Contemporary Review*, July-December 1892, pp. 849-854.

64 *VA*, 15 February 1849, p. 88.

65 Lewis Gompertz, *Fragments in Defence of Animals, and Essays on Morals, Soul and Future State* (London, 1852) and *Mechanical Inventions and Suggestions on Land, and Water Locomotion, Tooth Machinery, and various other branches of Theoretical and Practical Mechanics* (2nd edn, London, 1856).

66 *The Animals' Friend, or, The Progress of Humanity*, e.g., no. 9, pp. 21-28, 'Cowper Examined or, a consideration of the perfection of nature, as it relates to the moral progress of man, and to the welfare of all created beings'.

67 Turner, *Reckoning with the Beast*, pp. 39-43. Vegetarian members may have included Jane Hurlstone: her granddaughter recalled her as a founder of the RSPCA. Other vegetarians who are probably identifiable with supporters of Gompertz's society include R. Wainewright and Caleb Yewen.

68 *Journal of Health*, November 1856, p. 53.

69 See Anon., *A Plea for the Cattle. A Few Words, Addressed to the Upper and Influential Classes* (London, 1866).

70 Williams raised the vegetarian remedy in discussing slaughterhouses, *Animal World*, 1 July 1873, p. 109; 1 January 1874, p. 14 (where vegetarian creed and address were given); 1 July 1874, p. 110.

71 Address to RSPCA, June 1874, reprinted as advertisement in *Animal World*, 1 September 1874, p. 139, and in *Manifesto of the Vegetarian Society*.

72 During publication of articles about 'Cruelty in Secret Places', *Animal World* printed letters on Vegetarianism and Butchers: Alison Ivens, 1 October 1878, and T.W.L. Hayes, 2 December 1878, pp. 183-184.

73 *Vegetarian*, 10 March 1894, p. 114.

74 H. Newmarch, *WTE*, 6 January, 1889, p. 6.

75 Henry S. Salt commented, *Vegetarian*, 15 February 1896, p. 83 that zoophilists had appreciated vegetarian implications only in the last ten years.

76 *Vegetarian*, 20 November 1897, p. 654. The journal has been examined for 1896-1898. Vegetarian zoophilism was enjoined by Countess Wachtmeister, January 1898, p. 68, Ernest Bell, August 1898, pp. 201-202, and A.J.H. Crespi, September 1898, p. 220.

77 See Morris's letter of inquiry and suggestions in *DR*, January 1886, p. 23; J. Frewen Moor, *Thoughts Regarding the Future State of Animals* (Winchester, 1893). See *VM*,

April 1892 for the Dicky Bird Society established by the radical W.E. Adams in 1878, and *Vegetarian*, 4 July 1889, p. 360. A.M. Lewis, *Humanity and Vegetarianism* (a paper read at VFU, 26 May 1892, and reprinted as tract from *Vegetarian*), p. 6.
78   Dan Weinbren, 'Against *all* Cruelty: the Humanitarian League, 1891-1919', *History Workshop Journal* 38 (1994), pp. 86-101, on the League's programme and origins in Salt's reading of Williams' *Ethics of Diet*. See GMCRO-VS, G24/1/2/1 (London Auxiliary of the VS, Minutes; for Williams' letter, 22 July 1886, asking to be taken off the committee as he wished to devote himself to the humanitarian aspect of the subject; he agreed to be a nominal member.
79   *DR*, November 1878, p. 226.
80   *Shafts*, January 1897, pp. 24-5.
81   Proof copy of manifesto with pencil additions (1896), Johnson, Box 1; in 1898 this became the Humane Diet and Dress Department.
82   As reiterated in the republication of Salt's essay 'Humanities of Diet' as Humanitarian League tract 23. See Salt, ed., *The New Charter*. Of the six chapters, half were by vegetarians, but the food question was discussed in two other chapters.
83   *Humanity*, the League's journal, reviewed and recommended vegetarian works and engaged in controversies generated by non-vegetarians such as Sir H. Thompson. An essay by Ernest Axon marked the VS's anniversary, June 1897. Forward's lecture for the League at Tunbridge Wells was explicit about the League's vegetarian logic, see *Humanity*, December 1896, p. 175.
84   10 December 1896, cited in *VM*, February 1897, p. 41.
85   *VM*, 6 November 1897, p. 368.
86   *HH*, 1895, pp. 172-173 (interview with Salt). In 1899 this journal contained the leaflet *The Humanitarian League. What it Is and What it Is Not*.
87   'S', *Humanity*, November 1898, p. 83. There was a misunderstanding as a result of remarks in *Humanity*, see *Vegetarian* 3 December pp. 780-781 for Williams's call for vegetarians to join the League; and the journal's apology, 31 December p. 831.
88   'H.W.', *Humanity*, December 1898, pp. 95-6.
89   For pre-Darwinian evolutionary ideas in early nineteenth-century Britian see Adrian Desmond, *The Politics of Evolution. Morphology, Medicine, and Reform in Radical London* (London, 1989), which refers, pp. 185-186 to vegetarianism and anti-cruelty sentiment in anatomy schools in the 1830s. Though others applied 'Darwinism' to humanity, Darwin left out human origins from the *Origins of Species* (1859), but examined it in *The Descent of Man, and Selection in Relation to Man* (1871) and studied human-animal links in *The Expression of the Emotions in Man and Animals* (1872). Weinbren, 'Against *all* Cruelty', p.89 discusses the co-operative 'Greater Kinship' reading of Darwin. The 'sacredness of life for itself' and the idea of a web of dependency are seen as a post-Darwinist conceptualization of animal-mankind relations by Turner, *Reckoning with the Beast*, p. 127. The Catholic Dr T.L. Nichols criticized natural selection in *HH*, rejecting Darwin and Huxley as men of no faith who believed man descended through adaptation to circumstances from apes. Francis Newman's review of Gustav Schlickeysen's *Obst und Brod* identified its introduction of the Darwinian hypothesis as an act that would repel many from vegetarianism (*DR*, October 1877). Vegetarian attempts to clarify Darwin's position are noted in the Conclusion to this study. Alternative neo-Lamarckian versions of evolution allowed human will and idealism to play a part, and were

influential in the late-nineteenth century; see Ruth Livesey, *Socialism, Sex and the Culture of Aestheticism in Britain, 1880-1914* (forthcoming), with reference to Edward Carpenter. I am grateful to Dr Livesey for allowing me to see this research prior to publication. If there was ambivalence about animals (wider kinship/fears about animalization) this also existed in anti-vivisectionism, see French, *Antivivisection*, pp. 385-388.

90 'Thus Far!', *VM*, January 1894, pp. 8-10 [p. 9]. For similar treatment, see Mary Tudor Pole, 'The Evolutionary Aspect of Vegetarianism', *VM*, November 1899, pp. 389-392. For a standard view of survival of the fittest, and criticism of vegetarians, see David Balsillie, *The Ethic of Nature and its Practical Bearings* (Edinburgh, 1889), pp. 25-26.

91 J.S. Hibberd, *VA*, August 1849, p. 154.

92 Herbert Spencer, *Social Statics: or, The Conditions Essential to Human Happiness Specified, and The First of Them Developed* (London, 1851), pp. 411-412.

93 Thomas, *Man and the Natural World*, pp. 184-185; and Turner, *Reckoning with the Beast*, ch. 5, situate the movement in the context of revulsion to pain. For a recent examination of Victorian attitudes to pain, see Lucy Bending, *The Representation of Bodily Pain in Late Nineteenth-Century Culture* (Oxford, 2000).

94 Bending, *Representation of Pain*, p. 2.

95 Review of R. Fletcher, *A Few Notes on Cruelty to Animals*, in *The Athenaeum*, 5 February 1848, p. 141; 'The Height of Anarchy,' in *Punch's* Almanack for 1853; 'Height of Humanity,' in *Punch's* Almanac for 1882. For late-Victorian anti-sentimentalism see the war correspondent George W. Steeven's anonymous 'The New Humanitarianism', *Blackwood's Edinburgh Magazine* 163 (January 1898), pp. 98-106, which is also discussed in Bending, *Representation of Pain*, pp. 69-70. Henry S. Salt's reply, 'The Old Brutality,' *Humanity*, February 1898, pp. 12-13, was reprinted in several papers when *Blackwood's* refused to publish it.

96 Forward, *History*, p. 114. See the Reverend S. Barnett's comment, during the Ripper panic, quoted in Turner, *Reckoning with the Beast*, p. 134.

97 For instance *VM*, January 1853, supplement: p. 6. See Vic A.C. Gatrell, *The Hanging Tree. Execution and the English People. 1770-1868* (Oxford, 1994). The vegetarian Josiah Oldfield led the abolitionist society in the late-Victorian period.

98 *Nonconformist*, 11 June 1856, pp. 426-7.

99 *Healthian*, 1 July 1843, pp. 59-63.

100 See list in John Cassell's *Standard of Freedom*, 1 September 1849.

101 *VA*, 15 October 1848, p. 37; 15 November 1848, pp. 53-4; 15 March 1849, p. 93. See the quotation from J.P. Edwards's *Public Good* (supplement, 1850) in Alex Tyrrell, 'Making the Millennium: The Mid-Nineteenth Century Peace Movement', *Historical Journal* 21 (March 1978), pp. 75-95 [p. 88].

102 *VA*, 15 October 1848, p. 35. See *Journal of Health*, October 1855, p. 73 for Dornbusch's pacifism.

103 W.E. Aytoun, 'The Congress and the Agapedome', *Blackwood's Edinburgh Magazine*, September 1851 (vol. 70) p. 431. *Morning Chronicle*, 4 August 1851 (*VM*, November and December 1851: *Vegetarian Controversialist*, p. 17, p. 21) noted the resemblance between one public meeting and the Peace Congress. Bulwer-Lytton's bestselling *My Novel; or, Varieties in English Life* referred [see *Blackwood's Edinburgh Magazine* 70: 433 (November 1851), p. 573], to progressives such as the Quaker-seeming man

who asserted 'that the march of Enlightenment is a crusade for universal philanthropy, vegetable diet, and the perpetuation of peace, by means of speeches'.

104 *VM* advertised the *International Arbitration Association Journal* in 1887; *Vegetarian*, 8 June 1888, p. 359 printed the Peace Party's principles and objectives, vegetarians attended the 1894 Peace Congress, see *Vegetarian*, 15 September 1894, p. 439.

105 *HGA*, 15 August 1898, p. 94; *Vegetarian*, 2 October 1897, p. 540.

106 *The People's Advocate*, 1 January 1900, p. 5; *A Proposal for Restoring the Ancient Practices of Anthropophagy and Vivisection in their Just Development* (Johnson, Box 1) and published as I. Hay, *The Revival of Cannibalism: a Story of Coming Times* (London, 1885).

107 Henry Clubb believed violent animals existed through man's violence; see *VA*, 15 September 1848, p. 25, and response to this, e.g., 15 March 1849, p. 96.

108 See Lacy, 'The Vegetarian; or, a Visit to Aunt', pp. 411-412; and quotation from novel *Episodes in an Obscure Life* (1871), in *DR*, October 1881, pp. 209-210.

109 *VM*, June 1850, p. 92.

110 Thomas, *Man and the Natural World*, p. 288. On the idea of a return to the Adamic harmony of nature, see Stuart, *Bloodless Revolution*, p. 10, p. 19. See also the colour plates in *Bloodless Revolution*, reproducing paintings from the studio of Jan Breughel, of the Garden of Eden.

111 See Turner, *Reckoning with the Beast*; Moira Ferguson, *Animal Advocacy and Englishwomen, 1780-1900. Patriots, Nation and Empire* (Ann Arbor, 1998); and also Crossley, *Consumable Metaphors*, where 'the 'primary referentiality' in 'knowledge of animals' is 'overlaid with further levels of meaning' (p. 11), and animals 'serve to externalize human fears and wishes', p.15.

112 Mark Clement, 'Physical Puritanism and Religious Dissent: The Case of John Young (1820-1904), Sunderland Chemist and Druggist and Methodist Lay Preacher', *Social History of Medicine* 11:2 (August 1998), pp. 197-212.

113 Janet Oppenheim, *The Other World. Spiritualism and Psychical Research in England, 1850-1914* (Cambridge, 1985), p. 231. Emphasis on a *material* factor opened vegetarians themselves to a charge of materialism: e.g., G.J. Holyoake, *Reasoner*, 'Utilitarian Record', 1847, p. 95.

114 Early and mid-Victorian philanthropy conventionally incorporated prayers and appeals to scripture. In covering the vegetarian banquet in London, August 1851, the Paris *Journal des Debat*'s reporter thought the scriptural references were typical of English public banquets.

115 *VM*, December 1893, p. 439.

116 *VA*, 15 September 1848, p. 23.

117 Francis W. Newman, *Essays on Diet* (London, 1883) p. 13. See *Vegetarian*, 29 July 1892, p. 358 for W.G. Stubbs's opposition to the paper's Theatre section.

118 H.G. Wells, *Love and Mrs Lewisham* (London, 1900; first printed serially in the *Weekly Times* in 1899) p. 196. On Victorian Puritanism see Raphael Samuel, 'The Discovery of Puritanism, 1820-1914: A Preliminary Sketch,' in R. Samuel, (posthumously edited by Alison Light with Sally Alexander and Gareth Stedman Jones) *Island Stories: Unravelling Britain*. vol. 2 *Theatres of Memory* (London, 1998), pp. 276-322.

119 *VA*, 18 August 1848, advertisement for *Advocate*.

120 *VA*, May 1850, p. 112.

121 Horsell, *VA*, 15 January 1849, p. 72. See also Charles Lane, 'Physiological morality', *VA*, 15 October 1848, p. 42.
122 *Healthian*, February 1842, p. 23.
123 *Healthian*, 1 January 1843, p. 103.
124 See James C. Whorton, '"Christian Physiology": William Alcott's Prescription for the Millennium', *Bulletin of the History of Medicine* 49 (1975), pp. 466-431; Robert H. Abzug, *Cosmos Crumbling. American Reform and the Religious Imagination* (New York, 1994).
125 *Annual Register*, August 1824, p. 105; Robert Southey, 'The Roman Catholic Question', *Quarterly Review*, 38 (October 1828), p. 556. They had no national fame, but readers of Samuel Brown's essay would have learned of their existence. In 1836 the vegetarian-pacifist lecturer for the Anti-Slavery Society, George Pilkington, mentioned the sect in his autobiography, later excerpted in *VM*. The sect had abandoned vegetarianism by the time of its demise in 1932. Modern studies are: Peter J. Lineham, 'Restoring Man's creative power: the theosophy of the Bible Christians of Salford', in William J. Sheils, ed., *The Church and Healing*, pp. 207-223, which draws on Lineham's doctoral research on the English Swedenborgians (Sussex, 1978); Antrobus, *A Guiltless Feast*; and Samantha J. Calvert, 'A Taste of Eden: Modern Christianity and Vegetarianism', *Journal of Ecclesiastical History* 58: 1 (January 2007), which in part, discusses the Cowherdites. My thanks to Ms Calvert for a preview of this monograph.
126 The religious affiliations of 435 vegetarians were identified: 265 Cowherdites, 40 Quakers; 30 Anglican clergymen; 29 Unitarians; 26 Methodists (Primitive Methodists, Wesleyans, New Connexion); 17 Congregationalists; 9 Baptists; 9 Swedenborgians; 7 Roman Catholics; 2 Presbyterians; 1 Seventh Day Baptist family (Lt Richardson's family). There are, additionally, some 25 ministers whose denomination I have not identified. See Harrison, *Drink and the Victorians*, pp. 164-173 on denominational profile and ch. 8 on the relationship with religion; Lilian L. Shiman, *The Crusade against Drink in Victorian England* (Basingstoke, 1988), pp. 53-68 for responses to teetotalism by nonconformist churches.
127 Peter Collins, 'Quaker Plaining as Critical Aesthetic', *Quaker Studies* 5:2 (2001), pp. 121-139, discusses 'plainness' as a religious ideal, symbol of spirituality throughout history and aesthetic judgment.
128 William Bennett, *A Letter to a Friend, in reply to the question, What is vegetarianism?* (London, 1849).
129 *Truth-Tester*, n.s., vol. 1, 1847, p. 83.
130 See *International Magazine of Literature, Art and Science* (New York) 4:3 (October 1851), pp. 402-403, from Paris *Journal des Debats*, 'There were about four hundred persons present, as many women as men, a great many children, and a great many Quakers.'
131 For instance: *DR*, October 1862, p. 94; *DR*, March 1877, p. 44; *VM*, June 1898, p. 283.
132 *Vegetarian Society to the Society of Friends* (1880): 'This Association, we are glad to say, has never been without its supporters among the Society of Friends.' The Quaker journals (*The Friend*, *British Friend*) discussed vegetarianism only in correspondence in 1852 (*The Friend*, April-July). On efforts to establish a Quaker vegetarian society, see A.N. Brayshaw, *HGA*, 15 June 1900.
133 See *HGA*, September 1898, p. 103. The twelve are identified in my thesis.

134 *DR*, July 1887, p. 222; *DR*, February 1889, p. 47, citing coverage in *Nonconformist*, 6 December 1888; *Vegetarian*, 19 January 1889, p. 39; *Vegetarian*, 13 April, p. 231. The LVS moved into the Congregationalist Memorial Hall in 1889.
135 Forward, *History*, pp. 117-119. General Booth became vegetarian late in life. His son William Bramwell Booth and daughter-in-law were vegetarians, as was Frank Smith. See testimony of Staff Captain Ruth Tracy, *HH*, November 1899, p. 172.
136 *VA*, 15 October 1848 p. 37, p. 41; 15 April 1849, pp. 110. On Wesley's vegetarianism, see Kean, *Animal Rights*, pp. 18-21. See *VM*, December 1850, p. 154 on propaganda amongst Bible Christians of Cornwall.
137 Forward, *History*, pp. 116-117: 'The dignitaries of the Established Church do not appear to have been so favourably impressed by the truths of Vegetarianism as many of the dissenting clergy have been.' [p. 116] See *HGA*, December 1898, p. 142, for the Reverend A.M. Mitchell's comment. London vegetarians courted prominent Anglicans, see *HH*, 1887, p. 79.
138 See *DR*, May 1879, p. 105 on the Reverend H.J. Williams's projected vegetarian Lenten discourses. *DR*, November 1880, p. ix for the Reverend J.S. Jones's paragraph in Winchester *Diocesan Kalendar*. The Reverend A.M. Mitchell's annual parish letter was vegetarian. E.E. Kelly mentioned vegetarianism in sermons, *VM*, August 1898, p. 37.
139 Harry G. Levine, 'Temperance Cultures: Alcohol as a Problem in Nordic and English-Speaking Cultures', in Malcolm Lader, Griffith Edwards and D. Colin Drummond, eds, *The Nature of Alcohol and Drug-related Problems* (New York, 1993), pp. 16-36.
140 George Meredith, 'Jump-to-Glory-Jane' (1889), based on the New Forest Shakers. Orthodox Catholic response to 'heretical' vegetarianism in the early modern period, including the institutionalisation of abstinence via fast laws, is discussed in Stuart, *Bloodless Revolution*, pp. 150-154. See Crossley, *Consumable Metaphors*, p. 29, pp. 121-132, on the tension between mainstream Catholicism and the 'individual moral autonomy' expressed in the French animal protection movement.
141 See *Punch*, February 1879, 22 May 1886, p. 250; *DR*, January 1893, p. 37.
142 See Brown, 'Physical Puritanism' on the appearance of vegetable diet in school scripture reading.
143 On the dissolvent role of teetotalism, see Harrison, *Drink and the Victorians*, pp. 185-186. See 'On the permissions of the Mosaic Law', *VA*, 15 March 1849, pp. 94-95; 'G.W.W.', *British Controversialist*, 1850, p. 389: stressed mistranslation, historical formation of scripture and the nonscientific nature of scriptural knowledge.
144 E.g., 'B.W.P.', *British Controversialist*, 1850, pp. 309; see *MD*, 24 January 1890, p. 59 on the parading of reference to the 'fatted calf'.
145 Anon. (Richard Govett), *The Future Apostacy* (London, 1848), p. 38. See the review in *Truth-Tester*, n.s., vol. 2, 1848, p. 122. Simpson refers to this view in *VM*, July 1853, p. 31. Another association of new movements with false prophets of the latter days is 'A Tory Daniel' cited in *Chartist Circular*, 26 December 1840, p. 280. On Nebuchadnezzar, see *VM*, October 1894, p. 369.
146 Anon. (Richard Govett), *Vegetarianism. A Dialogue* (London, 1849), p. 13.
147 *Vegetarianism attacked and defended. Being a reprint of a controversy from the columns of the Glasgow Newspaper Press*, p. 4.

148 The Reverend Thomas Clarke of Ashford, Kent, *VA*, 15 April 1849, p. 110. See reverse of cover, *VM*, July 1850, for the Archbishop of Dublin's letter against the Society's treatment of scripture. Controversy over vegetarian reading of scripture surfaced in the *Bradford Observer*, see *VM*, April 1856, p. 26. *DR*, January 1862, pp. 12-13, reported that a 'popular lecturer' in Bradford thought vegetarianism insulted God. In *DR*, January 1867, p. 19, a Primitive Methodist preacher recalled his ministers' opinion that vegetarianism was contrary to the New Testament and inconsistent with being a preacher.
149 *HGA*, February 1896, p. 27.
150 *Vegetarian*, 1889, p. 106; pp. 394-395. For Hills, the 'unalterable adamant' was 'obeying the laws of God', see *Vegetarian*, 2 June 1892. To 'H.W's' criticisms that the *Vegetarian* was 'too secular' (3 December 1898, p. 767) the editor replied that the policy was to have a complete statement of the vegetarian case, in each number.
151 *VM*, January 1893, p. 19.
152 GMCRO-VS, G24/1/2/1, minute book of LVS, minutes 3 August, 24 September and 9 November 1888.
153 Twigg did not examine the *HGA*, or *Vegetarian*; see Twigg, 'The Vegetarian movement', p. 114, p. 293, p. 123. Her misinterpretation is repeated in C. Spencer, *The Heretic's Feast*, p. 293. See *Danielite Star*, 16 May 1887 (no. 1), p. 1 for the required declaration. Founded shortly afterwards, but soon distanced from the Order of the Golden Age, was John Todd Ferrier's 'Order of the Cross', see Calvert, 'A Taste of Eden', II.
154 *Vegetarian*, 19 November 1898, p. 745.
155 The phrase appears in *Vegetarian*, 4 January 1890, p. 13; the idea of a 'Gospel of Health' was repeated elsewhere, e.g., *Vegetarian*, 2 May 1890, pp. 263-264.
156 *New Age*, 13 May 1843, p. 15.
157 Isaac Taylor, *Ultimate Civilization and Other Essays* (London, 1860), p. 284.
158 *DR*, August 1890, p. 243. 'W', in *DR*, February 1886, p. 39, opposed 'the persistent attempts to make Vegetarianism a religious question'. See also C.H. Brooks, *Vegetarian*, 14 June 1894, p. 336.
159 *WTE*, 16 December 1888, p. 6 'excluding theology and idealism'; S. Soddy, in *Vegetarian*, 1888, p. 620 ('Neo-Vegetarian ...' is his phrase); Francis Newman, *DR*, February 1889, p. 46; and L. Large, *Vegetarian*, 9 February 1889, p. 91. T.R. Allinson, *Vegetarian*, 27 July 1889, p. 474 asserted he was as much an agnostic as a vegetarian. See *Vegetarian*, 30 January, p. 58 for one agnostic's response to a comment by Edward Maitland. Note also, *Vegetarian*, 1888, p. 3, the request of a 'friendly pastor' not to make a vegetarian lecture 'too high and lofty'.
160 Twigg, 'Vegetarian Movement', pp. 190-209. See also Twigg's essay, 'Food for Thought: Purity and vegetarianism', *Religion* 9 (Spring), 1979, pp. 13-35.
161 Oppenheim, *The Other World*, from whom the phrase 'surrogate faith' is derived; Logie Barrow, *Independent Spirits. Spiritualism and English Plebeians. 1850-1910* (London, 1986); Alex Owen, *The Darkened Room: Women, Power and Spiritualism in Late Victorian England* (London, 1989); Brian J. Gibbons, *Spirituality and the Occult. From the Renaissance to the Modern Age* (London, 2001).
162 Benjamin Morrell's *Spiritual Telegraph* and William Carpenter's *Spiritual Messenger*. Horsell's publications included Carpenter's *Communion with Ministering Spirits* (1858),

John Ashburner's *A Series of Essays. On the Connection between Mesmerism and Spiritualism* (1859) and Thomas Shorter's *Confessions of a Truth Seeker* (1859).

163 *Two Worlds*, p. 1.
164 Oppenheim, *The Other World*, p. 4; and Part II on the relationship between spiritualism, Christianity and freethought.
165 Oppenheim, *The Other World*, pp. 43-44.
166 'Dietetics in relationship to mediumship', *MD*, 20 January 1871.
167 See 'D.J.N', 'The Mediumship of George Spriggs', *Ark Review* (Noah's Ark Society for Physical Mediumship), 6:91, February 1998.
168 When it first appeared spiritualism benefited from superficial similarities with mesmerism, and continued to partner this and other medical unorthodoxies: see Oppenheim, *The Other World*, pp. 217-236; and Barrow, *Independent Spirits*, pp. 161-194; pp. 213-228.
169 *MD*, 6 September 1872, p. 349. See account of vegetarian food and discussion at Clapham Junction séance, *MD*, 5 June 1891, p. 362.
170 *Herald of Progress* (Gateshead) 1883 featured a contribution by J.J. Morse on 'Practical Vegetarianism' and advocacy from other vegetarians. See spiritualist fiction by Anna Kingsford, C.L.H Wallace, and the American William Wilberforce Colville's *Bertha. A Romance of Easter-tide* (London, 1884), published by Burns.
171 *MD*, 22 August 1890, p. 536.
172 *MD*, 12 October 1883, p. 641.
173 *MD*, 4 November 1892, p. 706.
174 *MD*, 13 June 1890, p. 370.
175 *FRM*, April-June 1884, p. 101.
176 *DR*, October 1866, pp. 121-122. The 'First Convention of Progressive Spiritualists' (1865) included 'dietetics' and hygiene as part of a proposed college.
177 See advertisements in *Spiritual Magazine*, 1863.
178 *Human Nature*, 1871, p. 330; *Vegetarian*, 14 January 1888, p. 7.
179 *MD*, 25 April 1879, republished, 20 March 1891, p. 183.
180 *MD*, 20 June 1888, front page, in large type.
181 *MD*, 17 July 1888, p. 450.
182 *MD*, 20 June 1890, p. 386.
183 *DR*, January 1893, p. 19.
184 *Vegetarian*, 16 March 1895, p. 133; *Vegetarian Review*, February 1895.
185 *The British Spiritual Telegraph*, 1 July 1858, p. 157. His friend William Tebb the anti-vaccinationist (and former vegetarian), a prominent spiritualist in the 1870s, befriended Adin Ballou, *The Practical Christian*'s editor, in the 1850s.
186 *MD*, 18 August 1871, p. 271, letter supporting Gerald Massey's lecture.
187 *Cooper's Journal*, 1850, p. 2. For his spiritualism, see Barrow, *Independent Spirits*, p. 61; *British Spiritual Telegraph*, 1857-1858.
188 Her career is discussed in Owen, *The Darkened Room*; and Barrow, *Independent Spirits*, pp. 222-224.
189 He is the fourth, unexplored member of the siblings discussed in Owen, *The Darkened Room*, ch. 4 (pp. 74-106).
190 *MD*, 11 May 1877, p. 295.
191 *MD*, 11 October 1878, p. 645.
192 Oppenheim, *The Other World*, p. 47.

193 Barrow, *Independent Spirits*, pp. 206-212; *MD*, 24 January 1873, p. 45, 27 February, pp. 10-11.
194 Barrow, *Independent Spirits*, p. 9, p. 16; and obituary in *DR*.
195 Barrow, *Independent Spirits*, p. 196, with photograph.
196 Charles Isham, *The Food That We Live On* (Northampton, n.d.), sold by Burns with 'A number of Tracts on Dietetic Subjects'.
197 Van Akin Burd, *Ruskin, Lady Mount Temple and the Spiritualists: an Episode in Broadlands History* (London, 1982).
198 *The New Age*'s motto, vol. 1, no. 1 (6 May 1843), was: 'If any man be in Christ he is a new creature: old things are passed away; behold all things are become new.' See Joscelyn Godwin, *The Theosophical Enlightenment* (Albany, 1994), pp. 228-230; and Jackie E.M. Latham, 'A Forgotten Theosopher: James Pierrepont Greaves', *Theosophical History* 8:8 (October 2001), pp. 221-230.
199 'Eirionnach', *Notes and Queries*, 2nd Series, no. 11, 11 May 1861, pp. 361-363.
200 Josiah Oldfield, 'Vegetarian Still', *Nineteenth Century*, August 1898, pp. 246-252 [pp. 246].
201 *Vegetarian*, 1 January 1898, p. 13.
202 Joy Dixon, *Divine Feminine. Theosophy and Feminism in England* (Baltimore, Maryland, 2001), pp. 132-134.
203 For instance, R. Undiano, *Vegetarian*, 27 April 1889, p. 259.
204 *Vegetarian*, 22 June 1889, pp. 396, letter from a 'Swedenborgian'.
205 *DR*, 1897, p. 63.
206 Dixon, *Divine Feminine*, p. 133.
207 Vegetarian-theosophists included Countess Wachtmeister, friend of Blavatsky and author of *Practical Vegetarian Cookery* (Theosophical Publishing Society, 1899). The homeopath Dr Leopold Salzer, president of Punjab VS, wrote *The Psychic Aspect of Vegetarianism*.
208 Address to the London Food Reform Society, first May meeting, reported in *FRM*, July 1881, p. 21.
209 H. Williams, *Food Reform Magazine*, October 1881, p. 62.
210 *The Gospel of the Holy Twelve* (1892), a humanitarian version of the gospels 'discovered' in 1881, in which Jesus teaches natural health reform and carnivorism is blamed on Satan.
211 See *DR*, October 1881, p. 202 and p. 218; activities included a banquet and quarterly papers: *DR*, May 1883, p. 132 and December 1883, p. 340.
212 *VM*, April 1896, p. 132; *Vegetarian*, 8 February 1896, pp. 69-70; *HGA*, February 1896, p. 23.
213 *HGA*, December 1899, pp. 134-136. The Order claimed no new morality or religion (*Vegetarian Review*, February 1896, p. 96).
214 *HGA*, December 1900, p. 150.
215 *DR*, October 1869, p. 126.
216 Henry S. Salt, *Seventy Years Among the Savages* (London, 1921), p. 173.
217 *MD*, 26 October 1888, p. 679.
218 Hynes, *Edwardian Turn of Mind*, p. 135; Mark Hamilton, 'Eating Ethically: "Spiritual" and "Quasi-Religious" aspects of Vegetarianism', *Journal of Contemporary Religion*, 15:1 (2000), pp. 65-83; and, on French occultist vegetarians, Crossley, *Consumable Metaphors*, pp.255-267.

Chapter Four

1 See Brian Harrison, 'A Genealogy of Reform in Modern Britain', ch. 6 in Christine Bolt and Seymour Drescher, eds, *Anti-Slavery, Religion and Reform. Essays in Memory of Roger Anstey* (Folkestone, 1980), pp. 119-148; and 'The Rhetoric of Reform in Modern Britain: 1780-1918', in Brian Harrison, *Peaceable Kingdom. Stability and Change in Modern Britain* (Oxford, 1982), pp. 378-443. Shared characteristics (and connections) with American reform should be recognized, see W.P. Garrison, 'The Isms of Forty Years Ago', *Harper's New Monthly Magazine* (New York), 60: 356 (January 1880), p. 192.
2 'Fadical' was coined by G. Dunn in 'A Defeated Transcendentalist', *Blackwood's Magazine*, February 1893, pp. 236-252.
3 Roy Porter, *The Greatest Benefit to Mankind. A Medical History of Humanity from Antiquity to the Present* (London, 1997), p. 390.
4 Roy Porter, in Roy Porter, ed., *The Cambridge Illustrated History of Medicine* (Cambridge, 1996), p. 116.
5 John F.C. Harrison, 'Early Victorian Radicals and the Medical Fringe' in W.F. Bynum and Roy Porter, eds, *Medical Fringe and Medical Orthodoxy* (London, 1987), pp. 198-215. For further exploration of the plebeian 'democratic intellect', see Barrow, *Independent Spirits*.
6 Prothero, *Artisans and Politics,* p. 263.
7 Royle, *Victorian Infidels*, p. 144; Harrison, *Drink and the Victorians*, pp. 184-185.
8 Royle, *Radical Politics*, p. 59.
9 *The Freethinker* 2 April 1893. Allinson joined the National Secular Society in 1890. See Allinson Papers, MS 3188, 17 January 1886; MS 3192, 2 February 1890, 31 March 1895.
10 Alex Tyrrell, *Joseph Sturge and the Moral Radical Party in Early Victorian Britain* (London, 1987). See also Alex Tyrrell, 'The Moral Radical Party and the Anglo-Jamaican campaign for the abolition of the Negro apprenticeship system', *English Historical Review* 99 (July 1984), pp. 481-502; Harrison, 'Genealogy of reform', pp. 131-3; and Trygve R. Tholfsen, *Working Class Radicalism in Mid-Victorian England* (London, 1976), ch. 4, for an important examination of middle-class social reformers and the 'religion of improvement'. One of Tholfsen's case studies is the ultra-reformer Joseph Cowen Jnr. of Newcastle upon Tyne, recipient of several vegetarian tracts. John Belchem, *Popular Radicalism in Nineteenth Century Britain* (Basingstoke, 1996), p. 97 situates vegetarianism within the 'expressive' wing of *middle-class* ultra-radicalism too. Tyrrell emphasized the continuing role of moral middle-class radicalism by reference to Frank Parkin, *Middle Class Radicalism* (Manchester, 1968) on CND activists. For the general history of 'pressure from without', and the shared characteristics of nonconformity, provincial vs. metropolitan etc., see Hollis, ed., *Pressure from Without*.
11 Tyrrell, *Joseph Sturge*, p. 5. See also Harrison, 'Genealogy of Reform', p. 134 on the 'symbolic character' of reforming crusades in general.
12 Tyrrell, *Joseph Sturge*, p. 121.
13 Tyrrell, *Joseph Sturge*, p. 144.
14 Tyrrell, *Joseph Sturge*, pp. 198-199. Neesom called for Sturge, Quakers and the Peace Movement to complete their work by converting to vegetarianism, see *VM*, September 1849, p. 13.

15 Henry James, *The Bostonians*, (serialized in *The Century Magazine*, 1885-1886, volume form 1886) in which Basil Ransom assumes Miss Birdseye's circle includes 'mediums, communists, vegetarians' (ch. 4).
16 George Hendrick, *H.S. Salt. Humanitarian Reformer and Man of Letters* (Urbana, Chicago, 1977); Stephen Winsten, *Salt and his Circle* (London, 1951), p. 61; Kean, 'The "Smooth Cool Men of Science". The Feminist and Socialist Response to Vivisection'.
17 Henry Snell, *Men, Movements and Myself* (London: J.M. Dent, 1936) p. 186, quoted (abridged) in Norman Brady, '"Shafts" and the quest for a new morality: an examination of the Woman Question in the 1890s as seen through the pages of a contemporary journal', M.A., University of Warwick, 1978.
18 'Vegetarianism', *The People*, 2:91, pp. 309-310 [p. 310]. See Barker's response to Dickens' attack on 'Whole Hog' reforms, in series 2, vol. 1 (no. 29), 27 September 1851, p. 225.
19 Jeremy Mason, *Oscar Wilde on Vegetarianism. An Unpublished letter to Violet Fane with an Introduction and Notes* (Edinburgh, 1991).
20 See Sidney Pollard's comment on Belchem's essay in the John F.C. Harrison *festschrift*, *Living and Learning*, in his review, *Labour History Review* 62, no. 3 (winter 1997), where vegetarianism is accepted as a source of radicalism frequently overlooked.
21 The association with late-eighteenth century radicals, such as J.J Rousseau or John Oswald, was not known by most critics. But see *Progress*, May 1886, where the fact that general opinion appeared to believe an English Revolution was 'within a measurable distance', made T.R. Allinson's Gospel of Brown Bread fitting: 'what more natural and proper than to have a Rousseau heralding the storm and proclaiming that we must undo the social contract, return to a state of primeval simplicity and set up Nebuchadnezzar as a vegetarian model'. See Allinson Papers, MS 3189.
22 See W.B. Withers, 'Progressivism of vegetarianism', *VA*, 1 July 1849, p. 134; and Bernard Henry in 'Letters', *History Workshop Journal*, Autumn 1978, p. 222 on his father, a socialist, vegetarian, anti-vaccinationist, anti-vivisectionist: 'as he explained to me, once you have challenged one belief you go on challenging'.
23 'Irenaeus', 'War and Woodcraft', *Blackwood's Edinburgh Magazine* 79 (April 1856), p. 395.
24 Salt, *Seventy Years*, p. 62. *Vegetarian*, 24 January 1888, p. 59 reported a Dr Tanner's view, in the American *Liberty*, that vegetarianism produced anarchists, see an anarchist vegetarian's reply.
25 *VM*, December 1856, p. 93.
26 Forward, *History*, p. 62.
27 *VA*, 15 August 1850, pp. 3-4, referring to the Manchester festival of 1849.
28 Belchem, '"Temperance in all things": vegetarianism, the Manx press and the alternative agenda of reform in the 1840s', pp. 149-160. Vegetarian claims echo teetotal, e.g., Thomas Smeeton, *The British League; or Total Abstainers' Magazine* 1847, p. 156.
29 *VA*, September 1850, p. 126. It would make 'every other good thing' easier to achieve, *VM*, 1 May, p. 37.
30 E.D.C. Butterfield, 'Tendency of Food Reform', *Food Reform Magazine*, January 1882, pp. 103-104.

31 For responses to vegetarianism as panacea, see 'Harold', *The British Controversialist*, 1850, pp. 230-231; and 'The Congress and the Agapedome,' *Blackwood's Edinburgh Magazine*, 70 (September 1851), pp. 359-378 [p. 431].
32 *To-day*, January 1887, p. 31.
33 French, *Antivivisection*, p. 231.
34 See Forward, *History*, ch. 8 [p. 62].
35 Hannah M. Wigham, *A Christian Philanthropist of Dublin* (London, 1886), pp. 13-14. Dr Tyrrell identifies Allen as a 'moral radical'. The label was picked up in Haughton's obituary, *DR*, 1 April 1873, p. 242. I am grateful to Dr Tyrrell for a copy of his paper, 'The Anti-everythingarians and the Moral Radical Party in early and mid-Victorian Britain' (July 1998).
36 See A.M. Schellenberg '"Prize the Doubt". The Life and Works of Francis William Newman', unpublished Ph.D. thesis, University of Durham, 1994, p. 94. See Isabel G. Sieveking, *Memoirs and Letters of Francis W. Newman* (London, 1909), p. 314, on the impact of publicizing the 'Antis I have been and am engaged!!'
37 *Punch*, 14 January 1865, p. 15, 'Anti-Everything Societies', condemning 'the fussy impertinence of restless and officious noodles' such as vegetarians and teetotallers. *HH*, October 1889, p. 111. See also *Vegetarian*, 8 December 1888, p. 566, reporting *Galignani* on Isaac Pitman as an 'anti-everythingist'. The label also appears in the anonymous vegetarian tract *Stomach Worship, A Growl* (1881), and Forward's *History*, p. 62.
38 Transcription of a clipping from *Weston-super-Mare Gazette*, in W.R. Richards of Martock's late-Victorian scrapbook, published on the Internet by Marijke Hysse (full reference in my Bibliography).
39 'The New Humanitarianism', *Blackwood's Edinburgh Magazine*, January 1898, pp. 98-106.
40 Haggard does not indicate they have been vegetarians, and Stephen is no longer teetotal. Another, sympathetic depiction, is cited in Clyde Binfield, '"I Suppose you are not a Baptist or a Roman Catholic?" Nonconformity's True Conformity', in Thomas C. Smout, ed., *Victorian Values* (Oxford, 1990), pp. 81-107 (p. 86), Gordon Stowell's *The History of Button Hill* (1929), set in late-Victorian Leeds and featuring a leather merchant whose support for 'rebellious and unpopular things' includes teetotalism, vegetarianism, Home Rule and women's rights.
41 *Vegetarian*, 7 December 1895, p. 598. In Harpur's case it was metrication, abolition of classical education and orthodox astronomy, drink and teetotal legislation, Saturday as the Sabbath, support for Salvation Army-made Matches, promotion of Oliver Cromwell as national hero and nationalization of property.
42 See *Report of the Proceedings of the Hartwell Peace and Temperance Festival* (London 1857-64). *Hartwell and Temperance Festival* (London, 1864), p. 5. Horsell, and fellow London vegetarian-phrenologist-temperance worker Jabez Inwards were frequent visitors to the festival. John Lee (1783-1866), antiquarian, scientist, barrister, advanced liberal, teetotaller and opponent of tobacco, see *DNB* entry (which ignores the festivals). Other topics featured there included anti-duelling, anti-slave trade, aboriginal protection, Ocean Penny Postage and Administrative Reform.
43 *Shafts*, November 1897, p. 305.
44 See *MD*, 3 July 1885, p. 429, 7 August 1885, p. 507, 6 November 1885, p. 713.
45 *VA*, 15 August 1850, p. 3.
46 *VM*, August 1850, p. 112.

47 Richard Cobden, quoted in Hollis, 'Pressure from Without: an introduction', Hollis, ed. *Pressure from Without*, p. 7. Note the assumption in *Vegetarian*, 11 July 1893, p. 334, J. Nugent's appeal for literature on Vegetarianism, Social Purity, Temperance, Tobacco, Antivaccination, Land Reform *etc., etc.,*' [my italics].
48 J. Passmore Edwards, *A Few Footprints* (London, 1905), where he neglects to mention his vegetarianism.
49 Tyrrell, 'Making the millennium: the mid-nineteenth century peace movement'.
50 On this perfectionism and post millennial 'march of mind', see Tyrrell and Pickering, '"In the Thickest of the Fight": the Reverend James Scholefield (1790-1855) and the Bible Christians of Salford', p. 465.
51 Charles Dickens, 'Whole Hogs', *Household Words*, no. 74, 23 August 1851, pp. 505-507.
52 *The Times*, 30 April 1846, p. 4.
53 *Bulletin of Labour History* 22 (Spring 1971), reporting a conference about millennialism and social reform in the early-Nineteenth century, pp. 4-5.
54 See Hibberd's comment on his ultra-reformer Jedihah Alger, 'Beans without bacon. A Pythagorean Romance,' in *The Golden Gate and Silver Steps with bits of tinsel round about it* (London, 1886), 'devoting the whole of his time to an indefinable cause called "Progress"'.
55 Royle, *Radical Politics. 1790-1900*, p. 13, p. 59. Holyoake identified as similar the antagonism of infidel and vegetarian towards, respectively, doctor and priest: *Reasoner*, vol. 6, 1849, p. 135.
56 'Progressist', *Water Cure Journal and Hygienic Magazine*, February 1848, pp. 257-259. See Barrow, *Independent Spirits*, p. 160 for the reliance on one's judgement, 'in other words ... epistemologically parallel in an activist way'.
57 'Vegetarianism', *The People* 2: 91, pp. 309-310.
58 *Animal World*, 1 January 1874, p. 14.
59 (1895) quoted in Harrison, *Drink and the Victorians*, p. 135. See also Horsell, *Board of Health*, p. 218, quoting D'Aubigne: 'To remain half way is a useless labour; in all things we must go right to the end.' A contemporary described Francis Newman as, 'Above all ... a Truthseeker', in William Robbins, *The Newman Brothers. An Essay in Comparative Intellectual Biography* (London, 1966), p. 164. J.F.C. Harrison has discussed the 'Truth-Seekers' of Leeds; and identified the organizing concept of faith in 'Man the Reformer'. See *Vegetarian*, 18 June 1898, p. 391, interview with the reformer J.M. Robertson, who deprecated teetotal/vegetarian fanaticism.
60 Alice F. Tyler, *Freedom's Ferment. Phases of American Social History from the Colonial Period to the Outbreak of the Civil War* (1944; New York, 1962), a pioneering survey of the Jacksonian 'ferment of reform', failed to treat seriously Grahamism and other physiological reforms apart from temperance; J.F.C. Harrison, *The Early Victorians* (London, 1971), p. 173 reappraised 'those isms with which we do not sympathise, and which appear too outlandish to be taken seriously'. See Tyrrell, *Joseph Sturge*, pp. 3-4 concerning Sturge's waning reputation.
61 Twigg, 'Vegetarian Movement', p. 23, rightly asserts that vegetarianism is a 'social phenomenon' and a 'choice made available within culture' and that discussion of personality adjustment and faddism is insufficient. Yet faddism and the language of faddism need examination.

62 Thus the popular *Science Siftings*, 'One-Idea People', 16 January 1897, cited in *Vegetarian*: vegetarians and the 'whole body of "professional" agitators and miscalled reformers are men of one idea'.
63 See J.H. Nightingale and C. Millward's farce, 'Bloomerism, or Follies of the Day', successfully performed at the Adelphi in 1851, which ridiculed the absurdities/mutual intolerances of vegetarianism, phonetics, the peace movement and women's rights: British Library, Lord Chamberlain's Plays, vol. 173, ff. l009(9).
64 G.J. Holyoake, *Sixty Years of an Agitator's Life*, 2 vols (London) II, defined a crank, p. 97, as 'one who mistakes his impressions for ideas, or, having ideas resting on proof only perceived by himself, insists, in season and out of season, on attention being given to them'.
65 Usage and definitions are from the *Oxford English Dictionary*, 2nd edition (1972-1986), and *Chambers's Etymological Dictionary of the English Language* (London, 1882).
66 See *Littell's Living Age*, 35:438, 9 October 1852, p. 35, from the *Journal of Psychological Medicine and Mental Pathology*, in which Samuel Laman Blanchard's vegetarianism is mentioned: 'an undoubted mark of eccentricity, whatever vegetarians may say or think'; T.P. Smith, 'Vegetarianism', *Fortnightly Review*, July-December 1895, pp. 752-764, on vegetarianism being regarded 'by most people as a sign of craziness' (and leading to mental and physical degeneration).
67 *MD*, 4 November 1892, p. 706.
68 Tyrrell, 'The Anti-everythingarians'.
69 *Vegetarian*, 10 February 1894, p. 65.
70 *VM*, October 1853, controversialist: p. 19, pp. 23-24.
71 Harrison, *Drink and the Victorians*, p. 149. See also his reference to 'distinctive personality', in Brian Harrison, 'Some Questions for the Local Historian', *The Local Historian* 8:5 (1968-1969), pp. 180-186: 'Many prominent temperance reformers verge on eccentricity; many were hydropathists, vegetarians or phrenologists.'
72 Crossley, *Consumable Metaphors*, p. 60, citing Chamfleury [J. F. Husson], *Les Excentriques* of 1852; Gleizes had been discussed as an eccentric in 1846, see *Consumable Metaphors*, p. 59. Jupille was recalled in the *Dublin Magazine* (1871), p. 134, and *Food Journal* in April 1872.
73 George J. Holyoake, *History of Cooperation*, vol. 1, p. 80, p. 217.
74 Howard Temperley, *British Anti-slavery. 1833-1870* (Harlow, 1972), p. 246. 'T.M. Jnr', *Vegetarian*, 18 February 1893, p. 81, called for fresh blood to replace worn out and crankish activists.
75 See *Vegetarian*, 1896 for correspondence about flat-earth, and dress reform efforts by W.A. Macdonald, of whom a friend declared, *Vegetarian*, February 1895, p. 20; 'Behold, there comes after me a mightier "crank" than I, the thongs of whose sandals I'm unworthy to untie!'
76 James Stuart Mill, *On Liberty* (1859); see *Drink and the Victorians*, p. 159. Mill tried vegetarianism for health, see *Vegetarian*, 8 June 1889, p. 355. *HH*, January 1897, p. 6 relates this defence to the life of pioneer vegetarians like James Salsbury.
77 For a parallel, see Tom Nairn, *The Enchanted Glass. Britain and its Monarchy* (1988; London, 1990), p. 54; note the reference to food-faddism.
78 Hibberd, 'Beans without bacon. A Pythagorean Romance'.
79 For Victorians, indicative of bohemianism or effeminacy. See Francis B. Smith, *Radical Artisan*, p. 17 (of W. J. Linton, *c*. 1838); *Punch*, January-June 1854; p. 97: 'The man who parts his hair down the middle.'

80 See *VM*, September 1898, pp. 429-431. Shelleyanism was the second most important factor in responses to an inquiry about the reason for conversion.
81 Thomas Hughes, *Memoirs of a Brother* (cited *DR*, September 1874, p. 106). See William Benzie, *Dr F.J. Furnivall. Victorian Scholar Adventurer* (Oklahoma, 1983), p.19-20. Furnivall, Charles Blachford Mansfield and Archibald Campbell are being alluded to.
82 Duncan failed to get a letter published in *Chambers' Edinburgh Journal* on beards after a correspondent called for a pro-beard society. His beard dismayed Holyoake, W. Lovett and others. Horsell's portrait embarrassed Henry Salt, *Vegetarian*, 11 December 1897, p. 694, since he seemed like a homicidal maniac. For reluctance to add the beard to other vegetarian crotchets, see *VM*, March 1854, p. 31 (and April, pp. 44-46). The *Monthly Homoeopathic Review* discussed the question, 1861, pp. 97-108.
83 *VM*, 1 July 1856, p. 62 (J.J. Beach); and *VM*, May 1935, p. 161, the Sheltons' recollection of their status in late Victorian Ely.
84 'IV: Times and Seasons', *Worcester Herald*, 5 August 1848, (p. 4 of unpaginated newspaper).
85 'Popular Literature–Tracts' *Blackwood's Edinburgh Magazine* 85:523 (May 1859), pp. 515-532. On the latent function of philanthropy and reform, see B. Harrison, 'Philanthropy and the Victorians', *Victorian Studies* 9:4 (June 1966), pp. 353-374.
86 See Edward F. Benson's *The Freaks of Mayfair* (London, 1916), and *Paying Guests. A Novel* (Leipzig, 1929).
87 *Report of the Proceedings of the Hartwell Peace and Temperance Festival* (London, 1857), p. 17.
88 *Vegetarian*, 23 February 1889, p. 123.
89 See Edward Carpenter, *My Days and Dreams, Being Autobiographical Notes* (London, 1916), ch. 10; Salt, *Seventy Years Among the Savages*, pp. 176-178. Salt was described as a 'compendium of cranks', his Humanitarian League a 'Cranks' Carnival' (see *Seedtime*, 1893, p. 9). See also C.W. Forward, *Vegetarian News*, 1921: on vegetarians with wild views 'who yet would solemnly remark that it was a pity there were so many "faddists" in our ranks'.
90 Daniel was employed by Walter Scott, the publisher of Tolstoy, and established his own company to promote Tolstoyanism. *The Crank. An Unconventional Magazine* (established 1904), edited by his wife F.E. Warland, promoted anarchism, pacifism and food reform.
91 *Vegetarian*, 22 June 1889, pp. 394-395.
92 *DR*, April 1868, pp. 34-37.
93 *DR*, February 1886, pp. 373-8.
94 *Vegetarian*, 15 June 1889, p. 378. Another anti-faddist was Forward; his *The Confessions of A Vegetarian*, *c*.1893, satirized 'going the whole gooseberry'.
95 *Vegetarian*, 11 June 1892, p. 286.
96 For some recent work on the relationship between 'moral' and 'institutional reforms' see the chapters in Burns and Innes, eds, *Rethinking the Age of Reform*.
97 'As political reform has its antecedent in social reform, so the latter has its antecedent in personal or moral reform,' *VA*, 15 December 1848, pp. 67-68; see also 'Moral Reform', 1 May 1850, p. 112; and 'Indirect advantages resulting from the temperance reformation', *Howitt's Journal*, 6 February 1847, pp. 76-78.
98 Tyrrell, *Joseph Sturge*, p. 473.

99 *The Oracle of Reason; or, philosophy vindicated*, 8 October 1842, p. 352.
100 Quoted in Gleadle, '"Our Several Spheres": Middle-class Women and the Feminisms of Early Victorian Radical Politics', p. 146.
101 Rowbotham and Weeks, *Socialism and the New Life*, p. 9; Terry Eagleton, 'The flight to the real', ch. 1 in Sally Ledger and Scott McCracken, eds, *Cultural Politics at the Fin de Siècle* (Cambridge, 1995), pp. 11-21.
102 Dornbusch moved to 'Vegetarian Villa'; see British Library. Add, 78156, f.29, letter to George Cruikshank, (24 April 1854).
103 *DR*, April 1880, p. 84. G.J. Holyoake identified republican involvement in diet, see Antony Taylor, '"The Nauseating Cult of the Crown": Republicanism, Anti-Monarchism and Post-Chartist Politics. 1870-1875', in David Nash and Antony Taylor, *Republicanism in Victorian Society* (Stroud, 2000), pp. 5I-71 [p. 63].

Chapter Five

1 *Punch*, 30 September, 1848.
2 *Times*, 13 January 1885; *Vegetarian Cookery, By a Lady* (6th edn, London), p. 38.
3 *DR*, February 1872, p. 10.
4 *Chambers's Edinburgh Journal*, 2 July 1881, pp. 430-432.
5 Charles Lane, *Dietetics. An Endeavour to Ascertain the Laws of Human Development* (London, 1849), p. 18.
6 *VA*, 18 August 1848, p. 5.
7 Johnson, Box 2, printed invitation, 29 July 1850.
8 *VA*, October 1848, p. 41.
9 *Vegetarian*, 2 October 1897, 'As others see us. The Press and the Congress.'
10 *Daily News*, 17 September 1897, quoted in *Vegetarian*, 2 October 1897.
11 Newnham-Davis, *Where and How to Dine in London* (London, 1899), pp. 92-93.
12 *Times*, 6 October 1891, p. 7; McDouall, *VM*, December 1898, p. 555.
13 *Times*, 20 August 1868, p. 8.
14 *VM*, February 1898, p. 60.
15 Jean O. Mill, *Reform Cookery Book* (1904; 4th edn, 1909).
16 In Beeton's *Household Management* from at least 1888. See *Mrs Beeton's Everyday Cookery and Housekeeping Book. New Edition, Revised and Greatly Enlarged* (London, 1890): advertisements highlighted 'Foreign and Vegetarian Cookery', p. lxviii praised the reform for extending use of vegetables, but p. lvi advised a mixed diet.
17 Preface, Mrs Bowdich, *New Vegetarian Dishes* (London, 1892), p. v.
18 James Simpson, 'Introduction', *Vegetarian Cookery. By a Lady* (6th edn, London), p. iii.
19 Smith, *Principles and Practice*, p. iii.
20 'Domestica', *The Vegetist's Dietary. Compiled, as nearly as possible, in accordance with the principles laid down by Sylvester Graham for the Vegetarian Society of England* (London: 1877), p. 78. The work had eight editions.
21 Preface, Mrs Bowdich, *New Vegetarian Dishes*, p. vi.
22 *Penny Vegetarian Cookery*, 8th edition, p. 4.
23 Review in *Food: A Monthly Journal of Dietetic Economy*, 15 April 1885, p. 175.
24 Charles W. Forward, *Practical Vegetarian Recipes. As Used in the Principal Vegetarian Restaurants in London and the Provinces* (London, 1891), p. 5, pp. 119-120.
25 Mary Pope, *Novel Dishes for Vegetarian Households* (Bradford, 1893), p. 107.
26 Arthur G. Payne, *Cassell's Vegetarian Cookery. A Manual of Cheap and Wholesome Diet* (London, 1895), p. 96.

27 Payne, *Cassell's Vegetarian Cookery*, p. 15.
28 Payne, *Cassell's Vegetarian Cookery*, ch. 9.
29 *How to Begin* (Manchester: VS), p. 7.
30 *VM*, 1898, advertisement for the *New Penny Cookery*.
31 Horsell, *Science of Cooking Vegetarian Food*, p. 4.
32 Pope, *Novel Dishes*, p. 6.
33 *VM*, November 1898, p. 521.
34 Orlebar, *Food for the People*.
35 *Food*, January 1887, p. 95.
36 See the cutlet recipes in Pope, *Novel Dishes*, pp. 100-102.
37 *Vegetarian*, 14 May 1898, p. 304; Mennell, *All Manners of Food*, p. 308.
38 Mars, 'À la Russe: The New Way of Dining.'
39 Payne, *Cassell's Vegetarian*, Preface, and p. 12.
40 *Vegetarian Advocate*, p. 63.
41 Dundee FRS, Minute Book.
42 Henry S. Salt, 'Food Reform', *Westminster Review*, October 1886.
43 Payne, *Cassell's Vegetarian Cookery*, p. 21.
44 *Vegetarian Advocate*, pp. 107-108.
45 *Vegetarian Advocate*, Hadleigh, p. 140.
46 See C.H. Collyns, *Simplicity of Tastes*; Francis W. Newman, *Essays on Diet*, ch. 1; and his letter in Helen Allingham and E.B. Williams, eds, *Letters of William Allingham* (London, 1911), pp. 248-249.
47 Mennell, *All Manners of Food*, p. 214.
48 *Daily News*, 23 June 1851, p. 3.
49 Others recommended foreign foodstuffs like macaroni, e.g. *Food Journal*, 1 January 1874, p. 448.
50 Payne, *Cassell's Vegetarian*, p. 131, p. 135, p. 183; Pope, *Novel Dishes*, p. 11.
51 Pope, *Novel Dishes*, p. 7.
52 *Gentleman's Magazine*, 'Scientific Notes' for January-June 1887, p. 611.
53 *Times*, 14 September 1984, p. 4.
54 See advertisement in *VM*, September 1898.
55 On Vejos, see the advertisement in the *Times*, 27 November 1897, p. 15.
56 Ideal Food Reform rejected chemical flour-raisers, yeast 'and other impurities', and made foods 'on scientific principles, which a great London "daily" has described as 100 Years in Advance of the Age'.
57 The Supremely Digestible Wholemeal Flour 'Nu-Era' was wheat flour finely ground to remove all irritating properties whilst containing the 'full food-value of the ripened grain'.
58 James H. Cook claimed (*How to Run a Health Food Store*) to have coined the phrase *c.*1898.
59 *DR*, March 1882, p. 67; July 1882, p. 150.
60 Advertisements in *Food Reform Magazine*, July-September 1884 for Nichols's sanitary goods, Tidman's sea salts (for baths); January-March 1885 for Scott's Pure Wheatmeal and Samuel Saunder's preserved fruits.
61 *DR*, April 1878, p. 76.
62 Mill, *Reform Cookery Book*.
63 See *Vegetarian*, 25 September 1897, International Vegetarian Congress.
64 *Vegetarian*, 2 October 1897, 'As others see us. The Press and the Congress'.

65 Pope, *Novel Dishes*, advertisements.
66 Joseph Edwards Papers, folder 3, letter of Charles E. Dawson to Edwards dated 7 December 1898.
67 Edward Bellamy, *Equality* (London, 1897), 'The Doctor's Easy Task', where botanist and chemist apply their skills, though to 'natural products'.
68 Winwoode Reade, *The Martyrdom of Man* (17th edn, London, 1903), p. 513.
69 Paul A. Pickering, 'Chartism and the "trade of agitation" in early Victorian Britain', *History* 76 (1996), pp. 221-237.
70 *Food*, December 1887, p. 341.
71 Timothy Morton, *Radical Food. The Culture and Politics of Eating and Drinking. 1790-1820* 3 vols (London, 2000), vol. 1, p. 7.
72 Smith, *Principles and Practice*, p. ii.
73 *Penny Vegetarian Cookery*, p. 10.
74 Hans J. Teuteberg, 'Agenda for a Comparative European History of Diet', in Teuteberg, ed., *European Food History. A Research Review* (Leicester: Leicester University Press, 1992), pp. 7-8.
75 Robert Thorne, 'Places of refreshment in the Nineteenth century', ch. 7 in Anthony D. King, ed., *Buildings and Society. Essays on the Social Development of the Built Environment* (London, 1980), footnotes Forward's *History* (where they are discussed, pp. 102-107). See Burnett, *Plenty and Want*, p. 229 on the new upper-class fashion for dining out. *DR*, January 1882, p. 41 refers to vegetarian diets published by demand in *Caterer and Hotel Proprietors Gazette*.
76 The British Workman teetotal public house organization's officers included vegetarian William Harvey. See Hall, *Coffee Taverns*; Mark Girouard, *Victorian Pubs* (London, 1975), p. 175. On fruit-rooms, see *Truth-Tester*, 15 March 1848, p. 88.
77 *VA*, September 1849 (Talfourd), October 1849; on Hollinworth's, 1 February 1850, pp. 62-64, reporting the *Manchester Examiner and Times*' comment on its 'admirable style'; advertisements in *VM*, January-March 1850, reverse of cover. See March 1850, p. 60 for vegetarian testimony by one converted by the Ordinary; *VM*, April 1851, p. 31 for Christmas dinner. See 'A Vegetarian Eating House', *Punch*, July-December 1854, p. 53 set, in Leeds.
78 *VA*, vol. 2, p. 13. The Coffee House was noted in *Family Herald*, 1851, p. 315.
79 In Edward Bulwer-Lytton, *Kenelm Chillingly. His Adventures and Opinions* (Leipzig, 1873, 4 vols), vol. 1, ch. 3, the hero stays at a Temperance Hotel catering for vegetarians and is offered stewed cauliflower and rice pudding.
80 *DR*, March 1876, p. 11, for restaurant arrangements at Liverpool, London, Manchester, and Newcastle.
81 *Food Reform Magazine*, July-September 1884, editorial notes. In August 1882 the *DR* estimated 3000 daily meals served nationally in vegetarian restaurants.
82 Nichols, *Penny Vegetarian Cookery*, p. 38, claimed a daily serving of 300 meals could easily be doubled or trebled.
83 Loose flyer, dated 30 January 1880, inserted in *HH*, February 1880.
84 See *Vegetarian*, 18 September 1897, p. 505 for interview with the current proprietor, F.E. Hansen, a 'burnt out' City man.
85 Orlebar, *Food for the People*, p. 81. Orlebar reprinted the bill of fare, p. 79.
86 *HH*, May 1908.
87 See photograph, Forward, *History*, p. 103. It was praised for its cleanliness, cosiness and elegance in the *City Press*, 9 October 1886.

88 See appreciative comments in J.J. Morse's 'Practical Vegetarianism', in the spiritualist *Herald of Progress*, 7 September 1883.
89 Arthur C. Doyle, 'The Red-headed League', *The Strand Magazine*, August 1891, pp. 198-199.
90 Twenty-five according to *MD*, 11 November 1887, p. 716. See Forward, *History*, p. 102 (and *Vegetarian Yearbook*, 1898) for a map of London restaurants.
91 See clipping in Bishopsgate Institute, 'Food Reform Company', *City Press*, 8 September 1890; *HH*, 1 March 1890, 'Unsymphonious Shareholders'; and *VM*, April 1888, p. 96. Forward attributed part of the failure of the Charing Cross venture to exorbitant rent.
92 See *Vegetarian*, 14 December 1889, p. 798; *HH*, 1 February 1890, p. 15.
93 *Vegetarian News*, March 1926, p. 85, from Morley Roberts. Hudson disliked vegetarian restaurants because of the food's indigestibility.
94 *DR*, February 1886. Formerly the Charing Cross Vegetarian Hotel; *Vegetarian*, January 1892; *VM*, August 1892, pp. 288-289 (Shelley); *Herald of the Golden Age*, January 1899, back cover and reverse.
95 *Vegetarian*, 2 March 1889, p. 134. It taught reading, writing, drawing, French, music and woodcarving.
96 James Burns, *MD*, 6 March 1891, p. 156.
97 See Johnson, Box I, advertisement for 'Arcadian' (proprietors Forster and Hazell) which included extracts from Sir H. Thompson on 'Food and Feeding'.
98 *HH*, 1 November 1888, p. 128.
99 H. Light, *Vegetarian*, 8 August 1896 spoke of the 'greater number' of proprietors being non-vegetarian.
100 *Vegetarian*, 5 September 1896.
101 GMCRO-VS, G24/1/2/1, minutes of the VS London Auxiliary, 7 January 1886, p. l6; 21 January 1886, p. 19.
102 'Vegetarianism in the City,' *City Press*, 8 April 1885, clipping in Bishopsgate Institute.
103 The need for speedy service is emphasized by H. Light, *Vegetarian*, 8 August 1896; and J.C. Wilson, *Vegetarian*, 4 May 1889, p. 282. See Bishopsgate Institute clippings from *City Press*, 16 September 1885 on the City Cafe Company; and 11 April 1888, the London Clerks café, for cheap non-vegetarian places for clerks and others in the City.
104 George Gissing, *The Private Papers of Henry Ryecroft* (1903; London, 1939), p. 231.
105 [F. Anstey], 'At a Vegetarian Restaurant', *Punch*, 17 December 1892, pp. 280-281.
106 *Vegetarian*, 18 September 1897, p. 505. Earlier customers ranged from 'ordinary shopmen and artisans' to intellectuals and students, see *HH*, March 1880, pp. 324-325.
107 *Vegetarian*, 2 October 1897, p. 537.
108 R.G. Abbott, *Vegetarian News*, autumn 1946, p. 159.
109 Reported by Nayler, *Vegetarian*, 23 April 1892, p. 195.
110 *Vegetarian*, 16 May 1896, p. 240.
111 C.W. Forward, *VM*, November 1896, p. 372, related declining membership to cheap refrigerated food, and uncompetitive prices in non-vegetarian restaurants now meat was at 'rock-bottom' prices.
112 *Vegetarian*, 15 March 1889, p. 170 (where the correspondent noted that non-vegetarian Lockarts charged 1*d* for porridge when vegetarians charged 3*d*); A.J.

Marriott, *Vegetarian*, 30 November 1889, pp. 762-763 (on closing time); Thomas Gent, 11 January 1890, pp. 28-29 (who recommended a charge of 1½d). On quantity, opening hours and 'delicacy', see Hubble, *Vegetarian*, 8 March 1890, pp. 156-157. See May, *Vegetarian*, 19 November 1898, p. 749, on the workingman's naturally conservative tastes.

113 *Figaro*, 25 December 1885, cited in *The Apple Tree Annual* (1887). One proprietor believed customers felt enabled to do better office work, see *Vegetarian*, 23 March 1889, p. 187.
114 *Esoteric*, January 1898, p. 302.
115 *Vegetarian*, 13 March 1897, p. 77; Forward, *History*, p. 105. Shaw partially attributed his vegetarianism to London vegetarian restaurants, see *Pen Portraits and Reviews by Bernard Shaw* (London, 1931, 1932), p. 453. Behramji M. Malabari, *The Indian Eye on English Life, or Rambles of a Pilgrim Reformer* (London, 1893), p. 46, suggested they employ Indian cooks for a time. The *Vegetarian* in 1898 reported Pheroze Langrana's experiment in establishing an Indian vegetarian restaurant.
116 Sandys Britton, *Food Reform Magazine*, April-June 1885, pp. 126-127.
117 Nathaniel Newnham-Davis, *Where and How to Dine in London* (London, 1899), p. 90; British Library, Evanion collection of ephemera, 6641 (1889).
118 On lack of female provision, see the anonymous *London at Dinner, or Where to Dine* (London, 1858), p. 11. See *The Food Journal*, 1 July 1872, p. 216, on the novelty of provision for ladies in City dining rooms.
119 Evanion Collection of Ephemera, 6510 ('Wheatsheaf', 1884); on shop assistants' starvation, see *The Clarion*, 5 October 1895, p. 320.
120 See William E.A. Axon's paper (read at a National Coffee Tavern Conference), *VM*, June 1890, pp. 166-172: (after London's 33) Manchester 7, Liverpool 2, Portsmouth 2, Belfast 1, Birmingham 1, Bristol 1, Leeds 1, Newcastle 1, Nottingham 1, Ventnor 1.
121 *VM*, July 1895, pp. 223-224.
122 Chapman started a hygienic and reform library here, see *VM*, July 1896, p. 235; on Nottingham see *Vegetarian*, January 1890.
123 The Portsmouth restaurants were patronized by dockyard workers, see W.C.F. Gunn, *Vegetarian*, 5 September 1896, p. 426.
124 A 'shilling Vegetarian ordinary' operated at Mrs Matthews' Restaurant in Princes Street in 1875, after discussion in *DR*, December 1874, p. 151.
125 *DR*, February 1884, advertisement. *Manchester Faces and Places* (Manchester, 1890-1897) vol. 4, pp. 13-14, states he served 750,000 meals in 1891. He published a vegetarian tract (*DR*, March 1880, p. 60).
126 Mary Ward, *The History of David Grieve* (London, 1892), pp. 251-252; pp. 256-257, pp. 351-352.
127 *DR*, February 1886, p. 58; on its role in local vegetarianism see *DR*, April 1882, p. 82.
128 *Vegetarian*, 23 October 1897, p. 585.
129 *Vegetarian*, 5 November 1898, advertisement on front cover.
130 *Vegetarian*, 29 October 1898, pp. 689-691.
131 James H. Cook, *How to Run a Health Food Store Successfully. By the Founder of the First* (Four Oaks, Warwick, c.1929); K. Keleny, *The First Century of Health Foods* (Stroud, 1996).

132 Cook, *How to Run a Health Food Store,* p. 121, drawn by the 'attractive manner' and a good table d'hôte at 1s 3d. The restaurant was, unlike store and hotel, unsuccessful and the whole business was sold in 1901.
133 *VM,* April 1895, p. 116; *Vegetarian,* 13 April, pp. 181-182.
134 David J. Jeremy, ed., *Dictionary of Business Biography. A Biographical Dictionary of Business Leaders Active in Britain in the Period 1860-1980,* vol. 4 (London, 1985), pp. 436-438.
135 *VM,* April 1895, p. 115.
136 *VM,* June 1895, pp. 222-223.
137 *Food Reform Magazine,* February 1879, pp. 21-22; *VM,* April 1890, p. 118; see *Vegetarian,* 20 April 1889, p. 246 on (temperance) *Refreshment News* report about a conference involving the Coffee Tavern Protection Society, at Charing Cross Vegetarian hotel. LVS secretaries wrote in *Refreshment News,* see *Vegetarian,* 1 June 1889, p. 342.
138 George J. Holyoake, *The Social Means of Promoting Temperance with remarks on errors in its advocacy* (London, 1859), p. 19.
139 Girouard, *Victorian Pubs,* p. 176; Thorne, 'Places of refreshment', p. 245.
140 'The Vegetarian Creed', *The Speaker,* reprinted in *Littell's Living Age,* vol. 216, issue 2792 (8 January 1898), p. 127.
141 Forward, *History,* p. 103, *Vegetarian,* 29 October 1898, p. 696.
142 *To-day,* January 1887, p. 31.
143 Newnham-Davis, *Where and How to Dine,* p. 89.
144 *Vegetarian,* 19 November 1898.
145 'T.M.', *Vegetarian,* 18 February 1891, p. 81, on grounds of expense and staleness. *Vegetarian,* 29 October 1898, p. 701.
146 *Vegetarian,* 29 October 1898, p. 701.
147 *HH,* March 1880, pp. 324-325.
148 'Fruges consumere nati', *Punch,* 20 November 1886, p. 244.
149 *DR,* May 1880. This was meant to inaugurate 'Food of Health Restaurants' in various parts of London, see 'Food of Health Restaurants', *City Press,* 3 May 1880. It did not remain purely vegetarian, see *DR,* February 1882, p. 41.
150 See James Epstein, 'Some organizational and cultural aspects of the Chartist movement, 1840-1848', in James Epstein and Dorothy Thompson, eds, *The Chartist Experience. Studies in Working-class Radicalism and Culture 1830-60* (London, 1982), pp. 221-268 for the idea of a 'movement culture'.
151 See Brian Harrison, 'Press and Pressure Group in Modern Britain', in Joanne Shattock and Michael Wolff, *The Victorian Periodical Press* (Toronto, 1982), pp. 261-295, on the inspirational, informative and integrative functions of this press [p. 282].
152 See Paul A. Pickering, 'Chartism and the "trade of agitation" in early Victorian Britain', *History* 76 (1996), pp. 221-237. 'Pro-vegetarian serials' are listed with vegetarian journals, in Appendix C of my thesis. See Forward, *History,* ch. 10 on vegetarian literature, and reproduction of covers to late Victorian papers, p. 88.
153 *VA,* editor's preface and farewell, 1850-1851.
154 Simpson apparently funded the *Truth-Tester,* see James Gaskill, *VM,* December 1859, p. 32.
155 See Horsell's ambitious plans for the journal, in note to subscribers, 1 August 1850.

156 *VA*, September 1849, p. 1, the *VM* was intended as a medium of information for those not yet convinced; the *VA* for convinced vegetarians, see *VM*, September 1849, p. 1. See the *VA*'s editorial preface and farewell, in final volume (1850-1851). Despite its demise, it was listed with the *Messenger* in *Moore's Almanac*, 1853.
157 Initially the publishers were Horsell, and William Bremner in Manchester, the printers were brothers Robert and Henry Clubb at Stratford St Mary 1849-1850. The first editor was Henry Clubb. 5000 copies of the first number were issued (December 1849, p. 26).
158 The supplement, *Vegetarian Controversialist* and *Vegetarian Treasury* was paginated for separate distribution. The *Controversialist* was for open discussion and response to periodicals and books; the *Treasury* (in small type) culled items from modern and ancient writings and published converts' experience.
159 The VS, concerned that a separate identity be preserved, set conditions and was cautious not to give a 'pledge' to Horsell. GMCRO-VS, G24/1/1/2, Minute Book, 1859-1875: 21 December 1859; 20 January, 23 July and 2 August 1860.
160 Tweedie was informed 'no change was possible at the present'. Published initially by Alexander Ireland, by 1865 the publishers were Job Caudwell in London, Bremner in Manchester, J. Dickson in Edinburgh and G. Gallie of Glasgow. Pitman shortly afterwards was the London publisher.
161 In 1871 the VS obtained estimates for the publication of 1000 monthly. The first number produced by Clark of Dunfermline (January 1872) was a 'disappointment'.
162 *DR*, March 1884. In November 1879, p. 232 the circulation was stated as 5000 per month.
163 *DR*, February 1884, p. viii.
164 This was Forward's idea, see *History*, p. 170. *VM*, December 1897, made clear that editorial control remained in Manchester. Amalgamation resulted in a size increase, typographic changes and inclusion of VFU reports. Financial and business responsibility was the Ideal Publishing Union's. However, no benefits being felt, as the *VM* reported, December 1898, p. 559, January 1899 saw a return to the old title.
165 *DR*, 1 April 1862, p. 38.
166 'Finger Posts of Progress,' *DR*, February 1874, p. 28.
167 *The Herald of Health. A Journal of Sanitary and Social Science*, 1 July 1875. Printed by Hay Nisbet, 219, George Street, Glasgow, (recommended to Nichols as 'good, honest, reliable', *HH*, December 1885, p. 139).
168 *Nichols' Journal of Sanitary and Social Science*, July 1873 (1*d*; the only number issued).
169 *HH*, August 1875, p. 24. Nichols and Co., at 23 Oxford Street, sold his products, including his bestselling books. The firm traded under his name after his direct association with it ceased, see *Vegetarian*, 11 September 1897, p. 489.
170 *HH*, 1 July 1875, p. 2.
171 *HH*, August 1875, p. 24.
172 *HH*, June 1876.
173 *Vegetarian*, 8 May 1897, p. 198; on making *HH* a weekly, see June 1876, p. 185.
174 *HH*, April 1881, p. 47 (*Norwich Argus*); *HH*, February 1885, p. 24 (*Christian Leader*).
175 Forward also 'wrote the chief part'. He recalled, *Vegetarian*, 11 September 1897, p. 489, his impetuous, often near-libellous approach and claimed for it 'very

striking results, especially in connection with the Vegetarian Society's operations in the Metropolis'.
176 *HH*, 2 June 1890, p. 71.
177 *The Gentleman's Journal*, 15 April 1895 described it as 'one of the most spirited, varied and useful two penny monthlies' (cited in *HH*, May 1895).
178 Subsequently published by the Philanthropic Press. On Yeats' illustrations in vegetarian journals, see Hilary Pyle, *Jack B. Yeats. A Biography* (London, 1970), p. 33.
179 *Burlington House, a magazine and critic of the Royal Academy Museum, University Learned Societies and Burlington Debating Association.* The British Library's damaged copy of vol. 1 (May 1878-1879) is the only surviving copy.
180 *MD*, 2 May 1878, p. 330, for an appreciative review by Chandos Leigh Hunt.
181 *Food Reform Magazine*, April-July 1882. Editorial comment.
182 GMCRO-VS, G24/1/2/1, 1887. See Forward, *History*, p. 91 on Curtice and *Vegetarian News*, December 1922, p. 374 for Forward's recollections of the journal.
183 'Personal Explanation', *Vegetarian*, 4 February 1888, p. 6; for further criticism of his writings, 9 February 1889, (Richard Gill, *pro*-Hills) p. 90 (p. 91, Leslie Large, *anti*), and Hills's reply, 16 February, p. 106.
184 *Vegetarian*, 16 March 1895, p. 127.
185 *Vegetarian*, 15 January, p. 41: Shaw; 29 January 1898, p. 73: Dadobhai Naoroji; 12 February, pp. 105-106: Reverend Russell Wakefield; 5 March, p. 153: W.T. Stead; 26 March, p. 199: Grant Allen; 16 April, p. 247: Reverend W.D. Morrison; 26 November, pp. 759-760: Haldane Macfall (stepson of novelist Sarah Grand); 31 December, p. 839: Cutcliffe Hyne.
186 E.g., *Vegetarian*, 23 August 1890, p. 537, 'Dockers Union Refusing Members'; 11 October 1890, p. 649, 'Free Trade vs. Protection' (Sime: about the McKinley Tariff); 18 October, p. 681 (Sime: Socialism and the Law); 29 November, p. 761, 'meat inspection' (Yeats). Sime was a leading illustrator of the period, Jack Yeats became a famous painter.
187 *Vegetarian*, January 1897 (Carmen Sylva, Queen of Rumania); 27 February 1897 ('Q'); 10 April 1897 (George Henty).
188 *Newspaper Press Directory* (London: C. Mitchell), 1889, p. 64; 1891, p. 74.
189 GMCRO-VS, G24/1/2/1, 22 October 1888.
190 Advertisement in Lt. Col. A. T. Wintle, *The Dietary of Troops* (London, 1892).
191 In R.E. O'Callaghan, *The Best Diet for a Working Man, with Month's Dietary* (London, 1891). See *Newspaper Press Directory*, 1899: 'A high class journal devoted to a crusade against the barbarisms of a carnivorous diet.'
192 *Vegetarian Yearbook*, 1898, advertisements overleaf of cover.
193 *Vegetarian*, 19 June 1897; *Vegetarian*, 1 January 1899, p. 1.
194 *Vegetarian*, 5 March 1898, p. 140.
195 *Vegetarian*, 3 December 1898, p. 767.
196 James S. Herron, *Vegetarian*, 24 February 1894, p. 96; see T.N. Roberts, *Vegetarian*, 19 April 1890, p. 254 for similar criticism of politics (and reports on 'intervarsity sports') in its new 'Mustard and Cress' section.
197 'The Vegetarian and Politics', *Vegetarian*, 26 April 1890, p. 269 see also 10 May, p. 300.
198 'C.R.H.L.,' *Vegetarian*, 3 March 1894, p. 109.
199 *Vegetarian*, 1890.

200 Bodington: *Vegetarian*, 15 December 1894, p. 616. On divorces, C.K. Murray, *Vegetarian*, 1 March 1890, p. 141. Walter Strafford, *Vegetarian*, 14 February 1891, p. 108; W.G. Stubbs, 29 July 1893, p. 358 on theatre.
201 Prospectus, *Vegetarian*, 9 December 1893; *VM*, February 1894, pp. 55-57. Hills owned 1000 of the 10,000 £1 shares and was chairman of the board of directors.
202 *The Merry-go-round. An Unconventional Journal* (January to June 1894). See *Vegetarian Review*, 1894, p. 551.
203 See *Vegetarian*, January 1898, p. ii; November 1898, p. 743. Other titles produced by the Depôt included the *White Ribbon*, *United Temperance Gazette* and *Medical Temperance Review*. The *United Temperance Gazette*, the organ of the National United Temperance Council established through Hills, had articles on vegetarianism in 1896-97.
204 Subtitled *The anti-alcohol, anti-tobacco, antivaccination, anti-vivisector, anti-physic and anti-gambling journal. The Organ of the Natural Living Society*, 3 August–21 September, 1889 (Curtice and Romeike).
205 *Hygienic Advertiser*, May 1891.
206 *Vegetarian*, 30 May 1891, p. 300.
207 *HGA*, 15 September 1899.
208 *MD*, 22 March 1895, p. 5. See 'appeal to active vegetarians' in *MD*, 1891, p. 81. Only excerpts in *MD* survive.
209 *Phonetic Journal*, 21 July 1900; it continued into the 1920s.
210 A Parsi, N.F. Bilimoria, translated articles for his vegetarian-temperance journal *Cherâg* c.1900. Stugelman of Calcutta canvassed subscribers and the membership lists 1905-1910 include Indian supporters. The paper was known in Montreal as a result of an enthusiastic member of the Order, the journalist Florence Helsby, see *HGA*, January 1905, p. 10.
211 See *Labour Annual* (edited and published by Joseph Edwards of Wallasey, Cheshire) 1899, p. 181; and British Library catalogue.
212 'The Editor', *Almonds and Raisins*, 1886. The earliest almanac was Horsell's *Illustrated Physiological and Vegetarian Almanac for 1850*. Nichols produced *Dr Nichols' Health Almanack*, c.1879-85. Smallman in Manchester, F.W. Smith in Leeds, and James Smith in Edinburgh c.1879 retailed localized issues. Sydney Young produced an *Almanac*, 1888-89. For criticism of the content see *Vegetarian*, 4 January 1890, p. 13. On Glendinning's work, see *MD*, 1891, p. 173. Forward edited the *Yearbook* 1889-93. It lapsed in 1894 and was replaced by an enlarged report before being revived in 1896. Forward also edited a *Vegetarian Birthday Book* (1898).
213 The Daisy Society, founded by W.M. Wright (see *Vegetarian*, 9 June 1888, p. 153), was funded by a legacy from the zoophilist Matilda Cooper.
214 *The Rainbow; The Children's Garden* (1900); *The Children's Realm* (1906-1914).
215 Posters survive in the Allinson Papers, and reproduced in the *Vegetarian*. Placards were used throughout the period; see *VM*, January 1859, p. 12 on a 'well-executed and short dialogue extensively posted on the walls of Leeds'.
216 *Reasoner*, vol. 9, 1850, p. 11: his depôt was advertised as 'liberal and progressive' in 1846.
217 William Love of Glasgow, son-in-law of Alexander Campbell, and agent c.1851. Bremner's address, 15 Piccadilly, was shared by the VS's corresponding secretary.
218 Osbond's 'Scientor House', *Labour Annual*, 1899, p. 168.

219 *VM*, 1859, at £12 monthly. A free-circulation list when the paper was re-launched included Iowan 'Trappists'.
220 *DR*, September 1873, p. 320.
221 *VM*, April 1889, p. 95.
222 *HGA*, January 1898, p. 6.
223 *HGA*, June 1898, p. 67.
224 *Vegetarian*, 19 April 1898, pp. 234-235.
225 On William Tebb's *Dietetic Journal* ever-circulator, *Phonetic Journal*, 1 August 1851, p. 120. See *VM*, March 1854, p. 25 for the Corresponding Secretary's ever-circulator. The *Phonetic Examiner and Aspirants' Journal* serialized a vegetarian paper *c.* July-August 1853.
226 'FRH,' *DR*, June 1884, p. 182; *VM*, September 1899, p. 300.
227 *VM*, July 1887, p. 204.
228 See *Labour Annual*, 1899, p. 133: 'as usual, the year's OBITUARY of the Reform Press is heavy'.

Chapter Six

1   For previous recognition of its propaganda aimed at the 'respectable working man' see Harrison, *Peaceable Kingdom*, pp. 170-1.
2   Dixon, *Divine Feminine*; Lucy Bland, *Banishing the Beast. English Feminism and Sexual Morality. 1885-1914* (London, 1995); Sandra S. Holton, *Suffrage Days: Stories from the Women's Suffrage Movement* (New York, 1996).
3   *DR*, April 1880, p. 80.
4   Allingham and Williams, eds, *Letters of William Allingham*, p. 249.
5   *VM*, November 1855, pp. 96-99.
6   See Gregory, 'Vegetarian Movement', Appendix A for occupations. Vegetarians' statistics aggregated women and class composition may be skewed by this.
7   *VM*, May 1854, pp. 41-45; *VM*, November 1854, supplement: p. 96; *VM*, 7 December 1854.
8   C.O.G. Napier, 'The Autobiography of a Vegetarian. A True Narrative of a Successful Career', republished in *Littell's Living Age* (New York), 12 August 1876.
9   Twigg, 'Vegetarian Movement', pp. 115-116. Clerks were the movement's major occupational group from the 1870s, though there was considerable variety in income and status.
10 Hau, *Cult of Health and Beauty in Germany*, ch. 1.
11 Annual reports 1866; 1869. Such an attitude risked alienating the public, as did dwelling on disasters; the *Glasgow Herald* posed as outraged by vegetarians' handling of rinderpest and potato blight and wages, see *DR*, April 1867, p. 37.
12 See William Sharman, *Plain Words to the Working Men of Sheffield now Abstaining from Dear Meat* (Sheffield, 1860); 'J.H.', *DR*, October 1880, p. 219; *Vegetarian*, 20 November 1897, p. 653 (May Yates exploiting the engineers' strike); *Vegetarian*, 5 November 1898, p. 729 (G. Cholwick Wade, of the Rhondda miners' strike).
13 *The Merry-go-round*, 1894, pp. 391-395; *VM*, January 1894, p. 11.
14 R.G. Abbott, *Vegetarian News*, autumn 1946, p. 159 alleged that the Works favoured vegetarians. See Forward, *History*, p. 150 on vegetarian ironworkers. On the Works' missions, see *MD*, 17 August 1888, p. 519; *Vegetarian*, 24 January 1891, p. 54. On Billericay, see *Vegetarian*, 23 April 1898, p. 264; p. 775. His opening essay in *Merry-go-round* examined unemployment and his *Vegetarian* advertised J.A. Hobson's *Poverty*. See notices on Booth, *Vegetarian*, 1891; East End lectures and

food: *Vegetarian*, 5 March 1892, p. 112; Alderman Phillips' East End stories appeared in *Vegetarian*; a Whitechapel society was planned, *Vegetarian*, 19 February 1898, p. 114. The 'Women's Vegetarian Union' had East End meetings; an associated East London Pure Food Depôt was established, see *HH*, August 1899, p. 120.

15 The *Hygienic Advertiser* included the *WTE* in the movement; its readership was lower middle class and working class. Its editor, E.J. Kibblewhite, was a vegetarian sympathizer who also edited *English Mechanic* and *Building News*, 14 October, 1888, p. 9.

16 Allinson Papers, MS 3189, 'The Gospel of Brown Bread', *Progress*, May 1889.

17 *English Mechanic and World of Science*, 4 October 1867, pp. 25-26; May 1879, p. 106.

18 Orlebar, *Food for the People*, p. 12. The anti-vegetarian *Food Journal*, 1 September 1873, p. 313, called servants 'gross animal feeders'. Several vegetarian servants' agencies were attempted. C.L.H. Wallace, in *HGA*, 1899, p. 117 (at the vegetarian congress) stressed her long and successful relationship with servants. See also *VM*, September 1894, pp. 317-319.

19 For instance William L. Sargant's *The Economy of the Labouring Classes* (London, 1857), pp. 165-170. Sargant, like many apologists, saw the value of animal food in digestibility and concentration, enabling the mechanic to work more hours and 'get through a greater quantity of work than would be possible with a vegetable diet'.

20 *FRM*, July 1881, p. 22 (a speech at VS May Meeting); *FRM*, July 1881, p. 3.

21 *FRM*, July 1881, p. 19 (Kerr); *VM*, March 1889, pp. 57-58 (Crespi, familiar with the Dorset 'poorer classes'); *Vegetarian*, 12 November 1898, p. 745 (T. May); *MD*, 22 February 1889, p. 116 (Burns). See also George Poyntz, *WTE*, 14 April 1889, p. 6.

22 See *VM*, March 1890, p. 79 for T.F. O'Connell of Glasgow's discovery that none of the factory workers he met knew about vegetarianism.

23 *DR*, 1880, pp. 249-249; 'Vegetarianism and the Working Class', *Vegetarian*, 28 April 1888, p. 59.

24 H. Mayhew, 'Of the diet, drink, and expense of living of the Street-Irish', p. 12; 'Evacustes' Phipson, of the Nationalization of Labour Society (a vegetarian), *VM*, April 1893, p. 151.

25 'A.W.', Darlington, *VM*, May 1859, p. 62 (on public banquets); H.G. Gibson, *VM*, June 1890, p. 157.

26 Burnett, *Plenty and Want*, p. 54.

27 'C.W.M.', in *VM*, August 1859.

28 See statements in '12 points why the Vegetarian Society claims the help of all', reproduced in propaganda and serial literature of the period. Vegetarianism featured in the *Agricultural Labourers' Union Chronicle*, see *DR*, 1 July 1873, pp. 292-293. See also debate on the parson-squire system in *Vegetarian*, 1892. The vegetarian Christian Socialist Reverend Oswald Birchall wrote in the Land Nationalization Society's journal, and articles promoted vegetarianism in the National Land Union monthly, see *HH*, September 1879, p. 251.

29 Various aspects to the perennial 'food question' appear in *Transactions of the National Association for the Promotion of Social Science*. Brown, *The Food of the People*, p. 43, claimed that 'English cookery among the humbler class is about the worst and most wasteful cookery in the world'. More sensitive is Edward Smith's *Practical Dietary for Families, Schools and the Labouring Classes* (London, 1864), pp. 203-204.

30 The children's writer and Fabian Edith Nesbit, and the novelist George Gissing, adopted vegetarianism because of straitened circumstances. In 1895, the periodical *New Age* recorded the vegetarian/milk-and-fruit experiments of 'a Bachelor Girl, – or, life in a London flat'.
31 'Thrift in Food', *FRM*, October 1881, pp. 50-51 [p. 51]. Its journal *Thrift* (January-March 1882) advertised food reform, its president chaired a vegetarian meeting, see *Vegetarian* 25 February 1888, p. 6. National economy and food supply feature in *Manchester Vegetarian Lectures* (Manchester, 1888).
32 E.J. Baillie, *VM*, January 1892, p. 10.
33 John Bruce Wallace, *Vegetarian*, 31 May 1890.
34 Benjamin W. Richardson, 'Thrift in relation to food', *Journal of the Society of Arts*, 1880, p. 383; Robert B. Marston, *War, Famine and Our Food Supply* (London, 1897). Hills invited Marston to write on the subject, see pp. 214-215.
35 Frances E. Hoggan, *Advantages of a Vegetarian Diet in Workhouses and Prisons* (London, 1883); William Couchman, *How to Marry and Live Well on a Shilling a Day* (Manchester, 1884); C.F. Corlass, *How do you spend your Wages?* See also *VM*, May 1887, pp. 146-147.
36 *Trewman's Exeter Flying Post*, 16 August 1882, p. 5, suggested testing the diet in prisons and penitentiaries.
37 *HH*, January 1880, pp. 300-301.
38 *Labour Annual*, 1898, p. 223, for the VS advertisement: 'The Society's Lecturer will be glad to book LECTURES in connection with ILP and other Socialist organizations.'
39 *VM*, January, p. 29; and March 1897, p. 95.
40 The Fabians' relationship with the pro-vegetarian 'Fellowship of New Life' is explored in the Mackenzies' *The First Fabians*. Colin Spencer's assertion that most Fabians were vegetarian is an exaggeration but Beatrice Webb, Bernard Shaw, Edith Nesbit, Frank Podmore and Swan *were* vegetarian. For the lower middle-class/middle-class location of the membership, see Eric J. Hobsbawm, *Labouring Men. Studies in the History of Labour* (London, 1964), pp. 250-271. The Manchester and District Fabian Society requested *HH*, see April 1892, p. 43.
41 Snell, *Men, Movements and Myself*, p. 186. On socialism as another *faddism* and 'faddist fanaticism', see Ernest B. Bax, *Essays in Socialism New and Old* (London, 1907), p. 79, pp. 100-101.
42 Friedrich Engels, 'On the History of Early Christianity', originally in *Die Neue Zeit*, 1894-1895.
43 E.g., *Clarion*, 23 January 1897, p. 80 (W.M. Farrington's letter). *Vegetarian*, 5 February 1898, p. 85 printed a letter which showed Blatchford's sympathies but socialist priority. Blatchford's *Sorcery Shop* (1907) presents an utopia without alcohol, tobacco and meat. The 1908 edition of his *Merrie England* carried this advertisement: 'Since "Nunquam" gave up meat, vegetarianism has made more rapid strides than before, especially among Social reformers.'
44 Harrison, *Late Victorian Britain. 1875-1901*, p. 146. On the van, see *VM*, e.g., July 1898, p. 290. J. Nugent advised vegetarians to emulate socialists' open-air meetings, *Vegetarian*, 25 July 1896, p. 358.
45 On Mann, see Chushichi Tsuzuki, *Tom Mann, 1856-1941. The Challenges of Labour* (Oxford, 1991), p. 11. Hardie supported the 'National Food Supply Association', *VM*, January 1894, p. 12. On the 'almost vegetarian' Walter Crane, see *Vegetarian*,

16 September 1898. James Burns said he was always confused with the socialist John Burns (who addressed a vegetarian meeting) see *MD*, 24 August 1888, p. 530.

46   The first oft-quoted condemnation (conversation recreated from a 'synthesis of information') appears in Winsten, *Salt and His Circle*, p. 64; for the other, see Henry M. Hyndman, *The Records of an Adventurous Life* (London, 1911), p. 306. The tendency was also criticized by Ernest B. Bax, *Outspoken Essays on Social Subjects* (London, 1897), pp. 117-133. Peter C. Gould, *Early Green Politics. Back to Nature. Back to the Land, and Socialism in Britain, 1880-1900* (Hassocks, 1988) treats socialism in a monolithic way and views interests such as Henry Salt's as oddities; for the importance of 'ethical socialism', see Yeo, 'A New Life: The Religion of Socialism', and the examination of socialism in relation to the 'faddism' of Bernard Shaw and Edward Carpenter, Ruth Livesey, *Socialism, Sex and the Culture of Aestheticism*, ch. 4. Livesey examines the opportunity in the ethical socialist movement before the Great War for the exploration and discussion of masculinity via Jaegerism, vegetarianism and sandal-wearing. Such fads could be presented in a way that responded to anxieties about bourgeois masculinity. I am grateful to Dr Livesey for the opportunity to read this research prior to publication. Later anti-vegetarian socialists include George Orwell (*The Road to Wigan Pier*) and Grayson, see Reginald Groves, *The Strange Case of Victor Grayson*, 1975, p. 80, cited Andrew J. Davies, *To Build a New Jerusalem. The British Labour Party from Keir Hardie to Tony Blair* (1992; London, 1996).

47   Samuel, 'The Discovery of Puritanism', pp. 276-322.

48   See the entry by Trevor Griffiths on (Charles) Allen Clarke, in the *ODNB* (Oxford, 2004). He promoted vegetarianism in his *Teddy Ashton's Journal*.

49   Kean, 'The "Smooth Cool Men of Science" ...', pp. 16-38; Livesey, *Socialism, Sex and the Culture of Aestheticism*, ch. 4. *Vegetarian*, 15 March 1890, p. 182, reported support by Bolton's *Labour Light*. Johnson, *WTE*, 28 June 1889, p. 11, claimed socialists were largely teetotal and 'more or less vegetarian', and 'almost invariably stout opponents of Vaccination and Vivisection'.

50   Henry S. Salt, 'Socialists and Vegetarians,' *To-day: The Monthly Magazine of Scientific Socialism*, vol. 6 n.s., no. 36, November 1886, pp. 172-174; 'Food reform', *Liberty*, 1883, pp. 334-338.

51   Vegetarianism cast as a response to unemployment was contrasted with 'being led astray by Socialist agitators', in *Food*, February 1878, p. 22. See *HH*, June 1888 onwards, on controversy generated by W.S. Manning's insensitivity at lectures before Battersea Social Democratic Federation branch.

52   *FRM*, December 1882, p. 88; R.E. O'Callaghan, *The Best Diet for a Working Man* (1889); *Vegetarian*, 9 February 1889, p. 90.

53   H. Davis, 'The Capitalistic Advantages of Vegetarianism', *Commonweal*, 28 August 1886, pp. 169-170; and subsequent comments from Axon, Buist, Domoney, Walkden, William Morris (25 September, p. 201). Critiques of thrift include April 1886, pp. 29-30 and 28 April 1888, pp. 132-133. Morris's astute comment that universal vegetarianism would perpetuate class distinctions in diet appears in Winsten, *Salt and His Circle*, p. 94. Morris apparently often dined with Salt at a vegetarian restaurant.

54   The *WTE*'s editor, 30 June 1889, p. 10 denied the same charge made in J.M. Davidson's 'The Old Order and the New', which it serialized. Henry S. Salt, 'Vegetarianism and Social Reform', in *A Plea for Vegetarianism and Other Essays*,

pp. 114-115, is another rebuttal. Henry L.J. Jones accepted the allegation in a letter to Joseph Edwards, 1 October 1893, (Johnson, Box 2), believing the 'ideal' results more important than social economics. Vegetarianism and other panaceas are rejected in Joseph Lane, *An Anti-Statist, Communist Manifesto* (London, 1887).

55 Karl Marx, *Capital*, Part VII, ch. 24, sections 3-4.
56 *The Book of Labour*, serialized in *Labour World*, 4 October 1890, p. 10; 'Among Women Workers': 15 November, p. 10, 21 February, p. 10. Sympathies were expressed by its successor, *The Sunday World*, in 1891.
57 *VM*, March 1892, p. 77.
58 *VM*, May 1887, pp. 130-131. *Arden*, the Greek journal was produced by Platon Drakoules, a pioneer Greek socialist who married Alice M. Lewis. See *Vegetarian News*, 1926, p. 265.
59 Henry S. Salt, 'Socialism and Vegetarianism', *Vegetarian*, 6 July 1889, and 12 April 1890, p. 229; Herbert Burrows, 'Socialism' *Vegetarian*, 26 August 1893, p. 401; W.A. Macdonald's articles on 'scientific communism' in *Vegetarian*, 1896; *FRM*, July-September 1883, pp. 15-16, for James Joynes' 'Remedies for Poverty' in which the insufficiency of socialism alone was asserted.
60 *Home Links* advertised Allinson's medical works, Humanitarian League and *Labour Annual* (see its advertisement in *Labour Annual*, 1898, p. 223). It aligned itself with abolition of punishments, spelling reform, international peace and Tolstoyanism.
61 *The Weekly Star*, 7 September 1889 and 31 August 1889. Alderman Phillips of West Ham was also an active supporter of the dockers' strike.
62 *The Co-operator and Herald of Health*, December 1863, p. 101, supported a vegetarian cookery book for co-operative libraries and planned a farthing book, see 'The Best and Cheapest Food', 1 January 1870, p. 6. On Lawrenson's activity see *Vegetarian*, 31 August 1889, p. 550. Vegetarian recipes include 20 October 1888, p. 1067, 3 November, p. 1115. Emily Sharland, editor of *Co-operative News*' 'Junior Page' converted after opening the page to vegetarians. See *VM*, January 1887, p. 20 for a 'co-operative society' near London joining VS; the Royal Arsenal Co-operative Society subscribed in 1892. The editor of Pickering Co-operative's local *Wheatsheaf* promoted vegetarianism, see *VM*, July 1899, p. 230. *VM* advertised the 'Co-operative Jewellers Association' in this period, and its donors included the Stockton Women's Co-operative Guild and Masborough Women's Co-operative Guild. *HH* was offered to co-operative societies, *Co-operative News*, 5 January 1889, p. 17.
63 *WTE*, 24 June 1888, p. 6; *WTE*, 8 July 1888, p. 6.
64 *WTE*, 9 September 1888, p. 6; *Co-operative News*, 29 September 1888, p. 985. Subsequent reports are in *WTE*, see also *Vegetarian* from 11 August 1888, p. 98 to 9 February 1889, p. 91. The society was registered as a co-operative organization, see *Co-operative News*, 2 March 1889, p. 195.
65 *Co-operative News*, 6 April 1889, p. 339; *Co-operative News*, 10 November 1888, p. 1127.
66 *Vegetarian*, 9 February 1889, pp. 90-91. Phillips planned a *Vegetarian Handbook and Directory*, see *VM*, January 1889, p. 17.
67 *Vegetarian*, 7 September 1889, p. 567; *VM*, January 1890, p. 28.
68 Samuel Smiles, in 'Home Power', *Character* (1878; London, 1902), p. 61.
69 Isabella Beeton, *Book of Household Management* (1861), ch. 25.

70 Twigg, 'Vegetarian Movement', pp. 171-175 briefly discusses feminism and female vegetarians. See Lenemen 'The Awakened Instinct', for the Edwardian period. Lenemen contributed vegetarians to Elizabeth Crawford, *The Women's Suffrage Movement: A Reference Guide* (London, 1998). Adams, *Sexual Politics of Meat*, pp. 166-185.

71 See *Shafts*, 19 November 1892, pp. 40-41; A.M. Lewis, *Humanity and Vegetarianism* (1892). This view was expressed in other zoophilist movements.

72 Brady, '"Shafts" and the quest for a new morality ...', for instance, suggests (p. 76) it was innovatory like 'new woman' novels, Ibsenism or 'rational' dress.

73 See Latham, *Search for a New Eden*; and Gleadle, '"The age of physiological reformers": rethinking gender and domesticity in the age of reform.' Women are little discussed in Antrobus, *Guiltless Feast*, but the contribution of one Cowherdite woman, at least, was important, since Martha Brotherton's influential vegetarian cookery book, first serialized in 1812, went through five editions by 1870.

74 'The Coming Woman', *Diogenes*, vol. 2, p. 181; *The Times*, 23 September 1853, p. 7. Cartoon representations of female vegetarians include 'Pleasures of Vegetarianism', *Punch*, 1852.

75 *Hartwell and Temperance Festival* (London, 1864), p. 5; Elizabeth Horsell, *The Penny Domestic Assistant and Guide to Vegetarian Cookery* (London, 1850).

76 *People's Magazine and Progressionist*, August 1854, p. 121, for her role. See *VA*, 1850, p. 66 on her 'kindness and hospitality in days gone by'.

77 *VA*, 1850, p. 104.

78 E.g., J.S. Hibberd, *VA*, 1850, p. 111; *VM*, May 1850, reverse of cover, for a working man's wife's opposition, despite 'what I ordered'; 'K.J.' of Rochdale, *VM*, October 1853, p. 24; 'the sex hardest to win over'; *DR*, October 1868, p. 127; A.F. Scott, *Vegetarian*, 16 March 1888, p. 173. Obviously 'domestic ties' might be *general family resistance* rather than female.

79 *VM*, April 1855, p. 32.

80 C.F. Corlass, *Intentional Oddity*, pp. 6-7 (Johnson, Box 1).

81 G. Dunn, 'A Defeated Transcendentalist', *Blackwood's Edinburgh Magazine*, February 1893, pp. 236-252. See E. Beavan, *Lil Grey, or Arthur Chester's Courtship* (London, 1878), p. 217 for the hero's relief in his bride's support.

82 *DR*, February 1882, p. 43, reporting letter in *Dundee Evening Telegraph*.

83 *VM*, June 1850, supplement: p. 15, is a rare report on efforts by a 'strong-minded and zealous woman, in circumstances of the greatest difficulty and opposition' to convert family, relations and servants.

84 See 'Parallel of the Sexes', *VA*, May 1850, p. 113.

85 Mrs Earle (Maria Theresa Earle) in *Vegetarian*, 5 November 1898, p. 712.

86 See the Reverend G.B. Watson, *VM*, October 1851, p. 85.

87 *VA*, 15 December 1848, pp. 65-66, possibly by Mrs Dornbusch.

88 Hibberd, *VA*, 1850, 'Women's Reformation', pp. 93-95; H.S. Clubb, *VA*, p. 141. Holyoake thought that a young lady in a butcher's shop was 'an incongruity that few can feel reconciled to,' *Reasoner*, 1850, p. 47; Burns: *MD*, 20 July 1888, p. 449, on the 'Progressive Food and Cooking Society'.

89 *VM*, January 1873, p. 12. Ladies, Amelia Lewis noted, felt raw meat 'indelicate and vulgar', *The Housekeeper*, 8 January 1876, p. 43. This rejection of meat is seen as expressive of sexual/physical phobias, by Adams, *Sexual Politics of Meat*, ch. 8.

90 Dornbusch, *VM*, October 1854, local operations, p. 84; on Mme Lamartine, see *VM*, June 1850, supplement: p. 15; and Crossley, *Consumable Metaphors*, pp. 111-113.
91 On comfortable confinements, see *VA*, 15 August 1850, p. 12. Elizabeth Martyn contributed vegetarian articles to *Mother's Companion*, 1890. An early appeal to women and mothers appears in 'A Child's Question', *VA*, 15 March 1849, p. 102.
92 Lane, *Dietetics*, p. 41; Freeston, *VM*, October 1867, p. 112; Horsell, *Science of Cooking Vegetarian Food*, p. 4. Feminist sentiment was expressed by G.J. Ford, *VA*, 1850, p. 63; Morgan, *DR*, January 1868, p. 7; and J.L. Barker, 'Women's Rights', *DR*, April 1869, pp. 40-47.
93 Some banquets were funded by women, see *VM*, May 1859, p. 62. On female entertainment, see *VM*, January 1854, pp. 13-14. Their presence was emphasized, with references to 'about half' at Liverpool, *VM*, April 1853, supplement: p. 7; a 'considerable number' at Malton, *VM*, January 1854, p. 4; a 'large number', p. 13; and the 'majority' in side-galleries at a Birmingham meeting, *VM*, December 1855, p. 67.
94 *The Times*, 2 August 1851, p. 8.
95 *VM*, September 1854, p. 76.
96 See Shiman, '"Changes are Dangerous": Women and Temperance in Victorian England.'
97 *The Lady's Newspaper*, 6 August 1853, p. 65; 'The Vegetarian System. By a Vegetarian', was serialized, August-September. The *Ladies' Own Journal* published material sent by a vegetarian, see *VM*, June 1854, p. 69.
98 See Alice M. Lewis, *Humanity and Vegetarianism*, p. 6: 'so few modern feminine advocates of the humaner diet'; Marie Joseph, *Shafts*, 11 February 1893, p. 237: 'Men are always first in food reform, – women come last as a rule.'
99 *VM*, November 1895, p. 348.
100 The president of the 'Women's Progressive Society', Mrs Snoad, was a sympathizer.
101 See Charles E. Dawson's *Vegetarian* covers (e.g., 2 May-12 September 1896 a barefooted girl with a basket of apples, pears), Forward's *Herald of Health* cover, and the *Hygienic Advertiser* cover.
102 See Lesley Hall's biography of Sibthorp, *Oxford Dictionary of National Biography*; *Vegetarian*, 12 May, p. 222; and Brady '"Shafts" and the quest for a new morality.' Sibthorp was a theosophist and joined Frances Swiney's eugenicist, feminist 'League of Isis'. On Swiney, see Barbara T. Gates, *Kindred Nature. Victorian and Edwardian Women Embrace the Living World* (Chicago, 1998) pp. 152-157. Swiney emphasized her vegetarian credentials in *Vegetarian*, 10 June 1899, p. 275.
103 *Home Links*, February 1898, p. 9.
104 Several had university education, which accords with the 'Girton Girl' stereotype. Alice Williams, Beatrice Lindsay, and Katharine Browning were Girtonians; *Punch*'s satire on female students incorporated a debate on vegetarianism, 25 December 1886, p. 304.
105 See C.W. Morley, *Vegetarian*, 9 November 1895, p. 544. In response to 'protest at the marriage bond', Chandos Wallace wrote *The Other New Woman*, see *VM*, August 1897, p. 303. Her 'New Woman Rational Cycling Society' championed rational attire. She felt female chauvinism harmed the cause, see *HH*, November

1895, p. 174, but supported women's full mental, physical and social development, see *Labour Annual*, 1899, p. 165.
106 New public prominence echoed the wider temperance world from *c.*1860, see Shiman, '"Changes are Dangerous" ... ' who points out (p. 206), that the B.W.T.A still had male domination in local activities and journalism.
107 See her *In My Lady's Chamber. A Speculative Romance, Touching a few Questions of the Day* (London, 1873). Her thesis (Paris, 1880) was translated into English. The *Perfect Way in Diet* (1882) heralded her major theosophic work, *The Perfect Way*.
108 *DR*, November 1882, p. 233.
109 Vegetarian from *c.*1888, she published *Vegetarianism in the Light of Theosophy* in the year of the WVU's establishment. She addressed the VS in 1897 and participated in the National Congress in 1899, see *The Times*, 12 September 1899, p. 9. See *Vegetarian*, 2 April 1898, pp. 215-216 for interview.
110 Lady Mount Temple's letters to Newman on vegetarianism were circulated in the press after publication in the *Pall Mall Gazette*, see *DR*, May 1882, p. 95, pp. 98-99.
111 Sandys Britton, *FRM*, April-June 1885, pp. 126-127.
112 *MD*, 25 April 1890, p. 263.
113 *Women's Penny Paper*, 10 August 1889, p. 7.
114 Brian Harrison, 'Women's Health and the Women's Movement in Britain: 1840-1940' in Charles Webster, ed., *Biology, Medicine and Society. 1840-1940* (Cambridge, 1981); Anne L. Scott, 'Physical Purity Feminism and State Medicine in Late Nineteenth-century England', *Women's History Review* 8:4 (1999), pp. 625-653; Mary A. Elston, 'Women and Anti-vivisection in Victorian England. 1870-1900', in Nicolas Rupke, ed., *Vivisection in Historical Perspective* (1987; London, 1990), pp. 259-294; Paul McHugh, *Prostitution and Victorian Social Reform* (London, 1980).
115 The American Mary Gove Nichols, married to T.L. Nichols, should also be included: see Brown 'Nineteenth-century American Health Reformers and the Early Nature Cure Movement in Britain'; Aspinwall, 'Social Catholicism and Health'; and Forward, *History*, pp. 45-46.
116 Adams, *Sexual Politics of Meat*, p. 174.
117 See the feminist *The Women's Penny Paper* and *Women's Herald* (1888-1893, launched and initially edited by F. Henrietta Müller, sister of a feminist vegetarian, and friend of Sibthorp), e.g., 10 August 1889, p. 7: A.M. Lewis's vegetarian address at the Paris Women's Congress; and 30 November 1889, p. 4: menu given at fashionable party (A.M. Lewis). It published interviews with women associated with vegetarianism or the WVU, like Chant.
118 E.g., *Dressmaker's Chart and Cutter* in 1894. There was coverage in the *Lady's Pictorial* (late 1894), and *The Queen*.
119 Beatrice Lindsay edited *DR*, and *Raisins and Almonds*, the Society's annual. She produced the movement's first history, *DR* 1885-1886. Herron's *Vegetarian Almanac* had many contributions by his wife.
120 The largely hostile Eleanor Orlebar felt they were an alternative career to governess for unmarried middle-class women, *Food for the People* (1879), p. 78. On waitresses, moving 'with a sweet but slightly mystic benignity', see *Punch*, 17 December 189, p. 280.
121 On female preparation, *Vegetarian*, 29 June 1889, p. 405; on cookery by the 'sterner sex', *VM*, December 1895, p. 405.

122 *DR*, November 1883, p. 311 (Annual Report): it was to provide 'practical help' in the 'peculiar department' identified with women.
123 These included Lady Paget, Sibthorp, Florence Bramwell Booth, Edith Carrington, Mona Caird (Forward, *History*, pp. 126-127 for her vegetarian son), Miss A.C. Woodward, A.M. Lewis.
124 *MD*, 27 June 1890, pp. 402-403.
125 See WVU material in Johnson, the only previous printed references are a brief entry in Peter Gordon and David Doughan, *Dictionary of British Women's Organizations. 1825-1960* (London, 2001) and Frank K. Prochaska, *Women and Philanthropy in Nineteenth Century England* (Oxford, 1980), p. 32.
126 *Shafts*, January 1894, p. 197. See interview, *Vegetarian*, 11 September 1897, p. 497.
127 Johnson, Box 1, letter to Joseph Edwards dated 24 October 1896.
128 *Vegetarian*, 11 September 1897, p. 491.
129 *Vegetarian*, 11 September 1897, p. 491.
130 Johnson, Box 1, *The Women's Vegetarian Union*, tract, n.d.
131 *Vegetarian*, March 1896, article by Veigelé, p. 122ff.
132 *Vegetarian Yearbook*, 1898.
133 Sixth Annual Report, March 1900-March 1901, p. 8.
134 *The Times*, 19 September 1898, p. 7.
135 *Shafts* in February and March 1897; see Johnson, Box 1, cards for November 1897.
136 Johnson, Box 1, 'Second Annual Meeting Agenda', 1897.
137 Third Annual Report, pp. 6-7. See the Depôt's price lists for 1897-8, and sheet on services supplied through the Agency, in Johnson, and advertisements in *Vegetarian Yearbook*, 1898 and *Home Links*. Box 3 has an advertisement for 'The Healtheries' at Praed Street, where Adrienne sold commodities and literature on 'all advanced subjects' connected with women, industrial and hygienic questions, and Tolstoy. See letter in *VM*, February 1898, and note in May, p. 238; Johnson, Box 1, MS Annual Report for year 1896-1897.
138 *Vegetarian*, 26 November 1898, p. 763.
139 *Vegetarian*, 7 January 1899, p. 11; Johnson, Box 2, letter to Joseph Edwards from Adrienne Veigelé, 30 November 1898, for affiliation of this society to WVU, she also founded a WIPU branch here.
140 Johnson, Box 2, pamphlet of 'Société Belge pour l'Étude de la Réforme Alimentaire', and a copy of *La Réforme Alimentaire* (no. 1, October 1897). On May Yates' lectures on bread reform and vegetarianism in Belgium, see *VM*, May 1893, pp. 184-185. On French vegetarianism in this period, see Crossley, *Consumable Metaphors*, ch. 13.
141 Johnson, Box 1, Women's Vegetarian Union, 1/2: 'Rules of the Union'.
142 Johnson, Box 1, invitation to evening meeting at Chandos Wallace's, November 1897, subject: 'Women as healers in the home.'
143 Adrienne contributed to *Shafts*, see 'Qualities admired by Men in Women and by Women in Men', April 1898, p. 137.
144 Joseph Edwards Papers, folder 2, card from Sibthorp dated 'Dec. 5'.
145 *Vegetarian Review*, April 1895. See Edward J. Bristow, *Vice and Vigilance. Purity Movements in Britain since 1700* (Dublin, 1977), p. 119. Her husband, subscriber to *DR* c.1873, was a professor of jurisprudence and member of Clementia Taylor's circle at Aubrey House, see Philippa Levine, *Feminist Lives in Victorian England. Private Roles and Public Commitment* (Oxford, 1990), p. 65.

146 Both agitated to close the Empire Theatre, 1894: see Bland, *Banishing the Beast*, pp. 105-107. On the National Society for Women's Suffrage executive, active in local government and agitating for women preachers, Chant was satirized in *Punch* as 'Prowlina Pry'.
147 She announced an 'autonomistic alliance' with Alfred Wastall, editor of Densmore's *Pure Food*) in 1898, see *Labour Annual* 1898, p. 153. On the League, see Brady, '"Shafts" and the quest for a new morality.'
148 Brady, '"Shafts" and the quest for a new morality,' p. 15.
149 *Vegetarian*, 7 December 1895, p. 606.
150 See *Home Links*, 20 December 1898, p. 143. See Allinson Papers, MS 3193, clipping from *Marylebone Times*, 5 February 1897, on WVU social held at their house, Spanish Place.
151 *Vegetarian*, 6 July 1895, p. 322, this took place at the WWCTU Convention, London 1895.
152 Beginning in 1895 with addresses at the conference on 'L'Alimentation et la Temperance', organized by president of the Belgian WCTU, Madame Chantraine, member of the Maternity Society and WVU.
153 *The Times*, 14 September 1894, p. 4. Boult, Chandos Wallace, Mrs Archibald Hunter, and May Yates also gave papers.
154 *Vegetarian*, 16 April 1898, p. 252.
155 *DR*, 1884, p. 373.
156 *Home Links*, January-March 1898. The *Daily Chronicle*, 7 September 1896, reported a meeting, see Allinson Papers, MS 3193.
157 *Shafts*, October-December 1899, p. 120, reprinted Mr and Mrs A.H. Curror's paper; and noted, p. 119, that the phrenologist Esther Higgs' *Woman the Individual* had been read to the Women's Progressive Union.
158 *Shafts*, September 1897, p. 255 for Brussels branch, whose rules were devised with advice from feminist leader Madame Popelin. See Johnson, Box 1, for leaflet for the 'Union des Femmes Végétariennes'.
159 *Shafts,* September- October, 1898.
160 Brady, '"Shafts" and the quest for a new morality,' p. 18. Somerset's *Woman's Signal* announced the existence of the WVU, 11 July 1895, p. 28.
161 Marion Leslie, 'A Peep at the Lady Pioneers,' *Hygienic Review*, July-December 1893. On Massingberd's vegetarianism see *Vegetarian*, 12 August 1893, p. 379. Chant was a Pioneer. Mrs Charles Mallet, a Pioneer (and Humanitarian Leaguer), supported the WVU and WIPU, see *VM*, February 1896, p. 63.
162 *Vegetarian*, 6 July 1895, p. 332.
163 Ruth Bordin, *Frances Willard. A Biography* (London, 1986) p. 208. Before Willard became vegetarian (*HGA*, 15 March 1898, p. 30) she and the WCTU had been hostile, see *VM*, January 1890, p. 23.
164 See *Woman's Signal*, 11 July 1895, p. 28; 21 November 1895, p. 321 for notices. It helped that the *Signal*'s editorial office was Memorial Hall. Reformed diet columns appeared in the WCTU's *Union Signal*, as noted in *HGA*, February 1896, p. 24.
165 *International Council of Women. Report of Transactions*, vol. 7 *Women in Social Life* (London, 1900) p. 183; p. 249. The pro-vegetarian Sarah Amos and Chant, and other vegetarians participated.
166 *Vegetarian*, 8 July 1899, p. 319.
167 Johnson, Box 3, MS First Annual Report, for the year 1896-1897.

168 *First Annual Report of the WVU* (March 1895-March 1896), Preface, p. iii.
169 Preface, *Fifth Annual Report of the WVU* (March 1899-March 1900), p. 3.
170 *Shafts*, 11 February 1893, p. 237. Beeby was a Humanitarian Leaguer.
171 The *Fifth Annual Report* thanked Stead for an office at *Review of Reviews*; on Leo: *Third Annual Report of the WVU* (March 1897-March 1898); Nugent wrote to *Shafts*, July 1895, p. 64 as a 'constant reader', advocating a female VS.
172 Mary Dawtrey, *FRM*, January 1882 (pp. 87-90), April 1882 (pp. 134-136).
173 *Vegetarian*, from 18 March 1893, had 'About Women – for Women' on topics such as female doctors and trade unions, and 'men as women saw them'. 'For the Ladies' appeared in *VM* in 1896, to address 'special needs', see 49th Report, *VM*, 1896, p. 320.
174 See *Vegetarian*, 9 December 1893, p. 592, p. 596: Eva McClaren and Mrs Morgan Browne on suffrage. A pro-franchise article appeared, 10 July 1897, p. 344.
175 *Vegetarian*, 4 June 1892, p. 267.
176 C.W. Morley, 'The Coming of the Woman', *Vegetarian*, 9 November 1895, p. 544.
177 *Vegetarian*, 11 September 1897, p. 491.
178 Kingsley contrasted Shelley and Byron, *Fraser's Magazine*, November 1853 in terms of effeminate 'gentle and sensitive vegetarian' and 'sturdy peer'. Adams, *Sexual Politics of Meat*, p. 38 quotes a comment of 1836 that 'Emasculation is the first fruit of Grahamism.'
179 Johnson, Box 1, 'Second Annual Meeting Agenda', 1897.
180 *Shafts*, July-September 1899, p. 88.
181 Johnson, Box 2, letter 16 November 1899.
182 *Vegetarian*, 16 June 1894.
183 Johnson, Box 2, letter 8 December 1900; Joseph Edwards Papers, folder 3, letters 18 September and 11 November 1901.

Chapter Seven

1 Brown, 'Physical Puritanism', p. 407.
2 Sir Henry Thompson, 'Why Vegetarian?' *The Nineteenth Century*, April 1898; Thompson, 'Why Vegetarian?' *The Nineteenth Century*, June 1898, pp. 966-976; J. Oldfield, 'Vegetarian Still', *The Nineteenth Century*, August 1898, pp. 246-252.
3 *DR*, June 1873, p. 281, noting the diet of Fuseli and Mrs Radcliffe.
4 *VA*, February 1850, pp. 81-82, responding to reference to *The Times*, 25 December 1849, on Shelley and J.E. Duncan. *VM*, September 1887, pp. 291-293. See 'A Lecture on Journalism', *Blackwood's Edinburgh Magazine*, 68, no. 422 (December 1850), p. 697 on young journalists, 'all mere moonshine – pure flatulency' due to vegetable diet.
5 Ruskin responded to a letter from the wife of Hume Nisbet, Helen Nisbet, in *Fors Clavigera*, Letter 90 (May 1883).
6 *Blackwood's Edinburgh Magazine*, 67, April 1850, p. 468: 'Roots are a windy, watery diet, they breed melancholy.'
7 *Blackwood's Edinburgh Magazine*, December 1856, p. 732.
8 On Romantic vegetarianism see Adams, *Sexual Politics of Meat* and Adams, 'Vegetarianism', in Laura Dabundo, ed., *Encyclopaedia of Romanticism. Culture in Britain, 1780s-1830* (London, 1992) pp. 594-595; Morton, *Shelley and the Revolution in Taste*; Henry S. Salt, *P.B. Shelley. Poet and Pioneer* (1896; London, 1924), p. 120; Peter Foot, *Red Shelley* (London, 1980); Mark Kipperman, 'Absorbing a Revolution:

Shelley Becomes a Romantic, 1889-1903', *Nineteenth Century Literature*, 47:2 (September 1992), pp. 187-211; Onno Oerlemans, 'Shelley's Ideal Body: Vegetarianism and Nature', *Studies in Romanticism*, 34:4 (winter 1995), pp. 531-552; and Part Three of Stuart's *Bloodless Revolution*.

9   Morton, *Shelley and the Revolution in Taste*, admits that vegetarianism largely attracted a 'fairly elite grouping' including professionals and upper-class radical freethinkers, 'The discourse of *bread* would have been more familiar to artisans and others in the labouring-class hierarchy', p. 5.

10 The scornful phrase was Kingsley's, *Fraser's Magazine*, November 1853. See Hector Waylen, 'A Few More Notes', *Vegetarian*, 1890, p. 15. Kingsley witnessed vegetarians in Christian Socialist circles; Francis Newman encouraged Mrs Kingsley to be vegetarian.

11 Morton, *Revolution in Taste*, p. 37 (Carlile quoted); see Foot, *Red Shelley*, pp. 228-241 on predominantly working-class enthusiasm for Shelley and *Queen Mab* (1813). Book 8 of *Queen Mab* envisions a vegetarian future, supported by a lengthy note, 17; also in 1813 Shelley published *A Vindication of Natural Diet*. His son tried twice to be vegetarian according to his letter to Kegan Paul, 14 November 1883, see *VM*, March 1891, p. 77. Shelley's friend E.J. Trelawny became vegetarian.

12 *VA*, 1848, p. 26. Note the possibility of critics of Shelley's diet in radical papers like the *Reasoner*, where Robert Beith, 10 June 1846, pp. 22-25 claimed his dietetic prejudices were confirmed by Shelley's writings.

13 *The Times*, 25 December 1850, p. 4.

14 George Buckley, *VM*, 1853. Shelley Centenary celebrations at 'Wheatsheaf', were widely reported, e.g., *New York Times* and *Pall Mall Gazette*. See G.B. Shaw's 'Shaming the Devil about Shelley', *The Albemarle Review*, September 1892 and 'On Going to Church', in *The Savoy*, January 1896. The VS published William E.A. Axon's *Shelley's Vegetarianism* (1891), a paper read to the Shelley Society.

15 *MD*, 17 February 1888, p. 104. See *MD*, 1 July 1892, pp. 407-408, p. 424, for Burns's scornful account of the Anniversary's treatment of Shelley in materialist and prosaic fashion.

16 Adherents influenced by Shelley included Charlotte Despard, see Andro Linklater, *An Unhusbanded Life. Charlotte Despard. Suffragette, Socialist and Sinn Feiner* (London, 1980), pp. 30-32. On the Shelleyanism of London radical clubs, see Stan Shipley, *Club Life and Socialism in Mid-Victorian London* (Oxford, 1971), p. 28. But H.J. Godbold, *VM*, August 1892, pp. 288-289, disavowed support for Shelley's views.

17 Edward Fitzgerald's vegetarian ditty appears in *Vegetarian*, 15 January 1898, p. 41. Tennyson's verse 'To E. Fitzgerald,' in *Tiresias and other Poems* (1885), records trial vegetarianism. References to vegetarianism also feature in verse by 'Violet Fane' ('A Fable,' from *Poems by Violet Fane*, 1892); George Meredith ('Jump to Glory Jane'); F.W.O. Ward ('Twixt Kiss and Lip,' 1890); and William Allingham ('Blackberries,' 1890).

18 See Angela Leighton, 'Introduction II,' in Angela Leighton and Margaret Reynolds, *Victorian Women Poets* (Oxford, 1995), p. xxxix.

19 Mary Howitt, 'The Cry of the Animals. A Poem' (London, 1900).

20 Reported in *HGA*, October 1910, p. 99.

21 LeeAnne M. Richardson, 'Naturally Radical: The Subversive Poetics of Dollie Radford', *Victorian Poetry* 38:1 (2000), pp. 109-124.

22 Mona Caird was an exception, see *Hygienic Review*, July-December 1893, pp. 12-19. Caird's fiction had no vegetarians until *The Great Wave*, 1931; but see references to slaughtered carcasses for dinner, in *The Daughters of Danaus* (1894). Olive Schreiner was sympathetic, see *Vegetarian*, 2 September 1893, p. 418; Sarah Grand was not, see interview, *Vegetarian*, 20 August 1898.
23 *DR*, May 1893, pp. 179-181.
24 Some sense of the extent of the pre-Victorian discourse on vegetarianism can most easily be gained from Stuart, *Bloodless Revolution*, in its examination of treatment of diet in early-modern works of travel literature, the literary impact of Dr George Cheyne's vegetable diet, the impact across Europe of Rousseauistic educational reform, and the 'counter-vegetarian' reactionary poetry of Alexander Pope, William Cowper, James Thomson and others, which Stuart points out (ch. 16), condemned animal cruelty but defended the right to kill and eat animals.
25 *The Times*, 13 January 1885, Exeter Hall meeting of the VS.
26 Augustus H. Keane, *Ethnology* (Cambridge, 1896), ch. 6; Friedrich Ratzel, *The History of Mankind* (translated from the German, vol. 1, London, 1896), p. 92. On diet and climate see John W. Draper, *History of the Intellectual Development of Europe* (2 vols, London, 1864), vol. 1, p. 26. On colonial acclimatization and diet, see William Z. Ripley, *The Races of Europe. A Sociological Study* (London, 1899), p. 563. William E.H. Lecky, in *History of European Morals from Augustus to Charlemagne* (London, 1869), vol. 1, p. 50, discusses animal rights and vegetarianism from a utilitarian viewpoint. Winwood Reade's influential *The Martyrdom of Man* posited a vegetarian future (17th edn, London, 1903), p. 513.
27 Alexis Soyer, *The Pantropheon, or History of Food and its Preparation* (London, 1853).
28 Volant and Watson, eds, *Memoirs of Alexis Soyer*. See *The Times*, 20 October 1858, p. 14.
29 George Dodd, *The Food of London. A Sketch of the Chief Varieties, Sources of Supply. Probable Quantities, Modes of Arrival, Processes of Manufacture etc.* (London, 1856).
30 *Illustrated London News*, 15 June 1851, p. 560.
31 Sargant, *Economy of the Labouring Classes*, ch. 8.
32 Macmillan, *The Promotion of General Happiness*. John M. Davidson, *The Old Order and the New. From Individualism to Collectivism*, serialized in *WTE* in 1889; the editor criticized his stance 30 June 1889, p. 10. Frederic Harrison, *Realities and Ideals. Social, Political, Literary and Artistic* (London, 1908) essay 14, 'The Veto on Drink.'
33 See Richard Govett, *Vegetarianism. A Dialogue* (*c.*1850); On *A Glance at Vegetarianism* (London, 1850), see *VA*, 1 April 1850, p. 98. Metters, *Strictures on animal and vegetable diet* (Uxbridge, 1847); reviewed in *Truth-Tester*, 1847, pp. 119-120; and *Temperance News and Weekly Journal of Literature and Humanity*, August 1846, p. 81. Anon., [J. Johnson] *The Vegetarian Fallacy* (1856); 'Beef-eater,' *The Vegetarian Humbug*, references in *VM*, 1855. A later tract was Charles R. Drysdale's *Vegetarian Fallacies* (London, 1890). Bernard Moncriff's *The Philosophy of the Stomach; or, an Exclusively Animal Diet* (London, 1856), referred to vegetarianism, pp. 69-70. W.J. Farmer reported receiving 'a pamphlet purporting to be a response to Tolstoi's *The First Step*', see *Vegetarian*, 25 February 1893.
34 *The Times*, 25 December 1850, p. 8 (pudding); 19 July 1851, p. 9; 26 July, 1 August 1851 (soirée); 29 December 1855, p. 4 (Simpson's London lecture); 3 April 1856, p. 3 (LVA meetings).

35 *The Times*, advertisements for Graham, *Truth-Tester*, *VA*, 21 February 1849, p. 10; 'W.H.J' seeking lodgings in Hampstead or Highgate, 5 September 1850, p. 2.

36 *Daily News* coverage cited in *VM*, October 1855 p. 90, November 1855, pp. 96-99. 23 October–27 September 1854 the *Nonconformist* published correspondence on vegetarianism and consumption. On the *Morning Advertiser*, see *VM*, September-December 1852, controversialist section, p. 19. The *Morning Chronicle* reported on vegetarianism 4 August 1851 (*VM*, November 1851: controversialist, p. 17). In 1850 there were two 'favourable' papers in *Reynolds's Newspaper*. Surprisingly, given its moral radical status, the only reported reference in the *Morning Star* was in November 1867 (*VM*, January 1868, pp. 19-20).

37 See Brian Maidment, 'Magazine of Popular Progress and the Artisans', *Victorian Periodicals Review* 17: 3 (1984), pp. 83-94.

38 *Household Words*, 23 August 1851, 'Whole Hogs'. See Graham Storey, Kathleen Tillotson and Nina Burgis, eds, *The Letters of Charles Dickens*, vol. 6 (Oxford, 1988), p. 457: 10 August 1851 to W.H. Wills. The editors note Clara Lucas Balfour's response, in J.S. Buckingham's *The Temperance Offering*. Dickens criticized Cruickshank's temperance fairy-tales by showing the absurdity of Robinson Crusoe retold with vegetarian, teetotal or pro-aboriginal moral, *Household Words*, 1 October 1853.

39 *The British Controversialist*, June-November 1851, II: pp. 226-230, 230-231, 265, 267-270, 307-309, 389-391, 426-430. On this journal, see Michael Wolff, *Victorian Periodical Newsletter* 2, June 1968, pp. 27-45.

40 *Family Herald*, 9 November 1850, pp. 444-445. *Chambers's Edinburgh Journal* extracted Smith's *Fruits and Farinacea* 3 and 13 January 1846, rejected the vegetarianism of Thomson's 'The Seasons', 16 May 1846 and published a 'Plea for a Vegetarian Diet' in 1850.

41 For *Athenaeum* reviews, see 15 November 1845; 8 August 1846; 28 August 1847; 4 May 1850 (Asenath Nicholson, Charles Lane); 15 December 1860.

42 See *VA*, 15 October 1848, pp. 34-35; 15 November 1848, pp. 51-52, for response to *Punch*.

43 References in the period 1848-1857 include: 'The Vegetarians', 20 September 1848, p. 140; 'Punch and the Vegetarians', January-June 1851, p. 101; 'The Vegetarians in the North', July-December 1853, p. 73; 'The Delights of Spring. A Song by a Vegetarian', 6 June 1857.

44 *The Times*, 10 August 1854, p. 13.

45 'Vegetative Ideas,' *Diogenes*, 19 March 1853, p. 129.

46 *VM*, June 1890, noted the vegetarian's risk of cancer was a 'standing dish for slack times' for the press.

47 *Vegetarian*, 5 March 1898, p. 145, 19 February, p. 130.

48 C.O.G. Napier, 'Autobiography of a Vegetarian', *Fraser's Magazine*, 1876; Henry S. Salt, 'Food Reform', *Westminster Review*, October 1886, pp. 483-499; Lady Paget, 'Vegetarian diet', *Nineteenth Century* 31 (April 1892), pp. 577-585; on the *Pall Mall Gazette*, see report in *DR*, January 1882, p. 42; publication of Newman-Mount Temple correspondence May 1882. E.T. Cook, formerly W.T. Stead's colleague at the *Pall Mall Gazette*, and editor of *Westminster Gazette*, attending an Ideal Club dinner said that, 'Personally, he was always glad to use what influence he had in forwarding the interests of the Vegetarian Society' (*Vegetarian*, 22 December 1894).

49 *Notes and Queries*, 30 August 1879, p. 167 (inquiry by Axon); 20 December 1883, p. 496 (inquiry by T.C. Hughes, BA); 12 January 1884, pp. 30-32 (replies).
50 *Illustrated London News*, 11 September 1897, p. 368; and 2 October 1897, p. 465. By contrast *Gentleman's Magazine*, favourable in the 1880s in scientific notes by a supporter, William Mattieu Williams, published Oldfield's 'History of a Beefsteak' (November 1895).
51 References appearing 1865-1900, fully detailed in my thesis, included: 'Anti Everything Societies,' 14 January 1865, p. 15; 'A Ballad of Salad,' 1 June 1889, p. 267; 'Why Vegetarians?' 11 June 1898, p. 274. Journals such as *Fun, Moonshine, Scraps, Funny Folks* featured humour involving vegetarians. The leading black-and-white artist, Phil May, drew a cartoon reproduced in the *Vegetarian*, September 1894, p. 419.
52 'Chronicles of Clovernook' appeared first in *The Illuminated Magazine*, and was reprinted in 1846 (Offices of *Punch*). The Owenite J.F. Bray's utopian satire, *A Voyage from Utopia* (1842, see M.F. Lloyd-Prichard's edition, London, 1957) condemned the fact that the majority in Britain and Ireland were restricted by poverty to a 'chiefly vegetable diet', p. 125.
53 Armytage, *Yesterdays Tomorrows*, Nan B. Albinski, *Women's Utopias in British and American Fiction* (London, 1988); Vernon L. Parrington, *American Dreams. A Study of American Utopias* (2nd edition, New York, 1964).
54 Edward B. Lytton, *The Coming Race* (1871; London, 1893).
55 William H. Hudson, *A Crystal Age* (London, 1887), pp. 54-55. Hudson's utopia rejected vivisection, p. 79. Hudson joined the Humanitarian League; his opinion of vegetarianism was low.
56 Edward Bellamy, *Equality* (London, 1897).
57 Robert Buchanan, *The Reverend Annabel Lee. A Tale of To-morrow* (London, 1898), p. 73.
58 George B. Shaw, *Immaturity* (1879; London, 1931), p. 55.
59 Samuel Butler, *Erewhon, or, Over the Range* (these chapters, 26 and 27, were additions to the acclaimed first edition of 1872, when republished by Grant Richards, 1901). See Henry Festing, *Samuel Butler. Author of Erewhon. 1835-1902. A Memoir* (London, 1919), 2 vols, vol. 2: pp. 373-374, and Festing, ed., *The Note-books of Samuel Butler* (1921; London, 1930), p. 361.
60 *Darkness and Dawn. The Peaceful Birth of a New Age* (London, 1884); *Paradise Found at the North Pole* (London, 1887); *The Angel and the Idiot. A Story of the Next Century* (London, 1890) reported in *VM*. Simon Landis's *The Social War of 1900* (Philadelphia, 1872) featured the vegetarian Dr Juno. The short-lived journal *The Utopian* (London, 1884) discussed vegetarianism.
61 David Brewster, *More Worlds than One. The Creed of the Philosopher and the Hope of the Christian* (London, 1854), p. 154.
62 'Saturn conquers Earth and makes its inhabitants Vegetarians,' *Punch's Almanac* for 1990 (reprinted in *Littell's Living Age*, 2 March 1861); J.C.E. Munro, *A Trip to Venus. A Novel* (London, 1897) noted in *VM*, January 1898, p. 5.
63 Octave Uzanne, 'The End of Books', *Scribner's Magazine* 16 (July-December 1894), pp. 221-231.
64 H.G. Wells, *The First Men in the Moon* (1901; London, 1925), p. 16.
65 Henry Rider Haggard, *She. A History of Adventure* (1887, London, 1894), p. 137. There was a year of essays on the novel's meaning, in *Vegetarian*, 1889.

66 A.W. Malcolmson, *The Aesthetic in Food* (Manchester, 1899), p. 9. The aesthetes, despite parodists' talk of 'vegetable passion' (by Gilbert and Sullivan's *Patience*), and feeding on lilies, had no strong connection with vegetarianism (though connected with dress reform). Salt complained about limited aesthetic support in 'Good Taste in Diet', *Food Reform Magazine*, October-December 1883.
67 Haggard wrote that he was theoretically a vegetarian, but not in the British climate, see *Vegetarian*, 23 February 1889, p. 122. Yva, in his later fantasy, *When the World Shook* (1919) is disgusted by the western characters' meat-eating.
68 *Vegetarian*, 2 October 1897.
69 Adams, *Sexual Politics of Meat*, pp. 105-107, pp. 127-129; Liz Jensen, *Ark Baby* (London, 1998).
70 Duncan, *Flowers and Fruits*; Fanny E. Lacy, 'The Vegetarian; or, a Visit to Aunt Primitive', *The Metropolitan Magazine*, April 1847, pp. 403-413; Sarah A. Clubb, *Good Influence. A Tale for the Young* (London, 1854); C.O.G. Napier, *Tommy Try* (London, 1869); 'Colossa' (Anna Kingsford) *In My Lady's Chamber. A Speculative Romance, Touching a Few Questions of the Day* (London, 1873), which first appeared in her *Lady's Own Paper*, 1872; Beavan, *Lil Grey; Or Arthur Chester's Courtship* (London, 1879); Arnold F. Hills, *Sunshine and Shadows* (1893); John A. Parker, *Ernest England* (London, 1895). Vegetarian poetry included Robert Sargeant, *The Revenge of the Beasts and other Vegetarian and Humanitarian Verses* (London, 1881); and [Harold Begbie?] *Odd Rhymes, Verses, Imitations, Jingles* (London, 1899).
71 On temperance fiction, see Carol Mattingley, *Well-tempered Women: Nineteenth Century Temperance Rhetoric* (Carbondale, Illinois, 1998), ch. 7.
72 See William M. Thackeray, *The Virginians* (1858) vol. 1, ch. 31, 'The Bear and the Leader', p. 243: defending 'Oenophilists' against teetotallers and vegetarians; Edward B. Lytton, *Kenelm Chillingley. His Adventures and Opinions* (Leipzig, 1873) vol. 1, p. 154.
73 Charles Dickens, *The Personal History of David Copperfield* (1849-50), ch. 36, 'A Little Cold Water.' *The Posthumous Papers of the Pickwick Club* (1837; Oxford, 1986) featured, ch. 20, p. 293, 'an elderly pimply-faced, vegetable-diet sort of man'. See 'Whole Hogs', *Household Words* 2: 74 (23 August 1851), pp. 505-507.
74 Charles Kingsley, *Alton Locke. Tailor and Poet* (1850; London, 1878), p. 28.
75 Kelty, *Visiting My Relations, and its Results; a series of small episodes in the life of a Recluse* (London, 1851).
76 'Zaidee: A Romance', *Blackwood's Edinburgh Magazine* 77:476 (June 1855), p. 680. Republished as a book, 1856. Mr Cumberland, a Fourierist dedicated to 'Nature', attempts the 'conversion of the world by vegetable diet'. [W.E. Aytoun] 'The Congress and the Agapedome,' *Blackwood's Edinburgh Magazine*, 70: 431 (September 1851), pp. 359-378; 'Pisistratus Caxton' [E. Bulwer-Lytton] 'My Novel; or Varieties in English Life', in *Blackwood's Edinburgh Magazine* 70: 433 (November 1851), p. 573, and subsequently republished as a book. See also Marmion W. Savage's popular novel, *Reuben Medlicott, Or The Coming Man* (London, 1852), where the eponymous hero takes up vegetarianism.
77 First appearing in serialized form, see Martin F. Tupper, 'The Rides and Reveries of Mr Aesop Smith', in *The Dublin University* Magazine, vol. 48 (July-December 1856), pp.660-661.
78 George Eliot, *Middlemarch. A Study of Provincial Life* (serialised, 1871-72; London, 1965), p. 203. The character Trawley is hot on the 'French social systems'. A

vegetarian American prophet figures in 'A Minor Prophet' in *The Legend of Jubal, and Other Poems* (London, 1874). Eliot read Brown's 'admirable article' before it was published in the *Westminster Review*, see Gordon S. Haight, ed., *The Letters of George Eliot* (London, 1954), vol. 2, p. 6.

79 'The Experiences of the A.C.', in Bayard Taylor, *Beauty and the Beast and Tales of Home* (New York, 1872); Orestes A. Brownson, *The Spirit-Rapper* (Boston, 1854), ch. 8, where Long, p. 98, an English 'Prophet of Newness', is an echo of Charles Lane. Brownson was a leading figure in this milieu before converting to Catholicism. The social reformer Lydia M. Child indicated pro-vegetarian sentiments in her Athenian *Philothea* (Boston, 1836). Louisa M. Alcott drew on her childhood experience of Fruitlands for her well-known story 'Transcendental Wild Oats' (*The Independent*, 18 December 1873).

80 'Radical Freelance', *The Philosophers of Foufouville* (New York, 1868), set in a community of Harmonians at New Jersey, p. 29.

81 'Whig Principles. What's Left of Them,' *United States Democratic Review*, 34:6 (December 1854), pp. 465-477.

82 See Stewart M. Ellis, *George Meredith* (London, 1920), p. 103 on the novel (completed 1874), Meredith's favourite. On his vegetarianism, see Salt, *Vegetarian*, 1912, p. 37; and Hyndman, *Records of an Adventurous Life*, pp. 85-86.

83 George Meredith, *Beauchamp's Career* (1875; London, 1902), p. 455-456.

84 The journalist Justin McCarthy observed in 'The Literature of the Victorian Reign' (*Appleton's Journal: A Magazine of General Literature*, pp. 541-542); this was a work that 'probably not one in every thousand novel-readers has even opened'.

85 Eliza Lynn Linton, *The Autobiography of Christopher Kirkland*, (London, 1885) vol. 3, p. 19. See Herbert van Thal, *Eliza Lynn Linton. The Girl of the Period* (London, 1979), pp. 142-154; Nancy F. Anderson, *Woman against Women in Victorian England* (Bloomington and Indianapolis, 1987), p. 180.

86 *Christopher Kirkland*, vol. 3, p. 55.

87 *Christopher Kirkland*, vol. 1, p. 191.

88 William F. Barry, *The New Antigone. A Romance* (London, 1887): the character Mr Mardol. John Sutherland, *The Longman Companion to Victorian Fiction* (1988; 1989), p. 459, characterizes this as a 'pro-Catholic novel of ideas'. By 1906 it had reached its seventh edition.

89 Mary Ward, *The History of David Grieve* (London, 1892), vol. 1, p. 338. See Enid H. Jones, *Mrs Humphry Ward* (London, 1973), pp. 91-97. *Vegetarian Review*, 1897, p. 534 noted Ward's association with Mancunian vegetarians two or three years before. Her brother William was vegetarian whilst at Oxford.

90 Forward, *History*, p. 166: photograph of Ward. Veigelé's depôt sold *David Grieve* c.1897.

91 Arthur Conan Doyle, 'The Red-headed League,' *The Strand Magazine* 2 (August 1891), pp. 198-199. A doctor, his autobiographical *The Stark Munro Letters* (1895) includes a recommendation to a patient of vegetarianism.

92 H.G. Wells, *Ann Veronica: a Modern Love Story* (1909; London, 1980) p. 111. Wells's Fabianism linked him to several vegetarians: see Norman and Jeanne Mackenzie, *The Time Traveller. The Life of H.G. Wells* (London, 1973), p. 62, p. 102, p. 174. See Peter Kemp, *H.G. Wells and the Culminating Ape. Biological Themes and Imaginative Obsessions* (London, 1982), pp. 15-17; and Wells's *A Modern Utopia* and other

Discussions, with its character the 'Voice of Nature' (1905; *The Works of H.G. Wells*, vol. 9, London, 1925), p. 60, pp. 106-113.

93 *The Curious and Diverting Adventures of Sir John Sparrow Bt., or, the Progress of an Open Mind* (London, 1902).
94 James Shirley Hibberd, 'Beans without bacon. A Pythagorean Romance', in *The Golden Gate and Silver Steps with Bits of Tinsel round about It* (London, 1886).
95 *The Odd Women* (1893; London, 1980), pp. 8, 12, 19, 23, 33; *The Private Papers of Henry Ryecroft* (London, 1903) 'Winter': ix, pp. 245-247; 'A Poor Gentleman' (1899; in *The House of Cobwebs and Other Stories*, London, 1906). Vegetarian communitarianism appears in *Will Warburton. A Romance of Real Life* (London, 1905). On Gissing's vegetarianism see comments in Jacob Korg, ed., *George Gissing's Commonplace Book* (New York, 1962), p. 67.
96 George Dunn, 'A Defeated Transcendentalist', *Blackwood's Magazine*, February 1893, pp. 236-252.
97 See Beatrice E. Kidd, *VM*, January 1899, pp. 28-29. *Vegetarian*, 2 October 1897, p. 539, saw incipient vegetarianism in George du Maurier, *The Martian* (1896). On Hardy, see Ronald D. Morrison, 'Humanity Towards Man, Woman, and the Lower Animals: Thomas Hardy's Jude the Obscure and the Victorian Humane Movement', *Nineteenth Century Studies* 12 (1998), pp. 64-82. Tolstoy's tract *The First Step* (which prefaced the Russian translation, 1892, of Williams' *The Ethics of Diet*) was printed by British vegetarians, see *VM*, March 1896 (essay by William E.A. Axon); and 1899 for serialization. *VM*, January 1851, p. 1, had identified literature in the 'spirit of vegetarian philosophy' in *Household Words* etc.
98 Henry James, *The Bostonians* (1896), Basil Ransom assumes Miss Birdseye's circle are 'mediums, communists, vegetarians' (ch. 4). James Snr. had known Sophia Chichester.
99 George Meredith, *The Ordeal of Richard Feverel* (1859); *One of Our Conquerors* (1892); Ella Hepworth Dixon, *My Flirtations* (1892).
100 Stories by Canon Victor L. Whitechurch featuring Hazell appeared in *The Royal Magazine* in 1905, and were collected as *Stories of the Railway*, 1912.
101 George Meredith, *One of Our Conquerors* (London, 1892), p. 61, p. 70, p. 98, p. 122, p. 209, p. 414.
102 British Library, Additional Manuscripts, 43037, ff.254-269: Lord Chancellor's Plays, vols 172-173, 'Bloomerism or Follies of the Day. A Farce. In one act'; 'The Vegetarian. A Serio-Comico-semi sentimental song', performed by Howard Paul in 'Patchwork', music and lyrics by Henry Walker, several editions (1859, 1869).
103 Edward F. Benson, *The Freaks of Mayfair* (London, 1916), and *Paying Guests* (London, 1929).
104 *The Lodger*, published in a magazine 1911 and republished as a book in 1913, was a bestseller. Sleuth, the killer, is a teetotaller, vegetarian and religious fanatic.
105 Daniel Karlin, 'The Rise and Fall of the Magnetic Fluid', *Times Literary Supplement*, 12 February 1999, p. 6.

Conclusion

1 Forward, *VM*, November 1896, p. 372. Josiah Oldfield stressed the 'extent to which public opinion and practice in matter of dietary' was affected beyond membership, *Encyclopaedia Britannica* ('Vegetarianism,' 10th edn, 1902-03). Qualified

praise in *The Times* and elsewhere for their philanthropic and educative work has already been cited.
2   *VM*, January 1892, p. 5.
3   Herbert Spencer identified advocacy of a low diet for children on hygienic grounds as originating in a convenient excuse for limited means, *Education: Intellectual, Moral, and Physical* (London, 1861), p. 153; Gissing, 'A Poor Gentleman' (1899); S.F. Bullock, *Robert Thorne. The Story of a London Clerk* (1907), cited in Richard N. Price, 'Society, Status and Jingoism: The Social Roots of Lower Middle Class Patriotism, 1870-1900', in Crossick, ed., *The Lower Middle Class in Britain*, p. 97.
4   Joseph Parker, *The Times*, 18 October 1900, p. 6; David A. Hamer, *The Politics of Electoral Pressure. A Study in the History of Victorian Reform Agitations* (Hassocks, 1977); Jon Lawrence, 'Class and Gender in the Making of Urban Toryism, 1880-1914', *English Historical Review* 108: 428 (July 1993), p. 637. Gladstone's support for fruit culture, if not vegetarianism, was noted in the *VM* obituary, July 1898, pp. 290-291.
5   Frances M. Lappe, *Diet for a Small Planet* (New York, 1971); Peter Singer, *Animal Liberation. A New Ethics for our Treatment of Animals* (New York, 1975).
6   Martin Daunton and Bernhard Reiger, eds, *Meanings of Modernity: Britain from the late-Victorian Era to World War II* (Oxford, 2001), p. 3; see S.S. Friedman, 'Definitional Excursus: The Meanings of Modern/Modernity/Modernism', *Modernism/Modernity* 8: 3 (2001), pp. 499-513; Marshall Berman, *All that is Solid Melts into Air. The Experience of Modernity* (1982; Harmondsworth, 1988).
7   Calhoun, 'What's new about new social movements?', pp. 385-427.
8   Thomas, *Man and the Natural World*, Twigg, 'Vegetarian Movement'.
9   Twigg, 'Vegetarian Movement', p. 64.
10 See Turner, *The Body and Society*, pp. 157-176.
11 Twigg, 'Vegetarian Movement', pp. 137-138; Ronald Pearsall, *The Worm in the Bud. The World of Victorian Sexuality* (1969; London, 1983), p. 196: citing Shaw's comment on the convenience of living like Christ, through modernization.
12 Morton, *Radical Food*, vol. 1, p. 7.
13 *Vegetarian Advocate*, 1 October 1849, p. 13: vegetarianism in relation to Manchester artisans; 15 August 1850, p. 3: concerning support in counting houses, iron manufactories, overheated mills.
14 Turner, *The Body and Society*, pp. 157-176.
15 Turner, *Reckoning with the Beast*, p. 33.
16 Sally Ledger, *The New Woman. Fiction and Feminism at the Fin de Siècle* (Manchester, 1997), ch. 6.
17 *HGA* even described itself in 1899 as 'the record of a Fin de Siècle protest against the inhumanity of the Age in general and Carnivorism in particular'.
18 A development at odds with definitions of modernity which marginalize the irrational, see Daunton and Reiger, eds, *Meanings of Modernity*, p. 7.
19 Amelia Lewis, *National Food and Fuel Reformer*, 8 January 1876, p. 149.
20 Anna Kingsford, in *Westminster and Foreign Quarterly Review*, October 1874, p. 510.
21 Forward, *Fifty Years of Food Reform*, ch. 1.
22 'The novelty of the Nineteenth Century', *HH* flyer, 1 February 1880.
23 See Josiah Oldfield, 'Vegetarian Still', *The Nineteenth Century*, August 1898, pp. 246-252.

24 'Vegetarianism' by J.E. Smith, *Family Herald*, 9 November 1850, pp. 444-445; Lane, *Dietetics*, p. 39.
25 *Medium and Daybreak*, 22 August 1890, p. 539.
26 George Dornbusch, *VM*, June 1852; John Madge, *Vegetarian*, 15 April 1893, p. 189 and Forward, *HGA*, vol. 1, no. 2, p. 27 on the 'age of movements'.
27 *VA*, 1 April 1850, pp. 99-101.
28 *Westminster Review*, October 1874, p. 514.
29 *Reasoner*, vol. 3, 1847, pp. 447-449.
30 *The Healthian*, May 1842, p. 44.
31 Alex Owen, 'Occultism and the "Modern Self" in *Fin de Siècle* Britain', in Daunton and Reiger, eds, *Meanings of Modernity*, p. 74.
32 Oldfield, 'Vegetarian Still', p. 252; letter from William E.A. Axon, 17 August 1880 in Frederick Burckhardt and Sydney Smith, eds, *A Calendar of the Correspondence of Charles Darwin, 1821-1882* (2nd edn, Cambridge, 1994), p. 533; and the letter from Darwin to Karl Höchberg on vegetable diet, 25 February 1879 (in response to Höchberg's inquiry about man's adaptation to mixed diet, p.503) which appeared in *HH*, n.s., 31 (1880), p. 180. A.T. Wintle identified the vegetarian movement's rise with evolution, *Dietary of Troops*, p. iii. Another vegetarian treated diet from an 'evolutionary standpoint', *Vegetarian*, 25 January 1894, p. 39.
33 Henry S. Salt, 'Food Reform', *Westminster Review*, October 1886, pp. 483-499.
34 See advertisements in *HH*, 1895 for Wallace Air Bread 'mixed by machinery'. See Salt, 'Food Reform', p. 496, for faith in human ingenuity in the creation of substitutes.
35 See also 'Minor Hugo', *Hints and Reflections*, vol. 3, Part I.I, p. 8.
36 See Hills, *Natural Food of Man*, p. 46. On the clash between science and zoophilists, see Turner, *Reckoning with the Beast*, pp. 95-120.
37 Turner, *Reckoning with the Beast*, p. 99.
38 'B.W.P.' in *British Controversialist*, 1850, p. 309.
39 See for instance, G.S. Jealous, *Journal of Health*, vol. 9, n.s., pp. 144-147.
40 *MD*, 10 October 1890, p. 652. In the early-nineteenth century, Eileen Yeo has argued, it was a 'still molten situation', and talk of 'escape' and 'adjustments' to capitalism in this period are simplistic, 'Robert Owen and Radical Culture', in Pollard and Salt, eds., *Robert Owen*, p. 106.
41 Berman, *All that is Solid Melts into Air*, p. 23. See also Klaus Eder, *The Social Construction of Nature. A Sociology of Ecological Enlightenment* (London, 1996), p. 136, for this sense that vegetarianism represented a 'counter-current' within and integral to modernity.
42 Calhoun, 'What's new about new social movements?'
43 See, for instance, the statement quoted in *Vegetarian*, 27 May 1893, p. 249: 'It is a very great satisfaction to find the educated West taking such intelligent interest in one of the cherished institutions of the East.'
44 See *Bloodless Revolution* for the impact on western philosophers and a wider reading public, of early-modern travel writing, with its revelation of Hindu *ahisma*, or non-violence to living things. Stuart stresses the 'ancient history of passionate curiosity' behind this cross-cultural experience in the form of Pythagorean and neo-Platonist associations (pp. 40-44) and also examines the role played by Orientalism in the Romantic era. See his important brief discussion about the question of 'genuine

influence' as opposed to the Saidian formulation of Orientalism, in ch. 4, note 3, pp. 523-524.
45 Lane, *Dietetics*, p. 6.
46 See J.E.B. Mayor's comment, *Vegetarian*, 7 January 1888, p. 4: about the East's resistance to western barbarities such as beef and brandy 'which follow and dishonour the standard of the Cross'.
47 *Edinburgh Weekly Herald*, reported in *VM*, December 1855, pp. 104-105; *VM*, 1 August 1857, p. 102, quoting the *Glasgow Daily Bulletin*.
48 E.g., Henry S. Salt, *A Plea for Vegetarianism* (1886); A.M.S. Roskruge, *The Most Eccentric Book Ever Published* (London, 1895), p. 34.
49 'Vegetarianism' by J.E. Smith, *Family Herald*, 9 November 1850, pp. 444-445.
50 T.P. Smith, *Fortnightly Review*, July-December 1895, p. 763; H. Thompson, 'Why "Vegetarian"?', *The Nineteenth Century*, April 1898, p. 569.
51 Thompson, 'Why Vegetarian?', *The Nineteenth Century*, June 1898, p. 973.
52 Granville, *Westminster Review*, December 1893, quoted in *Vegetarian*, 11 January 1894, p. 22. Vegetarians responded by characterizing their age as one of decadent dyspeptics, see Oldfield, 'Vegetarian Still', p. 251. For degeneration or regression as *part* of evolution, see David Trotter, *The English Novel in History. 1895-1920* (London, 1993), ch.7, 'Degeneration.'
53 *Food*, May 1887, p. 102.
54 Florence Fenwick-Miller, *Illustrated London News*, quoted in *Vegetarian*, 12 September 1896.
55 George W. Foote, in Henry S. Salt, ed., *The New Charter. A Discussion of the Rights of Men and the Rights of Animals* (London, 1896). Brown's essay on 'Physical Puritanism', referred to the 'sweet-minded botanical livers of those aeons'.
56 Nordau, *Degeneration*, p. 209.
57 *Vegetarian*, 28 January 1888, p. 4.
58 *VA*, June 1850, p. 140, William Cross.
59 Forward, *Fifty Years of Food Reform*, Preface.

BIBLIOGRAPHY

Archives
Bishopsgate Institute Library, London
    George Howell Collection, newspaper clippings on vegetarian restaurants.
    G.J. Holyoake, Diary 1849.
Bodleian Library, University of Oxford
    Johnson Collection of Printed Ephemera: Vegetarian Societies, boxes 1-3.
British Library
    Evanion Collection of Ephemera: vegetarian advertisements, 1884-1889.
    Lord Chancellor's Plays, vol. CLXXII and CLXXIII: 'Bloomerism or Follies of the Day. A Farce. In one act', Add. 43037, ff.254-269; 'The Vegetarians' altered from 'Travelers [sic] beware', Add. 43037, ff.183-197b.
    Add. 78156, Cruikshank Letters, f.29. Letter from George Dornbusch to George Cruikshank, (24 April 1854).
Co-operative Union Library
    Robert Owen Papers.
Dundee City Archives
    Dundee Dietetic Reform Society Minutes and Accounts Book, 1877-1883.
Greater Manchester County Records Office
    Vegetarian Society Archive.
Liverpool Records Office
    Joseph Edwards Papers.
Manx National Heritage, Douglas, Isle of Man
    Pierre H.J. Baume Papers.
Trinity College, Cambridge
    J.E.B. Mayor Papers.

University of Edinburgh
  Thomas R. Allinson Papers.
University of Southampton Special Collections, Broadlands Records
  Mount Temple Papers.
Private collections
  Job Caudwell Papers George Dornbusch Papers.

Journals, serials and newspapers

1. *Vegetarian*

Almonds and Raisins
Annual Report of the WVU
The Apple Tree Annual
The British Vegetarian
Burlington House
The Children's Garden
The Children's Realm
Daisy Basket. For Children
The Danielite Star
Dietetic Reformer and Vegetarian Messenger
The Food Reform Magazine / Food Reform Journal
Health Reform
The Healthian
The Herald of Health
The Herald of the Golden Age
The Hygienic Advertiser
The Hygienic Adviser
The Hygienic Review
Ivy Leaves
The Merry-go-Round
The New Age and Concordium Gazette and Temperance Advocate
Nichols' Journal of Sanitary and Social Science
The Scottish Health Reformeer
The Truth-Tester, Temperance Advocate and Healthian Journal
The Vegetarian
The Vegetarian Advocate, late Truth-Tester
The Vegetarian Messenger
The Vegetarian Messenger and Dietetic Reformer
The Vegetarian Messenger and Health Review
The Vegetarian News
The Vegetarian Review
The Vegetarian Yearbook
The Weekly Star and Vegetarian Restaurant Gazette

2. *Physical Puritanism*

The Abstainer and Temperance Physician
The Alliance
The Anti-Vaccinator and Public Health Journal
Dr Skelton's Botanic Record and Family Herald
The British Anti-Tobacco Journal
The British League; or Total Abstainers' Magazine
Hahnemannian Flysheet
The Hydropathic Record
The Journal of Health
The Journal of Health and Phrenological Magazine
The Journal of Health, Medical Eclectic and Phrenological Journal
The Journal of Health, Medical Eclectic and Vegetarian Messenger
Livesey's Moral Reformer
The London and Lincolnshire Mirror of Tee-Totalism
Monthly Homoeopathic Review
The National Temperance Chronicle
Notes of a New Truth. A Monthly Journal of Homoeopathy
The [People's Magazine and] Progressionist
The Provincial Homeopathic Gazette
Report of the Proceedings of the Hartwell Peace and Temperance Festival
Staunch Teetotaller
Teetotal Journal, or General Temperance Library
Temperance Lancet
Temperance News and Weekly Journal of Literature and Humanity
The Teetotal Progressionist
The Temperance Star
The Truth-Seeker
United Temperance Gazette

The Vaccination Inquirer and Health Review
The Water Cure Journal and Hygienic
   Magazine
The Zoist

3. Other progressive and reform journals

Some Account of the Progress of the Truth as it is in Jesus
The Animal World
The Animals' Friend
The Animals' Friend, or The Progress of Humanity
The Beehive
The Bohemian. An Unconventional Newspaper
The Bond of Brotherhood
The British Friend
The British Spiritual Telegraph
The Chartist Circular
The Clarion
The Commonweal
The Co-operator [and Herald of Health]
   continued as *The Anti-Vaccinator*
Cooper's Journal
Co-operative News
The Crank. An Unconventional Magazine
The Divinearian, or, Apostle of the Messiahdom
Douglas Jerrold's Weekly Newspaper
Educational Circular and Communist Apostle
The English Leader
The Esoteric
The Family Herald
The Fonotypic Journal
Food and Health Leaves
The Friend
The Friend of the People
The Helper: a journal of human improvement
The Herald of Co-operation and Organ of the Redemption Society
The Herald of Progress
Home Links
The Housekeeper. A Domestic Journal
Howitt's Journal
Human Nature
Humanity. The Journal of the Humanitarian League
The Labour Annual
The Lady's Own Paper
Liberty
Light
The Light of Reason
The London Phalanx
The Medium and Daybreak
The Moral World
The Morning Star, or Herald of Progression.
The Movement
The National Food and Fuel Reformer
National Reformer and Manx Weekly Review
The New Age
The New Moral World
New Order
The Oracle of Reason
The Peace Advocate and Correspondent
The People
The People's Advocate
The People's Journal
The People's Press
The Phonetic Journal
The Phonetic News
The Pioneer and Weekly Record of Movements
The Precursor of Unity
Present Day
The Promethean
The Public Good
The Reasoner
The Red Republican
Refreshment News
Report of the Bread Reform League
Shafts
The Shepherd
The Socialist
The Spirit of the Age
The Spirit of the Times
The Spiritual Magazine
The Standard of Freedom
The Sun Beam
The Truth Promoter
The Truth Seeker
The Two Worlds
The Weekly Tribune
The Women's Penny Paper
The Woman's Signal and *Signal Budget*
The Working Bee and Herald of the Hodsonian Community
The Zoophilist

4. Others

All the Year Round
Annual Register
Associated Medical Journal
The Athenaeum
The British Controversialist
British Medical Journal
Chambers's Edinburgh Journal
Cheltenham Free Press
Daily News
Diogenes
Dublin University Magazine
Dublin Medical Press
Dundee Year Book
Economy
English Mechanic and World of Science
Food: A Monthly Journal of Dietetics
Food, Water, and Air in Relation to the Public Health
Fraser's Magazine
Gentleman's Magazine
Illustrated London News
Journal of the Society of Arts
The Lady's Newspaper
The Lancet
Littell's Living Age
Manchester Guardian
News of the World
The Nonconformist
The Northern Star
Notes and Queries
The Nursing Record and Hospital World
Penny Illustrated Paper
Proceedings of the Medical Society of London
Provincial Medical and Surgical Journal
The Public Health
Punch
Saturday Review
The Times
Weekly Dispatch
Worcester Herald

Vegetarian Books

1. Vegetarian tracts/items by vegetarians

ANDREW, A., *Vegetarianism and Evolution, or, what is Vegetarianism?* (London: Millington, 1887).
ANON., *Prospectus for the Establishment of Concordium* (London: W. Strange, 1841).
ANON., *A Brief Account of the First Concordium* (London: Concordium, 1843)
ANON., *The Manual of Vegetarianism. A Complete Guide to Food Reform* (London: Hygienic Publishing Union, 1890).
ANON., *Repertoire Programme. Essays, Songs, Recipes* (London: LVS, n.d.).
ANON., *How to Begin* (Manchester: VS, n.d.).
'A. S. H.,' *Fruit the Proper Food of Man* (Manchester: VS, 1888).
'A VEGETARIAN', *Stomach Worship, A Growl* (Liverpool: Howell/London: Simpkin, Marshall, 1881).
AXON, W.E.A., *Corn or Cattle* (Manchester: Heywood, 1887).
—— ed., *Manchester Vegetarian Lectures. First Series* (Manchester: VS, 1888).
—— *Vegetarianism and National Economy: A Lecture Delivered in the Brotherton Hall, Manchester, on May 25th, 1887* (Manchester: VS, 1889).
—— *Vegetarianism and the Intellectual Life: A Lecture Delivered in the Brotherton Hall, Manchester, on Nov. 8th, 1887* (Manchester: VS, 1889).
—— *Shelley's Vegetarianism* (Manchester: VS, 1891).
—— *Fifty Years of the Vegetarian Society* (Manchester: VS, 1897).
—— *Sixty Years of the Vegetarian Society* (Manchester: VS, 1907).
BAKER, A., [writing as 'Domestica'] *The Vegetist's Dietary. Compiled, as nearly as possible, in accordance with the principles laid down by Sylvester Graham for the Vegetarian Society of England* (London: Tweedie, 1877).

BAKER, T., *A Battling Life* (London: Kegan Paul, Trench, 1885).
BARHAM, F.F., 'A Memoir of the late James Pierrepont Greaves Esq.' in *An Odd Medley of Literary Curiosities*, part 2 (London: the Author, 1845).
BEARD, S.H., *Is Flesh-Eating Morally Defensible?* (6th edn; Ilfracombe, OGA)
BEAVAN, E., *Lil Grey; or, Arthur Chester's Courtship* (London: S.W. Partridge, 1878).
BENTLEY, J., *State of Education, Crime etc. Etc ...Or, education as it is; ought to be; and might be* (London: Longman, 1842).
―― *Gems of Biography. My Life. During Infancy. Boyhood. Youth.* 'Vol. 1' (London: J. Bentley, 1856).
BOWDICH, E.W., *New Vegetarian Dishes* (London: G. Bell, 1892).
[BROTHERTON, M.,] *Vegetarian Cookery. By a Lady. With an Introductory Explanation of the principles of vegetarianism by the late James Simpson*, 6th edn (London: F. Pitman, 1866).
CAIRD, M., *Beyond the Pale. An Appeal on Behalf of the Victims of Vivisection* (London: W. Reeves, 1897).
CAMPBELL, A., *Letters and Extracts from the MS Writings of James Pierrepont Greaves* (London: Concordium/John Chapman, 1842-5).
CARPENTER, E., *England's Ideal and other Papers on Social Subjects* (London: Swan Sonnenschein, Lowrey, 1887).
―― *My Days and Dreams. Being Autobiographical Notes* (London: G. Allen and Unwin, 1916).
CARPENTER, R.L. ed., *Memoirs of the Life and Work of Philip Pearsall Carpenter* (London: Kegan Paul, 1880).
CAUDWELL, J., *Vegetarian Cookery for the Million* (London: Caudwell, six editions 1864-1865).
CLUBB, S.A., *Good influence. A Tale for the Young, who are willing to seek the stepping stone to health, intelligence and happiness, with an appendix* (London: Isaac Pitman).
COLLYNS, Rev. C.H., *Simplicity of Tastes* (2nd edn, revised, Manchester and London, 1879).
COOK, J.H., *How to Run a Health Food Store Successfully. By the Founder of the First* (Four Oaks, Warwick: Pitman Health Food Company).
COUCHMAN, W., *Man's Best Diet and Twenty Years' Trial of It* (Dunfermline: W. Clark, 1873).
―― *How to Marry and Live Well on a Shilling a Day* (11th edn, Manchester: VS, 1890).
DENSMORE, E., *How Nature Cures ... a New System of Hygiene* (London: Swan Sonnenschein, 1891).
―― *An Exposition of the Non-Starch Food System* (London: L.N. Fowler, 1891).
―― *Dr Allinson and Dogmatism* (London: L.N. Fowler, 1893).
DRIVER, J., *The Nature of Tobacco* (London: Burns, Nichols, 1881).
DUNCAN, J.E., *Flowers and Fruits, or Poetry, Philosophy, and Science* (London, 1843: printed for the author).
FORSTER, T.I.M., *Medicina Simplex; or, The Pilgrim's Waybook* (London: Keating and Brown, 1832).
FORWARD, C. W., *Practical Vegetarian Recipes. As used in the Principal Vegetarian Restaurants in London and the Provinces* (London: J.S. Virtue, 1891).
―― *Fifty Years of Food Reform. A History of the Vegetarian Movement in England* (London: Ideal Publishing Union, 1898).
―― *The Vegetarian Birthday Book* (London, 1898).

GOMPERTZ, L., *Fragments in Defence of Animals, and Essays on Morals, Soul and Future State; from the Author's Contributions to the Animals' Friend Society's Periodical* (London: Horsell, 1852).
GRAHAM, S., *Lectures on The Science of Human Life* (London: Horsell, 1854).
GROOM-NAPIER, C. O., *Tommy Try* (London: Chapman and Hall, 1869).
—— *Vegetarianism the Cure for Consumption* (Dunfermline, W. Clark: 1879).
—— *Vegetarian and Temperance Fête to His most serene Highness Prince of Mantua and Montferrat, was held at Greenwich, in a Pavilion specially erected, on Monday, April 21st 1879* (Dunfermline: W. Clark, 1879).
—— *Vegetarianism in the Bible: by the Prince of Mantua and Montferrat* (Dunfermline: W. Clark, 1879).
—— *Vegetarian and Temperance Fête to 335 Welsh Miners* (Dunfermline: W. Clark, 1879).
—— *Visions of the Interior of the Earth and of Past, Present and Future Events* (London: Simpkin, Marshall, 1894).
HANSARD, L.J. [as 'Minor Hugo'], *Hints and Reflections to Railway Travellers*, 3 vols (London: George Earle, 1843) vol. 3.
HARE, E.C., *Memoirs of Edward Hare CSI* (London: Grant Richards, 1900).
HARVEY, F.R., *Incontrovertible Facts in Relation to Diet* (Andover: F.R. Harvey, 1881).
HAUGHTON, S., *Memoir of James Haughton, with extracts from his private and published letters* (Dublin: Ponsonby, 1877).
HIBBERD, S., *Porphyry on Abstinence from animal food, translated from the Greek; being a carefully revised and amended text* (London: Horsell, 1851).
HILLS, A.F., *Essays on Vegetarianism, being a Collection of Articles Contributed to 'The Vegetarian'* (London: Ideal Publishing Union, 1895).
—— *Natural Food of Man* (Office of *The Vegetarian*, Memorial Hall, 1893).
—— *Reaction, a Speculation* (Office of *The Vegetarian*, Memorial Hall, 1893).
—— *Principles and Practice* (Office of *The Vegetarian*, Memorial Hall, 1893).
HORSELL, E., *The Penny Domestic Assistant and Guide to Vegetarian Cookery* (London: Horsell, 1850).
[HORSELL, W.], *The Life and Labours of Jabez Inwards* (London: W. Horsell, n.d.).
—— *The Board of Health and Longevity, or Hydropathy for the People* (London: Houlston and Stoneman, 1845).
—— *Cholera Prevented by the Adoption of a Vegetarian Diet; and cured by a Judicious Application of the Hydropathic Treatment* (London: W. Horsell, 1849).
—— *The Science of Cooking Vegetarian food: also the rise and progress of the Vegetarian Society, twelve reasons for not eating flesh, and answers to twenty objections to the vegetarian practice* (London: W. Horsell, 1856).
HOWITT, M., *Mary Howitt. An Autobiography*, 2 vols. (London: William Isbister, 1889).
HOYLE, W., *Remedies for the Poverty, Degradation and Misery which Exist* (London: Simpkin, Marshall, 1882).
INWARDS, J., *Memorials of Temperance Workers* (London, S.W. Partridge,1879).
ISHAM, C., *The Food that We Live On* (2nd edn, Northampton: Law, n.d.).
JONES, R., *Vegetarianism with Special Reference to its Connection with Temperance in Drinking* (Melbourne and Sydney: George Robertson, 1888).
KINGSFORD, A., [as 'Colossa'] *In My Lady's Chamber. A Speculative Romance, Touching a few Questions of the Day* (London: J. Burns, 1873).
—— *The Physiology of Vegetarianism* (Manchester: V.S., 1886).
—— *The Perfect Way in Diet. A Treatise Advocating a Return to the Natural and Ancient Food of our Race* (London, Kegan Paul, Trench, 1881).
—— *Health, Beauty and the Toilet* (London: F. Warne, 1886).

—— 'The Best Food for Man', *Westminster Review*, October 1874, p. 511.
LACY, F.E., 'The Vegetarian; or, a Visit to Aunt Primitive', *Metropolitan Magazine*, April 1847, pp. 403-413.
LANE, C., *Dietetics. An Endeavour to Ascertain the Laws of Human Development* (London: Whittaker, 1849).
LAWSON, W., C.D. Hunter and others, *Ten Years of Gentleman Farming at Blennerhasset with Co-operative Objectives* (London: Longman, Green, 1874).
LEES, F., *Dr Frederic Richard Lees* (London: H.J. Osborn, 1904).
LEES, F.R., *An Argument on Behalf of the Primitive Diet of Man* (London: F. Pitman, 1857).
LESTER, H.F., *Behind the Slaughterhouses* (London: W. Reeves, 1892).
LEWIS, A.M., *Humanity and Vegetarianism, being a paper read before the Vegetarian Federal Union* (London: L.V.S., 1892).
LONGMAN, F., *Fifteen Years Fight against Compulsory Vaccination* (London: F. Longman, 1900)
LONGSTAFFE, J. H. *Fifteen Reasons for Abstaining from the Use of the Flesh of Animals as Food. An Essay* (London: J. Caudwell, 1860).
MACDONALD, W. A. *Humanitism: the Scientific Solution of the Social Problem* (London: Trubner, 1890).
—— *Science and Ethics. Being a series of six lectures delivered under the auspices of the Natural Law Research League* (London: Swan Sonnenschein, 1895).
MAITLAND, E. *Anna Kingsford. Her Life, Letters, Diary and Work* 2 vols, (London: George Redway, 1896).
—— and E. Carpenter, *Vivisection. Two Essays* (London: W. Reeves, 1893).
MALCOLMSON, A.W., *The Aesthetic in Food* (Manchester and London: VS, 1899).
MANSELL, T., *Vegetarianism and Manual Labour. A lecture delivered in the Brotherton Hall, Manchester, on April 10th, 1888* (1897).
MAYOR, J.E.B., *Social Changes in Sixty Years* (Manchester: Vegetarian Society, 1897).
MILL, J.O., *Reform Cookery Book* (1904; 4th edn, 1909).
NEVILL, J.H.N., *The Biology of Daily Life* (London: Kegan Paul, Trench, Trubner, 1890).
NEWMAN, F.W., *Essays on Diet* (London: Kegan, Paul, Trench, 1883).
NICHOLS, T.L., *Behaviour: a Manual of Manners and Morals* (London: Longman, Green, 1874).
—— *Eating to Live. The Diet Cure: an Essay on the Relations of Food and Drink to Health, Disease and Cure* (London: Nichols, 1877).
—— *How to Live on 6d a Day* (London: Nichols, 1878).
—— *Dr Nichols' Penny Vegetarian Cookery. The Science and the Art of Selecting and Preparing a Pure, Healthful, and Sufficient Diet* (different editions from 1884).
O'CALLAGHAN, R.E., *The Best Diet for a Working Man, with Month's Dietary* (London: LVS, 1891).
OLDFIELD, J., *The Best Way to Begin Vegetarianism* (London: 'Vegetarian' Office).
—— *A Groaning Creation* (London: Ideal Publishing Union/W. Reeves, E.W. Allen, 1895).
—— 'Vegetarianism', *Encyclopaedia Britannica* (10th edn, 1902-03).
OUSELEY, G.J.R., *England Regenerated, through Justice to Ireland, or a Programme of Reforms, proposed to a Reformed Parliament. With Appendices on Food and Drink Reform, Burial and Cremation* (3rd edn, London: Nichols, 1888).
—— *The Gospel of the Holy Twelve known also as the Gospel of the Perfect Life. Edited by a Disciple of the Master from eastern and western sources* (Paris: Order of At-one-ment, 1901).
OWEN, T., *Personal Reminiscences of Oswestry Fifty Years Ago* (Oswestry: Owen, 1904).

PARKER, J.A., *Ernest England; or a Soul laid Bare* (London: Leadenhall Press, 1895).
PAYNE, A.G., *Cassell's Vegetarian Cookery. A Manual of Cheap and Wholesome Diet* (London: Cassell, 1895).
PITMAN, I. ed., *Memorial of Francis Barham* (London: Pitman, 1873).
POPE, M., *Novel Dishes for Vegetarian Households* (Bradford: Lund, 1893).
REED, T.A., *A Biography of Isaac Pitman* (London: Griffin and Furran, 1890).
[ROSKRUGE, A.M.S.], *The Most Eccentric Book Ever Published. The Cloven Hoof. A Literary Novelty reviewing the Odd Humours of Some Very Old Friends* (London: Ideal Publishing Union, 1895).
RUSHTON, A., *My Life. As Farmer's Boy, Factory Lad, Teacher and Preacher* 'vol. 1' (Manchester: S. Clarke, 1909).
SALT, H.S., *A Plea for Vegetarianism and Other Essays* (Manchester: VS, 1886).
—— ed., *The New Charter. A Discussion of the Rights of Men and the Rights of Animals* (London: Geo. Bell and Sons, 1896).
—— *Humanities of Diet* (London: Reeves, 1897).
—— *The Logic of Vegetarianism. Essays and Dialogues* (London: Ideal Publishing Union, 1899).
—— *Seventy Years Among the Savages* (London: George Allen and Unwin, 1921).
SHARMAN, W., *Plain Words to the Working Men of Sheffield now Abstaining from Dear Meat: with an appendix on what to eat and how to cook it* (Sheffield, J. Chapman, 1860).
[SIMPSON, J.], *The Products of the Vegetable Kingdom vs the Flesh of Animals as Food 'Part I'* (London: Whittaker, 1847).
—— *A Few Recipes of Vegetable Diet with Suggestions for the Formation of a Dietary, from which the Flesh of Animals is Excluded* ...(London: Whittaker, 1847).
SMITH, J., *Fruits and Farinacea The Proper Food of Man* (London: John Churchill, 1845).
—— *The Principles and Practice of Vegetarian Cookery. Founded on Chemical Analysis, and Embracing the Most Approved Methods of the Art* (London: Simpkin, Marshall, 1860).
STORIE, J., *The Dietetic Errors of the People the Cause of the Increase of Mortality from Diseases of the Respiratory Organs* (East Linton: J. and W. Storie, 1866).
SUTTON, H.S., *The Evangel of Love* (London: C.A. Bartlett, 1847).
TARRANT-SIDDONS, T., *Food Reform Cookery Book* (London, 8th edn, 1889).
TAYLOR, A., *Memories of a Student* (London: Simpkin, Marshall, 1895).
[VASEY, G.], *Illustrations of eating. Displaying the Omnivorous Character of Man* (London: J.R. Smith, 1847).
[VASEY, G.], *Individual Liberty, Legal, Moral and Licentious; In which the political fallacies of J.S. Mill's essay 'On Liberty' Are Pointed Out* (London: George Vasey, 1867).
WALLACE, C.L.H., *366 Menus. Each consisting of a soup, a savoury course, a sweet course, a cheese course, and a beverage, with all their suitable accompaniments, for every day in the year, no dish or beverage being once repeated, all arranged according to the season, and without the introduction of fish, flesh, fowl, or intoxicants* (London: Wallace, 1885).
WALSH, W., *My Spiritual Pilgrimage. From Sectarianism to Free Religion* (London: Free Religious Movement, 1925).
WARD, W.G., *Food for the Million, Letters to 'The Times' with other Selections* (London: F. Pitman, 1880).
WEILSHAUSER, E., *Der Vegetariener. Zeitschrift fur Naturgemasse Nahrund Lebensweise* (Berlin: Zahn, 1876).
WILLIAMS, H., *The Ethics of Diet. A Catena of Authorities deprecatory of the Habit of Flesh-eating* (London: Pitman, 1883).
WILSON, J., *Joseph Wilson. His Life and Work* (London: Lund, Humphries, n.d.).

WINTLE, A.T., *The Dietary of Troops* (London: The 'Vegetarian' office, 1892).
WRIGHT, H.G., Miss Wright and assistants, *Exposition of an Educative Effort at Alcott House Ham Common, near Richmond, Surrey* (London: Torras, 1839).

2. Vegetarians in fiction

BARRY, W.F., *The New Antigone. A Romance* (London: Macmillan, 1887).
BEGBIE, H., *The Curious and Diverting Adventures of Sir John Sparrow Bt., or, the Progress of an Open Mind* (London: Methuen, 1902).
BELLAMY, E., *Equality* (London: Heinemann, 1897).
BENSON, E.F., *The Freaks of Mayfair* (London: T.N. Foulis, 1916).
—— *Paying Guests* (London: Hutchinson, 1929).
[BLACKWELL, A.], *Ellen Braye, or, The Fortune-Teller* (London: Saunders and Otley, 1841).
BROWNSON, O.A., *The Spirit-Rapper* (Boston: Little, Brown, 1854).
BUCHANAN, R., *The Reverend Annabel Lee. A Tale of To-morrow* (London: C.A. Pearson, 1898).
BUTLER, S., *Erewhon, or, Over the Range* (1872; London: Penguin, 1977).
CHILD, L.M., *Philothea* (Boston: Otis, Broaders, 1836).
DOYLE, A.C., 'The Red-headed League,' *The Strand Magazine*, August 1891.
ELIOT, G., *Middlemarch. A Study of Provincial Life* (1871-1872; London: Penguin, 1965).
—— 'A Minor Prophet' in *The Legend of Jubal, and Other Poems* (London and Edinburgh: W. Blackwood and Sons, 1874).
GISSING, G., *Demos. A Story of English Socialism* (1886; London: Smith, Elder, 1897).
—— *The Odd Women* (1893; London: Virago, 1980).
—— *The Crown of Life* (London: Methuen, 1899).
—— 'A Poor Gentleman' (1899; reprinted in *The House of Cobwebs and Other Stories*, London: Constable, 1906).
—— *The Private Papers of Henry Ryecroft* (1903; London: Archibald Constable, 1939).
—— *Will Warburton. A Romance of Real Life* (London: Archibald Constable, 1905).
HAGGARD, H.R., *She. A History of Adventure* (1887; London: Longmans, Green, 1894).
HIBBERD, J.S., 'Beans without bacon. A Pythagorean Romance,' in *The Golden Gate and Silver Steps with bits of tinsel round about it* (London: E.W. Allen, 1886).
HUDSON, W.H., *A Crystal Age* (London: T. Fisher Unwin, 1887).
JAMES, H., *The Bostonians* (1885-6; Harmondsworth, Penguin, 1984).
KELTY, M.A., *Visiting My Relations, and its Results; a series of small episodes in the life of a recluse* (London: William Pickering, 1851).
KINGSLEY, C., *Alton Locke. Tailor and Poet* (1850; London: Macmillan, 1878).
LINTON, E.L., *The Autobiography of Christopher Kirkland*, (London, 1885).
LOWNDES, M.B., *The Lodger* (Leipzig: Tauchnitz, 1913).
LYTTON, E.B. [as 'Pisistratus Caxton'], *My Novel; or, Varieties in English Life*.
—— *The Coming Race* (London: George Routledge, c.1893).
—— *Kenelm Chillingly. His Adventures and Opinions* (Leipzig: Bernhard Tauchnitz, 1873).
MEREDITH, G., *The Ordeal of Richard Feverel* (1859; London: Chapman and Hall, 1890).
—— *One of Our Conquerors* (London: Chapman and Hall, 1892).
—— *Beauchamp's Career* (1897; London: Archibald Constable, 1902).
MOOR, J.F., *Thoughts Regarding the Future State of Animals* (Winchester: Warren, 1893).
OLIPHANT, M., 'Zaidee: A Romance', *Blackwood's Edinburgh Magazine*, December 1854-December 1855.
'RADICAL FREELANCE', *The Philosophers of Foufouville* (New York: G.W. Carleton, 1868).
ROWE, R., *Episodes in an Obscure Life* (London: Bungay, 1871).

SAVAGE, M.W., *Reuben Medlicott, Or The Coming Man* (London: Chapman and Hall, 1852).
SHAW, G.B., *Immaturity* (1879; London: Constable, 1931).
TAYLOR, B., *Beauty and the Beast and Tales of Home* (New York, 1872).
'TEMPLE CHAMBERS', *The Works of 'Temple Chambers'*, vol.1: *The family of Smith, or Milk and Eggs. An entirely original and largely vegetarian comic opera in two acts* (Surbiton: Bull and Son, 1903).
UZANNE, O., 'The End of Books', *Scribner's Magazine* 16 (July-December 1894), pp. 221-231.
WARD, H., *The History of David Grieve* (3 vols, London: Smith, Elder, 1892).
WELLS, H.G., *Love and Mr Lewisham* (1898; London and New York: Harper and Brothers, 1900).
—— *The First Men in the Moon* (1901; *The Works of H.G. Wells*, Atlantic Edition, vol. 6, London: T. Fisher Unwin, 1925).
—— *Ann Veronica* (1909; London: Virago, 1987).
ZANGWILL, I., *The Children of the Ghetto. A Study of a Peculiar People* (1892; London: W. Heinemann, 1897).
—— *Without Prejudice* (London: T. Fisher Unwin, 1896).
—— *The Grey Wig: Stories and Novelettes* (London: Macmillan, 1903).

3. Articles and chapters on vegetarianism

ANON., 'Vegetarianism', *Household Words* (May-Oct 1881), 28 May 1881, pp. 96-97.
ANON., 'The Roving Englishman. The Philosophy of Dining', *Household Words*, no. 131, 1853, p. 231.
ANON., 'Dornbusch', *Chambers's Edinburgh Journal*, no. 914, 2 July 1881, pp. 430-432.
ANON. [Samuel Brown], 'Physical Puritanism', *The Westminster Review* 57, April 1852, pp. 405-42 [reprinted in *Littell's Living Age* 34: 426, July 17 1852, pp. 129-143].
ANON., 'Singular Sects', *Howitt's Journal*, 18 September 1847, pp. 180-182.
ANON., 'City', *The Popular Encyclopaedia, or, Conversations Lexicon* (new edn, London: Blackie, 1873-76), half-volume III, pp. 365-367.
ANON., 'The Fall of Rome', *Blackwood's Edinburgh Magazine*, 59, no. 368 (June 1846), p. 697.
ANON., 'A Lecture on Journalism', *Blackwood's Edinburgh Magazine*, 68, no. 422 (December 1850).
ANON., 'The Congress and the Agapedome', *Blackwood's Edinburgh Magazine*, September 1851 (vol. 70).
ANON., 'War and Woodcraft', *Blackwood's Edinburgh Magazine*, April 1856.
ANON., 'Popular Literature – Tracts', *Blackwood's Edinburgh Magazine*, May 1859.
ANON., 'The New Humanitarianism', *Blackwood's Edinburgh Magazine*, January 1898, pp. 98-106.
ANON., 'The Vegetarian Creed', *Littell's Living Age*, vol. 216, issue 2792, 8 January 1898, p. 127 (from *The Speaker*).
ANON., 'Whig Principles. What's Left of Them', *United States Democratic Review* 34: 6 (December 1854), pp. 465-477.
BAGWELL, E., 'Quakerism in Ireland', *Fortnightly Review*.
CONWAY, M.D., 'South Coast Saunterings in England', *Harper's New Monthly Magazine* 39: 231, August 1869, pp. 330-353.
—— 'Sheffield – A Battlefield of English Labour', *Harper's New Monthly Magazine*, April 1868, pp. 594-605.

DAVIES, C.M., *Heterodox London, or Phases of Free Thought in the Metropolis* 2 vols (London: Tinsley Brothers, 1874), vol. 2.
DICKENS, C., 'Whole Hogs', *Household Words* no. 74, 23 August 1851, pp. 505-507.
DUNN, G., 'A Defeated Transcendentalist', *Blackwood's Magazine*, February 1893, pp. 236-252.
GARRISON, W. P., 'The Isms of Forty Years Ago', *Harper's New Monthly Magazine* 60: 356, January 1880.
[GOVETT, R.,] *Vegetarianism. A Dialogue* (London: Campbell, 1849).
GROOM-NAPIER, C.O., 'Autobiography of a Vegetarian. A true Narrative of a successful career reported by C.O.G. Napier of Merchiston, F.G.S.', *Fraser's Magazine* [reprinted in *Littell's Living Age* 130: 1679, 12 August 1876, pp. 427-434].
KINGSFORD, A., 'The Best Food for Man,' *Westminster Review* 102, October 1874, pp. 500-514.
OLDFIELD, J., 'Vegetarian Still', *The Nineteenth Century*, August 1898, pp. 246-252.
SALT, H.S., 'Food Reform', *Westminister Review*, October 1886, pp. 483-499.
SHAW, G.B., 'Shaming the Devil about Shelley', *The Albermarle Review*, September 1892, reprinted in *Pen Portraits and Reviews by Bernard Shaw* (London: Constable, 1931, 2).
SMITH, T.P., 'Vegetarianism', *Fortnightly Review*, July-December 1895, pp. 752-764.
SOUTHEY, R., 'The Roman Catholic Question', *Quarterly Review* 38 (October 1828), p. 556.
THOMPSON, H., 'Why "Vegetarian"?' *The Nineteenth Century*, April 1898, pp. 557-569.
—— 'Why Vegetarian?' *The Nineteenth Century*, June 1898, pp. 966-976.
TUPPER, M.F., 'The Rides and Reveries of Mr Aesop Smith', in *The Dublin University Magazine* vol. 48 (July-December 1856), pp. 660-661.

4. Other primary literature

ADAMS, W.E., *Memoirs of a Social Atom* (1903; New York: Augustus M. Kelley, 1968).
'AMICUS CURIAE', *Food for the Million. Maize against Potato* (London: Longman, Brown, 1847).
ANON., *A Plea for the Cattle. A Few Words, Addressed to the Upper and Influential Classes* (London: S.W. Partridge, 1866).
ANON., *International Council of Women. Report of Transactions*, 7 vols, vol. 7 *Women in Social Life* (London: T. Fisher Unwin, 1900).
ANON., *London at Dinner, or Where to Dine* (London: R. Hardwicke, 1858).
ANON., *The National Temperance Congress* (London: National Temperance Publishing Depot, 1884).
ANON., *Royal Album of Arts and Industry of Great Britain* (London: Wyman, 1887).
ANON., *Transactions of the National Association for the Promotion of Social Science, 1860* (London: Parker, 1861).
BALSILLIE, D., *The Ethic of Nature and its Practical Bearings* (Edinburgh: David Douglas, 1889).
BARKER, J.T. ed., *The Life of Joseph Barker. Written by Himself* (London: Hodder and Stoughton, 1880).
BAX, E.B., *Essays in Socialism New and Old* (London: E. Grant Richards, 1907).
—— *Outspoken Essays on Social Subjects* (London: W. Reeves, 1897).
BEACH, T.M. ['Henri le Caron'] *Twenty-five Years in the Secret Service. The Recollections of a Spy* (London: W. Heinemann, 1892).

BEATTY-KINGSTON, W., *Intemperance. Its causes and its remedies* (2nd edn, London: George Routledge and Sons, 1892).
BEETON, I., *Book of Household Management. Comprising information for the mistress ... Also, sanitary, medical, & legal memoranda; with a history of the origin, properties, and uses of all things connected with home life and comfort* (London: S.O. Beeton, 1861).
—— *Mrs Beeton's Everyday Cookery and Housekeeping Book. New Edition, Revised and Greatly Enlarged* (London: Ward, Lock, n.d.)
BLATCHFORD, R., *Merrie England* (London: The Clarion Press, 1908).
BONNER, H.P., *Charles Bradlaugh* (1894; London: Fisher Unwin, 1902).
BRAY, J.F., *A Voyage from Utopia* (1842; M.F. Lloyd-Prichard's edition, London: Lawrence and Wishart, 1957).
BREWSTER, D., *More Worlds than One. The Creed of the Philosopher and the Hope of the Christian* (London: John Murray, 1854).
BROWN, J., *The Food of the People. A Letter to Henry Fenwick Esq. MP* (London: Longman, Green, 1865).
BURN, J.I., *Familiar Letters on Population, Emigration, and Home Colonization* (London: Hatchard, 1832).
BUTLER, S., *The Way of All Flesh* (1903; Harmondsworth: Penguin, 1986).
CARLYLE, T., *Past and Present* (1843).
CHADWICK, E., *Report on the Sanitary Condition of the Labouring Population of Great Britain* (1842; this edn, M.W. Flinn, ed., Edinburgh: Edinburgh University Press, 1965).
CHISHOLM, C., *Comfort for the Poor! Meat Three Times a Day!!* (London: Ollivier, 1847).
COLT, M.D., *Went to Kansas, Being a Thrilling Account of an Ill-fated Expedition to that Fairy Land, and its Sad Result* (Watertown: L. Ingalls, 1862).
COOKE TAYLOR, W., *Notes on a Tour in the Manufacturing Districts of Lancashire; in a Series of Letters to his Grace the Archbishop of Dublin* (London: Duncan and Malcolm, 1842).
COULING, S., *History of the Temperance Movement in Great Britain and Ireland; from the Earliest Date to the Present Time* (London: W. Tweedie, 1862).
DICKENS Jnr., C., *Dickens's Dictionary of London. An Unconventional Handbook* (London: 'All the Year Round' office, 1879).
DODD, G., *The Food of London. A Sketch of the chief varieties, sources of supply. Probable quantities, modes of arrival, processes of manufacture etc ...* (London: Longman, Brown, Green and Longman, 1856).
DRAPER, J.W. *History of the Intellectual Development of Europe* (2 volumes, London: Bell and Daldry, 1864).
DRYSDALE, C.R., *The Population Question According to T.R. Malthus and J.S. Mill* (London: Standring, 1892).
DUNGLISON, R., *Medical Lexicon. A Dictionary of Medical Science*, 9th edn revised (London: Sampson Low, 1853).
EDE, W.M., *Cheap Food and Cheap Clothing. To Which is added Hints for the Management of Penny Dinners for Schoolchildren* (London: W. Scott, 1884).
EWART, J., *Meat Production. A Manual for Producers, Distributors, and Consumers of Butchers' Meat* (London: Crosby Lockwood, 1878).
FAWCETT, H., *Pauperism: Its Causes and Remedies* (London: Macmillan, 1871).
FISHER, J., *Where shall we get Meat? The Food Supplies of Western Europe being letters written in reply to the question, where is England to get Meat?* (London: Longman, Green, 1866).
FOWLER, T., *Progressive Morality. An Essay in Ethics* (London: Macmillan, 1884).

BIBLIOGRAPHY 283

FRETWELL, J., *Johannes Ronge and the English Protestants*, reprinted from the *Unitarian Review* (1888).
FROST, T., *Forty Years' Recollections: Literary and Political* (London: Sampson Low, 1880).
—— 'Social Utopias', *Chambers's Papers for the People* no.18 (1850), pp. 1-32.
GASKELL, E., *North and South* (1854; London: Penguin, 1970).
GIBBINS, H. DE B., *The English People in the Nineteenth Century. A Short History* (London: A and C. Black, 1898).
GRAHAM, S., *A Lecture to Young Men* (London: Strange, 1843).
GRAY, J., *The Social System. A Treatise on the Principle of Exchange* (Edinburgh: Tait, 1831).
HAGGARD, H.R., *Dr Therne* (London: Longmans, Green, 1898).
HALL, E.H., *Coffee Taverns, Cocoa Houses and Coffee Palaces. Their Rise, Progress, and Prospects; with a Directory* (London: S.W. Partridge, 1878).
HARDY, T., 'The Dorsetshire Labourer', *Longman's Magazine*, July 1883.
HARRISON, F., *Realities and Ideals. Social, Political, Literary and Artistic* (London: Macmillan, 1908).
HASSALL, A.H., *Food and its Adulterations; comprising the reports of the analytical Sanitary Committee of 'The Lancet'* (London: Longman, Brown, Green and Longmans, 1855).
HOGG, C., *On the Management of Infancy. With Remarks on the Influence of Diet and Regimen* (London: John Churchill, 1849).
HOLYOAKE, G.J., *The Social Means of Promoting Temperance with Remarks on Errors in its Advocacy* (London: Watts, c.1860).
—— *A History of Co-operation* (London: Trübner, 1879).
—— *The Jubilee History of the Leeds Industrial Co-operative Society from 1847 to 1897* (Leeds: Central Co-operative Offices, 1897).
—— *Sixty Years of an Agitator's Life* (London: T. Fisher Unwin, 1892).
HOOD, E. P. ed.,, *The Moral Reformer's Almanac. A Manual of Advancement and Civilisation for 1850* (London: C. Gilpin, 1850).
HUDSON, T., *Recollections and Random Reflections by Thomas Hudson* (London: Tweedie, 1875).
JEFFERIES, R., *Hodge and his Masters* (London: Smith, Elder, 1884).
JERROLD, T., *Our Kitchen Garden. The Plants We Grow and How to Cook Them* (London: Chatto and Windus, 1881).
KEANE, A.H., *Ethnology* (Cambridge: Cambridge University Press, 1896).
KOLB, G.F., *The Condition of Nations Social and Political With Comparative Tables of Universal Statistics* (London: G. Bell, 1880).
LANE, J., *An Anti-Statist, Communist Manifesto* (London: J. Lane, 1887).
LAW, J.T., *Law's Grocer's Manual. A Practical Guide for Tea and Provision Dealers* ...(Liverpool: J.T. Law, 1896).
LECKY, W.E.H., *History of European Morals from Augustus to Charlemagne* (London: Longman, Green, 1869), 2 vols, vol. 1.
LEWES, G.H., *The Physiology of Common Life* (2 vols, Edinburgh and London: W. Blackwood, 1859), vol. 1.
—— 'Theories of Food', *Blackwood's Edinburgh Magazine* 8: 542 (December 1860).
LINTON, W.J., *Memories* (London, Lawrence and Bullen, 1895).
MACAULAY, T.B., *History of England from the Accession of James II* vol. 1(1848; 10th edn, London: Longman, Brown, Green and Longmans, 1861).
MACMILLAN, M., *The Promotion of General Happiness. A Utilitarian Essay* (London: Swan Sonnenschein, 1890).

MALABARI, B.M., *The Indian Eye on English Life, or Rambles of a Pilgrim Reformer* (London: A. Constable, 1893).
MARSTON, R.B., *War, Famine and our Food Supply* (London: Sampson, Low, Marston, 1897).
MARX, K. and F. Engels, *The German Ideology*, written 1846; reprinted in vol. 5 of *The Collected Works of Karl Marx and Frederick Engels* (London: Lawrence and Wishart, 1976).
—— *Heroes of the Exile* (1852); in vol. 11 of *The Collected Works of Karl Marx and Friedrich Engels* (London: Lawrence and Wishart, 1979), pp.227-326.
MAYHEW, H., *London Labour and the London Poor* (London: Griffin, Bohn, 1861), vol. 1.
METCALFE, R., *The Rise and Progress of Hydropathy in England and Scotland* (London: Simpkin, Marshall, 1906).
MONCRIFF, B., *The Philosophy of the Stomach; or, an Exclusively Animal Diet* (London: Longman, Brown, Green and Longman, 1856).
MULHALL, M.G., *England's New Sheep Farm* (London: Edward Stanford, 1882).
MUSHET, D., *The Wrongs of the Animal World. To which is subjoined the speech of Lord Erskine on the Same Subject* (London: Hatchard and Son, 1839).
NEWNHAM-Davis, N., *Where and How to Dine in London* (London: Grant Richards, 1899).
NORDAU, M. S., *Degeneration* (translated from the second German edition 1895; Lincoln: University of Nebraska Press, 1993).
ORLEBAR, E.E., *Food for the People. Or Lentils, and other Vegetable Cookery* (London: Sampson, Low, 1879).
OWEN, R., *A New View of Society and Other Writings* (ed. with Introduction by G. Claeys) (1813 and after; London: Penguin, 1991).
PEARCE, W., *The Treatment and Cure of Diseases Incidental to Sedentary Life* (London: Groombridge, 1854).
PERRYCOSTE, F. H., [as 'A. Freelance'] *Towards Utopia* (London: Swan Sonnenschein, 1894).
PILKINGTON, G., *The Doctrine of Particular Providence* (London: Effingham Wilson, 1836).
—— *Travels through the United Kingdom* (2nd edn, London: Edmund Fry, 1839).
RATZEL, F., *The History of Mankind* (translated from the German; London: Macmillan, 1896).
READE, W., *The Martyrdom of Man* (17th edn, London: Kegan Paul, Trübner, 1903).
RIPLEY, W.Z., *The Races of Europe. A Sociological Study* (London: Kegan Paul, Trench, Trübner, 1899).
RUSKIN, J., *Fors Clavigera* (E.T. Cook and A. Wedderburn, eds, *The Works of John Ruskin. Library Edition*, vol. 29, London: George Allen, 1907).
SARGANT, W.L., *The Economy of the Labouring Classes* (London: Simpkin, Marshall, 1857).
SEYMOUR, H., *An Examination of the Malthusian Theory* (London, 1889).
SHAW, G.B., 'The Sanity of Art. An Exposure of the Current Nonsense about Artists Being Degenerate' (1895; reprinted in G.B. Shaw, *Major Critical Essays*, London: Constable , 1932), pp. 281-332.
SIMMONDS, P.L., *The Animal Food Resources of Different Nations* (London: E and F.N. Spon, 1885).
SMILES, S., *Character* (1878, London: John Murray, 1902).
SMITH, E., *Practical Dietary for Families, Schools and the Labouring Classes* (London: Walton and Maberley, 1864).
SMITH, W.A., *'Shepherd' Smith the Universalist. The Story of a Mind* (London: Sampson Low, Marston and Company, 1892).

SOUTHEY, R., 'The Roman Catholic Question', *Quarterly Review* 38 (October 1828).
SOYER, A., *The Pantropheon, or History of Food and its Preparation* (London: Simpkin, Marshall, 1853).
SPENCER, H., *Social Statics: or, The Conditions Essential to Human Happiness Specified, and The First of Them Developed* (London: John Chapman, 1851).
—— *Education: Intellectual, Moral, and Physical* (London: G. Manwaring, 1861).
SWANN, E.G. *The Bread Question; or, Where the Shoe Pinches* (London: Society of Emmet, 1855).
TAYLOR, I., *Ultimate Civilization and Other Essays* (London: Bell and Daldy, 1860).
URE, A., *The Philosophy of Manufactures: or, an Exposition of the Scientific, Moral, and Commercial Economy of the Factory System of Great Britain* (3rd edn, continued by P.L. Simmonds; London: H.G. Bohn, 1861).
VOLANT, F. and J.R. Watson eds, *Memoirs of Alexis Soyer with Unpublished Receipts and Odds and Ends of Gastronomy* (London: W. Kent, 1859).
WALLACE, A.R., *My Life. A Record of Events and Opinions* 2 vols (London: Chapman and Hall, 1905).
WIGHAM, *A Christian Philanthropist of Dublin* (London: Hodder and Stoughton, 1886).
WILLIAMS, T., *A Sketch of the Relations which Subsist between the Three Kingdoms of Nature* (Swansea: J. Williams, 1844).
WINSKILL, P. T., *The Comprehensive History of the Rise and Progress of the Temperance Reformation* (Warrington: P.T. Winskill, 1881).
—— *The Temperance Movement and its Workers. A Record of Social, Moral, Religious and Political Progress* (London: Blackie, 1892).
WOLFF, M.P., *Food for the Million. A Plan for Starting Public Kitchens* (London: Samson Low, 1884).

Secondary Works
1. Books and essays in books
ABZUG, R.H., *Cosmos Crumbling. American Reform and the Religious Imagination* (Oxford: Oxford University Press, 1994).
ADAMS, C.J., *The Sexual Politics of Meat. A Feminist-vegetarian Critical Theory* (1990; New York: Continuum, 1994).
—— 'Vegetarianism', in Laura Dabundo, ed., *Encyclopaedia of Romanticism. Culture in Britain, 1780s-1830* (London: Routledge, 1992).
ALBINSKI, N.B., *Women's Utopias in British and American Fiction* (London and New York: Routledge, 1988).
ALLINGHAM, H., and E.B. Williams, eds, *Letters of William Allingham* (London: Longman, Green, 1911).
ANDERSON, N.F., *Woman against Women in Victorian England* (Bloomington and Indianapolis: Indiana University Press, 1987).
ANON., *Fifty Years of the Bread and Food Reform League* (Norwich: Jarrold, 1928).
ANON., *A. Neave Brayshaw. Memoir and Selected Writings* (Birmingham: Woodbrooke Extension Committee of the Society of Friends, 1942).
ANTROBUS, D., *A Guiltless Feast. The Salford Bible-Christian Church and the Rise of the Modern Vegetarian Movement* (Salford: Salford City Council, 1997).
ARMYTAGE, W.H.G., *Heavens Below. Utopian Experiments in England 1560-1960* (London: Routledge and Kegan Paul, 1961).
—— *Yesterdays Tomorrows. A Historical Survey of Future Societies* (London: Routledge and Kegan Paul, 1968).

ASHE, G., *Gandhi. A Study in Revolution* (London: Heinemann, 1968).
ASHTON, R., *Little Germany. Exile and Asylum in Victorian England* (Oxford, Oxford University Press, 1986).
ASPINWALL, B., 'Social Catholicism and Health' in W.J. Sheils, ed., *The Church and Healing* (Oxford: Basil Blackwell, 1982).
BAKER, A., *The Life of Sir Isaac Pitman* (London: Isaac Pitman and Sons, 1930).
BARKAS, J., *The Vegetable Passion. A History of the Vegetarian State of Mind* (London: Routledge and Kegan Paul, 1975).
BARROW, L., 'Determinism and environmentalism in socialist thought', pp. 194-214 in R. Samuel and G.S. Jones, eds, *Culture, Ideology and Politics. Essays for Eric Hobsbawm* (London: Routledge and Kegan Paul, 1983).
—— *Independent Spirits. Spiritualism and English Plebeians. 1850-1910* (London and New York History Workshop Series: Routledge and Kegan Paul, 1986).
—— 'An imponderable Liberator: J.J. Garth Wilkinson', in R. Cooter ed., *Studies in the History of Alternative Medicine* (Basingstoke and London: Macmillan Press, 1988), pp. 88-117.
—— 'Why were most medical heretics at their most confident around the 1840s? (The other side of mid-Victorian medicine)', in R. French and A. Wear, eds, *British Medicine in an Age of Reform*, (London: Routledge, 1991), pp. 165-182.
BECKSON, K., *London in the 1890s. A Cultural History* (London and New York: W.W. Norton, 1992).
BELCHEM, J., *Popular Radicalism in Nineteenth Century Britain* (Basingstoke: Macmillan, 1996).
—— '"Temperance in all things": Vegetarianism, the Manx press and the alternative agenda of reform in the 1840s', ch. 11 in M. Chase, I. Dyck eds, *Living and Learning: Essays in Honour of J.F.C. Harrison* (Aldershot: Scolar Press, 1996), pp. 149-162.
BENDING, L., *The Representation of Bodily Pain in Late Nineteenth-Century Culture* (Oxford: Clarendon Press, 2000).
BENN, E.J.P., *Confessions of a Capitalist* (London: Hutchinson, 1925).
BENNETT, J., 'The London Democratic Association 1837-41: a Study in London Radicalism' ch. 3 in Epstein and D. Thompson, eds, *The Chartist Experience* (London: Macmillan, 1982), pp. 87-119.
BENZIE, W., *Dr F. J. Furnivall. Victorian Scholar Adventurer* (Oklahoma: Pilgrim Books, 1983).
BERMAN, M., *All that is Solid Melts into Air. The Experience of Modernity* (1982; Harmondsworth: Penguin, 1988).
BESTOR, A.E., *Backwoods Utopias. The Sectarian and Owenite Phases of Communitarian Socialism in America, 1663-1829* (Philadelphia, London and Oxford: University of Pennsylvania Press, 1950).
BINFIELD, C., '"I Suppose you are not a Baptist or a Roman Catholic?' in T.C. Smout, ed., *Victorian Values* (Proceedings of British Academy 78; Oxford University Press for the British Academy, 1990), pp.81-107.
BLAND, L., *Banishing the Beast. English Feminism and Sexual Morality. 1885-1914* (London: Penguin, 1995).
BLIX, G., ed., *Symposia of the Swedish Nutrition Foundation, VIII, Food Cultism and Nutrition Quackery* (Uppsala, 1970).
BOLSTERLI, M.J., *The Early Community at Bedford Park. The Pursuit of 'Corporate Happiness' in the First Garden Suburb* (London: Routledge and Kegan Paul, 1977).

BONDFIELD, M., *A Life's Work* (London: Hutchinson, *c*.1948).
BONNER, H.P., *Charles Bradlaugh. A Record of his Life and Work* (1894; London: T. Fisher Unwin, 1902).
BORDIN, R., *Frances Willard. A Biography* (London and Chapel Hill: University of North Carolina Press, 1986).
BRADLEY, I., *The Call to Seriousness. The Evangelical Impact on the Victorians* (London: Jonathan Cape, 1976).
BRIGGS, A., *The Age of Improvement.1793-1867* (1959; London: Longman, 1993).
BRIGGS, J., *A Woman of Passion. The Life of E. Nesbit, 1858-1928* (London: Hutchinson, 1987).
BRISTOW, E.J., *Vice and Vigilance. Purity Movements in Britain since 1700* (Dublin: Gill and Macmillan, 1977).
BURCKHARDT, F. and S. Smith eds, *A Calendar of the Correspondence of Charles Darwin, 1821-1882* (2nd edn, Cambridge: Cambridge University Press, 1994).
BURD, Van Akin., *Ruskin, Lady Mount Temple and the Spiritualists. An Episode in Broadlands History* (London: Brentham Press, 1982).
BURNETT, J., *Plenty and Want. A Social History of Diet in England from 1815 to the Present Day* (London: Thomas Nelson and Sons, 1966), and 3rd edn, 1989.
BURNETT, J., and D.J. Oddy, *The Origins and Development of Food Policies in Europe* (London: Leicester University Press, 1994).
BYNUM, W.F., and R. Porter, eds, *Medical Fringe and Medical Orthodoxy. 1750-1850* (London: Croom Helm/Wellcome Institute Series in History of Medicine, 1987).
BYNUM, W.F., S. Lock, and R. Porter, eds, *Medical Journals and Medical Knowledge* (London: Routledge, 1992).
CAINE, B., *English Feminism. 1780-1980* (Oxford: Oxford University Press, 1997).
CARPENTER, K.J., *Protein and Energy. A Study of Changing Ideas in Nutrition* (Cambridge: Cambridge University Press, 1994).
CARSON, G., *Cornflake Crusade* (London: Victor Gollancz, 1959).
CAYLEFF, S.E., *Wash and Be Healed. The Water Cure Movement and Women's Health* (Philadelphia: Temple University Press, 1987).
CEVASCO, G.A., ed., *The 1890s. An Encyclopedia of British Literature, Art and Culture* (New York and London: Garland, 1993).
CHASE, M., *'The People's Farm'. English Radical Agrarianism* (Oxford: Clarendon Press, 1988).
—— 'Republican Movement or Moment', ch. 4 in D. Nash and A. Taylor, eds, *Republicanism in Victorian Society* (Stroud: Sutton, 2000), pp. 35-50.
CHENEY, E.D., *Louisa May Alcott. Her Life, Letters, and Journals* (1889; London: Sampson Low, 1890).
CHESTERTON, G.K., *George Bernard Shaw* (1910; London: J. Lane, Bodley Head, 1935).
—— *Autobiography* (London: Hutchinson, 1936).
CLAEYS, G., *Citizens and Saints. Politics and Anti-politics in Early British Socialism* (Cambridge: Cambridge University Press, 1989).
CLARKSON, L.A., and E. Margaret Crawford, *Feast and Famine. Food and Nutrition in Ireland. 1500-1920* (Oxford: Oxford University Press, 2001).
COOK, E.T., and A. Wedderburn, eds, *Works of John Ruskin. The Letters of John Ruskin*, vol. II, 1870-1889 (London: G. Allen, 1909).
COOTER, R., ed., *The Cultural Meaning of Popular Science: Phrenology and the Organization of Consent in Nineteenth Century Britain* (Cambridge: Cambridge University Press, 1984).

—— *Studies in the History of Alternative Medicine* (Basingstoke and London: Macmillan Press/St Anthony's College, Oxford, 1988).
—— *Phrenology in the British Isles. An Annotated Historical Biobibliography and Index* (Metuchen, New Jersey and London: Scarecrow, 1989).
COUSTILLAS, P., ed., *London and the Life of Literature in late Victorian England. The Diary of George Gissing, Novelist* (Hassocks: Harvester Press, 1978).
CROSSICK, G., ed., *The Lower Middle Class in Britain, 1870-1914* (London: Croom Helm, 1977).
CROSSLEY, C., 'Attitudes towards Animals and Vegetarianism in Nineteenth Century France', ch. 6 in M. Cornick and C. Crossley, eds, *Problems in French History* (Palgrave: Basingstoke, 2000), pp. 81-103.
CROSSLEY, C., *Consumable Metaphors. Attitudes towards Animals and Vegetarianism in Nineteenth-Century France* (Oxford, Bern: Peter Lang, 2005).
CRUIKSHANK, R.J., *Charles Dickens and Early Victorian England* (London: Isaac Pitman, 1949).
DAVIES, A.J., *To Build a New Jerusalem. The British Labour Party from Keir Hardie to Tony Blair* (1992; London: Abacus Books, 1996).
DAVIES, B., 'Empire and Identity: the "case" of Doctor William Price', in D. Smith, ed., *A People and a Proletariat. Essays in the History of Wales, 1780-1980* (London: Pluto Press, 1980).
DAVIES, J., *The Victorian Kitchen* (London: BBC Books, 1989).
DAUNTON, M., and B. Rieger, eds, *Meanings of Modernity: Britain from the late Victorian Era to World War II* (Oxford: Berg, 2001).
DESMOND, A., *The Politics of Evolution. Morphology, Medicine, and Reform in Radical London* (London: University of Chicago Press, 1989).
DINGLE, A.E., *The Campaign for Prohibition in Victorian England. The United Kingdom Alliance, 1872-1895* (London: Croom Helm, 1980).
DIXON, J., *Divine Feminine. Theosophy and Feminism in England* (Baltimore, Maryland: Johns Hopkins, 2001).
DRUMMOND, J.C., and A. Wilbraham, *The Englishman's Food. A History of Five Centuries of English Diet* (1939; London: Jonathan Cape, 1964).
DUNBAR, C., *A Bibliography of Shelley Studies: 1823-1950* (New York: Garland Publishers, 1976).
DUNCAN, D., *Life and Letters of Herbert Spencer* (1908; London: Williams and Norgate, 1911).
DYER, J.C., *Vegetarianism: an Annotated Bibliography* (London/Metuchen, New Jersey: Scarecrow, 1982).
EAGLETON, T., 'The flight to the real', ch. 1 in Sally Ledger and S. McCracken, eds, *Cultural Politics at the Fin de Siècle* (Cambridge: Cambridge University Press, 1995), pp.11-21.
EDER, K., *The Social Construction of Nature. A Sociology of Ecological Enlightenment* (London: Sage, 1996).
EDWARDS, J.P., *A Few Footprints* (London: Clement's House, 1905).
ELLIS, R.H., *The Casebooks of Dr John Snow* [*Medical History* supplement 14] (London: Wellcome Institute for the History of Medicine, 1994).
ELLIS, S. M., *George Meredith* (London: Grant Richards Ltd, 1920).
ELSTON, M.A., 'Women and Anti-vivisection in Victorian England. 1870-1900', in N. Rupke, ed., *Vivisection in Historical Perspective* (1987; London and New York: Routledge, 1990), pp. 259-294.
ENSOR, R.C.K., *England 1870-1914* (1936; Oxford: Clarendon Press, 1963).

EPSTEIN, B.L., *The Politics of Domesticity. Women, Evangelism, and Temperance in Nineteenth Century America* (Middleton, Connecticut: Wesleyan University Press, 1981).
EPSTEIN, J., 'Some organizational and cultural aspects of the Chartist movement, 1840-1848' in J. Epstein and D. Thompson, eds, *The Chartist Experience. Studies in Working-class Radicalism and Culture 1830-60* (London: Macmillan, 1982), pp. 221-268.
FAHEY, D.M., *Temperance and Racism. John Bull, Johnny Reb, and the Good Templars* (Lexington: University Press of Kentucky, 1996).
FERGUSON, M., *Animal Advocacy and Englishwomen, 1780-1900. Patriots, Nation and Empire* (Ann Arbor, Michigan: University of Michigan Press, 1998).
FESTING, H., *S. Butler. Author of Erewhon. A Memoir* (London: Macmillan, 1919), 2 vols, vol. 2.
—— (ed.), *The Note-books of Samuel Butler* (1921; London: John Cape, 1930).
FIDDES, N., *Meat. A Natural Symbol* (London: Routledge, 1991).
FOGARTY, R.S., *Dictionary of American Communal and Utopian History* (Westport, Connecticut and London: Greenwood Press, 1980).
FOOT, P., *Red Shelley* (London: Sidgewick and Jackson, 1980).
FORD, F.M., *The Soul of London. A Survey of a Modern City* (London: Alston Rivers, 1905).
FRAISSE, G., and M. Perrot, eds, *A History of Women in the West. IV. Emerging Feminism from Revolution to World War* (Cambridge, Mass., and London: Harvard University Press, 1993).
FRANCIS, W.J., *Reminiscences* (privately printed, Southend on Sea, n.d.).
FRASER, W.H., *Alexander Campbell and the Search for Socialism* (Manchester: Holyoake Books, Co-operative Union Ltd, 1996).
FREEMAN, S., *Mutton and Oysters. The Victorians and their Food* (London: Gollancz, 1989).
FRENCH, R. and A. Wear, eds, *British Medicine in an Age of Reform* (London: Routledge, 1991).
FRENCH, R.D., *Antivivisection and Medical Science in Victorian Society* (Princeton and London: Princeton University Press, 1975).
GAFFYN, J., and D. Thomas, *The Centenary History of the Co-operative Women's Guild* (Manchester: Co-operative Union, 1983).
GANDHI, M.K., *An Autobiography. The Story of my Experiments with Truth* (1927-9; Boston: Beacon Press, 1957).
GATES, B.T., *Kindred Nature. Victorian and Edwardian Women Embrace the Living World* (Chicago and London: University of Chicago Press, 1998).
GATRELL, V.A.C., *The Hanging Tree. Execution and the English People. 1770-1868* (Oxford: Oxford University Press, 1994).
GIBBONS, B.J., *Spirituality and the Occult. From the Renaissance to the Modern Age* (London: Routledge, 2001).
GIBSON, A. and T.C. Smout, 'From Meat to Meal: Changes in Diet in Scotland', ch. 2 in C. Geissler and D.J. Oddy, eds, *Food, Diet and Economic Change. Past and Present* (Leicester, London and New York: Leicester University Press, 1993), pp.10-34.
GINSWICK, J., ed., *Labour and the Poor in England and Wales, 1849-51* (London: Frank Cass, 1983).
GIROUARD, M., *Victorian Pubs* (London: Studio Vista, 1975).
GLEADLE, K., *The Early Feminists. Radical Unitarians and the Emergence of the Women's Right Movement. 1831-51* (London: Macmillan, 1995).
—— '"Our Several Spheres": Middle-class Women and the Feminisms of Early Victorian Radical Politics', in K. Gleadle and S. Richardson, eds, *Women in*

British Politics, 1760-1860. The Power of the Petticoat (Basingstoke: Palgrave, 2001), pp. 134-152.

— '"The age of physiological reformers": rethinking gender and domesticity in the age of reform', ch. 8 in A. Burns and J. Innes, eds, *Rethinking the Age of Reform* (Cambridge: Cambridge University Press, 2003), pp. 200-219.

GOODMAN, J., *Tobacco in History. The Cultures of Dependence* (London and New York: Routledge, 1993).

GOODWAY, D., *London Chartism, 1838-1848* (Cambridge: Cambridge University Press, 1982).

GOULD, P.C., *Early Green Politics. Back to Nature, Back to the Land, and Socialism in Britain, 1880-1900* (Hassocks: Harvester Press, 1988).

GRAY, B.K., *A History of English Philanthropy. From the Dissolution of the Monasteries to the Taking of the First Census* (London: P.S. King, 1905).

GREENSLADE, W., 'Fitness and the Fin de Siècle', ch. 2 in J. Stokes, *Fin de Siècle/Fin du Globe. Fears and Fantasies of the late Nineteenth Century* (London: Macmillan: 1992).

GREGERSON, J., *Vegetarianism. A History* (Fremont, California: Jain Publishing, 1994).

GRUGEL, L.E., *George Jacob Holyoake. A Study in the Evolution of a Victorian Radical* (Philadelphia: Porcupine Press, 1976).

GURNEY, P., *Co-operative Culture and the Politics of Consumption in England, 1870-1930* (Manchester: Manchester University Press: 1996).

HAIGHT, G.S., ed., *The Letters of George Eliot* (London: Oxford University Press, 1954), vol. 2.

HALEY, B., *The Healthy Body and Victorian Culture* (Cambridge, Massachusetts: Harvard University Press, 1978).

HAMER, D.A., *The Politics of Electoral Pressure. A Study in the History of Victorian Reform Agitations* (Hassocks: Harvester Press, 1977).

HARDY, D., *Alternative Communities in Nineteenth Century England* (London: Longman, 1979).

HARPER, G.M., *Yeats's Golden Dawn* (London: Macmillan, 1974).

— *Yeats and the Occult* (1975; London: Macmillan, 1976).

HARRIS, S.H., *Auberon Herbert. Crusader for Liberty* (London: Williams and Norgate, 1943).

HARRISON, B., *Drink and the Victorians. The Temperance Question in England, 1815-1872* (London: Faber and Faber, 1971).

— *Dictionary of British Temperance Biography* (Sheffield: Society for the Study of Labour History, 1973).

— 'A Genealogy of Reform in Modern Britain', ch. 6 in Christine Bolt and Seymour Drescher, eds, *Anti-Slavery, Religion and Reform. Essays in Memory of Roger Anstey* (Folkestone, 1980), pp. 119-148.

— 'Women's Health and the Women's Movement in Britain: 1840-1940', ch. 1 in C. Webster, ed., *Biology, Medicine and Society. 1840-1940* (Cambridge: Cambridge University Press, 1981).

— *Peaceable Kingdom. Stability and Change in Modern Britain* (Oxford: Clarendon Press, 1982).

— 'Press and Pressure Group in Modern Britain', in J. Shattock and M. Wolff, *The Victorian Periodical Press* (Toronto and Buffalo: University of Toronto Press/ Leicester University Press, 1982), pp. 261-295.

HARRISON, J.F.C., *A Study in the English Adult Educational Movement* (London: Routledge and Kegan Paul, 1961).

BIBLIOGRAPHY

—— *Robert Owen and the Owenites in Britain and America. The Quest for the New Moral World* (London: Routledge and Kegan Paul, 1969).
—— *The Early Victorians. 1832-1851* (London: Weidenfeld and Nicolson, 1971).
—— 'Early Victorian Radicals and the Medical Fringe', in W.F. Bynum and R. Porter, eds, *Medical Fringe and Medical Orthodoxy, 1750-1850* (London: Croom Helm, 1987), pp.198-215.
—— *Late Victorian Britain, 1875-1901* (London: Fontana Press, 1990).
HAU, M., *The Cult of Health and Beauty in Germany. A Social History, 1890-1930* (Chicago and London: University of Chicago Press, 2003).
HAYLER, M.H.C., *The Vision of a Century. 1853-1953* (London: The United Kingdom Alliance, 1953).
HEARL, T.W., *William Barnes. 1801-1886. The Schoolmaster* (Dorchester: Longmans, 1966).
HEASMAN, K., *Evangelicals in action. An Appraisal of their Social Work in the Victorian Era* (London: Geoffrey Books, 1962).
HEELAS, P., *The New Age Movement. The Celebration of the Self and the Sacralization of Modernity* (Oxford: Blackwell, 1996).
HENDERSON, A., *G.B. Shaw: Man of the Century* vol. 1 (New York: Da Capo Press, 1972).
HENDRICK, G., *H.S. Salt. Humanitarian Reformer and Man of Letters* (Urbana, Chicago and London: University of Illinois, 1977).
HOBSBAWM, E.J., *Labouring Men. Studies in the History of Labour* (London: Weidenfeld and Nicolson, 1964).
HOLLIS, P., ed., *Pressure from Without in Early Victorian England* (London: E. Arnold, 1974).
HOLROYD, M., ed., *The Genius of Shaw. A Symposium* (London: Hodder and Stoughton, 1979).
—— *Bernard Shaw* vol. 1 *1856-1898, The Search for Love* (1988; New York: Vintage Books).
HOLTON, S.S., *Suffrage Days: Stories from the Women's Suffrage Movement* (New York: Routledge, 1996).
HOPPEN, K.T., *The Mid-Victorian Generation, 1846-1886* (Oxford: Clarendon Press, 1998).
HURLSTONE, K., ed., *William Hurlstone, Musician. Memorials and Records by his Friends* (London: Cary, *c.*1940).
HYNDMAN, H.M., *The Records of an Adventurous Life* (London: Macmillan, 1911).
HYNES, S., *The Edwardian Turn of Mind* (Princeton: New Jersey: Princeton University Press, 1968).
IRVINE, W., *The Universe of George Bernard Shaw* (1949; New York: Russell and Russell, 1968).
JACKSON, H., *The Eighteen Nineties. A Review of Art and Ideas at the Close of the Nineteenth Century* (1913; London: Pelican Books, 1950).
JAY, H., *Robert Buchanan. Some Account of his Life, His Life's Work, and His Literary Friendships* (London: T. Fisher Unwin, 1903).
JONES, E.H., *Mrs Humphry Ward* (London: Heinemann, 1973).
JONES, H.F., *Samuel Butler. Author of Erewhon. A Memoir* 2 vols, vol. 2. (London: Macmillan, 1919).
JOYCE, J., *Ulysses* (Everyman's Library edition, London: David Campbell Publishers, 1994).

KALIM, M.S., *The Social Orpheus. Shelley and the Owenites* (Lahore: Research Council, 1973).
KAMM, J., *Rapiers and Battleaxes. The Women's Movement and its Aftermath* (London: George Allen and Unwin, 1966).
KEAN, H., *Animal Rights. Political and Social Change in Britain since 1800* (London: Reaktion Books, 1998).
KELENY, K., *The First Century of Health Foods* (Stroud, Gloucester: Nuhealth Books, 1996).
KELVIN, N., ed., *The Collected Letters of William Morris* vol. 2, *1881-1884* (Princeton: Princeton University Press, 1987).
KEMP, P., *H.G. Wells and the Culminating Ape. Biological Themes and Imaginative Obsessions* (London: Macmillan, 1982).
KESTER, S.R., *Utopian Episodes. Daily Life in Experimental Colonies Dedicated to Changing the World* (Syracuse, New York: Syracuse University Press, 1993).
KIDD, B.E., and M.E. Richards, *Hadwen of Gloucestershire. Man, Medico, Martyr* (London: John Murray, 1933).
KORG, J., ed., *George Gissing's Commonplace Book* (New York: New York Public Library, 1962).
KUMAR, K., *Utopia and Anti-Utopia in Modern Times* (Oxford: Basil Blackwell, 1987).
LAPPE, F.M., *Diet for a Small Planet* (New York: Friends of the Earth/ Ballantine Books, 1971).
LATHAM, J.E.M., 'Fruitlands: a postscript', in J. Myerson, ed., *Studies in the American Renaissance* (Charlottesville: University Press of Virginia, 1995), pp. 61-66.
—— *Search for a New Eden. James Pierrepont Greaves (1777-1842): The Sacred Socialist and His Followers* (London: Associated University Presses, 1999).
LAURENCE, D.H., *Bernard Shaw. Collected Letters. 1874-1897* (London: Max Reinhardt, 1965).
—— *Bernard Shaw. A Bibliography* (Oxford: Clarendon Press, 1983).
LEDGER, S., *The New Woman. Fiction and Feminism at the Fin de Siécle* (Manchester: Manchester University Press, 1997).
LEE, A., *Rosemary and Laurels. The Life and Times of William and Mary Howitt* (Oxford: Oxford University Press, 1955).
LEVINE, H.G., 'Temperance Cultures: Alcohol as a Problem in Nordic and English-Speaking Cultures', in M. Lader, G. Edwards and D. Colin Drummond, eds, *The Nature of Alcohol and Drug-related Problems* (New York, 1993), pp. 16-36.
LEVINE, P., *Feminist Lives in Victorian England. Private Roles and Public Commitment* (Oxford: Basil Blackwell, 1990).
LINKLATER, A., *An Unhusbanded Life. Charlotte Despard. Suffragette, Socialist and Sinn Feiner* (London: Hutchinson, 1980).
LIVESEY, R., *Socialism, Sex and the Culture of Aestheticism in Britain, 1880-1914* (Oxford University Press, 2007).
LOCK, S., L.A. Reynolds and E.M. Tansey, eds, *Ashes to Ashes. The History of Smoking and Health* (Amsterdam: Rodopi, 1998).
LONGMATE, N., *The Waterdrinkers. A History of Temperance* (London: Hamish Hamilton, 1968).
LOOSLEY, S.G.H., *Wycliffe College, the First Hundred Years* (Stonehouse: Wycliffe College, 1982).
LUPTON, D., *Food, the Body and the Self* (London: Sage Publications, 1996).
MACKENZIE, N., and J. Mackenzie, *The Time Traveller. The Life of H.G. Wells* (London: Weidenfeld and Nicolson, 1973).

—— *The First Fabians* (London: Weidenfeld and Nicolson, 1977).
MARLAND, M.H., *Medicine in Wakefield and Huddersfield, 1780-1870* (Cambridge: Cambridge University Press, 1987).
MARSH, J., *Back to the Land. The Pastoral Impulse in England, from 1880 to 1914* (London: Quarto, 1982).
MARSTON, R.B., *The Dust of Combat. A Life of Charles Kingsley* (London: Faber and Faber, 1959).
MARTIN, D., 'Land Reform', ch. 6 in P. Hollis, ed., *Early Victorian England* (London: Edwin Arnold, 1974) pp. 131-158.
MARWICK, W.H., *The Life of Alexander Campbell* (Glasgow: Glasgow and District Co-operative Association, 1964).
MASON, M., *The Making of Victorian Sexual Attitudes* (Oxford and New York: Oxford University Press, 1994).
MATTHEISEN, P.F., A.C. Young and P. Coustillas, eds, *The Collected Letters of George Gissing* vol. 2 *1881-1885* (Athens, Ohio: Ohio University Press, 1990).
—— *The Collected Letters of George Gissing* vol. 7 *1897-1899* (Athens, Ohio: Ohio University Press, 1995).
—— *The Collected Letters of George Gissing* vol. 8 *1900-1902* (Athens, Ohio: Ohio University Press, 1996).
MATTINGLEY, C., *Well-tempered Women: Nineteenth Century Temperance Rhetoric* (Carbondale: Southern Illinois University Press, 1998).
MCCABE, J., *Life and Letters of G.J. Holyoake* (London: Watts, 1908).
MCCALMAIN, I., *Radical Underworld. Prophets, Revolutionaries and Pornographers in London, 1795-1840* (Cambridge: Cambridge University Press, 1988).
MCHUGH, P., *Prostitution and Victorian Social Reform* (London: Croom Helm, 1980).
MCLAUGHLIN, T., *A Diet of Tripe. The Chequered History of Food Reform* (Newton Abbot: David and Charles, 1978).
MELLER, H.E., *Leisure and the Changing City. 1870-1914* (London: Routledge and Kegan Paul, 1977).
MENNELL, S., *All Manners of Food. Eating and Taste in England and France from the Middle Ages to the Present* (Oxford: Basil Blackwell, 1985).
MENNELL, S., and A. Murcott, A.H. Van Otterloo, *The Sociology of Food. Eating, Diet and Culture* (London: Sage, 1992).
MINGAY, G.E., *Rural Life in Victorian England* (1971; Stroud: Alan Sutton, 1990).
MORTON, T., *Shelley and the Revolution in Taste, The Body and the Natural World* (Cambridge: Cambridge University Press, 1994).
—— (ed.), *Radical Food. The Culture and Politics of Eating and Drinking. 1790-1820* 3 vols, vol. 1, *Ethics and Politics* (London and New York: Routledge, 2000).
MUMFORD, L., *The City in History* (1961; London: Pelican, 1979).
MURPHY, C., *The Women's Suffrage Movement and Irish Society in the Early Twentieth Century* (London: Harvester Wheatsheaf, 1989).
MURPHY, M., ed., *Asenath Nicholson's Annals of the Famine in Ireland* (Dublin: Lilliput Press, 1998).
NAIRN, T., *The Enchanted Glass. Britain and its Monarchy* (1988; London: Picador, 1990).
NELSON, C., 'Care in feeding: vegetarianism and social reform in Alcott's America', in C. Nelson and L. Vallone, eds, *The Girls Own. Cultural Histories of the Anglo-American Girl, 1830-1915* (Athens, Georgia/London: University of Georgia Press, 1994), pp. 11-33.
NEWTON, S.M., *Health, Art and Reason. Dress Reformers of the Nineteenth Century* (London: John Murray, 1974).

NICHOLLS, P.A., *Homoeopathy and the Medical Profession* (London: Croom Helm, 1988).
NISSENBAUM, S., *Sex, Diet and Debility in Jacksonian America. Sylvester Graham and Health Reform* (Westport, Connecticut, London: Greenwood Press, 1980).
OPPENHEIM, J., *The Other World. Spiritualism and Psychical Research in England, 1850-1914* (Cambridge: Cambridge University Press, 1985).
OUEDRAOGO, A.P., 'The social genesis of western vegetarianism to 1859', in R. Dare, ed., *Food, Power and Community. Essays in the History of Food and Drink* (Adelaide: Wakefield Press, 1999), pp. 154-166.
VAN OTTERLOO, A.H., *Eten en eetlust in Nederland (1840-1990)* (Amsterdam: Bert Bakker, 1990).
OWEN, A., *The Darkened Room. Women, Power and Spiritualism in Late Victorian England* (London: Virago, 1989).
PARRINGTON, V.L., *American Dreams. A Study of American Utopias* (1947; 2nd enlarged edn, New York: Russell and Russell, 1964).
PEARSALL, R., *The Worm in the Bud* (1969; London: Penguin, 1983).
PERKIN, H., *The Origins of Modern English Society, 1780-1880* (London: Routledge and Kegan Paul, 1969).
PERREN, R., *The Meat Trade in Britain. 1840-1914* (London: Henley and Boston: Routledge and Kegan Paul, 1978).
PETERSEN, C. (ed. A. Jenkins), *Bread and the British Economy, c.1770-1870* (Aldershot, Hampshire: Scolar Press, 1995).
PICKERING, P.A., *Chartism and the Chartists in Manchester and Salford* (Basingstoke: Macmillan Press, 1995).
PIERSON, S., *British Socialists. The Journey from Fantasy to Politics* (Cambridge, Massachusetts and London: Harvard University Press, 1979).
PODMORE, F., *Robert Owen. A Biography* 2 vols (London: George Allen and Unwin, 1906).
PORTER, R., *Health for Sale. Quackery in England 1660-1850* (Manchester: Manchester University Press, 1989).
—— ed., *The Medical History of Waters and Spas* (London: Wellcome Institute for the History of Medicine, 1990).
—— 'The People's Health in Georgian England', ch. 6 in T. Harris, ed., *Popular Culture in England, c.1500-1850* (Basingstoke: Macmillan, 1995), pp. 124-142.
—— ed., *The Cambridge Illustrated History of Medicine* (Cambridge University Press, 1996).
—— *The Greatest Benefit to Mankind. A Medical History of Humanity from Antiquity to the Present* (London: Harper Collins, 1997).
PROCHASKA, F.K., *Women and Philanthropy in Nineteenth Century England* (Oxford: Clarendon Press, 1980).
PROTHERO, I.J., *Artisans and Politics in Early 19th Century London. John Gast and his Times* (Folkestone: Dawson, 1979).
PURVIS, J., *Hard Lessons. The Lives and Education of Working Class Women in Nineteenth Century England* (London: Polity Press, 1989).
PYLE, H., *Jack B. Yeats. A Biography* (London: Routledge and Kegan Paul, 1970).
READ, D., *The English Provinces* (London: E. Arnold, 1964).
REDFERN, P., *Journey to Understanding* (London: George Allen and Unwin, 1946).
RICHARDSON, E., and C. Willis, eds, *The New Woman in Fiction and Fact. Fin-de-Siecle Feminisms* (Basingstoke: Palgrave, 2001).
RITVO, H., *The Animal Estate. The English and other Creatures in the Victorian Age* (Cambridge, Massachusetts and London: Harvard University Press, 1987).

ROBBINS, K., *Nineteenth Century Britain. Integration and Diversity* (Oxford: Clarendon Press, 1988).
ROBBINS, W., *The Newman Brothers. An Essay in Comparative Intellectual Biography* (London: Heinemann, 1966).
ROBSON, J.M., ed., *Collected Works of J.S. Mill* vol. 27. *Journals and Debating Speeches* (Toronto and Buffalo: University of Toronto Press, 1988).
ROGERS, B., *Beef and Liberty* (London: Chatto and Windus, 2003).
ROGERS, H., "'The Prayer, the passion and the reason" of Eliza Sharples: freethought, women's rights and republicanism, 1832-52', ch. 2 in E. Yeo, ed., *Radical Femininity. Women's Self-Representation in the Public Sphere* (Manchester: Manchester University Press, 1998), pp.52-78.
ROMEIN, J.M., *The Watershed of Two Eras. Europe in 1900* (Middleton, Connecticut: Wesleyan University Press, 1978).
ROTHSTEIN, T., *From Chartism to Labourism* (London: Lawrence, 1929).
ROWBOTHAM, S., and J. Weeks, *Socialism and the New Life. The Personal and Sexual Politics of Edward Carpenter and Havelock Ellis* (London: Pluto Press, 1977).
—— "'Our Party is the People": Edward Carpenter and Radicalism in Sheffield', ch. 8 in J.G. Rule and R. Malcolmson, eds, *Protest and Survival. The Historical Experience. Essays for E.P. Thompson* (London: Merlin Press, 1993), pp. 257-278.
ROYLE, E., *Radical Politics. 1790-1900. Religion and Unbelief* (London: Longman, 1971).
—— *Victorian Infidels. The Origins of the British Secularist Movement, 1791-1866*, (Manchester: Manchester University Press, 1974).
—— 'Owenism and the Secularist Tradition: The Huddersfield Secular Society and Sunday School', ch. 14 in *Living and Learning: Essays in Honour of J.F.C. Harrison* (Aldershot: Scolar Press, 1996), pp. 199-217.
—— *Robert Owen and the Commencement of the Millennium: A Study of the Harmony Community* (Manchester: Manchester University Press, 1998).
RUBINSTEIN, D., *Before the Suffragettes. Women's Emancipation in the 1890s* (Brighton: Harvester Press, 1986).
RULE, J.G., 'Regional variations of food consumption amongst agricultural labourers, 1790-1860', in W. Minchinton, ed., *Exeter Papers in Economic History. Agricultural Improvement: Medieval and Modern* (Exeter: University of Exeter, 1981).
RULE, J.G., and R. Malcolmson, eds, *Protest and Survival. The Historical Experience. Essays for E.P. Thompson* (London: Merlin Press, 1993).
RUSK, R.L., *The Letters of Emerson*, vol. 3 (New York: Columbia University Press, 1939).
RUSSELL, B., *Autobiography* (1967; London: Unwin Paperbacks; 1978).
ROSS, E., *Love and Toil. Motherhood in Outcast London, 1870-1918* (New York: Oxford University Press, 1993).
RUPKE, N., ed., *Vivisection in Historical Perspective* (1987; London and New York: Routledge, 1990).
SALAMAN, R., *The History and Social Influence of the Potato* (Cambridge: Cambridge University Press, 1949).
SALT, H.S., *P.B. Shelley. Poet and Pioneer* (1896; London: George Allen and Unwin, 1924).
SAMUEL, R., 'The Discovery of Puritanism, 1820-1914: A Preliminary Sketch', in A. Light with S. Alexander and G. Stedman Jones, eds, *Island Stories: Unravelling Britain*. vol. 2 *Theatres of Memory* (London and New York: Verso, 1998), pp. 276-322.
SANBORN, F.B., *Bronson Alcott at Alcott House, England and Fruitlands, New England 1842-1844* (Cedar Rapids, Iowa: Torch Press, 1908).

SAVILLE, J., 'J.E. Smith and the Owenite Movement 1833-34,' in S. Pollard and J. Salt, eds, *Robert Owen: Prophet of the Poor. Essays in Honour of the Two Hundredth Anniversary of His Birth* (London: Macmillan, 1971), pp. 115-144.
SAXE WYNDHAM, H., *William Lambe MD ... A Pioneer of Reformed Diet* (London: LVS, 1940).
SCHWARTZKOPF, J., *Women in the Chartist Movement* (Basingstoke: Macmillan, 1991).
SCOLA, R., *Feeding the Victorian City. The Food Supply of Manchester, 1770-1870* (Manchester: Manchester University Press, 1992).
SEARLE, G.R., *Morality and the Market in Victorian Britain* (Oxford: Clarendon Press, 1998).
SHAW, N., *Whiteway. A Colony in the Cotswolds* (London: C.W. Daniel, 1935).
SHIELS, W.J., ed., *The Church and Healing* (Oxford: Basil Blackwell, 1982).
SHI, D.E., *The Simple Life. Plain Living and High Thinking in American Culture* (Oxford, New York: Oxford University Press, 1985).
SHIMAN, L.L., *The Crusade against Drink in Victorian England* (Basingstoke: Macmillan, 1988).
—— '"Changes are Dangerous": Women and Temperance in Victorian England', ch. 8 in G. Malmgreen ed., *Religion in the Lives of English Women, 1760-1930* (London: Croom Helm, 1986), pp. 193-215.
SHIPLEY, S., *Club Life and Socialism in Mid-Victorian London* (Oxford: Ruskin College, 1971).
SIBLY, W.A., *Vegetarianism and the Growing Boy* (Manchester and London: VS/LVS, 4th edn, 1942).
SIEVEKING, I.G., *Memoirs and Letters of Francis W. Newman* (London: Kegan Paul, 1909).
SIMS, G.R., *My Life. Sixty Years Recollections of Bohemian London* (London: Eveleigh Nash, 1917).
SINGER, P., *Animal Liberation. A New Ethics for our Treatment of Animals* (New York: New York Review, 1975).
SLATER, J., ed., *The Correspondence of Emerson and Carlyle* (New York and London: Columbia University Press, 1964).
SMITH, F.B., *Radical Artisan. William James Linton, 1812-1897* (Manchester: Manchester University Press, 1973).
—— *The People's Health. 1830-1910* (London: Croom Helm, 1979).
SMITH, V., 'Physical Puritanism and Sanitary Science: Medical and Immaterial Beliefs in Popular Physiology, 1650-1840', in R. Cooter ed., *Studies in the History of Alternative Medicine* (Basingstoke and London: Macmillan Press, 1988), pp. 174-197.
SMITH, W.S., *The London Heretics 1870-1914* (London: Constable, 1967).
SNELL, H., *Men, Movements and Myself* (London: J.M. Dent, 1936).
SOUTHGATE, D., 'Edwin Scrymgeour (1886-1947). Prohibitionist and Politician', in *Three Dundonians* (Dundee: Abertay Historical Society Publication, 1968), pp. 16-22.
SPENCER, C., *The Heretic's Feast. A History of Vegetarianism* (London: Fourth Estate, 1993).
—— *British Food. An Extraordinary Thousand Years of History* (London: Grub Street, 2002).
STEWART, W.A.C., and W.P. McCann, *The Educational Innovators. 1750-1880* (London: St Martin's Press, 1967).
STOKES, J., *Fin de Siècle/Fin du Globe. Fears and Fantasies of the late Nineteenth Century* (Macmillan, 1992).

STOREY, G., K. Tillotson and N. Burgis eds, *The Letters of Charles Dickens* vol. 6 *(1850-1852)* (Oxford: Clarendon Press, 1988).
STUART, T., *The Bloodless Revolution. Radical Vegetarians and the Discovery of India* (London: HarperCollins, 2006).
SUTHERLAND, J., *The Longman Companion to Victorian Fiction* (1988; Harlow: Longman, 1989).
TAYLOR, A., '"The Nauseating Cult of the Crown": Republicanism, Anti-Monarchism and Post-Chartist Politics. 1870-1875', ch. 5 in D. Nash and A. Taylor, eds, *Republicanism in Victorian Society* (Stroud: Sutton, 2000), pp. 51-71.
TAYLOR, B., *Eve and the New Jerusalem. Socialism and Feminism in the Nineteenth Century* (London: Virago, 1983).
TAYLOR, M., and M. Wolff, *The Victorians since 1901. Histories, Representations and Revisions* (Manchester and New York: Manchester University Press, 2004).
TEMPERLEY, H., *British Anti-slavery. 1833-1870* (Harlow: Longman, 1972).
TENNYSON, G.B., and U.C. Knoepflmacher, eds, *Nature and the Victorian Imagination* (Berkeley, London: University of California Press, 1977).
TERHUNE, A.M., and A.B. Terhune, eds, *The Letters of Edward Fitzgerald. Volume 1: 1830-1850* (Princeton, New Jersey: Princeton University Press, 1980).
TEUTEBERG, H.J., 'Agenda for a Comparative European History of Diet', introductory chapter in Teuteberg, ed., *European Food History. A Research Review* (Leicester: Leucester University Press, 1992).
THISTLEWAITE, F., *America and the Atlantic Community. Anglo-American Aspects, 1790-1850* (New York and Evanston: Harper Torchbooks, 1963).
(First published as *The Anglo-American Connection in the Early Nineteenth Century*, University of Pennsylvania Press, Oxford University Press, 1959).
THOLFSEN, T.R., *Working Class Radicalism in Mid-Victorian England* (London: Croom Helm, 1976).
THOMAS, K., *Religion and the Decline of Magic. Studies in Popular Beliefs in Sixteenth and Seventeenth Century England* (1971; London: Penguin, 1991).
—— *Man and the Natural World. Changing Attitudes in England, 1500-1800* (London: Allen Lane, 1983).
THOMAS, O., *Frances Elizabeth Hoggan. 1843-1927* (Newport, Monmouth: R.H. Jones).
THOMPSON, E.P., *The Making of the English Working Class* (London: Gollancz, 1964).
THOMSON, P., *George Sand and the Victorians. Her Influence and Reputation in Nineteenth Century England* (London and Basingstoke: Macmillan, 1977).
THORNE, R., 'Places of Refreshment in the Nineteenth Century,' ch. 7 in A.D. King, ed., *Buildings and Society. Essays on the Social Development of the Built Environment* (London: Routledge and Kegan Paul, 1980), pp. 228-53.
TREUHERZ, J., *Pre-Raphaelite Paintings for the Manchester City Art Gallery* (London: Lund Humphries, 1980).
TROTTER, D., *The English Novel in History. 1895-1920* (London and New York: Routledge, 1993).
TSUZUKI, C., *Edward Carpenter. 1844-1929. Prophet of Human Fellowship* (Cambridge: Cambridge University Press, 1980).
—— *Tom Mann, 1856-1941. The Challenges of Labour* (Oxford: Clarendon Press, 1991).
TURNER, B.S., *The Body and Society. Explorations in Social Theory* (1984; London: Sage, 1996).
—— *Regulating Bodies. Essays in Medical Sociology* (London and New York: Routledge, 1992).

TURNER, J., *Reckoning with the Beast: Animals, Pain and Humanity in the Victorian Mind* (London, Baltimore: Johns Hopkins University Press 1980).
TWIGG, J.M., 'Vegetarianism and the Meanings of Meat' in A. Murcott ed., *The Sociology of Food and Eating* (Aldershot: Gower, 1983), pp. 18-30.
TYLECOTE, M., *The Mechanics' Institutes of Lancashire and Yorkshire Before 1851* (Manchester: Manchester University Press, 1957).
TYLER, A.F., *Freedom's Ferment. Phases of American Social History from the Colonial Period to the Outbreak of the Civil War* (1944; New York: Harper and Row, 1962).
TYRRELL, A., *Joseph Sturge and the Moral Radical Party in Early Victorian Britain* (London: Croom Helm, 1987).
TYRRELL, I., *Woman's World. Woman's Empire. The Woman's Christian Temperance Union in International Perspective, 1880-1930* (Chapel Hill and London: University of North Carolina Press, 1991).
VAN THAL, H., *Eliza Lynn Linton. The Girl of the Period* (London, 1979).
VINCENT, D., ed., *Testaments of Radicalism. Memoirs of Working Class Politicians. 1790-1885* (London: Europa, 1977).
VISSER, M., *The Rituals of Dinner* (Toronto: HarperCollins, 1991).
WALKOWITZ, J.R., *Prostitution and Victorian Society. Women, Class, and the State* (Cambridge: Cambridge University Press, 1980).
WALTERS, K.S., and L. Portmess, eds, *Ethical Vegetarianism. From Pythagoras to Peter Singer* (Albany, New York: State University of New York Press, 1999).
—— *Religious Vegetarianism. From Hesiod to the Dalai Lama* (Albany, New York: State University of New York Press, 2001).
WARD, M., *G.K. Chesterton* (London: Sheed and Ward, 1945).
WATTON, J.K., *Fish and Chips and the British Working Class, 1870-1940* (Leicester, London and New York: Leicester University Press, 1992).
WEBSTER, C., ed., *Biology, Medicine and Society. 1840-1940* (Cambridge: Cambridge University Press, 1981).
WEEKS, D., and J. James, *Eccentrics* (London: Weidenfeld and Nicolson, 1995).
WHATLEY, C.A., D.B. Swinfen and A.M. Smith, *The Life and Times of Dundee* (Edinburgh: John Donald, 1993).
WHORTON, J.C., *Crusaders for Fitness. The History of American Health Reformers* (Princeton, New Jersey: Princeton University Press, 1982).
WILDE, O., *Oscar Wilde on Vegetarianism. An Unpublished letter to Violet Fane with an Introduction and Notes by Jeremy Mason* (Edinburgh: Tragara Press, 1991).
WILSON, C.A., ed., *Luncheon, Nuncheon and Other Meals. Eating with the Victorians* (Stroud: Alan Sutton, 1994).
WILSON, D.A., *Carlyle on Cromwell and Others* (London: Kegan Paul, Trench, Trubner, 1925).
WINSTEN, S., *Salt and his Circle* (London: Hutchinson, 1951).
WINTER, A., *Mesmerized. Powers of Mind in Victorian Britain* (Chicago and London: University of Chicago Press, 1998).
WOODRING, C.R., *Victorian Samplers* (Lawrence: University of Kansas Press, 1952).
WRIGHT, T.R., *The Religion of Humanity. The Impact of Comtean Positivism in Victorian Britain* (Cambridge: Cambridge University Press, 1986).
YARMOLINSKY, A., *A Russian's American Dream* (Lawrence: University of Kansas Press, 1965).
YEO, E., 'Robert Owen and Radical Culture', in J. Pollard and J. Salt eds, *Robert Owen. Prophet of the Poor. Essays in Honour of the Two Hundredth Anniversary of His Birth* (London: Macmillan, 1971).

YOUNG, G.M., *Portrait of an Age* (London: Oxford University Press, 1977).

2. Articles in journals

ANON., *Bulletin of Labour History*, no. 22, Spring 1971, report from conference 15 November 1970, on millenialism and social reform in the early nineteenth century, pp. 4-5.
ANON., 'The Mediumship of George Spriggs', *Ark Review* (Noah's Ark Society), February 1998.
ARMYTAGE, W.H.G., 'The Journalistic Activities of J. Goodwin Barmby between 1841 and 1848,' *Notes and Queries*, April 1956, pp. 166-169.
BECK, A., 'Issues in the Anti-Vaccination Movement in England', *Medical History* 4 (1960), pp. 310-321.
BELCHEM, J., 'The Neglected "Unstamped": The Manx Pauper Press of the 1840s', *Albion* 24: 4 (Winter 1992), pp. 605-616.
BERGMAN B.P., and S.A. Miller, 'Historical Perspectives on Health. The Parkes Museum of Hygiene and the Sanitary Institute', *Journal of the Royal Society of Health* 123: 1 (March 2003), pp. 55-61.
BERRIDGE, V., 'Victorian Opium Eating: Responses to Opiate Use in Nineteenth-Century England', *Victorian Studies* 21: 4 (summer 1978), pp. 437-461.
BEVIR, M., 'The Rise of Ethical Anarchism. 1885-1900', *Historical Research* 69 (1996), pp. 143-165.
—— 'Annie Besant's Quest for Truth: Christianity, Secularism and New Age Thought', *Journal of Ecclesiastical History* 50: 1 (January 1999), pp. 63-93.
BRANG, P., 'Even without Pineapples. Vegetarianism in Russian Life and Literature', *European Vegetarian* 23 (2000).
BROWN, P.S., 'Nineteenth-century American Health Reformers and the Early Nature Cure Movement in Britain', *Medical History* 32 (1988), pp. 174-194.
—— 'Medically Qualified Naturopaths and the General Medical Council', *Medical History* 35 (1991), pp. 50-77.
CALHOUN, C., 'New Social Movements of the Early 19th Century', *Social Science History* 17: 3 (1993), pp. 385-427.
CALVERT, S.J., ' A Taste of Eden: Modern Christianity and Vegetarianism ', *Journal of Ecclesiastical History* 58: 1(January 2007), pp.1-21.
CANDY, C., 'Relating Feminism, Nationalism and Imperialism: Ireland, India and Margaret Cousin's Sexual Politics', *Women's History Review* 3 (March 1994), pp. 581-594.
CLAEYS, G., 'John Adolphus Etzler, Technological Utopianism, and British Socialism: The Tropical Emigration Society's Venezuelan mission and its Social Context, 1833-1848', *English Historical Review* 101 (1986), pp. 351-375.
CLEMENT, M., 'Physical Puritanism and Religious Dissent: the Case of John Young (1820-1904), Sunderland Chemist and Druggist and Methodist Lay Preacher', *Social History of Medicine* 11: 2 (August 1998), pp. 197-212.
COLLINS, P., 'Quaker Plaining as Critical Aesthetic', *Quaker Studies* 5: 2 (2001), pp. 121-139.
CROSFIL, M.L., 'Henry Mudge, Surgeon and Teetotaller', *Journal of the Royal Institution of Cornwall*, n.s. 11: 3 (1996), pp. 50-64.
—— 'Dr. Ralph Barnes, the medical apostle of temperance', *Journal of Medical Biography* 5: 2, May 1997, pp. 73-79.
CROSSLEY, C., 'Food and Salvation: Jean-Antoine Gleizes (1773-1843) and Vegetarianism', *Romance Studies* 13 (winter 1988), pp. 7-21.

D'ANIERI, P., C. Ernst and E. Kier, 'New Social Movements in Historical Perspective', *Comparative Politics* July 1990, p. 445-458.
DONOVAN, J., 'Animal Rights and Feminist Theory', *Signs* 15: 2, pp. 350-375.
DURBACH, N., 'Working class resistance to compulsory vaccination', *Social History of Medicine* 13: 1 (2000), pp. 45-62.
EBSTEIN, E., 'Historical Notes on Vegetarianism', *Medical Life* 31 (1924), pp. 469-472.
FIDLER, G., 'The work of Joseph and Eleanor Edwards, two Liverpool enthusiasts', *International Review of Social History* 24 (1979), pp. 293-313.
FINLAY, M.R., 'Quackery and Cookery: Justus von Liebig's Extract of Meat and The Theory of Nutrition in the Victorian Age', *Bulletin of History of Medicine* 66 (1992) pp. 404-418.
FRIEDMAN, S.S., 'Definitional Excursus: The Meanings of Modern/Modernity/ Modernism', *Modernism/Modernity* 8: 3 (2001), pp. 499-513.
GAMBONE, J.G., ed., 'Kansas – A Vegetarian Utopia: The Letters of John Milton Hadley, 1855-6', *Kansas Historical Quarterly* 38: 1 (1972), pp. 65-87.
GREGORY, J.R.T.E., 'Some Account of the Progress of the Truth as it is in Jesus': The White Quakers of Ireland', *Quaker Studies* 9:1 (2004), pp. 68-94.
GEORGE, K.P., 'Should Feminists be Vegetarians?' *Signs* 19: 2 (1994), pp. 405-434.
HAMILTON, M., 'Eating Ethically: "Spiritual" and "Quasi-Religious" aspects of Vegetarianism', *Journal of Contemporary Religion*, 15:1 (2000), pp. 65-83.
HARRISON, B., 'Philanthropy and the Victorians', *Victorian Studies* 9:4 (June 1966), pp. 353-374.
— 'Some Questions for the Local Historian' *The Local Historian* 8:5 (1968-1969), pp. 180-186.
— '"A world of which we had no conception": Liberalism and the Temperance Press, 1830-1872', *Victorian Studies* 13: 2 (1969-1970), pp. 125-158.
— 'Animals and the State in nineteenth century England', *English Historical Review* 88 (October 1973), pp. 786-820.
HAY, S., 'The Making of a late Victorian Hindu: M.K. Gandhi in London, 1888-1891', *Victorian Studies* 33:1 (1989), pp.74-98.
HAYNES, A., '"Murderous Millinery": the Struggle for the Plumage Act, 1921', *History Today* 33 (July 1983), pp. 26-30.
HENRY, B., 'Letters', *History Workshop Journal* (Autumn 1978), p. 222.
HICKMAN, R., 'The Vegetarian and Octagon Settlement Companies', *Kansas Historical Quarterly* 2: 4 (1933), pp. 377-385.
HOLTON, S., 'Silk dresses and lavender kid gloves. The wayward career of Jessie Craigen', *Women's History Review* 5:1 (1996), pp. 129-150.
HUI-LI, C., 'A Union of Christianity, Humanity, and Philanthropy: The Christian Tradition and the Prevention of Cruelty to Animals in Nineteenth-Century England', *Society and Animals. The Journal of Human-Animal Studies* 8: 3 (2000), pp. 265-285.
JÜTTE, R., 'The Historiography of Nonconventional Medicine in Germany', *Medical History* 43 (1999), pp. 342-358.
KARLIN, D., 'The Rise and Fall of the Magnetic Fluid', *Times Literary Supplement*, 12 February 1999, p. 6.
KEAN, H., 'The "Smooth Cool Men of Science": The Feminists and Socialist Response to Vivisection,' *Historical Journal* 40 (1995), pp. 16-38.
KIPPERMAN, M., 'Absorbing a Revolution: Shelley Becomes a Romantic, 1889-1903', *Nineteenth Century Literature* 47: 2 (September 1992), pp. 187-211.

KITSON-CLARK, G.S.R., 'Hunger and Politics in 1842', *Journal of Modern History* 25 (1953), pp. 355-374.
KNAPP, V.J., 'The Democratisation of Meat and Protein in Europe,' *The Historian* 59: 3 (Spring 1997), pp. 541-551.
LATHAM, J.E.M., 'Emma Martin and Sacred Socialism: the correspondence of James Pierrepont Greaves', *History Workshop Journal* 38 (1994), pp. 215-217.
—— 'The Political and the Personal: the Radicalism of Sophia Chichester and Georgiana Fletcher Welch', *Women's History Review* 8: 3 (1999), pp. 469-487.
LAWRENCE, J., 'Class and Gender in the Making of Urban Toryism, 1880-1914', *English Historical Review* 108: 428 (July 1993), pp. 629-652.
LENEMEN, L., 'The Awakened Instinct: vegetarianism and the women's suffrage movement in Britain', *Women's History Review* 6: 2 (1997), pp. 271-287.
LIVESEY, R., 'Morris, Carpenter, Wilde, and the Political Aesthetics of Labour', *Victorian Literature and Culture* 32: 2 (2004), pp. 601-616.
MACKENZIE, N., 'Percival Chubb and the founding of the Fabian Society', *Victorian Studies* 23:1 (autumn 1979), pp. 29-55.
MAIDMENT, B., 'Magazines of Popular Progress and the Artisans', *Victorian Periodicals Review* 17: 3 (1984), pp. 83-94.
MEYER-RENSCHHAUSEN, E., and A. Wirz, 'Dietetics, health reform and social order: vegetarianism as a moral physiology. The example of Maximilian Bircher-Benner (1867-1939)', *Medical History* 43 (1999), pp. 323-341.
MORRISON, R.D., 'Humanity Towards Man, Woman, and the Lower Animals: Thomas Hardy's Jude the Obscure and the Victorian Humane Movement', *Nineteenth Century Studies* 12 (1998), pp. 64-82.
NICHOLLS, D., 'Richard Cobden and the International Peace Congress Movement, 1848-1853', *Journal of British Studies* 30: 4 (October 1991), pp. 351-376.
OERLEMANS, O., 'Shelley's Ideal Body: Vegetarianism and Nature', *Studies in Romanticism*, 34: 4 (winter 1995), pp. 531-552.
OUEDRAOGO, A.P., 'De la secte religieuse à l'utopie philanthropique. Genèse sociale du végétarisme occidental', *Annales HSS* 4 (July-August 2000), pp. 825-843.
PECKHAM, M., 'Victorian Counter-culture', *Victorian Studies* 18: 3 (March 1975), pp. 253-276.
PEPPER, S., 'Allinson's Staff of Life', *History Today* 42 (October 1992), pp. 30-35.
PICHARDO, N.A., 'New Social Movements: A Critical Review', *Annual Review of Sociology* 23 (1997), pp. 411-430.
PICKERING, P.A., 'Chartism and the "trade of agitation" in early Victorian Britain', *History* 76 (1996), pp. 221-237.
PICKERING, P.A., and A. Tyrrell, '"In the Thickest of the Fight": the Reverend James Scholefield (1790-1855) and the Bible Christians of Salford', *Albion* 26: 3 (Fall 1994), pp. 461-482.
PORTER, D., and R. Porter, 'The Politics of Prevention: Anti-Vaccination and Public Health in Nineteenth Century England', *Medical History* 32 (1988), pp. 231-252.
POSTMUS, B., 'Mr Harmsworth's Blue Pencil: "Simple Simon" Revisited', *The Gissing Journal*, 31: 1 (January 1995), pp. 1-10.
PRICE, R., 'Hydropathy in England. 1840-1870', *Medical History* 25 (1981), pp. 269-280.
RANLETT, J., 'Checking Nature's Desecration: late Victorian environmental organization', *Victorian Studies* 26 (winter 1983), pp. 197-222.
RICHARDSON, L.M., 'Naturally Radical: The Subversive Poetics of Dollie Radford', *Victorian Poetry* 38: 1 (2000), pp. 109-124.

ROYLE, E., 'Chartists and Owenites – many parts but one body', *Labour History Review* 65:1 (spring 2000), pp. 2-21.
RUDRUM, A., 'Ethical Vegetarianism in Seventeenth Century Britain: its Roots in Sixteenth Century European Theological Debate', *Seventeenth Century* 18:1 (2003), pp. 76-92.
SAGER, E.W., 'The Social Origins of Victorian Pacifism', *Victorian Studies* 23 (winter 1980), pp. 211-236.
SCOTT, A.L., 'Physical Purity Feminism and State Medicine in Late Nineteenth-Century England', *Women's History Review* 8: 4 (1999), pp. 625-653.
SHAABAN, B., 'Shelley and the Barmbys', *Keats-Shelley Journal* 41 (1992), pp. 122-138.
SHAW, C.E., 'Identified with the One: Edward Carpenter, Henry Salt and the Ethical Socialist Philosophy of Science', *Prose Studies. History Theory* 13: 1 (May 1990), pp. 33-57.
SHYROCK, R.H., 'Sylvester Graham and the Popular Health Movement, 1830-1870', *The Mississippi Valley Historical Review* 18: 2 (September 1931), pp. 172-183.
STARICK, J.E.D., 'Love at First Beet: Vegetarian Critical Theory Meets Dracula', *The Victorian Newsletter* 89 (Spring 1996), pp. 23-29.
SWIFT, R., 'Food Riots in Mid-Victorian Exeter, 1847-67', *Southern History* 1980, pp. 101-127.
TWIGG, J.M., 'Food for Thought: Purity and Vegetarianism', *Religion* 9 (Spring 1979), pp. 13-35.
TYRRELL, A., 'Making the Millennium: The Mid-Nineteenth Century Peace Movement', *Historical Journal* 20:1 (March 1978), pp. 75-95.
—— 'The "Moral Radical Party" and the Anglo-Jamaican campaign for the abolition of the Negro Apprenticeship system', *English Historical Review* 99: 392 (July 1984), pp. 481-502.
TYRRELL, I., 'The Temperance Movement and Smoking in Australia: Themes and Implications for the Study of Drugs and Social Reform Movements', *The Social History of Alcohol Review* 38-39 (1999), pp. 28-34.
WALKER, R.B., 'Medical Aspects of Tobacco Smoking and the Anti-Tobacco Movement in Britain in the Nineteenth Century', *Medical History* 24 (1980), pp. 391-402.
WEINBREN, D., 'Against *all* Cruelty: the Humanitarian League, 1891-1919,' *History Workshop Journal* 38 (1994), pp. 86-101.
WHORTON, J.C., '"Christian Physiology": William Alcott's Prescription for the Millennium', *Bulletin of the History of Medicine* 49 (1975), pp. 466-431.
WILKINSON, A., 'The Preternatural gardener: the life of James Shirley Hibberd', *Garden History* 26: 2 (winter 1998), pp. 153-175.
YEO, S., 'A New Life: The Religion of Socialism in Britain. 1883-1896', *History Workshop Journal* 4 (Autumn 1977), pp. 5-56.

Unpublished material

ANON., 'Quaker Concern for Animals' (Friends' House Library, London).
BRADLEY, J., 'Medicine on the Margins: Hydropathy in Britain, 1840-1860', abstract of conference paper, 'Plural Medicine – Orthodox and Heterodox Medicine in Western and Colonial Countries During the 19th and 20th Centuries', University of Southampton, September 1999.

BRADY, N., '"Shafts" and the quest for a new morality: an examination of the Woman Question in the 1890s as seen through the pages of a contemporary journal', M.A., University of Warwick, 1978.
BURNETT, J., 'The History of Food Adulteration in Great Britain in the Nineteenth Century, with Special Reference to Bread, Tea and Beer', Ph.D., London School of Economics, 1958.
CLEMENTS, M., 'Sifting Science: Methodism and Natural Knowledge in Britain. 1815-1870', D. Phil., University of Oxford, 1996.
CULE, J., 'Dr William Price (1800-1892) of Llantrisant. A Study of an eccentric and a biography of a pioneer of cremation', M.D. thesis, University of Cambridge, 1960.
GREGORY, J.R.T.E., 'The Movement against Capital Punishment in Britain, 1846-1868', M. Phil., University of Cambridge, 1997.
LANGDON, J.C., 'Pocket Editions of the New Jerusalem: Owenite Communitarianism in Britain. 1825-1855', D. Phil., University of York, 2000.
MARSDEN, B., 'Fighting Cruelty: Lewis Gompertz, the morals of mechanism, and the Animals' Friend Society for the Prevention of Cruelty to Animals.'
SCHELLENBERG, A.M., '"Prize the Doubt". The Life and Works of Francis William Newman' Ph.D., University of Durham, 1994.
TWIGG, J.M., 'The Vegetarian movement in England from 1847-1981: a study of the structure of its ideology', Ph.D., London School of Economics, 1982.
TYRRELL, A., 'The Anti-everythingarians and the Moral Radical party in early and mid-Victorian Britain' Leeds conference on Radical Cultures, July 1998.

Material published on the Internet

ANON., Catalogue notes on the 'Nederlandsche Vegetariersbond', International Institute of Social History.
http://www.iisg.nl/collections/vegetariersbond
(accessed 16 March 2004).
BEBEL, A., 'Free Development of the Individual', 2: 'Revolution in Food' (1879).
http:www.marxists.org/archive/bebel/1879/woman-socialism/ch03b.htm.
DAY, J., Transcription of the Diary of Charles Walker of Worcester, 1851.
http://homepage.which.net/~j.day/WALKER.htm
(accessed May 2002).
HUYSSE, M., Transcription of newspaper clippings from the scrapbook assembled by William Robert Richards of Martock (1869-1957).
http://www.genealogyhelp.co.uk/Martock%20Web%20Site/diaries%20and%20scrap%20books.htm
(accessed July 2006).

Reference Works

The Dictionary of National Biography (London, Smith, Elder and Co., 1885-1960).
The Dictionary of Welsh Biography Down to 1940 (London: Honourable Society of Cymmrodorium, 1959).
The Oxford Dictionary of National Biography (Oxford: Oxford University Press, 2004-2006)

Manchester Faces and Places (Manchester: Hammond, 1890-1897), vol. 4.
Who was Who vols. 1-5 (London: A and C. Black, 1920-1961).
BAYLEN, J.O., and N.J. Gossman, eds, *Biographical Dictionary of Modern British Radicals II*. (Hemel Hempstead: Harvester Wheatsheaf, 1984).
BELLAMY, J.M., and J. Saville, eds, *Dictionary of Labour Biography*, vol. 2 (London and Basingstoke: Macmillan Press, 1974).
—— *Dictionary of Labour Biography*, vol. 8 (London and Basingstoke: Macmillan Press, 1987).
—— *Dictionary of Labour Biography*, vol. 9 (London and Basingstoke: Macmillan Press, 1993).
BOASE, F., *Modern English Biography. Containing many thousand concise memoirs of persons who have died between the years 1851-1900, with an index of the most interesting matter* 6 vols (Truro: Netherton and Worth, 1892-1921).
CRAWFORD, E., *The Women's Suffrage Movement: A Reference Guide* (London: University College London Press, 1998).
DOUGHAN, D., and D. Sanchez, *Feminist Periodicals, 1855-1984* (Hassocks: Harvester, 1987)
GORDON, P., and D. Doughan, *Dictionary of British Women's Organizations. 1825-1960* (London: Woburn Press, 2001).
HARRISON, R., G.B. Woolven, R. Duncan, eds, *Warwick Guide to British Labour Periodicals* (Hassocks: Harvester Press, 1977).
JEREMY, D.J., ed., *Dictionary of Business Biography. A Biographical Dictionary of Business Leaders Active in Britain in the Period 1860-1980*. 5 vols, vol.4 (London: Butterworths, 1985).

INDEX

Abzug, Robert H. 100
Adams, Carol 4, 161, 165-166, 173, 182
aesthetics of food 17, 126, 181
Alcott, Bronson 23-25
Alcott, William Andrus 23, 100
Allinson, Thomas R. 79, 80, 84, 103, 112, 133, 136, 143, 146-147, 155, 159, 169
Allinson, Anna 160, 169, 173
allopathy 70, 73-74, 82
American vegetarianism and reforms 3, 22-23, 74, 80, 100, 104, 107, 113, 118, 146, 148-149, 161, 168, 185
Amos, Sarah Sheldon 169
Anglicanism and Anglicans 39, 101-102, 101n126, 146
animal welfare (*see also* zoophilia) 5, 88-96, 162, 167, 171, 189
Ann Veronica (H.G. Wells) 184
Anthropological Society 45-46
anthropology 39, 176
anti-everythingarianism 115-119
anti-tobacco movement 9, 33, 45, 58, 77-78, 110, 114, 117, 147
anti-vegetarian tracts 177
anti-vivisection and anti-vivisectionists 5-6, 10, 61, 65, 83, 88-89, 93-95, 104, 109, 115-116, 119, 123, 144, 158, 165, 170-171, 176, 188, 192
aristocracy 19, 70, 112, 114, 152, 190
astrology 108
Aurora Villa 46, 48
Aveling, Edward 90, 93
Axon, William E.A. 192
Aytoun, William 98, 182

Baker, Amy, *known as* 'Domestica' 128
Baker, Thomas 75, 125
Barker, Joseph 30, 114, 119
Barker, Thomas Halliday 77
Barham, Francis Foster 25
Barkas, Thomas P. 52
Barmby, Goodwyn and Catherine 29, 30-31
Barnardo, Dr Thomas 145
Barnes, Reverend William 39
Barnesley, William 40
Barry, William 183
Baume, Pierre Henri 47, 77, 120
Beach, John 34, 43
Beale, Abigail 30
Beard, Sydney Hartnoll 56, 109
beards 24, 28, 30, 121
Bedborough, George 149
Beeby, Eleanor 172
beef, roast 13
Beeton, Isabella 18, 128, 161
Begbie, Harold 184
Beketon 193
Bell, Ernest 93, 128
Bellamy, Edward 133, 147, 181
Bennett, William (and family) 46, 101
Benson, E.F. 122, 186
Bentley, Joseph 46
Besant, Annie 66, 104, 108, 164, 171
Bible Christians, *see* Cowherdites
Blatchford, Robert 158
Blennerhasset Festival 51, 117
bloodsports 95
Bond, Hannah 27, 31
Bondfield, Margaret 64, 170

Booth, General William 155
Bormond, Joseph 34, 44, 51
Boult, Frances L. 106, 149, 165
Bower, Samuel 27, 125
Brady, Norman 169
Bremner, William 149
Brewster, Sir David 181
British and Foreign Society for the Promotion of Humanity 24
British Medical Journal 86
Brotherton, Joseph 16n77, 31-32, 74, 77, 126
Brotherton, Martha 128-129
Brown, Samuel 35, 70-71, 75, 103, 174, 176, 178
Browning, Robert 25
Brownson, Orestes 183
Bruce, Mrs F.J. 127
Buchanan, Robert 181
Burlington House 144
Burns, James 51, 64, 102, 105-106, 120, 147, 156, 163, 165, 175
Burritt, Elihu 98, 113
Butchers 88, 90-92, 97
Butler, Samuel 17, 179, 180-181

Caird, Mona 147, 175
Calhoun, Craig 189, 193
Campbell, Alexander 24, 27, 30
capital punishment 1, 5, 32, 40, 52, 58, 93, 97, 118, 122
Carlile, Richard 28, 175
Carlyle, Thomas 13, 25, 69, 73
Carpenter, Edward 9, 55-56, 122, 135, 170, 175
Catholics 41, 46, 102, 102n140
Caudwell, Job 9, 47, 78
Chadwick, Edwin 17, 85
Chant, Laura Ormiston 169
Chartism and Chartists 6, 12, 28, 30, 35, 38-39, 35, 44-45, 52, 56, 59, 77, 112-113, 120, 180, 182
Chichester, Sophia 22, 24
cholera 80-83, 179
Christian Socialism 47, 121, 125, 184
Claridge, Captain R.T. 73
Clarion movement 65, 158-159
Clark, Reverend James 57, 131
Clarke, (Charles) Allen 158
Clayden, Peter W. 40

clerks 65-66, 136-138, 156, 174, 188, 190
clothing reform vii, 1, 30, 92n41, 115, 121n75, 170, 180
Clubb, Henry S. 33-34, 44, 178
Clubb, Robert T. 44
Clubb, Sarah 44, 182
Cobbett, William 13
coffee taverns 140
Colegate, Isabel 182
Coles, Caroline and Emily Coles 170
Collyns, Reverend Charles Henry 60, 130
Communitarianism (*see also* Concordium, Fruitlands, Hampston Wick, Harmony, Manea Fen and Little Bentley) 21-30, 37, 44, 50, 100, 107, 113, 118, 120, 157, 182-184, 188, 192-193
Concordium 21-31, 44-45, 47, 73, 77, 92, 98-99, 107, 161, 181
Congregationalism 54, 60, 63, 66, 101, 101n.126
Contagious Diseases Act 55, 115, 123, 165
Cook, James H. 133, 138
Cook, Thomas 149
Cookery (non-vegetarian) 12, 14, 17-18, 20
Cooper, Matilda 95
co-operative movement 12, 16, 26, 29, 51, 61, 112, 121, 157, 159-160, 166, 168
Co-operator, The 52, 143, 159
Corn Laws 12, 33, 38, 40
Couchman, William 49
countryside and rural life 19, 36-7, 66, 145, 156
Cousins, James Henry, and Margaret Cousins 61
Cowherdites 5, 9, 21, 30-32, 35, 38-39, 44, 71, 74, 77, 80, 101-102, 101n126, 110, 161
Cox, Harold and Mrs Harold Cox 170
Crank, The 122
Crawcour, Isaac Lionel 84
Crespi, Dr Alfred 156
Cruikshank, George 47
culinary nationalism 11, 13
Curtice, Edward 144

cycling 166
Daisy Society 148
Daniel, Charles William 122
Danielite Herald 147
Danielites, Order of 75-76, 89, 103, 109, 147
Darwin, Charles 73, 96, 96n89, 192
Davidson, John M. 159, 177
Davie, John 52, 57, 74
Davitt, Michael 159
Daw, John James 120
Dawson, Charles 147
degeneration 180, 194
Densmore, Emmet 80, 105
Detrosier, Rowland 5n19
Dick, Colin Mackenzie 45
Dickens, Charles 12, 90, 118, 178, 182
Dictionary of National Biography 10
Dietetic Reformer 35, 51, 103, 142-143
Dixie, Lady Florence 93
Dixon, Ella Hepworth 185
Dixon, Joy 108
Dodd, George 90, 177
Dorcas, Mrs 48
Doremus, Franklin Pierce 122
Dornbusch, Amalie 48, 126
Dornbusch, George 45-50, 78, 81, 98, 106-107, 123, 125-126, 152
Duncan, James Elmzlie 29, 49, 120-121, 141, 175, 182
Dundee Vegetarian and Food Reform Society 58-60

Eamonson, Charlotte 168
Earle, Mrs Charles William 162
eccentricity 20, 120, 121, 141, 175, 182
Edwards, John Passmore 47, 113, 118, 155
Edwards, Joseph 158, 166
effeminacy and masculinity 173, 176, 183
Eliot, George 183
Elmy, Elizabeth Wolstenholme 171
emigration 12, 28-29, 39n147, 41
empire, colonies and imperialism 3, 12, 71, 86, 131, 147, 174, 193
Engels, Friedrich 25, 36, 44, 158
environmentalism 4, 93
Erewhon 180-181
ethnology 176

Etzler, J.A. 28-29
evolution 96, 192, 194
Exhibition, Great (1851) 49, 113, 131, 177
exhibitions, international 15, 134
exhibitions, vegetarian 63, 132

Fabians 7, 9, 157
faddism 119-123, 158, 174, 188
family 3, 13, 43, 52, 65, 68, 125, 134, 155, 162, 187
Farrington, William 54
Fellowship of the New Life 65
feminism 4, 7, 29, 55, 152, 161, 163, 165-166, 169-173, 182, 184
Fitzgerald, Edward 176n17
flat-earth 121
food, and adulteration 13, 16-17, 19, 37, 81, 177
— and health stores 132
— and middle class 16, 18-20, 130
— supply 12, 14, 157, 177
— and technology 4, 19, 133
— and Victorians 11-20
— and working class 12-20
Food Reform Journal 144
Ford, G.J. 23
Ford, Isabella 170
Forward, Charles W. 5, 63-64, 67, 81, 93, 102, 114, 129, 136, 140, 144, 147, 150, 194
freethought 38, 45, 76, 103-104, 112, 119, 135
French, Richard D. 93-94, 116
French, and French cuisine 13, 16-18, 20
— and vegetarianism 3, 121, 144
Frost, Thomas 26
fruitarianism 11, 84, 184
Fruitlands 23
Fruits and Farinacea 39, 83n114, 83n116
Furnivall, Frederick J. 47, 125

Galpin, William 24, 27, 29-30
Gamgee, Professor John 13
Gammage, Robert 28
Gandhi, Mahatma 3, 137
Gassion, Alfred 41, 50
German vegetarians 3, 11, 47, 144, 153, 168, 194

Gilpin, Charles 113
Gissing, George 66, 136, 175, 184, 188
Glendinning, Andrew 107, 134-137, 148
Gompertz, Lewis 94, 192
Gooch, Edmund T. 45
Gottschling, Andreas 92, 159, 164, 172
Govett, Richard 102
Greaves, James Pierrepont 21-27, 29-30, 44-46
Greenwell, Dora 176
Graham, Sylvester, *and* Grahamism 3, 23, 43, 72-73, 79, 80, 92, 100, 106, 113, 128, 144, 183
Griffin, Nathaniel 43, 152
Grub 150

Hadwen, Dr Walter 75, 84
Haggard, Henry Rider 116, 181, 186
hair 29-30, 121
Harmony Hall 26-27, 45
Hansard, Luke 39, 92
Hampton Wick community 24
Hardie, James Keir 158
Harding, Emily 165
Hardy, Thomas 185
Hare, Edward 126
Harpur, Caldwell 116, 126
Harrison, Brian 5
Harrison, Frederic 177
Harrison, John F.C. 112
Harvey, William 32, 74, 77, 115
Haughton, James 73, 77, 83, 116
Hazell, Thorpe 185
Hawkins, Ellen 165
Health, or Physiological Association (1842) 23-24
'Healtheries' (International Health Exhibition, 1884) 134
Henty, George 93, 145
Herald of Health 64, 79-80, 143-144
Herald of the Golden Age 103, 147-149, 192
Herron, John S. 60-61, 148
Hibberd, James Shirley 45, 47, 121, 163, 184, 110, 169
Hills, Arnold Frank 54, 62-65, 67, 74, 76, 78-80, 85, 93, 102, 106, 122, 138, 144-145, 154-155, 169, 171, 188
hippophagy 15

Hogg, Charles 84
Hoggan, Frances 165
Holmes, Sherlock 135, 184
Holyoake, George Jacob 16, 24-27, 30, 76, 121, 123, 139
Home Links 159, 164
homeopathy 45, 70-73, 108, 113
homosociality 165
Horebites, Order of 77
Horsell, Elizabeth 43, 48, 162, 189
Horsell, William 52, 72-74, 77, 94, 98, 104, 107
Howitt, Mary 46, 176
Hoyle, William 40, 77
Hudson, William Henry 135, 181
Human Nature 51, 105, 110
Humanitarian League 64, 91, 95-97, 109, 117, 135, 147, 158, 165-166
humanitarianism 89, 94-98, 109, 117, 177, 181, 185, 188, 191, 193
Hurlstone, Frederick Yeates 45, 47
Hurlstone, Jane Coral 47-48, 126, 162, 189
hydropathy 23, 31, 70-73, 84, 104-105, 113, 119, 143, 175,
Hyndman, Henry 114, 158

Ideal Club 64, 154, 172
Ideal Publishing Union 76, 146
Independent Labour Party 35, 54, 157, 168
India and vegetarians 4-5, 68, 144, 147, 193, 193n44
industrialization and industrial revolution 16, 34, 36-37, 189, 190
insanity 30, 120
International Order of Good Templars and Good Templars 55, 58, 60-61, 66, 76, 103, 107, 109, 144, 157, 168
Irish 12, 14, 61, 143, 155
Irish Vegetarian Union 60
Ironside, Isaac 29-30
Isham, Sir Charles 108
Ivy Leaf Society 149, 165

Jacob, Joshua 30
James, Henry 113, 185
Jewish method of slaughter 91
Joyce, James 61
Joynes, James L. 144, 175
'Jumpers' 102

INDEX

Kellogg, John Harvey 131, 147
Kelty, Mary Anne 26, 182
Kerr, Norman 76, 84, 155
King, Maude Egerton 176
Kingsford, Anna 84, 92-94, 104, 108-109, 144, 155, 164-165, 172, 176, 191-192
Kingsley, Charles 28, 182
Knight, Joseph 58, 148
Kress, Daniel H. 147

Lacy, Fanny E. 31, 47, 182
'late Victorian revolt' 6, 65, 110
Labour Annual 149, 157-158, 166
Lamartine, Alphonse de 163
Lambe, William 24, 71, 83-84
Lancet, The 16, 70, 82-83, 86
land reform 14, 63, 145, 156, 160
Lane, Charles 23-24, 27, 31, 90, 126, 193
Larner, James 40
Latham, Jackie E.M. 22
Lawrenson, Mary 159
Lawson, William 51
Lee, John 117
Lees, Frederic R. 77, 119
Leo, Alan (William Allan) 108, 172
Lewes, George H. 41, 121, 176
Lewis, Alice Marie 95, 106, 165
Lewis, Amelia (Louisa Freund) 191
Liebig, Justus von 12, 33, 83, 192
Lindsay, Beatrice 148, 166
Linton, Eliza Lynn 183
Linton, William 26
Little Bentley 29-30
Livesey, Joseph 77
London/National Food Reform Society 13, 62-63, 122, 134, 144, 156, 158, 164
London Vegetarian Society 5, 9, 62-65, 68, 78, 94, 103, 123, 136, 145, 166, 170, 173
London, East End 145, 155, 159, 165, 168
London, vegetarian branches 64-65
Longman, Frederick 98
Longstaffe, J.H. 39
Lord, Frances 117
Lytton, Edward Bulwer 180-182

Macaulay, Thomas 19
Macdonald, William Allan 121n75, 133
Mayhew, Henry 14, 156
Maitland, Edward 93-94, 104, 108
Malins, Joseph 76, 138
Malthusian crisis and neo-Malthusianism 11-12, 14, 147, 169
Manning, William S. 160
Manea Fen 26
Mann, Tom 158
Marshall, Forbes 58, 80
Marx, Karl 25, 44, 159
Massingberd, Emily L. 171
Maternity Society 79, 163, 170
Maurier, George du 185
Mawson, John 40, 73, 98
May, Ernest 147
Mayor, Professor John E.B. 62, 145
McCaughey, Leonard 58, 60, 139
McDouall, Adelaide 169-170, 172
meat, necessity of for health 82, 87, 155, 177, 194
— supply of, *and* growth in consumption of, 13-16, 18-19, 37, 62, 66, 155, 191
— female aversion to, 163
medical botany 74, 80
medical orthodoxy 73, 78-87
Medium and Daybreak 105, 107, 110
Mennell, Stephen 130
Meredith, George 102, 175, 183, 185
mesmerism 70-73, 105, 108, 119, 175
Methodism and methodists 37-38, 54-55, 73-74, 101, 101n126
Middle class 140
Mill, John Stuart 110
Mill, Jean 127, 132
millennium 118, 194
modernity, *see* vegetarianism and modernity
moral radicalism 6, 112-113
Morisonianism 72
Morley, Samuel 76
Morris, Reverend Francis Orpen 95
Morris, William 158
Morton, Timothy 133, 190
Mount Temple, Lady 108, 164
Munro, John 181
mutual improvement 36, 43-44, 55

Napier, Charles Ottley Groom- 57, 62, 75, 144, 153
National Food Supply Association 154
Natural Living Society 80, 103, 147, 159
nature and mankind 37, 55, 98, 133, 189, 190, 193
Nayler, John 54
Neesom, Charles 28, 45, 77
Nesbit, Edith 7, 175
New Age 6
New Age, The 22-23, 25, 27-29, 192
new social movements 4
Newman, Francis W. 52-53, 55, 61, 76, 80, 82, 89, 93-94, 99, 116, 122, 126, 130, 152, 163
Newnham-Davis, Nathaniel 137
Newnes, George 139
Nichols, Mary Gove 144
Nichols, Thomas Low 55, 57, 64, 66, 79, 80, 84, 132-135, 143-145
Noble, John 40
'Nonconformist conscience' 99
Nordau, Max 6, 194
Nugent, John 172
Nunn, Martin 62

O'Callaghan, John Barry 160
occult 104-110
Octagon settlement 44-45
Oldfield, Josiah 79, 84, 95-97, 108-109, 117, 147, 173, 192
Oldham, William 24-25, 31
Oliphant, Margaret 182
opium 115, 118, 183
Order of At-Onement 109
Order of the Golden Age 56, 102, 109
Orlebar, Eleanor 155
Orwell, George 158n46
Ouseley, Gideon 109
Owen, Robert 22, 25, 29-30
Owenism and Owenites 6, 21, 23-24, 26-29, 35, 45-46, 48, 71, 77, 104, 107, 112, 118

Paget, Lady Wahlburga 97
Palmer, Joseph Gunn 31
Parker, Margaret 58
Payne, Arthur 129-130

peace movement 23, 32-33, 38-40, 43, 58, 98, 101, 113, 115, 117-118, 122, 149, 178
Pengelly, J. Isaac 55-56, 147
Perkin, George 41, 43, 152, 155
Perkin, William H. 84n221
personal reform 112-113
phonetic reform 9, 23, 32, 41, 44-46, 107, 121, 150
phrenology 39, 45, 51, 58, 70, 72, 113, 118, 171, 147
physical education 168
physical puritanism 7, 29, 35-37, 69-71, 75, 103, 105, 108, 115-117, 152-153, 174, 194
Pilkington, George 101n125
Pioneer Club 171-172
Pitman, Benn 44
Pitman, Isaac 44, 138
Pitman, Henry 44
Pope, Mary 129-131, 133
press, on vegetarianism 177-180, *see also under The Times, Lancet, British Medical Journal*
Price, William 56, 120
Priestman, John 39
Progressive Food and Cooking Society 105
Punch 20, 34, 48, 66, 71, 116, 125, 179-182, 185
Puritanism 18, 55, 146, 169

quackery 69-70, 83, 86, 133
Quakers 6, 31, 36, 39, 46, 54, 58, 101, 101n126, 170
Quakers, White 29-30, 37, 44, 102

race 14, 174, 177, 193
radicalism 5-6, 12, 35-36, 40, 54, 59, 111-115, 123, 184
Radford, Dollie 150
Radford, E.N. 150
Reade, Winwoode 133
Reid, Katharine 170
Reid, Robert 40, 134
republicanism 62, 123n103, 143, 185
restaurants, non-vegetarian 136
Richardson, Sir Benjamin 85
Richardson, T.W. 76, 92, 147
Richmond, David 107
rinderpest 14

INDEX

Ripper, Jack the 97n96
Romanes, Kenneth 11
Romantic age and romanticism 5, 133, 175
Romein, Jan 3
Ronge, Johannes 46
Royal Society for the Prevention of Cruelty to Animals 94-95
Ruskin, John 54-55, 108, 175
Russell, Bertrand 155
Russell, George ('A.E.') 169
Russian vegetarians 3, 65

Salsbury, James 144
Salt, Henry 14, 82, 86, 95-96, 114, 122, 130, 144, 158, 175, 182, 192
Salvation Army 56, 101, 116n41, 155
Samuel, Fanny 107, 170
Sand, George 48
Sandau, Mathilde Wolff van 170
Scholefield, James 31
science 77, 103, 121, 162, 166, 173, 177
Scotland, diet 14
Scottish Food Reform Society 57, 130
Scottish Vegetarian Union 57
Scripture and Bible 4-5, 89n4, 73, 102-103, 114
Scrymgeour, James 59
Selous, Frederick 93
self-help 6, 12, 16, 28, 75, 82, 111-112, 123, 151, 153,
Seventh Day Adventists 131, 133
Shafts 7, 117, 158-159, 164, 166, 169, 171-173
Sharman, Reverend William 39
Shaw, George Bernard 7, 9, 150, 172, 175, 181
Sheldrick, Richard 150
Shelley, Percy Bysshe 5, 25, 28-29, 49, 71, 114, 121, 135, 175-176
shorthand 44, 52, 147, 150
Sibthorp, Margaret Shurmer 158, 164, 166, 169, 171
Sime, Sidney H. 145
Simpson, James 30-34, 38-41, 44, 48-51, 68, 72, 75, 77, 81, 83, 92, 98-99, 105, 128, 141, 149, 163, 188
slaughterhouses 89, 91, 94, 177
Smallman, Frederick 138-139
Smiles, Samuel 16, 38, 161

Smith, Edward 83
Smith, James 'Elishama' or 'Shepherd' Smith 25, 194
Smith, John of Malton 39, 128, 133, 177
Smith, W.G. of Kingston 121
Snow, John 83
Socialism ('scientific' and late-Victorian) 7, 55, 104, 114, 123, 140, 157-159, 171
Somerset, Lady Henry 171
'somatic society' 7
Southey, Robert 101
Soyer, Alexis 19, 176
Spencer, Colin 4, 18, 24
Spencer, Herbert 97, 136, 188
spiritualists and spiritualism 6, 34-35, 41, 45-46, 51, 56-57, 72, 96, 104-110, 152, 164, 171-172, 183, 186, 191
Stead, William T. 110, 172
Stollmeyer, Cornelius F. 28
Struve, Gustav 44, 47
Sturge, Joseph 6, 112-113
Sutton, Henry Septimus 26, 77
Swan, Henry 54
Swedenborgianism 5, 21, 41, 44, 55-56, 60-61, 101, 101n126, 106, 110, 118

Taylor, Bayard 183
Taylor, G.B. 117
Taylor, Isaac 103
Taylor, William Cooke 36
Tebb, William 75
Tegetmeier, Edith 170
temperance and teetotalism 1-8, 23, 26, 29-30, 32-40, 44-46, 49, 51, 54, 57-61, 63, 66-67, 70, 72, 75-78, 85, 100, 102-204, 112, 117-118, 123, 134, 139, 142, 144, 146, 158, 165-166, 168, 171, 177
Tennyson, Alfred 73, 176n17
Thames Ironworks 154
Theobald, William 107
theosophy 61, 104, 108, 148, 170, 184, 191
Thompson, Sir Henry 85, 194
thrift 2, 12, 16-17, 46, 56, 62, 64-66, 75, 130, 142, 151, 156-157, 177, 184, 188
Thrift Society 156-157

Times, The (London) 20, 49, 51-53, 66, 77, 83-84, 118, 120, 127, 155, 163, 175, 177
Tolstoy, Leo and Tolstoyanism 60, 65, 146, 148, 159, 168, 185
Towgood, Frederick 45
Truth-Tester, The 30, 45, 129
Tupper, Martin 183
Turley, William 45-46, 107
Turner, Bryan 7, 190
Turner, James 190
Twigg, Julia M. 2, 4, 37-38, 43, 103, 119, 153, 161, 189
Tysoe, Charles 37-38
Two Worlds, The 95

Unitarians 29, 40, 54-55, 73, 101, 101n126
United Kingdom Alliance 32-33, 40, 48, 55, 77
urbanization 7, 10, 16, 20, 36-37, 69, 189
utopia 6, 25-26, 28, 133, 180-82

vaccination and anti-vaccination 56, 60-61, 65, 67, 74-75, 83-84, 95, 107, 110, 115-117, 122-123, 143-144, 147, 158, 165, 192
Vasey, George 46
veganism 11, 76, 99
Vegetarian, The 63, 144-146
Vegetarian Advocate, The 72-74, 78, 82-84, 92, 94, 96, 100, 105, 128, 141, 149, 162, 174, 177-178
Vegetarian, almanacs 60, 148
— cookery 125-131
— decline 50-52
— derivation of word 10-11
— *Depôt* (Horsell's) 45
— doctors (*see also* Thomas Low Nichols and T.R. Allinson) 83-84
— *Federal Union* 53, 64, 67, 89, 145
— fiction 182
— hospitals 64-65, 79, 98
— hotels 55, 63, 134-135, 137-139
— *Messenger* 50, 72, 74, 80, 89, 93, 114, 141-143, 159, 170, 172
— orphanage 157
— poetry 175-176
— press 141-150

— prosopography 10
— *Rambling Society* 64, 105, 160, 166
— restaurants 134-141
— revival 6, 21, 53, 61
— schools 56
— *Society* 2-3, 30-31, 34-35, 46, 52, 54, 62, 64, 67-68, 78, 94-95, 114, 158, 164
— substitutes 92, 131-134
— *Yearbook* 148, 172
Vegetarianism, *and* agriculture 37, 146
— *and* capitalism 7, 37, 113, 153, 158-159, 190
— *and* class, 151-153, *see also* middle class, working class, *and* capitalism
— *and* fish 89, 131
— *and* gender 4, 151, 160-173, 188
— *in* Ireland 30, 35, 60-61, 92, 139, 168
— *and* Liberals 33, 113, 159, 188
— *in* London 45-50, 61-67, 76, 92, 106-107, 126, 135, 142, 154, 156, 178
— *in* Manchester 38, 40, 48, 51, 54, 61-63, 77, 82, 134, 138-139, 190
— *and* manual labour 46, 151, 155
— *and* modernity 189-194
— *and* mortality 81
— *in* northern England 35-38, 188
— *and* radicalism (*see also* Chartism, Christian Socialism, Co-operative movement, Socialism) 111-115
— *in* Scotland 34-35, 57-60, 130, 147
— *and* servants 52, 66, 130, 141, 150, 155
— size of movement 3, 42-43, 52, 65, 67-68
— size of female membership 164
— social base of 43, 46, 151-153
— *and* theatre 50, 145-146, 181, 185
— *in* western England 40-42, 50, 55-56
— *in* Wales 35, 56, 82
Veigelé, Adrienne 61, 170-171, 173
Veigelé, Alexandrine 166-169, 171-173
Viettinghoff, Graf Johan von 45, 47, 73, 83-84
Fane, Violet (Marie Montgomerie Currie) 114
Virchow, Rudolf 193
virtuoso, religious 100
'vital' foods 80
Vril-ya 181

Wade, G. Cholwick 56
Walkden, Charles 159
Walker, Charles 50
Wallace, Alfred Russel 96
Wallace, Chandos Leigh Hunt 56, 80, 107, 123, 129, 132-133, 144, 164-166, 169-170, 172, 189
Wallace, Joseph 56, 164
Wallace, Reverend John Bruce 60-61
Walsh, Reverend Walter 60
Ward, Mrs Humphry (Mary Arnold) 81, 138, 183
Ward, William Gibson 53, 57, 155-156
Wardlaw Best, Emma 169, 171
Wells, H.G. 98-99, 180-181, 184
Wesley, John 101, 190
White Quakers, *see under* Quakers
White, William 48, 75, 106
Wilde, Oscar 114
Willard, Frances 170-171

Williams, Reverend Henry John 109
Williams, Howard 94, 96, 109, 119
Williams, William Mattieu 131
Wilson, Joseph 39, 43, 52
Withers, William B. 31, 34
Women's Vegetarian Union 9, 64, 78, 108, 144, 166-171
World's Women's Christian Temperance Union 78, 168, 171
Wright, Henry Gardiner 23
Wright, John 118

Yates, May (Mary Ann Yates Corkling) 168-171, 173, 189
Yeats, Jack B. 91, 144-145

Zangwill, Israel 185
Zimpel, Charles Franz 47
Zoophilia 5, 37, 88-103, 153, 157, 172, 176, 190